THE JOY OF BIRD FEEDING

THE JOY OF BIRD FEEDING

The Essential Guide to Attracting and Feeding Our Backyard Birds

Jim Carpenter

Founder of Wild Birds Unlimited

SCOTT & NIX, INC.

NEW YORK

To my mother Elaine Steed and my grandmother Helen Carpenter,
who inspired and supported me in so many ways

A SCOTT & NIX EDITION

PUBLISHED BY

SCOTT & NIX, INC.
150 W 28TH ST, STE 1900
NEW YORK, NY 10001
SCOTTANDNIX.COM

FIRST EDITION MAY 2017

ISBN 978-1-935622-61-1

WILD BIRDS UNLIMITED®
AND ITS LOGO ARE REGISTERED TRADEMARKS OF
WLD BIRDS UNLIMITED, INC.

SCOTT & NIX, INC. BOOKS
ARE DISTRIBUTED TO THE TRADE BY

INDEPENDENT PUBLISHERS GROUP (IPG)
814 NORTH FRANKLIN STREET
CHICAGO, IL 60610
800-888-4741
IPGBOOK.COM

FRONTISPIECE: NORTHERN CARDINAL BY JIM CARPENTER

THE PAPER OF THIS BOOK IS FSC CERTIFIED, WHICH
ASSURES IT WAS MADE FROM WELL MANAGED FORESTS
AND OTHER CONTROLLED SOURCES.

PRINTED IN CHINA

Contents

Foreword

Why feed the birds?

Joy and awe

I FEED THE BIRDS because it brings me joy. I never tire of watching the same beautiful birds every day, all year long. Every season, I also get to see new birds and different behaviors. I hope to see Carolina Chickadees, Northern Cardinals, and American Goldfinches every time I look out the window. On a very special day, I might see a Brown Creeper sneaking in for a bite of my Bark Butter.

All this and more comes to me while I'm comfortably inside my house, outside on the deck, or working around the house and garden.

I've titled this book *The Joy of Bird Feeding*. From planning out my bird feeding stations to buying the products, filling the feeders, and watching the birds, I find joy in all of it. This hobby sparks different kinds of joy: There is the pleasure of thoughtful planning, followed by the relaxing and informative experience of shopping in my Wild Birds Unlimited store. Then I have the delight of filling the feeders and adjusting the foods and feeders with the seasons. Finally, I get the daily reward of watching the birds. All that joy is why I feed the birds.

Watching birds at your feeders fills the spaces in your day. Every time you glance out the window, you are blessed with a little bit of nature. A quick look at the feeders might be all you need to move you through the spaces between your daily activities—or you might pause for a few seconds, rack up 10 or 12 views of various birds flitting in and out, and then carry on with your day.

Even that little pause brings great joy. It might even help you concentrate when you go back to your tasks. Researchers at the University of Melbourne recently found that when students were assigned repetitive tasks and then given a 40-second break to look at a beautiful flowering roof, their concentration and performance were better than those of another group who looked at plain concrete. I think a 40-second break watching birds at feeders would have the same effect.

I like watching birds at the feeders while I am doing chores. My wife, Nancy, is very happy when I volunteer to wash the dishes, a task I often take on just so I can watch the birds out our kitchen window. Whatever chores you are doing, a quick glance at the feeders is a wonderful break. Watching birds at the feeders can bring joy to just about any activity at your home, even chores, indoors or out.

Chickadees are my favorite birds. The more I watch them, the more I am in awe of what these little puffs of feathers can accomplish, especially in the winter. Chickadees weigh less than half an ounce, and yet they manage to thrive in incredibly challenging conditions. Right in the middle of a blizzard, with the howling wind and snow freezing you to your bones as you shovel the walk or fill the feeders, you might hear a flock coming towards you through the woods, calling *chick-a-dee-dee!* The chickadees take turns, landing one or two at a time on your feeder, picking out a seed, and flying away to peck it into smaller pieces.

Now, I know that the birds are not really "happy" or "cheerful" to be out in the blizzard, but they seem to be saying, "Oh, is it snowing? It's a good day to sing a song." It cheers me up, and even though I may be no warmer than I was before, I feel warmer on realizing that I really have nothing to complain about. In fact, I can turn it all around and think, "Oh, is it snowing? I think I will enjoy the chickadees."

The mixture of the daily, the new, and the seasonal is what makes this hobby so engaging. Even if I see chickadees every day, they behave differently every day, even more so in different seasons. They might visit the feeders only a few times a day, as in the summer, or they might show up every 15 minutes, as in the winter. Sometimes they seem to get along with each other, and at other times it is obvious that they have a very definite hierarchy to determine which "alpha" chickadee gets first dibs at a feeding spot or observation point. Sometimes the flock is only chickadees, and sometimes they show up in a mixed foraging flock with titmice, nuthatches, and Downy Woodpeckers. The members of the flock are always busy chatting and calling, all in their own language, with each species behaving in its own way. And then, just as suddenly as they arrived, they all depart.

If I am lucky, I hear the primitive call of the Pileated Woodpecker. And then one of these giants, 30 times heavier than a chickadee, swoops in to the tree next to the feeders, cackles as it checks out the scene, and flies the remaining few feet to the suet feeder. There it is, just a few feet from where I am standing at the window! If the chickadees are joyful, the pileateds are magnificent. These living dinosaurs nearly take my breath away at what nature has produced. You never know what is going to happen out on the feeders.

Because watching birds is such a joyful activity, feeding them is one of the easiest ways to introduce children to nature. Children enjoy the entire process, from visiting the store to buying the food to filling the feeders and watching the birds. With a bit of work and patience, you can even take it a step further and teach the birds to grab a seed out of a child's hand.

Watch that joyful expression!

People who can't get out much especially enjoy feeding the birds. Those who spend a lot of time at home, such as the elderly or infirm, find that watching birds at the feeders greatly enhances their lives every day. You might want to place a bird feeding station outside a relative or friend's room at their home or nursing center. For many years, I delivered bird seed to an elderly customer who could no longer drive to the store on the other side of town. Her husband had passed away and eventually her beloved dog died, but she still had the joy of the company of the birds. My joy came from providing this joy to her.

Across North America, over 180 bird species can be attracted to yards with the right food, water, and shelter. In any given yard, you can attract 60, 100, or even more kinds of birds. That's a lot of joy and awe, all of it right outside your window.

Giving back to nature

Some people feed the birds because they feel that they are giving back to nature, replacing resources that have been lost to the birds as civilization creeps in. Think of the positive effect that thousands or even millions of backyards can have on bird conservation. Some think of bird feeding as a personal sustaining relationship with nature. This relationship can remain just that—personal—or you can become part of the larger picture of conservation by participating in citizen science projects that help inform decision-makers on how to save our diminishing natural habitats.

Our efforts to create inviting habitats in our yards and to provide food and water actually do make a difference. In his recently published book *Subirdia*, John M. Marzluff, a professor at the University of Washington, describes how he and his students found a greater diversity of birds on the suburban edges of towns—subirdia—than in urban centers or even pristine natural areas. "Realizing that a wide variety of birds live in self-sustaining populations in subirdia highlights the conservation value of our neighborhoods. Stewardship of these lands helps keep common and resilient birds abundant. By buffering climatic extremes and providing steady sources of food and water, the places we call home also provide backup breeding reserves for birds that thrive in wilder habitats."

Continue a rich hobby heritage

In their 2015 book, *Feeding Wild Birds in America*, Baicich, Barker and Henderson detail the long heritage of feeding birds, which began in the late 1800s. Bird feeding has grown tremendously in recent years and serves as a way to connect people to birds.

Helping the birds at critical times

One Wisconsin study showed that Black-capped Chickadees gathered only 21 percent of their food at winter bird feeders; the rest was from natural sources. Birds do not become addicted to bird feeders, and they always know how to fend for themselves in the wild.

However, when snow and ice cover up wild food sources and temperatures plunge, supplemental food can help wild birds survive. Birds need to go to sleep with a belly full of food to supply body heat through 14-hour nights, and they need to restock as soon as possible the next morning. Blizzards can make finding food very difficult at the very time birds need even more. Supplemental feeding helps birds in this critical survival situation.

A 2008 study conducted in the United Kingdom found that birds that frequented feeders in the winter had better breeding success in the spring. Another study published in 2015 found a consistent pattern of greater overall health for the birds at sites where supplemental feeders were present. Even though wild birds can take care of themselves, there are certain critical times when our feeders actually help them survive and reproduce.

Refuge and relaxation

For some birdwatchers, the hobby provides a refuge from the complexities of the modern world. By taking the time to buy the products, plan their placement in the yard, keep the feeders full, and watch the birds that arrive, hobbyists can create a mental and physical sanctuary in their own backyards.

I combine my feeding hobby with bird photography, and the time I spend waiting and watching completely absorbs my attention while the rest of the world fades away. By really observing the lives of the birds at the feeders and in the forest around our house, I see things I would not ordinarily see, such as the feeding rhythms of mixed flocks of chickadees, titmice, and nuthatches: when the flock flies off, I know I have 15 minutes to get a warm cup of coffee before more birds arrive for the next photo session.

You can feel equally close to the birds' activities by intentionally taking the time to sit outside and watch the feeders—no newspaper, no magazine, no camera, no cell phone or digital device. Simply watch the birds. It is incredibly relaxing, just the break you need from your busy life.

Combined with gardening

Bird feeding is often combined with gardening and, boy, does that ever make sense. Truly useful habitat for the birds combines food, shelter, water, and places to raise their young. We can provide for many of these needs, but the birds still have to have trees, bushes, perennials, annuals, and "wild places" to thrive.

Why plant a garden just for food and beauty? Bring it to life with birds when you are planning your plant selections and landscape.

Why did I write this book?

To share the joy

In 1981, I opened a tiny bird feeding store and named it Wild Birds Unlimited. Of course I hoped to earn a living, but I also wanted to do something with meaning for me and my customers. I wanted to share the joy of feeding birds with everyone who visited and with my larger community. Eventually, our little shop grew into over 300 stores, and our store owners and their staffs now spread the joy of feeding birds throughout North America.

Still, there is no way you can learn everything about this hobby by visiting a specialty store—no more than you can learn everything about photography by visiting a camera shop. The general principles of bird feeding hold true everywhere, so you can use this book to learn both basic and advanced principles, then stop by a local bird feeding specialty store for advice about the birds in your region and the best ways to attract them in your yard.

To generate respect for the hobby

When I opened that first store, the hobby of bird feeding was very poorly served by retail outlets. The only place to find truly good merchandise and advice was mail order outlets, but the high cost of shipping seed made the products quite expensive. Local outlets such as hardware, grocery, and garden stores carried bird feeding supplies as an afterthought, and only after the season for grass seed, fertilizer, and lawn chemicals was past.

Those stores that did carry bird seed made it available only in fall and winter. Even though high-quality seeds such as sunflower and nyjer (thistle) were usually available, most of the bird seed tonnage sold was an inexpensive "wild bird mix." "Who would spend money on a handout?" was the thinking. Full of cheap fillers that the birds did not eat, these mixes were a waste of money and a disservice to bird feeding hobbyists and the environment. Think of all the resources wasted on seed that birds do not eat: thousands of acres of farm land, thousands of gallons of fuel to plant, harvest, and transport the seed, thousands of square feet of silos and warehouse space, and thousands of man hours of labor are wasted on seed that just lies scattered on the ground.

Back in 1981, birdwatching in general was kind of uncool, thanks in no small part to media depictions of birdwatchers as somewhat geeky. If you are old enough, you might remember the character of Jane Hathaway in "The Beverly Hillbillies." Who wanted to be like her and her little-old-lady-in-tennis-shoes friends?

Overall, the hobby of bird feeding got little respect from most manufacturers or from the general public. I set out to change the perception of bird feeding from a cheap "handout" to a hobby deserving the same respect as gardening, fly-fishing, or photography. I decided to carry only high-quality food, feeders, and accessories, and to give customers my best advice for enjoying the hobby.

I quickly found out that many people were very pleased to have a local store where they could buy the good stuff and just "talk birds." And of course, there were many who sought advice about the seemingly impossible task of defeating the squirrels "stealing" their bird seed.

In some cases, it was clear that people enjoyed feeding birds but wouldn't admit it for fear of being deemed geeky. Well, when you could walk into my retail store and see a 30-year-old guy (non-geeky, or at least I thought so) who said it was really cool to talk about and feed the birds, perceptions started to change. It was OK for my customers to admit that they really liked birds and watched and fed them.

To empower you to make good decisions

Any hobby is more enjoyable when you know how to make good decisions about the equipment and how to use it. Unfortunately, the majority of bird feeding products offered in many non-specialty retail outlets have not improved much since 1981. Over 50 percent of all bird seed sold today is still "wild bird mix," with its contents determined more by price point than by the needs of birds. Many feeders are still poorly constructed and hard to fill, hang, and clean.

In most of those non-specialty outlets, there is no one on the floor to answer your questions or direct you to the best products for your needs. You are left hoping that the retailer has chosen good products to offer. You are also left trusting that whatever the packaging says about the product is accurate. In most retail outlets, the hobby still gets no respect. You are on your own in those places—so the better informed you are, the better the choices you will make. Fortunately, today there are many bird feeding specialty stores, along with some hardware and garden centers, where you can find both good products and pertinent, helpful advice.

My goal in writing this book is to continue sharing the joy of birds and generating respect for the hobby of bird feeding. I want to empower you to make good decisions as you buy products for your bird feeding station and to be a thoughtful strategist as you decide how to attract a special bird or solve a specific problem.

It's time to bring joy into your life through the hobby of bird feeding!

1 The five steps to bird feeding mastery

THE PATH FROM beginner to expert bird feeding hobbyist is just five steps long.

Step 1: Offer feeder-free bird food to discover which foods work.

The basis for everything else in bird feeding is an understanding of which foods actually attract the birds in your yard. You first need to put out a variety of foods, with no feeders to obstruct the birds' view. Offer samples of all the basic foods to entice as many species as possible. Then study Chapter 3 to identify the birds that have accepted each of the foods.

Step 2: Continue to offer the foods that worked.

Which foods were eaten, and which birds brought you the greatest pleasure? Based on your observations, you can decide which foods you want to continue providing; this knowledge in turn will guide your purchase of appropriate feeders. If you want even more out of the hobby, you can move on to step 3.

Step 3: Consider the 12 elements of a thoughtful bird feeding station.

This is where the fun really begins! By keeping these 12 elements in mind, you can become a thoughtfully strategic bird feeder, considering exactly which food and feeder combinations are most likely to bring in daily, seasonal, and rare birds. You will be thoughtful about where to place your feeders, how to create an inviting and safe environment for the birds, and how to solve basic problems.

Step 4: Improve your habitat to attract even more birds.

At this point in your journey, you want to look at ways to improve your overall habitat to provide natural food, water, cover, and places to raise young.

Step 5: Become seasonally savvy.

Now you'll focus on getting even more in tune with the natural world. You will learn to expand and scale back your food and feeder set-up with the seasons. As you learn the annual patterns of migrating birds, you can anticipate their arrival and departure in spring and fall, changing your food and feeders to accommodate their annual movements. You will be ready for "big events" such as blizzards, ice storms, and drought.

What time of year is best to start feeding the birds?
It is okay to start offering food any day of the year, but your results might differ from one season or another because of migration and other factors. Overall, a good time to start feeding is when seasons change, especially summer to fall and winter to spring. But remember: Any day you decide to start is a good day, because you are now feeding the birds!

Step 1: Offer feeder-free foods to discover what works.

How soon will birds come to the feeder-free food?

It might take a while for the birds to find their new pantry—it can be a few days or even a week or two before you see your first visitors. Keep the food fresh, and the birds will come.

The first step to a truly joyful hobby experience is taking three or four weeks to find out which bird foods work for the birds in your yard. Take careful notes to record which birds are attracted to which foods. This knowledge will last you a lifetime, and it is well worth the time you spend to acquire it.

The best way to find out what your local birds like is to offer bird food that is not enclosed by a feeder—feeder-free foods! Backyard birds find food by sight, and if you offer foods on a tray or in the form of bird food cylinders, with nothing to come between the birds and the food, you make it especially easy for the birds to see and select their favorites. This is the simplest way to discover the best choices for your bird feeding station.

When you put food in a feeder of any type, the birds may not see it right away. In fact, my advice for helping birds find a new hopper or tube feeder is to place food on a tray next to the feeder. Feeder-free food is much more easily seen as the birds fly by.

Even though I call this "feeder-free food," it is true that the tray method and the bird food cylinder method involve putting the food on something, such as a tray or a cylinder holder. The point is that there is nothing to obstruct the birds' view of the food choices.

Method 1: The food tray

Your first task is to buy or build a tray, which can be as simple as a two-foot by-six-inch board or as elaborate as a neatly mortised shelf divided into compartments. Birds are very comfortable feeding from a tray: they can easily see any other birds that might be aggressive, and they can quickly decide whether they want to stay or leave. And with a tray feeder, you can spy every bird that visits your buffet.

You can mount the tray on a stand, place it on a deck railing, or hang it from a low tree branch. You will find that the money or time put into a durable, well-made tray pays off in the long run: a tray is one of the best possible feeders, and should be standard equipment at any feeding station.

Once your tray is in place, offer samples of the six most popular foods. You can generally find small bags of each at your bird food supply store, and a couple can probably be found in your local grocery store, too. The six sample helpings should include representatives of all the principal categories of food attractive to birds: seeds, nuts, fats, fruits, and nectar.

1. **Sunflowers** Black oil sunflower seeds, or sunflower without shells, called sunflower chips, kernels, or hearts.

2. **Millet** White proso millet.

3. **Peanuts** Unsalted, roasted, or blanched and broken into pieces.

4. **Fats** A suet blend cake or other fat, such as suet nuggets, Jim's Birdacious Bark Butter, or Jim's Birdacious Bark Butter Bits. Remember to break suet cakes into small chunks.

5. **Fruit** Raisins, orange halves, grape halves, blueberries, cherry halves. A combination of fruits is best, but always include orange halves.

6. **Nectar** In regions and seasons where hummingbirds are likely to be present. Granted, it's difficult to offer this food without a feeder. Use a simple hummingbird feeder with lots of red in the feeder parts but no red dye in the sugar solution, which is made of 4 parts water to 1 part sugar.

If you offer equal amounts of each food, say a half of a cup each morning, you can compare what is left over at the end of the day and quickly determine how much the birds like each food. If it rains or snows, you will probably need to dry the tray and replace all of the food.

This selection has a good chance of bringing in any bird that likes to eat seeds, nuts, fats, fruit, or nectar. You will also attract many insect-eating birds, such as woodpeckers, which are also attracted to suet and peanuts. Keep notes on your visitors and the end-of-day amounts in the tray for at least three or four weeks. The information in that notebook will guide you for as long as you feed birds in this location.

Buffet blend

Another way to create a buffet is to use a blend. Some blends include sunflower seeds, millet, peanuts, suet nuggets, and fruit. Each food type is pretty easy to identify as a bird picks it up, so you can spread the blend out on your tray and observe which birds eat which food. If you cannot watch the birds, you can take note of the leftover food at the end of the day. The uneaten foods should be avoided in future purchases. Millet, though, is often not eaten by birds that come to elevated trays: Pour any remaining millet onto the ground or a ground-level tray, and see whether ground-feeding birds clean it up quickly.

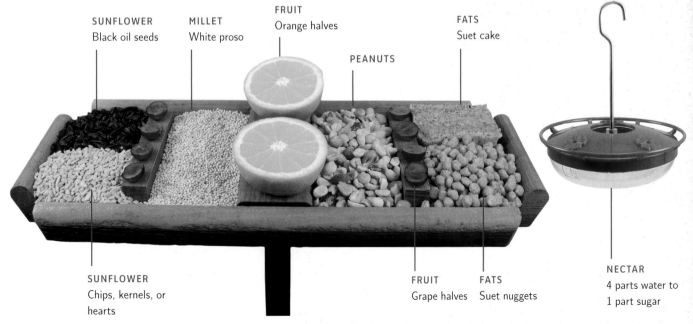

SUNFLOWER
Black oil seeds

MILLET
White proso

FRUIT
Orange halves

PEANUTS

FATS
Suet cake

SUNFLOWER
Chips, kernels, or hearts

FRUIT
Grape halves

FATS
Suet nuggets

NECTAR
4 parts water to 1 part sugar

Method 2: The bird food cylinder

The other feeder-free method to discover birds' preferences is much simpler, though the materials might be harder to find. The cylinder method is similar to the tray method, but it takes bird food in a different direction: vertical.

Circular cakes called "bird food cylinders" hold the seed together with a natural protein binder. Cylinders can contain seeds, suet, nuts, or various combinations of those ingredients. Cylinders are available in several sizes, but it is best to use the small cylinders, which are sometimes sold as Stackables.

You also need a feeder designed to hold the cylinders with a rod running through the hole in each cylinder's center. One advantage of this method: You can hang your offering from a tree branch, a shepherd's crook pole, or your house's overhang, any of which may be easier than finding a pole for a tray.

Look for these bird food cylinders:

1. **No-mess blend** Most no-mess cylinders are made of sunflower chips, with a few nuts and fruit pieces such as raisins or cherries.

2. **Suet** Most suet in cylinder form will be a dough that is suitable for feeding year-round and will not melt in summer heat.

3. **Peanuts and tree nuts** These cylinders include peanuts and a variety of tree nuts, such as walnuts, Brazil nuts, cashews, and pecans.

Cylinders are easy to hang
If hanging a feeder is easier than mounting a tray on a pole, then use the cylinder method to find out which birds eat the various foods.

FRUITS
Orange half, grapes, etc.

FATS
Suet dough

SUNFLOWERS
Sunflower chips and other ingredients

NUTS
Peanuts and tree nuts

To round out the offering during the summer, or in areas with warmer climates year-round, you will need:

4. **Nectar** Your solution should be mixed out of 4 parts water to 1 part sugar, with no red dye. This will require its own feeder, of course.

5. **Fruit** You can offer raisins, orange halves, grape halves, blueberries, or cherry halves on a tray or on top of the nectar feeder.

Food cylinders are very visible to the birds, so they can quickly find the foods they prefer. The cylinders make it even easier than a tray for you to see which foods have been eaten the most: the one that gets smaller fastest is the most popular food in your yard.

• • • • • • • • • • • • • • • • • •

Keep a list of the birds and the foods eaten

To identify the birds coming to your tray or cylinders, spend some time with Chapter 3, where you will find photos and information about 182 species that visit bird feeders. That chapter also points you to digital resources that can help with bird identification—sometimes a tricky matter if you're new to birdwatching.

During the three or four weeks that you are experimenting with the tray or cylinder method, keep track of the birds and the foods they are eating. Especially make note of the foods that your favorite birds prefer. No matter which method you use, you now know the proper foods for the birds in your yard.

Some species are consistently among the first to check out a new source of food. Depending on

where you live, chickadees, nuthatches, doves, or sparrows might be among the first to find your tray or cylinder.

Cylinder insight
Food cylinders are very visible to birds, so they can quickly find the foods they prefer, such as the Red-bellied Woodpecker, White-breasted Nuthatch and Downy Woodpecker above.

Step 2: Continue feeding the foods that work.

The purpose of step 2 is twofold: With the appropriate food in good feeders, you can have a very joyful hobby experience that lasts for years. You also will experience some of the issues, frustrations and opportunities that occur with bird feeding, and then you will be better prepared to use all of the information in this book.

Choices after using the tray method

After three or four weeks with the tray method, you will want to keep providing the foods that attract the most customers and the specific birds you most enjoy watching. You can provide foods separately, or you might opt for a high-quality blend that includes most or all of the foods preferred by your target birds.

If you have found that all of the items were eaten to some extent, then you can find or create blends with at least four or five of the foods. Avoid buying any mixes that list milo, wheat, or cracked corn as the first or second ingredient as these are not attractive to most target birds and will be scratched onto the ground uneaten.

You can also offer only no-mess blends, thus avoiding a pile of sunflower and millet shells under the feeders. You might see good results on adding a small amount of dried fruit to the no-mess blend. If your birds have also eaten your fat offering, continue with a suet-blend cake, suet nuggets added to a seed blend, suet nuggets on a tray, or a spreadable suet smeared on tree trunks.

When you are looking at the ingredients of various blends, do not let yourself be tricked into believing that a certain brand is superior because its manufacturer has "fortified" the seeds. You'll see later that with the sole exception of calcium

Rebel birder?

If you skipped Step 1 (see page 14), you can take my word that the foods suggested for the test will work in just about any yard. Buy a high-quality hopper or tube feeder and fill it with a blend that contains sunflower seeds, peanut pieces, and a little white millet. If the blend already includes safflower—also a good food—go ahead and buy it. Offer a fat of some sort, fruit, and, if you know that hummingbirds and orioles are around, sugar water, too.

Be a wise guy in the bird food aisle

For more details on how to be a wise bird food buyer, see Chapter 9. Learn to buy what actually works!

HIGH QUALITY BLENDS

This blend includes sunflower, sunflower chips, safflower, and peanuts.

This very good no-mess blend contains food without shells including sunflower chips, peanuts and hulled millet.

This no-mess blend includes added fruit, suet nuggets, and calcium.

during the nesting season, there is no need to add vitamins or minerals to food for wild birds.

If you open a bag of bird food and smell a sickly sweet scent, you're not detecting the fragrance of real fruit but an artificial flavoring added to make you think the food is especially attractive to the birds. Most backyard birds can't smell, so this perfume is meant to fool you, not to benefit the birds.

Feeder decisions

The tray is an excellent feeder, but it has its drawbacks. It probably needs to be filled daily, and it does not protect food from rain, snow, or wind. However, I do recommend the tray, because it is definitely the most popular feeder among the birds. They prefer its ease of landing and the wide-open space that allows them to scratch around for their favorite food.

Carolina Chickadee (in flight) and Tufted Titmouse (perched) enjoy a no-mess blend with sunflowers, peanuts, tree nuts, raisins, dried cranberries, and dried mealworms.

American and Lesser Goldfinches enjoying and fussing over the sunflower chips in a no-mess blend with sunflower chips, peanuts, hulled millet, and suet nuggets.

Now might be a good time to invest in a larger feeder that holds more food and offers protection from the elements. You will probably want a tube feeder or a hopper feeder. Either will work for blends with mostly sunflower seed, but hopper feeders tend to be better than tubes if the blend contains larger pieces such as tree nuts or fruit. If you really enjoyed watching the jays eat peanuts during your test, then buy a feeder designed to hold just peanut pieces or peanuts in the shell.

Tube feeders work well for blends combining sunflower, peanut pieces, and safflower; each of these flows easily through the small feeder ports. If you choose a seed blend with millet, though, I would recommend a tray or hopper feeder. Millet eaters such as Dark-eyed Juncos are normally ground-feeders, and they prefer trays and hoppers to tube feeders. If you add a large tray to a tube feeder, offer the millet only in the tray. (An exception to this last advice: Painted Buntings love millet and will eat it from a tube feeder.)

Goldfinches, highly desirable visitors that often travel in large flocks, will eat sunflower seeds at your tray, but what they really like is nyjer seed, which was not included in the test. Placed on a tray, nyjer tends to blow away, or is scattered so much that you cannot see whether it was eaten or not. If you have goldfinches coming to your tray, I

American and Lesser Goldfinches (above) love nyjer in a tube feeder designed especially for this small nutritious seed. Hopper feeders (right) with large capacities work well with most foods you choose to continue offering.

Peanuts-in-the-shell (above) are best offered in their own feeder. Peanut halves and pieces (top right) can be offered in a variety of feeders with mesh openings sized just right. Suet-blend cakes (bottom right) can be offered in a variety of feeders that hold the food and are comfortable for woodpeckers to land on.

recommend buying a tube feeder designed to hold nyjer or a blend of nyjer and fine sunflower chips.

You can provide fats, such as suet-blend cakes, in many kinds of feeders, from simple wire cages to tail-prop feeders and fancy metal containers. You can continue to use the tray for suet nuggets, and also spread Bark Butter on a tree trunk or a specially designed feeder.

Immature Rufous Hummingbird (top) on leak- and ant-proof nectar feeder. Baltimore Oriole (bottom) on nectar feeder that also provides orange halves and jelly.

The nectar feeder used in the test will continue to attract hummingbirds. Look for a design that is leak-proof and easily cleaned. If orioles showed up, they might visit an additional sugar-water feeder designed for their larger bills, with areas to hold fruit or grape jelly.

Choices after using the bird food cylinder method

The test with the three stacking cylinders showed you which birds like sunflower seeds, suet, and nuts. If you offered sugar-water and fruit near the cylinders, then you also know which species like those foods. You have two options now: Continue feeding only cylinders, or offer the same foods loose in hopper, tube, and tray feeders.

The easy convenience of bird food cylinders might really appeal to you, or their ability to entice a variety of birds might have impressed you. The neat thing is that each 10-ounce stackable cylinder has a larger counterpart. If you have determined that your birds liked the small no-mess cylinder, you can buy a 2¼-pound no-mess cylinder at specialty stores. Some of the cylinders are even available in 4¼-pound sizes—ideal for feeding while you are away on vacation.

Feeder decisions: You may have used a very simple feeder to hold the cylinders during the test. While you can certainly keep on using that feeder, you might enjoy exploring your options. There are many feeders designed to hold cylinders, from practical-looking versions that cover the food and provide perches to quite fancy ones that combine beauty with larger landing areas for the birds.

Again, if the nectar feeder you used in your test attracted birds, then continue to use it. You can also offer fruits on a separate tray or on an oriole feeder with sections that hold fruit and jelly.

Tufted Titmouse, Downy Woodpecker and Carolina Chickadee on a variety of stackable food cylinders (above) and (below) on a larger cylinder that contains sunflower chips, nuts and fruit.

Downy Woodpecker (left) enjoying a suet blend cylinder and Northern Cardinal (right) at a seed blend cylinder. Note the circular wire perch feature incorporated into the design of this hanging feeder.

Summary of Steps 1 and 2

With the results of your food tests in hand, you know which foods bring the most birds to your yard. You have gradually learned how to identify many of your backyard birds. And you have selected feeders that will continue to attract your favorite birds.

If you followed the tray method or the bird food cylinder method and then used that data to create a feeding station, you are already far more knowledgeable about feeding the birds than many other hobbyists. Now you can make wise decisions when you buy food in any store.

When you are ready to increase your mastery of the bird feeding hobby, pull this book back out and go on to read steps 3, 4, and 5. With the information you find there, you can establish a thoughtful bird feeding station, improve your habitat for the birds, and learn how to become seasonally savvy.

"Old school" versus "new school" bird food choices

Old school

When I started selling bird food in 1981, I saw very few high-quality seed blends in local stores. Most knowledgeable hobbyists did not buy blends, but offered individual foods in separate feeders. They would pour black oil or striped sunflower into their hopper or tube feeders, throw out millet or cracked corn for ground-feeding birds, and offer nyjer (thistle) seed in a finch tube and a suet cake in a suet feeder.

This simple strategy works very well for many of today's hobbyists, too. But I call this feeding style "old school" because it no longer provides hobbyists with the greatest joy. The hobby has come incredibly far in the past 30 years, and there are now many foods and techniques that can bring greater pleasure to backyard birdwatchers.

I have also observed:

▶ Old school hobbyists do not change their feeding selection with the seasons, except to add hummingbird and fruit feeders.

▶ Old school birdwatchers usually use only seeds with shells. When the birds remove the shells, they create a mess under the feeders and on any surface near the feeders, such as sidewalks, decks, and patios.

▶ Old school hobbyists often use inexpensive feeders that are difficult to fill and clean and do not last very long out in the elements.

New school

The past 30 years has seen real changes in bird food and feeder options. Today's hobby takes advantage of high-quality seed blends created for different purposes, regions, and seasons. For example, many seed blends are "no-mess": because all the shells have been removed, everything in the package is edible and there are no shells to pile up under the feeders.

The new school style includes a variety of foods alongside loose seeds, seed blends, and suet cakes. Bird food cylinders and cakes are designed to include some or all of the major food groups. Even insects are available now, including live mealworms that can be offered in small dishes, and dried mealworms to be added to loose seed blends or cylinders and cakes.

Suet blends come in many more forms now, including cylinders, bite-size bits, and even spreadable varieties.

New school hobbyists might offer loose seed blends or bird food cylinders that include dried fruit pieces. They often provide peanuts (in or out of the shell) and tree nuts, either separately or in loose seed blends and cylinders. Many new school birdwatchers also put out foods that include calcium, whether year-round or just during the nesting season to help female birds with egg formation.

In this modern version of the hobby, the old rules of "which bird comes to which feeder" are changed. Every bird in your yard—except the sugar-water fans—can visit a single feeder that can hold every food that attracts the local birds. A loose seed blend or a bird food cylinder can include every seed type— oil sunflower, safflower, millet, and others—as well as peanuts and tree nuts, fruit pieces, suet nuggets, and dried mealworms.

Even though one feeder can serve many species, a variety of feeders at several feeding stations can entice even more birds for the birdwatcher's enjoyment. The idea of multiple bird feeding stations that change with the seasons, solve various problems, and are placed in the best locations for observation is an important part of new school thinking.

New school bird feeding also considers the birds' needs more carefully, ensuring that they have safe places to land and hide before and after they visit the feeders. With the birds' well-being in mind, hobbyists choose feeders that are designed to weather the elements, are easy to clean, and even have anti-microbial protection built in.

Step 3: Consider the 12 elements of a thoughtful bird feeding station

You have been feeding the birds for a while, using the appropriate foods for local birds and a feeder that works well. This is as far as many hobbyists get, because it seems to be getting the job done: luring birds into view. But I want to lead you to the next level of expertise.

Now you will really think about each of your choices, you will be thoughtful in every decision affecting your bird feeding station. Your knowledge of which foods work well in your yard will help you make the best decisions when faced with the thousands of feeders, poles, baffles, and other accessories on the market.

1. Foundational feeder

This feeder should hold a seed blend that attracts 80 percent of the local birds. It should be able to feed many birds at one time and hold enough seed to last four or more days without refilling. Many feeders can serve as a foundational feeder, including wooden hoppers, large tube feeders, and bird food cylinders.

2. Tray feeder

This option—often called a platform feeder or bird table—can hold one or more types of seed, blends, or specialty foods. Tray feeders, my favorites for viewing the birds and their behavior, are not used often enough by hobbyists. Because a tray feeder's capacity is low and the food can get wet or be covered by snow, it needs to be filled every day or two.

3. Fat feeder

These feeders hold one or more of the many options of "fat," including suet-blend cakes, plugs, and cylinders. Alternately, Bark Butter is a great fat source that can be spread on tree trunks, and suet nuggets can be made available on tray feeders.

5. Nectar, jelly, and fruit feeders

In hummingbird and oriole season, a nectar feeder should be used to hold a fresh solution of 4 parts water to 1 part table sugar. If you live on the Pacific or Gulf Coast, your hummingbird season is year-round. Orioles sip sugar-water out of nectar feeders, but they also eat fruit and jelly, which you can offer in a separate feeder. Some feeders, like the one shown above, have room for all three: sugar water, jelly, and fruit pieces.

4. Finch feeder

Designed for nyjer seed or nyjer blends, this feeder attracts finches whenever they are present in your area. Finches will eat other foods, such as sunflower, but they really respond to nyjer seed.

6. Snack, specialty, and convenience feeders

These feeders add variety at different seasons, or are very convenient to fill with food. The menu here can feature peanuts, mealworms, whole or cracked corn, wildlife blends, seed and nut blend cylinders, suet cylinders, and fat cylinders. The almost endless options include small-bird-only feeders, window feeders, and squirrel feeders.

7. Water

Year-round source of water. Water can attract as many birds to your yard as food offerings and often attracts birds that do not normally visit your feeders such as migrating warblers and thrushes. Choose from hundreds of birdbath options, from ground-level to pedestal-based to ones that attach to deck rails. It is important that the birds are able to land comfortably and bathe in a water depth appropriate to their size. The basin should be easy to empty and clean.

8 & 9. Nearby landing spots

Perching branches. One of the most important elements of your bird feeding station, nearby branches can double or even quadruple the number of birds visible at one time. Individual birds and flocks need branches for perching or gathering as they prepare to visit feeders and as they leave. Natural or man-made, perching branches are also used by chickadees and titmice to crack open seeds or nuts grabbed from the feeders. Hummingbirds use perching branches as observation and resting spots.

Vertical landing spots. Some birds such as woodpeckers and nuthatches prefer vertical landing surfaces. Your perching branches might have a vertical central trunk, or you can attach a slab of tree bark or wooden plank to a feeder pole. A feeder with a vertical wooden landing surface can also serve this purpose. Woodpeckers use these vertical landing spots as they approach the feeders or await their turn at the fat feeders. Nuthatches typically prefer to land upside down on a bark-like surface and then fly to the feeder.

10 & 11. Feeder locations

Thoughtful feeder placement. When deciding where to put your feeders, you need to consider several factors, including the birds' easy and safe access to the feeders, their visibility from your principal observation points, ease of filling and cleaning, and the proper distance from trees, windows, and low shrubs.

Multiple feeding stations and diverse heights. The more feeding stations and the wider variety of feeder heights, the more birds will come to the feeders. Birds of different species are more comfortable gathering in one area if the feeders offer perches at a variety of heights.

12. Basic critter solutions

Station is free of squirrel, chipmunk, raccoon, nuisance bird, and cat problems. These are universal problems that can be solved, or nearly solved, with simple strategies. The goal is to maximize your joy in viewing your favorite birds, to minimize frustrations and feeder damage, and to eliminate any dangers to the birds.

Feeders should be within 3 feet of windows or further than 10 for the safety of the birds that might get spooked. Having feeders in both places attracts a larger number and variety of birds. The feeder on the pole in the background is protected by a raccoon baffle.

I use my second floor deck for 11 feeders (above). It is all visible from our kitchen windows and is raccoon-proof. (Notice even the railing is a tray feeder.) I also have feeders in the side and front yards.

Squirrels (right) are the number one nuisance at feeders. See Chapter 7 for detailed ways to defeat them and other critters at your feeding stations.

Step 4: Improve your bird habitat to attract even more birds

With what is often called "birdscaping," you can do more to make your yard more bird-friendly and to entice an even greater variety of birds. I have always felt that we should consider the birds' entire habitat, not just feeders, houses, and baths. I started selling "Bushes for Birds" in my first year of business and have always promoted filling in the following plant niche categories in your yard. The wonderful thing is that when you create a refuge for the birds, you are also creating a refuge for yourself.

Habitat diversity

Every living thing needs the right environment if it is going to survive and thrive. The greater the habitat diversity, the greater the variety of birds that find their needs met by it.

Many birds that do not commonly come to feeders—such as warblers and flycatchers—are attracted to a birdscaped habitat. I know a couple who bought a house surrounded by a small grassy yard with a few yews near the house. They drafted a bird-friendly plan to include woody plants, perennials, annuals, and vines. Within two years, the number of bird species seen in their yard skyrocketed from 20 to 75. Something interesting was happening in their yard every day of the year, because it served as an oasis for resident and migrant birds in the middle of an otherwise uniformly landscaped subdivision.

Plants

I recommend the following to create a diverse and bird-friendly landscape:

▶ Woody plants ranging from small bushes to medium-size trees and shade trees. Plant both evergreens and deciduous trees. Plan for fruit, berries, and nuts during summer, fall, and winter. Also plan in some dense woody places for birds to hide.

▶ For hummingbirds, butterflies, moths, and bees, plant perennials of various heights that flower at different times. Also include perennials that produce seed heads for birds.

▶ Beautifully colored, rapidly growing annuals with flowers to attract hummingbirds, butterflies, and bees and produce seed heads that provide food and nesting material for birds such as goldfinches.

▶ Vines that offer flowers, fruits, berries, or dense leafy areas for hiding and nesting.

▶ Grassy areas in full sun. On a chemical-free lawn, you still want to see American Robins pulling up a worm.

A diverse offering of native plants that offer hiding places, berries, flower seeds and nectar greatly increases the diversity of wildlife that visits your yard.

▶ Shade- and sun-loving varieties. Choose plants that do best in sun, partial sun, and shade, depending on the situation of your yard.

▶ Four seasons of food. Plan for annuals, perennials, vines, and woody plants to provide flowers, seeds, fruits, and nuts at all seasons, and fibers for nests in the breeding period.

I always recommend choosing plants native to your region, as they are natural components of the local ecosystem. Native plants also have less need than non-natives for chemical protection from native pests, and require less water in drought.

You need to freshen up the water in a birdbath every few days to prevent mosquitoes from breeding and to clean out any droppings. If you add an element of motion—a bubbler, a water dripper, or a mister—you may attract more birds. In climates with freezing temperatures, a bird bath heater can keep the water thawed for thirsty birds.

Shelter

Birds need shelter and perches in the form of brushy, twiggy, grassy, viney, or dense foliage. Such areas provide natural food sources and protect the birds from predators as they hunt for food. Flocking birds need areas where the entire group can assemble for conversation and squabbles.

I highly recommend woody plants of all sizes near your bird feeding area. Ground-flocking birds, such as Dark-eyed Juncos, prefer to use low shrubs while moving to and from feeders. If cats roam in your yard, though, be sure to place your feeders at least 10 feet away from low cover; this keeps cats from easily creeping up on birds on the ground underneath feeders.

Before and after eating at the feeders, songbirds prefer to use perching sites on medium-size trees such as dogwoods, viburnums, or scrubby and even dead junipers. Woodpeckers and larger birds such as jays prefer bigger trunks and more open branches.

Cedar Waxwings (above left) are sure to visit your berry trees such as this Serviceberry. American Robins (above right) can enjoy water year-round in a bath equipped with a heating element.

Food

All these plants provide fruit, nuts, seeds, sap, and buds, and also host insects that become food as eggs, larvae, pupae, and adults.

Bird feeders supplement the natural foods in and around your yard.

Water

If your yard does not have a natural water source, then you need to provide a water feature. This could be a simple birdbath made out of a pottery saucer, a beautiful concrete bath on a pedestal, or an entire recirculating system with a waterfall, stream, and pond.

Larger songbirds also like high branches and treetops. They use them to announce their presence to other birds and to get a good look around, making sure there are no predators on the ground or in the sky.

In harsh winter weather, your visitors will seek spots that keep them safe from the worst of the wind and cold. In hot and arid climates, the birds need shady sites to stay out of the mid-day heat and shrubby areas to hide from night-time predators.

Brush piles are man-made shelters for the birds. Stack dead and living branches into a large pile that has many entrances and exits and provides cover from the elements. Brush piles are especially useful as shelter from predators and harsh weather.

This yard has a very effective mixture of plant types with dense cover, open areas and water. And, it's also a refuge for people!

Nesting areas

Birds need places to create nests and materials to build nests. Their nests are placed in many places ranging from right on the ground to small bushes, trees and vines, to tall shade trees and large saguaro cactus. They make nests out of materials such as dried grass, twigs, sticks, animal hair, moss, lichens, spider silk, plant fibers, feathers, and much more.

You can help nesting birds by setting out natural fibers such as short wool threads, dog fur, and horse hair. Cavity-dwelling birds use nest boxes placed in suitable locations; wrens, chickadees, and bluebirds are the easiest to lure to appropriately sized boxes. You might also have the good fortune to house woodpeckers or owls in larger boxes.

Chemicals

The best option is to use as few chemicals as possible on a birdscaped yard, even if the yard has a few weeds and grubs and looks a bit messier. With fewer or no chemicals, the soil and plants will host a larger supply of native insects and other organisms that the birds depend on. It is best for the birds to not have any pesticides on the surfaces of any berries and fruits they consume. I prefer a grassy yard with a few dandelions, which also has robins pulling up worms and bluebirds dropping down on insects, to a perfectly green lawn with no natural ecosystem.

Step 5: Become seasonally savvy

Being "seasonally savvy" means that you adjust your feeding program to suit the behavior of the birds over the course of the changing seasons. Local activity levels, migration, food preferences, and weather introduce constant variation and change. When you know how to embrace and benefit from these seasonal transitions, you'll experience even more joy. As a seasonally savvy hobbyist, you keep your foundational feeder and fat feeder active all year and:

▶ Increase the number of feeders and foods when activity is greatest—such as when large flocks show up or finch irruptions occur—and when extreme weather arrives.

▶ Change the types of feeders and food as migrating birds arrive and depart, as

fledglings are leaving the nest, or as seasonal habits change.

▶ Decrease the number and types of feeders and food during periods of low activity.

Most hobbyists have learned to be seasonally savvy to some extent. For instance, most folks in Indiana know that Northern Cardinals are there year-round, Dark-eyed Juncos are there only from fall to spring, and Ruby-throated Hummingbirds are there only from late spring to early fall. Even with this knowledge, most hobbyists change their feeding stations only by adding hummingbird feeders during the spring and summer seasons.

While that is appropriate, you can be much savvier than that. For instance, when it snows in Indiana, the first birds on the feeders the next

When you are prepared, your feeders are still very easily accessible (left) even after a snowstorm. Spring (right) brings beauty and migrating birds to your feeders!

morning—even before sunrise—are Northern Cardinals. If you are savvy about the season, you anticipate this behavior, keep an eye on the weather reports, and stock up on several types of bird food. The night before a storm, you fill up the foundational feeder and the others while hoping that a few of the food ports will not be plugged with snow in the morning. That way, you get to enjoy the marvelous show of cardinals the next morning while sipping a warm cup of coffee.

After the snow stops and you have ventured outdoors, you remove any snow clogging the feeders and, most importantly, add at least one tray feeder to the station. You might fill it with sunflower seeds, peanuts, and suet nuggets before going outside, or you might turn a flat deck railing or bench into a super-large tray feeder—which is where most of the action will take place after a snowstorm.

When Dark-eyed Juncos arrive in fall, you alter your feeding program to include more millet in a feeder where the millet will be knocked onto the ground. When the juncos depart, you decrease the millet.

Just before the hummingbirds arrive, you position your nectar feeders in last year's spots so that returning adults find your offering. When the young hummingbirds leave the nest, you should double or triple the number of feeders in your yard, since there are more hummingbirds to feed. As migration nears, competition for nectar becomes fierce.

You take care of the basic needs of your resident birds when you use the same feeders year-round, but to be seasonally savvy, you must adjust to the season and the changing needs of your resident birds; in addition, new birds arrive or leave or pass through in migration. I always have quite a

This stump on our deck (far left), normally holds coffee cups in the summer, but becomes a Dark-eyed Junco feeder in the winter. After a blizzard and extreme cold, I use all available feeders including this hummingbird feeder base (middle) to hold suet nuggets for the Carolina Wren. I even use our saucer snow sled (far right) as a giant tray feeder the morning after a big snow. Tufted Titmice and Carolina Chickadees find it quickly.

I always turn the deck rail (left) into a feeder after snowstorms. The Northern Cardinals flock to this rail feeder. Pine Siskins (right) can arrive in large flocks every other winter or so in some areas. Double or triple the finch feeders so all can feed.

Scrub Jays love whole peanuts and will cache them for future dining.

A covered tray holds mealworms for baby Eastern Bluebirds fed by parents.

cakes in a suet feeder will probably work well all year. In the northern states, a finch feeder will work all year long, whereas in the southeastern states, where goldfinches appear only in the winter, a finch feeder will bring in visitors only in the cooler months.

What seasonally savvy means

You have at least one foundational feeder and one fat feeder that you use all year long, and you have a variety of feeders and foods that you seasonally add, change, or subtract from your station. Here are a few seasonally savvy activities:

▶ Where goldfinches, Pine Siskins, and other finches live year-round, keep a finch feeder up every day of the year. Where they occur only seasonally, offer finch food only during those seasons.

▶ If you see large numbers of jays in the area, perhaps a gathering of young juveniles, add whole peanuts to your offering on a tray or in a special feeder, then sit back and enjoy the show. In fall or winter, the jays will cache many of the peanuts for later consumption.

▶ In irruption winters, when winter finches move south, or when your local goldfinches are especially numerous, you might want to hang several finch feeders to really enjoy the show.

▶ Where hummingbirds and orioles are present only in summer or migration, put out nectar feeders a week or two before their normal arrival. Also offer fruit and jelly, which can be as attractive to orioles as nectar.

few feeders in reserve for the needs of the various seasons and pull them out as necessary. Some foods and feeders are very likely to work all year, with the most constant being your foundational feeder with the foundational feeder blend and whatever fat feeder you are using. For example, a high-quality blend in a large hopper and nutty suet

- When it is very cold, add more high-fat food for extra calories.

- In the nesting season, add high-protein foods and foods with added calcium for egg production and nestling growth.

- If you see insect-loving birds like bluebirds in your yard, add mealworms or a source of fat, such as Bark Butter Bits, in a special bluebird feeder.

- In an extended drought, increase your water offering. This brings more birds in for food as well.

- Some foods are better than others for new hatchlings. Insects are highly favored, so mealworms are at-tractive to parents feeding young. Jim's Birdacious Bark Butter and Bark Butter Bits are also excellent for nestlings: they are highly nutritious, easily carried to the nest, and easily swallowed.

- When mockingbirds and catbirds are present, offer them fresh or dried fruits and berries on a tray. Cat-birds are somewhat shy, but will often come to Bark Butter on the side of a tree.

- You may notice a high level of chickadee activity in the fall, but you might not know that many of the seeds the birds take are being stored for a later meal. Give them their own small-birds-only feeder full of sunflower seeds in the shell, as these are better for caching.

- In spring, summer and fall, migrating and resident warblers are attracted to running water. Add a water dripper to your birdbath to create the sound of dripping water, and keep a close eye out to see the beautiful warblers coming to this water source. You might also smear some Bark Butter on tree trunks, as that is one of the few foods that attract warblers.

- When young woodpeckers emerge from the nest, there might be extremely high activity at the suet or other fat feeders. Add one or two extra feeders for at least six weeks to enjoy the activity of several woodpecker species.

I always like to offer lots of different foods in various feeders in the winter.

A fledgling male Downy Woodpecker (left) is fed Bark Butter by his dad. Water in a bird bath attracts the Clark's Nutcracker (right) during dry times in the Colorado foothills.

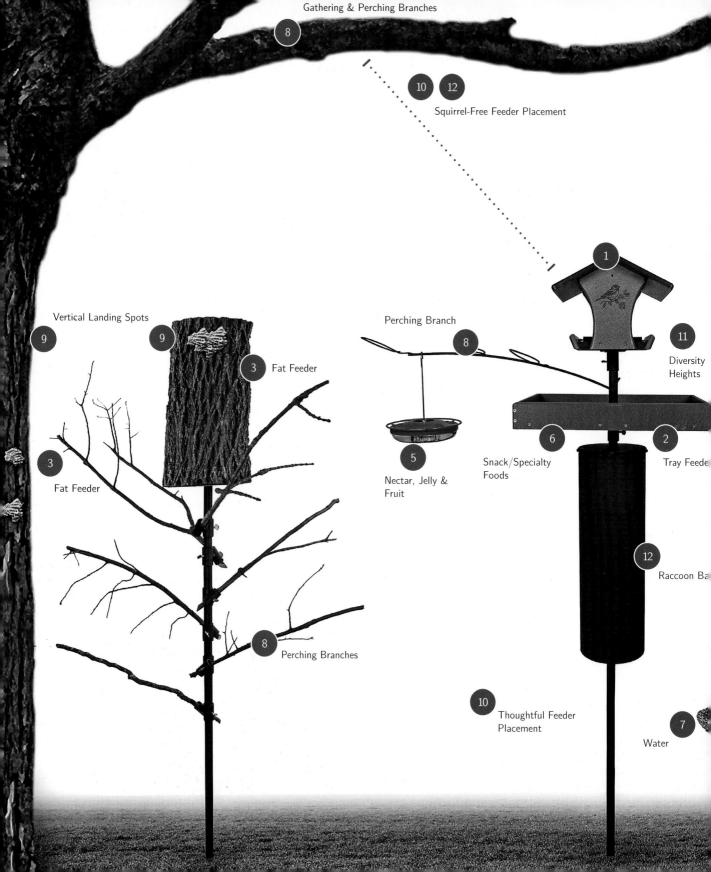

Gathering & Perching Branches

8

10 12

Squirrel-Free Feeder Placement

1

11

Diversity Heights

Vertical Landing Spots

9

9

3 Fat Feeder

Perching Branch

8

3

Fat Feeder

5

Nectar, Jelly & Fruit

6

Snack/Specialty Foods

2

Tray Feede

12

Raccoon Ba

8 Perching Branches

10

Thoughtful Feeder Placement

7

Water

6 Snacks/Convenience

3 Fat Feeder & Vertical Landing Spot

6 Snacks & Specialty Feeder

4 Finch Feeder

12 Squirrel Baffle

10 **12** Cat-safe Feeder Placement

11 Multiple Bird Feeding Stations Around House

8 Perching Branches

Feeder Choices
1. Foundational feeder
2. Tray feeder
3. Fat feeder
4. Finch feeder
5. Nectar, jelly, and fruit feeder
6. Snacks/specialty/convenience

Water
7. Source of water year-round

Nearby Landing Surfaces
8. Perching branches
9. Vertical landing spots

Feeder Locations
10. Thoughtful feeder placement
11. Multiple feeding stations

Basic Problems Solved
12. Station is free of basic problems like squirrels, raccoons, and cats.

I have found that when I pay thoughtful attention to my bird feeding station, I get to see the greatest variety of birds each time I look out the window.

Use these 12 elements of a thoughtful bird feeding station to guide your thinking about your own station so that you have the greatest joy and your birds can feed comfortably and safely.

2 Thoughtful bird feeding station elements in detail

THE 12 ELEMENTS of a thoughtful bird feeding station work in harmony to increase the wonderful views you have of the birds and their behavior. These elements also limit issues and frustrations—always a good thing. Of course, you can pick and choose which elements are suitable to your yard, but I have found the greatest joy when I take advantage of all of the elements at the same time.

Feeder choices

1. Foundational feeder

This is your Grand Central Station, with lots of activity and lots of birds coming and going at all times! It's open 24/7 and caters to a diverse population. The foundational feeder contains a high quality blend of food that attracts 80 percent of the local seed- and nut-eating birds. It can feed many birds at one time, and can go for four or more days without refilling. The food should be a blend tested in your yard and demonstrated to appeal to the largest selection of seed- and nut-eating birds.

A foundational feeder holds enough bird seed blend for at least four days and can feed many birds at one time.

A large wooden hopper feeder with a good blend of sunflower, safflower, peanuts, and a bit of millet can satisfy these requirements, especially if it has many places for birds to land and perch while eating.

Any food and feeder combination that serves the purpose can be your foundational feeder: a large tube feeder with a tray, a large hopper feeder, or a large bird food cylinder or seed cake. You might have a giant and beautiful gazebo feeder or a timed-release seed feeder that dispenses food over a period of several weeks.

Why is it so important to have a foundational feeder? As much as I enjoy feeding the birds, I can't always tend to the feeders every day, so it is important that I have at least one feeder that does not have to be filled very often. If your feeders are empty in between fillings, the birds will not be as constantly active as they are at a feeder that dependably provides food every day. Empty feeders = no joy! The birds will return after you refill an empty feeder, but it might take a few days for full activity to be renewed.

This is the most important feeder to place where it is easy to fill and easy to see. Whether you are just walking by the window, fixing dinner, washing dishes, or watching TV, you are sure to get a quick bird sighting every time you glance outside.

Foundational feeder examples (above): large hanging tube, XL bird food cylinder, and large mesh sunflower/blend feeder. Three or four species can easily feed at the same time from these feeders. Smaller foundational feeders (below) accomadate two to four birds at a time, depending on the species.

2. Tray feeder

Even "ground dwellers" like juncos will come up to tray feeders, especially if the snow has covered sources of food on the ground. On this day, the light, dry snow did not cover or moisten the food so these "Pink-sided" variety of Dark-eyed Juncos were able to dine even during the snow fall.

What's my favorite feeder? A simple tray. Here's why: A tray feeder gives you the best view of the action at the feeding station. There are no hoppers, tubes or seed cakes to block your view of any of the birds that land on the tray. You get to observe the most action for the time you have to sit and watch the birds.

I have a foundational feeder feeding the birds every day, but when I am home, I always put snacks on the tray feeder and then sit back to watch the show. When the snacks run out, the foundational feeder is there to keep the birds engaged.

You will see more interesting bird interactions on the tray than on any other feeder. The tray feeder is what I call the community feeder, where the greatest number of species come to find food. Birds seem to feel very comfortable on trays; they can see in all directions at all times while flying to and from the tray and grabbing their food. At the tray, birds can see other members of their species and interact as dictated by seasonal hormones or by the hierarchy established in the flock. Birds can also watch for other, larger species that might

"bully" them off the tray or even attack them. All songbirds need to watch out for hawks, and a tray gives them the clearest view of their surroundings—a tray gives a clear view of all that is around so the birds can interact, bully, or hide as needed.

You can put just about any kind of food on a tray, where it will attract a much wider variety of birds than the foundational feeder. Offer seeds of all types along with tree nuts, peanuts, fruit, dried mealworms (or live ones if the tray has steep, slippery sides), suet, suet nuggets, and Bark Butter. We often call these foods "snacks," since they will probably last for only a few hours and need to be replenished daily. If I'm out of snack foods, I will put the same food on the tray and in the foundational feeder—just so I can see all the action at the tray.

I cannot say it often enough: Every feeding station needs a tray feeder. So I will say it again: Every feeding station needs a tray feeder!

Blue Jays (top left) fuss over peanuts; Cassin's Finches (top right) interact noisily as a flock on the tray feeder; White-breasted Nuthatch, Hairy Woodpecker and Carolina Chickadee (bottom right) share a tray full of various snacks; Northern Cardinal and House Finch (bottom left) quietly feed together on a tray that has a weather dome that can also be lowered to keep out larger birds.

3. Fat feeder

Downy or Hairy, Red-bellied or Gila, woodpeckers are beautiful year-round visitors to my feeding station and probably to yours, too. If you provide fats, you will be filled with pleasure at the sight of woodpeckers and many other insect-eating birds.

Most feeding stations should have a constant supply of at least one of the many choices of "fat." Although we typically think of suet-blend cakes as the main fat choice, there are many types of fat available. We also typically think of fats as being mainly used to attract woodpeckers, as it is usually their favorite food. In fact, suet and the other fats attract a variety of species from most of the families that come to feeders. Many of the birds that visit feeders eat both seeds and insects from natural food sources, and the fats are very attractive to birds that normally seek insects as part of their diets.

The longest-lasting of the fatty foods, suet blend cakes and cylinders are standard offerings. There are many kinds of suet and suet-cake feeders for you to choose from. Suet cylinders have a hole in the center, so the same feeder can be used for seed or suet cylinders.

Suet plugs placed into holes in real branches or similar-looking man-made materials work very well since the vertical hanging branch simulates a natural tree trunk. Depending on the level of activity, suet plugs can last several days.

A few years ago, I introduced a new category of fat to the market. Jim's Birdacious Bark Butter is essentially "spreadable suet" that can be applied to tree trunks, branches, and feeders. The combination of suet, peanut butter, and cornmeal is attractive to many birds that eat seeds, nuts, and insects. I am especially proud of its appeal to many birds that otherwise rarely come to feeders, including warblers, thrushes, catbirds, thrashers, and creepers. This product has expanded the species list of backyard bird feeders more than any other food with over 140 bird species across North America having been observed eating it.

Pole-mounted suet cake feeder with Downy Woodpecker and Carolina Wren (left); suet cylinder cylinder with Downy Woodpecker (right).

Should you feed peanut butter? Birds really like peanut butter, but it is hard for them to swallow and can gunk up their feathers. It is best to use Bark Butter or your own blend of peanut butter, suet, and cornmeal, which is much better for the birds than peanut butter alone.

Suet plug feeder with female Downy Woodpecker top left); natural branch as Bark Butter feeder with male Downy Woodpecker and Carolina Chickadee (top right); hanging double suet cake feeder with tail-prop for male Pileated Woodpecker (bottom left); Bark Butter feeder on top of pole with male Downy (left) and Hairy (right) Woodpeckers (bottom right).

American Goldfinches in summer plumage on a mesh finch feeder.

4. Finch feeder

Go for the gold—goldfinches, that is! Beautiful in summer and interesting all year long, these appealing little finches are on the must-see list everywhere.

Many types of finches visit our feeders, and they will eat just about any high-quality blend in your foundational feeder, especially one with hulled sunflower seeds. However, I have always found that the smaller finches, most of them exclusively seed-eaters, like to have their own feeder with their favorite food. The best food to attract them is the tiny black seed called nyjer, which for many years was known by its agricultural name, niger, or "thistle." (Nyjer is a registered trademark of the Wild Bird Feeding Industry.) The best feeder for the very small nyjer seed is a tube feeder with tiny little holes called a Finch Feeder. "Thistle" finch socks also work well but are less durable.

Goldfinches like to travel and dine together, spending their days moving from field to field. If you give them their own finch feeder, you get a better show as a large flock of two to three dozen individuals dominates your feeders. They constantly interact with each other while flying to and from the feeder and while on the feeder. If you see several species of finches present—such as American Goldfinches, Lesser Goldfinches, and Pine Siskins—they will flock and feed together, and this is best observed on a finch feeder.

Finches are also attracted to "finch blends," usually a blend of nyjer and fine sunflower chips. Don't buy a finch blend with anything more than these two ingredients: the additions are likely "fillers." Finch blends work well in finch feeders unless rain or humidity moistens the chips and they gum up. Nyjer seed has shells that can pile up beneath the feeder; to avoid a mess, use only fine sunflower chips in a finch feeder or, in moist and humid regions, use shelled whole sunflower chips in a tube feeder with larger holes.

Keep finch feeder food fresh!
Finches are picky, and if the food has been in the tube for too long, they just won't eat it. If there is uneaten food in in your finch feeder and you have not seen any finches on the feeder for three weeks, you need to replace the food. If the seed has molded or clumped, clean the feeder with a 10 percent bleach solution to prevent the fresh seed from being contaminated.

American and Lesser Goldfinches on a finch sock and finch tube feeder.

A high-perch
hummingbird feeder
with a built-in anti-
ant moat attracts
a Broad-tailed
Hummingbird.

5. Nectar, jelly, and fruit feeders

You hear the hum first. Then a tenth of an ounce of
amazing bird lands on your feeder. Wow!

A flash of black and orange flies by. An oriole
perches on your feeder to enjoy the oranges, nectar,
and grape jelly.

Hummingbirds and orioles are just too cool to
be missed.

Hummingbirds are present year-round in the
Southwest and on the Gulf and Pacific Coasts. In
the rest of the U.S. and Canada, we generally see
hummers only in the summer; the duration of their
stay is shorter the farther north they go. To take full
advantage of your local hummingbird season, offer
sugar-water in a hummingbird feeder.

Perhaps no other feeder category varies so
much in design and construction materials.
Hummingbird feeders range from the totally practical to the totally artsy. Both extremes can work
for the birds, but what should be important to you
is that the feeders be easy to fill and clean and give
great views of the birds.

The recipe for nectar is simple: four parts water
to one part table sugar, with no red dye. Keep it
fresh by cleaning the feeder and changing the nectar regularly, every two days in very warm climates
and no less frequently than every five days elsewhere. That is all the hummingbirds need from us,
because they satisfy their other nutritional needs
by eating tiny insects.

Put your feeders up before the expected arrival

Oriole feeders often have pegs for orange halves and saucers for jelly (left), attractive to these two Baltimore Orioles. Other oriole feeders (right) offer nectar with room on the top for jelly and fruit, visited by this male and female Hooded Oriole.

date, and keep a fresh supply of nectar out for several weeks after the last hummingbird observations in your area. To determine these dates for your region, consult the online resources included on page 393 under Other General References.

Hummingbird species that are otherwise rare in your region may visit your feeders in late fall. Rufous Hummingbirds, for instance, regularly show up east of the Mississippi between October and December, weeks or months after the last Ruby-throated Hummingbird has left. These wanderers can be especially hungry, but they have few options in the wild once nectar-producing flowers have disappeared for the season.

Orioles migrate north at about the same time as hummingbirds. As long as you are mixing sugar-water for the hummers, you might as well put out nectar for the orioles, too. Where hummingbird feeders tend to be bright red, oriole feeders are bright orange, echoing the color of such desirable fruits as oranges and papayas. The oriole feeder has larger holes in the sugar-water chamber to let the bird's larger bill get to the liquid. Orioles are readily attracted to the 4 to 1 water-to-sugar hummingbird formula, but they also drink up a more dilute mix of 6 to 1.

The many species of orioles are also attracted to fruit, with oranges a consistent favorite. They eat red cherries, dark red grapes, apples, papaya, and mulberries, too. If you put the fruit on a tray or another feeder designed to offer orange and apple

halves, the orioles will find your feeding station very attractive. A bonus: These fruits can attract other visitors such as Northern Mockingbirds, Gray Catbirds, Verdins, American Robins, or thrashers.

Orioles also love grape and other flavors of jelly, which can be offered in any shallow container that does not leak. The best oriole feeders have a chamber for nectar and indentations in the lid for fruit and jelly—plus a moat to keep ants off the birds' sweet treats.

Decorative hummingbird feeders come in all types of materials and sizes.

6. Snack/specialty/convenience feeders

When is your bird feeding station like a fisherman's tackle box? Every day! As seasons change, the bird situation in your yard changes. Just like a fisherman, you bring out different lures and you "fish" in a different way.

Snack and specialty feeders and foods are your main tools for being seasonally savvy. They bring more diversity to your feeding stations and more joy to your hobby.

Even though your foundational, fat, and finch feeders satisfy most of your regular visitors, you can add to or change your overall menu to attract more of the resident birds and seasonal birds as they arrive.

I include these feeders and foods in the snack/specialty/convenience category, a very large category indeed. It includes all the products we call specialty feeders: small-bird-only feeders, peanut feeders, window feeders, corncob feeders, squirrel feeders, and more.

This category also includes such specialty foods as peanuts and tree nuts, hot pepper foods, and snack foods like dried fruit. It also covers insect products such as mealworms, grubs, and larvae, whether alive or dried, and kitchen scraps such as pumpkin, watermelon, and cantaloupe seeds, dried bagels, and even baked potatoes.

The items in this category let you customize your feeding for your particular region. For instance, in the winter in Colorado and North Carolina, you could use the same foundation, fat, and finch feeders. In North Carolina, though, you might find that Eastern Bluebirds are especially plentiful at that season, so you would want to bring out your mealworm feeders and fill them daily. You would also want to put suet nuggets on a tray or inside a bluebird feeder. During that same winter in the Colorado foothills, you might find

Mealworm feeders (top left) attract warblers and other insect-loving birds. Peanut feeders (bottom left and right) can be made out of metal mesh sized just right.

Small perching birds easily use this kind of feeder (top right) while large birds have a hard time clinging to the perching area.

that Mountain Bluebirds are not very common, but Steller's Jays, Clark's Nutcrackers, and Black-billed Magpies are abundant. So you would provide peanuts in the shell and peanut halves, and then sit back and watch the show as these very intelligent birds empty the feeders in just a few hours.

This category also includes convenience feeders, which hold bird food cylinders and cakes and can be quickly and easily refilled. These convenient foods are also small, making them easy to buy and store. You might use larger sizes of these same foods in your foundational feeder, but I add and subtract seed, nut, and suet cylinders all through the year depending on weather and bird abundance.

These products can include a wide variety of ingredients, so you can offer many small cylinders with different ingredients as special "snacks."

Window feeder (top) attaches with suction cups for very close viewing. Woodpecker feeder mounted on tree (bottom left) is a very natural feeder for woodpeckers and nuthatches as they can cling to the tree or the feeder to dine. Multiple hanging tray feeder (bottom right) offers four different kinds of specialty treats.

Bird food cylinders are convenient for many reasons

▶ They take up very little space in your garage or cabinet, yet they last as long as loose seed that weighs four times more. I estimate that a two-pound seed and nut cylinder will last as long as eight pounds of similar-quality loose seed.

▶ When seed is bound together in the cylinder, it takes longer for the birds to peck off and eat each seed.

▶ You do not have to fill your feeder as often as with loose seed.

▶ Cylinders and cakes are also very easy to place on the feeder. Just remove the wrapper and place the cake in the cage or the cylinder on the rod.

Water

7. Year-round water

This beautiful American Robin is a mess! When he takes a bath, he dips and twirls to work the water through his feathers. Then he shakes it all out, spinning water everywhere and looking totally discombobulated. After leaving the birdbath, he carefully preens every feather, applying oil and putting the feathers back into place. Now his feathers are fully prepared for flight.

Birds need water all year, making a water source an essential part of your feeding station and one of the major components of any backyard habitat. Most feeder visitors will also take advantage of the water, and as a bonus, it can also attract birds that rarely or never come to the feeders. For instance, robins generally shy away from feeders, but they absolutely love to take baths, and this is the most reliable way to see them near your feeding station.

In the summer, water needs to be replaced every few days to remain fresh, clean, and free of mosquito larvae. In the winter, it needs to be not only fresh but thawed; you can use a heated birdbath or put an electric de-icer in the basin. Your birdbaths are very important in extended periods of cold,

dry weather, when natural water sources are hard to find. During these times, your birdbath may be more active than your feeders.

During times of drought, your bath becomes a magnet for many species of birds. For instance, in the Southwest, Gambel's Quail, Curve-billed Thrasher and Greater Roadrunner are attracted to your water source at any time, but especially during a drought.

Water can be supplied to your bird habitat in a birdbath, small pool, recirculating waterfall, or shallow dish, or by a dripper or mister.

Still water is fine, but the birds like flowing water, dripping water, and misting water most of all.

Water that moves and makes a sound is a game changer, greatly increasing the number and variety of birds that visit. Movement and noise can be achieved with a dripper attached to your hose to release a drop of water every few seconds. Birds find the birdbath more easily when they can hear the drop hitting the water below and see the ripples move across the surface. The drops also keep the water fresh by slowly replenishing the contents of the birdbath. You can achieve the same results by hanging a plastic gallon jug of water above your

A built-in heater thaws the water all winter.

birdbath and punching a small hole in the bottom.

A mister sprays a fine mist into your birdbath instead of releasing a drop. The birds will stand under the mist to take their bath right there. This method uses more water per hour, an important consideration in many areas. A mister can also be set up to spray branches or leaves; hummingbirds will fly back and forth through the mist and land on the branch for their bath, a really cool sight.

Birdbaths are available in countless styles and can be made of concrete, pottery, ceramic, resin, glass, or plastic. A birdbath should be no deeper than three inches. A gentle slope from the rim to the middle is best, because the birds can find the depth that is best for their bath. If your birdbath is too deep or has steep, straight sides, a few rocks in the bottom will help birds comfortably reach the water.

A small dish attached to your feeding pole will provide water for a day. A specially designed cup mounted on top of the pole can hold a hummingbird feeder with an ant moat, providing a quick and convenient drink for small birds such as chickadees.

Since birdbaths are used both for bathing and for drinking, the water should be changed often and droppings removed. Clean the bath daily if it is heavily used, or every few days if it is visited less frequently. It is best to keep the birdbath in a shady spot to reduce the growth of algae and microbes. Use a brush to scrub away droppings and algae every time the bath is refilled. It is wise to do a deeper cleaning with a solution of ten percent bleach every two to three weeks; be sure to rinse the birdbath well before refilling it.

A mister (left) greatly increases the attractiveness of a bath to birds. A dripper (right) creates sound and water movement that is attractive to birds.

Nearby landing surfaces

8. Perching branches

I almost cut down that unsightly dead juniper bush in Colorado, but I just never got around to it. In Indiana, my favorite 70-foot pignut hickory blew over in a big wind, barely missing the second-story deck, the house, and the hot tub. Those two near-misses opened my eyes to what I now know are some of the most important yet unheralded additions to a feeding station.

When I started to really look at that unsightly dead juniper, I realized it was constantly used by the birds visiting my feeding station. The Steller's Jays would land on the top branches, call out to all that would hear, fly in to the feeding station, and land on the tray feeder. Mountain Bluebirds, American and Lesser Goldfinches, Pine Siskins, House and Cassin's Finches, and five varieties of Dark-eyed Juncos all hung out in its branches. They were constantly interacting as a flock, calling to announce their presence or issue a predator alert. That juniper had more birds on it than the feeders did! It gave me a great view into their social behavior and the chance to see three or four times as many birds out the window. What a mistake it would have been to cut it down.

The pignut hickory stood right off our deck in Indiana. It shaded the deck, provided the squirrels an annual bounty of nuts, and gave the birds a place to land as they came into the feeders. Over the many years I was testing Jim's Birdacious Bark Butter, that was the tree I used—and it enticed the

A dead juniper provides many perching branches for birds that arrive alone or in flocks.

The top branches from my fallen hickory tree (left) works well to provide perching branches and vertical landing spots. A 30 foot forest-grown maple tree (middle) set up next to my second floor deck is a woodpecker and nuthatch favorite landing spot. A perching tree (right) can be made out of an iron pole with real branches.

rarely seen Brown Creepers to dine on the spreadable suet. In fact, it is the bark of that very tree that appears on the Bark Butter label.

What a loss, I thought, looking at the fallen giant. I wanted to replace it, but how could I plant another 70-foot tree? I grabbed my chain saw and cut out a 10-foot section of gnarled branches. I dragged the branches up onto the deck and attached them about 6 feet from the feeders. Later, I cut down a 30-foot forest-grown sugar maple and mounted it on the other side of the feeders.

All I wanted was a keepsake of my favorite hickory tree, but what I found out truly surprised me. Thanks to these twisted branches near the feeders, the number of birds I could see out my window tripled. Instead of landing 20 feet above the deck, they were landing at eye level in the hickory branches or on the maple trunk, before and after visiting the feeders.

Black-capped Chickadees, Red-breasted and White-breasted Nuthatches, and Tufted Titmice, which before had flown to a distant perch to crack open their sunflower seeds, now went to the nearby branches, where they could be watched pecking away at the food.

I decided to conduct several 15-minute studies of the birds approaching and leaving the feeders. My very unscientific observations showed that two out of three birds coming to the feeders landed first on either the nearby scraggly hickory branches or the tall maple trunk and branches. One out of two birds flew to these branches when they left the feeders, and only then continued into the woods.

My quick studies supported what I see every day: If you provide gathering and perching branches, the birds will fly to them, deem the feeder safe, and then fly to it. A nearby tree or bush also gives the birds a safe place to go to if they feel threatened.

These branches can be living or dead. For flocking and ground-dwelling birds, a thick bush is the best pre-landing spot. Dark-eyed Juncos, sparrows, and finches love to congregate in low vegetation as they move to and from the feeders. Larger trees, dead or alive, are best for attracting Northern Cardinals, jays, grosbeaks, and tree-dwelling species such as chickadees, woodpeckers, and titmice. The closer to the feeders you place the branches, the better they work.

What can you do if you don't have a dead juniper, or you can't cut the top branches out of a hickory tree? It is easy to make your own tree with real or artificial branches. You can use a full-sized, well-branched dead tree if you can find one in a forest—or beside a garden center's dumpster. You can also combine components of Wild Bird Unlimited's Advanced Pole System. With the main feeder pole augered into the ground, you can make a tree by adding metal branches or attaching real branches to the pole with metal holders.

You can also use a pole to support a large dead branch placed upright in the ground. Keep in mind that perches for gathering and perching work best when they are three to six feet away from the feeders. If squirrels are a problem, you might need to install a baffle on the pole below the branches. Once this "tree" is in place, you may see two to four times as many birds at a time at your feeding station. For instance, instead of seeing one chickadee quickly grabbing a seed and flying away, you will have one at the feeder and another on the branches. Finches love branches where the whole flock can gather, so instead of seeing only the six on the feeder perches, you might have those six on the feeder and another dozen or more gathering in the branches and interacting with each other as they await their turn on the feeder.

Four species (top)—Downy Woodpecker, Carolina Chickadee, House Finch and American Goldfinch—are making use of this perching branch set-up. Hardware (left) for attaching perching branches to pole.

Perching space for all
With perching branches near feeders, you may see two to four times as many birds at a time at your feeding stations. Left to right: Lazuli Bunting, Red-headed Woodpecker, American Goldfinch, Black-headed Grosbeak, Red-bellied Woodpecker, Stellar's Jay, and Clark's Nutcracker. Bottom right: Lazuli Buntings, American Goldfinches, and Black-headed Grosbeak.

Sixteen American Goldfinches and a single Pine Siskin (opposite page) are gathered at this set-up with plenty of perchng space.

9. Vertical landing spots

As a final tribute to my Bark Butter hickory tree, I asked the tree-removal crew to cut out a few slabs of bark, which I mounted on my feeder poles above the raccoon baffles. That way, I could still feed Bark Butter on my favorite tree's bark. Interestingly, I observed something new: The woodpeckers and nuthatches coming to the bark slab for spreadable suet liked having a vertical landing surface. They first landed on the small vertical slab of bark and then went on to the suet feeder or other feeders—again and again.

A slab of bark, a vertical 1-by-6-inch cedar board, or the vertical portions of your perching branches can provide a vertical landing spot. Before visiting the other feeders, woodpeckers and nuthatches will land here, check out the lay of the land, see which other birds are present, decide if everything is safe, select the feeder they want to visit, and then fly the remaining few feet.

These birds naturally use vertical surfaces out in the woods. The woodpeckers land head-up, the nuthatches head-down. With a vertical landing spot at the feeders, the birds give more extended views; nuthatches spend twice as long in the feeding area as when they fly directly to and from the feeder. And when the Pileated Woodpecker lands on this vertical surface, I hold my breath and don't move.

Slab of hickory bark with a portion of Bark Butter.

Woodpeckers and nuthatches love to land on vertical surfaces prior to visiting feeders or to dine on Bark Butter on those vertical surfaces. Rough surfaces are best for them to grip to.

Why do woodpeckers and nuthatches land differently?

Woodpeckers have evolved to hunt for insects on tree trunks by going up and around trees while using their rigid tail feathers for support. Nuthatches have evolved to seek food while going down the trunk, and have no need to brace themselves with their short tail. Because they hunt in different directions on the same trunk, each kind of bird discovers different insects in the bark crevices, and thus they are able to share the same tree as a food source.

Vertical landing spots can be fat feeders, offering suet plugs or Bark Butter. Pileated Woodpecker (top left); Red-headed Woodpecker (top right); White-breasted Nuthatch (bottom left); White-breasted Nuthatch and Downy Woodpecker.

Thoughtful Bird Feeding Station Elements in Detail 63

Feeder locations

10. Thoughtful feeder placement

Hang your feeders from a tree. Place a pole in the ground. Mount them on a fence, wall, or window. Or put a pole on your deck railing. There is almost always a way to put your feeders exactly where you want them.

The most important considerations:

▶ The birds have easy and safe access to the feeders.

▶ You can see the birds from your windows.

▶ You can see the birds from your patio or deck.

▶ You can fill and clean the feeders easily.

▶ The feeders are sheltered from the weather.

▶ They are at a proper distance from branches to discourage leaping squirrels.

▶ The feeders are sheltered from the weather.

▶ The feeders are at a suitable distance from one another.

▶ The feeders and landing areas are at a variety of heights.

▶ They are at an appropriate distance from windows.

My deck feeders (above left and bottom right) are about 10 feet from our windows and provide a great view of the birds from several places in our home.

Let's start by taking a look at your house and where you might put feeders so you can watch the birds from inside.

The birds have easy and safe access to the feeders.

Even a yard that is completely barren of plants can still attract birds to a feeding station—but not as well as a yard with landscaping and places to land and hide. If trees or bushes are already available in one spot, you might choose to put your feeders there, near the natural vegetation, saving the effort of creating perching areas. Wood, wire, or split rail fences are also excellent perches, readily used by birds near the feeding station.

Safe access means that the birds can easily see and hide from a predator, whether a hawk from above or a cat from below.

You can see the birds from your windows.
Where do you spend the most time in your house? The kitchen, family room, den, breakfast nook, bedroom? Do you want to be able to sit down to watch, or do you enjoy the show while you are washing dishes or preparing dinner? Are you going to watch the birds while you are out on your deck or patio? Which part of your yard has the most vegetation that is most likely to attract birds? Do you want to have feeding stations in several places to maximize the variety and number of birds you can see at any one time? Do you want to avoid placing feeders near walks, patios, flowerbeds, or pools to keep them free of shells or droppings?

In most yards, the best places for feeders are

fairly obvious, and there will be only a couple of places that are truly excellent. The best location is where you can most easily observe the birds from the spot where you spend the most time.

GROUND-LEVEL WINDOWS. If your chosen window is at ground level, you have the most choices for your feeder station setup. You can put your feeders on a pole or poles, or hang them from tree limbs. Feeders can be located very close to the window or 10 feet away or more. There are even feeders that attach right to the window.

DECK-LEVEL WINDOWS. If your preferred observation windows look out onto a second-story deck, you might have fewer choices for feeders and placement, but you can still create a wonderful station. My deck has been my main area for bird feeding for nearly 30 years. You need to be able to easily fill the feeders and keep raccoons from messing with your setup; it is also important to keep the deck clean of seeds and droppings.

Feeders are excellent for learning about nature with grandparents (above) and even entertain the young ones during a morning snack (below left).

You can see the birds from your patio or deck.
You might want to place your feeders so that you can enjoy the birds while relaxing, cooking, or hanging out on your patio, deck, lanai, screened porch, or balcony. The same fundamental consideration applies here as when you are watching from inside: where do you have the best view of the birds as they approach and use the feeders? But there are a few additional things to keep in mind, too.

Since each bird has its own "personal space away from humans" requirement, the feeders need to be a certain distance away from your favorite seat. Some birds, such as hummingbirds, will feed within a few feet of you. Others, such as chickadees, nuthatches, and Downy Woodpeckers, will visit the feeders even if you only are 5 or 6 feet away. Northern Cardinals and Red-bellied Woodpeckers, in contrast, are very cautious, and may visit only if the feeders are at least 10 feet away and you can remain very still and quiet. It really is fun to have the birds visit when you are outside with them, so make sure to place the feeders at the correct distance from your seat.

You can fill and clean the feeders easily.
No matter where you place the feeders, you need easy access to fill them up. And every few weeks, you will need to clean them. I like to have a dry spot where I can put the food containers while I am filling the feeders. This is easy on my deck, but out in the yard it might be helpful to have a stepping stone near the feeders. Place the container on the stone, and you won't have any mud or ground litter to clean off the bottom later.

I have seen feeder stations where the feeders were so high on a pole that they required a ladder for access. If you make it too hard to fill your feeders, you won't do it very often, and the feeders will sit empty. You also want to be able to get to the feeders quickly and safely in rainy or snowy weather.

Since most of my feeders are on my deck, I have a hose outlet very near the feeder station. This lets me blast out the feeders occasionally and clean any bird droppings or seed shells from the floor of the deck and deck rails. I keep two cleaning brushes near the hose: one for the feeders and deck and one for the birdbath. This way I don't contaminate the birdbath water with anything I clean off the feeders or deck.

The feeders are sheltered from the weather.
If you live where extreme weather is frequent, such as unrelenting rain, strong winds, or blizzards, then shelter is a big consideration. You don't want the seed to be wet, blown out, or covered in snow. In high winds and blizzards, a sheltered feeder is a welcome respite for the birds, and it will be heavily visited.

In areas where such conditions are rare, it is not necessary to have wind-proof or blizzard-proof feeding stations. But still be prepared to move your feeders to a sheltered area on the infrequent nasty day, even if it is not ideal for viewing from your windows. Don't worry about the squirrels getting some goodies; in these conditions, it should be a free-for-all. All creatures need food in extreme weather.

They are at a proper distance from branches to discourage leaping squirrels.

If you feed the birds, you probably feed other hungry wild animals, too. Many hobbyists decide that that is OK, while others make it a life goal to never feed squirrels. Since we are talking about feeder placement here, you need to know that it is important to maintain certain distances off the ground and away from trees, decks, and window sills.

Squirrels can jump 3½ feet straight up, so if the top of your squirrel baffle is 4 feet off the ground, your food is safe. However, they also jump from above or from the side. If the tree or window sill is 10 feet away, you won't have any leaping squirrels; it's just too far. What if a tree branch is directly overhead? Gravity is our friend here: if the distance to the feeder is too great, a squirrel can drop too quickly and injure itself. They know this, too, and they don't usually take the chance. Generally, if the branch is at least 8 or 10 feet above the feeder, squirrels just stay in the tree. For more about squirrels, turn to Chapter 7.

How close can feeders be to each other?

This is a really great question, and the answer depends on your feeding situation. If you have room to spread your feeders out, then do so. If you have only a small area and you can put up only one pole, then it is just fine to put many feeders with different foods all on that pole. I have placed as many as nine feeders and food types on the same pole on my deck. Note: If you ever see signs of stress or disease in the birds, then immediately reduce the number of feeders in one area and spread the feeding stations out. You'll find more about that situation in Chapter 10.

If you notice that one individual is dominating your feeding station, then space out your feeders to give the other birds a shot. If a Northern Mockingbird is scaring away all the other birds, then you need at least two feeding stations as far apart as possible, perhaps one on each side of your house, making it difficult for the mockingbird to defend them all.

I always advise having several feeding stations for the greatest hobby enjoyment. However, you can do quite well with one feeding station with feeders and foods that attract six or seven species at the same time.

There is a diversity of heights of the feeders and landing areas.

Birds of different species are more comfortable gathering together if the feeders offer multiple heights and sight lines. I have found that the birds like to choose from several levels to land on or feed from. For instance, when I put out a tray feeder, I also provide several other feeders—wooden hoppers, finch feeders, tail-prop suet feeders—and a fake metal branch, all at different heights so that several species can comfortably use the feeding station. The various heights and sight lines mean that they are not all forced to interact on the tray. That diversity of heights and landing areas means that I get to see more birds.

Windows: How close and how far away are they?

Your feeders should be either within 3 feet of your windows or more than 10 feet away. Avoid placing feeders in the 3- to 10-feet zone.

The distance between your windows and your feeders is not just about your view; it is a safety issue for the birds.

In my experience, resident backyard birds fly into windows for two primary reasons: hormones and panic.

HORMONES. In spring, male birds competing for breeding territories chase each other. Sometimes they are so intent on the chase that they forget about the nearby building, and seeing only the reflections of yard and sky, they hit the window at

Migration and windows
One study estimated that 365 to 988 million birds die each year on hitting residence windows in the U.S.; most of the victims are migrants. That is a huge toll, averaging two to nine birds at each house each year. The windows of houses and other buildings are one of the most significant man-made causes of bird mortality. If you find that migrating or resident birds are striking your windows, you should do your best to disrupt or disguise the reflection, as described in Chapter 8 on page 338 and study the resources available on the American Bird Conservancy web site (www.abcbirds.org).

full speed. It was very sad one spring to find two male Indigo Buntings that had flown into a picture window during such a chase. That window now has shiny tape streamers, and there have been no other accidents. Whatever your feeder's location, birds with breeding on the brain may hit windows.

PANIC. A flock of birds on your feeders will panic when a hawk flies by, when you open doors or windows, or when they hear loud noises. The birds fly off in all directions. If they work up enough speed, they can be injured when they hit the window. My office windows are floor-to-ceiling glass with a mirrored surface on the outside, potentially the worst possible situation for the birds. But by adhering to the right distances for feeder placement, I have very few window strikes.

Why the closer-than-3-feet-and-farther-than-10-foot advice?

1. When feeders are closer than 3 feet, a few panicked birds may fly into the window, but they can't gain enough momentum to hurt themselves, and usually bounce off uninjured.

2. When feeders are farther than 10 feet from the window, panicked birds may spook towards the window, but they have time to make a sharp turn and avoid hitting it.

If you are still seeing window kills, then move your feeders closer or farther from the windows until you have solved the problem. If resident or migrating birds are hitting your windows with some frequency, there are various window treatments that make the window more noticeable or that decrease the deceptive reflections of your yard and the sky (see page 338.)

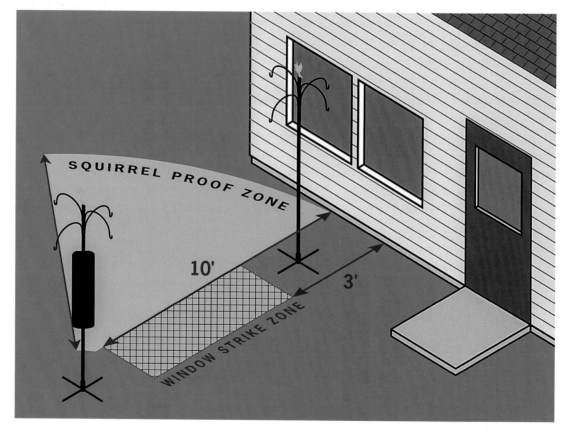

Bird feeders should be within 3 feet or farther than 10 feet from windows for bird safety. Hanging feeders on poles above a baffle should be 10 feet or more from windows or squirrels will jump from the window sill onto the feeders.

11. Multiple bird feeding stations

The more feeding stations you have, the more birds will come to your feeders.

I usually have about 15 feeders going at any one time in my forested Indiana yard. I'm nuts, but it brings me joy.

My feeders are not all in the same place. I organize them into three distinct bird feeding stations: two stations on our 60-foot-long second-story deck, and one on the edge of the woods in front of the house, visible from our front windows. In really active periods, such as snowstorms, I add stations at the side of the house and in a little dogwood tree by the front door to take care of all the hungry birds the morning after.

The two stations on the deck, both easily seen from our kitchen and our deck's dining table, are very different. One is the major setup, with my foundational feeder and many fat, specialty, finch, and other feeders; it is raccoon-proofed to keep them from destroying the feeders every night. The other station is a covered tray feeder with snacks; because that food has usually been eaten up by the end of the day, the feeder does not need to be raccoon-proof. Just for fun, I change the snacks every week or so, and add feeders as the season dictates: a hummingbird feeder in the summer, and seed or finch tubes and a Bark Butter feeder in the winter. One hummingbird feeder certainly attracts the hummers, but I always have at least three in three different areas. That way, no dominant hummer can keep the others away, and I get to see three times as many birds!

I also think strategically about what it takes to restock all of my feeding stations. I might have to carry five or six kinds of food to my main station on the deck, but I have to carry only one to three foods to my auxiliary stations. That way, I can fill all the feeders quickly without carrying every food to every station.

A variety of feeders and water sources in several locations attracts the most birds!

Basic critter solutions

12. Station is free of squirrel, chipmunk, raccoon, nuisance bird, and cat problems

It's your feeding station, so you should feed whoever you want to feed. All the basic problems with unwanted feeder visitors can be solved fairly easily, letting you enjoy the sight of the birds you want to see dining. Chapter 7 discusses how to solve (or nearly solve) all sorts of problems, so I won't go into much detail at this point.

Choosing the right combinations of feeder, pole, baffle, dome, hanger, and food can generally keep unwanted critters off your feeders.

To avoid feeding the birds you just don't want to feed, you can usually find a technique that at least decreases the amount they eat and their

dominance at the feeder. Cages to exclude larger birds, domes that slide down to allow only small birds, weight-sensitive perches, and careful food choices—offering the foods your unwanted guests do not like and avoiding those they do—are a few of the strategies.

Outdoor cats are a serious problem. American Bird Conservancy estimates that domestic cats kill 1½ to 4 billion wild birds each year in the U.S. alone. The ABC's Cats Indoors campaign seeks to address this issue.

The strategies described in Chapter 7 can help protect birds as they approach and leave the feeders and while they are eating. If outdoor cats roam near your feeders and you cannot change the situation, you can make it very difficult for the cats to kill your visitors.

Not today, Mr. Squirrel! Most tube feeders can be purchased or retro-fitted with a squirrel-excluding cage that has mesh sizes large enough for small birds to feed.

The Outfitter

The Outfitter is one of my favorite bird feeders, as it can incorporate many of the 12 elements of a thoughtful bird feeding station. I designed and patented it in the late 1990s to be as simple or as complex as the hobbyist desired, with the possibility of offering different foods in different feeders as the birds change through the seasons. The Outfitter lets you include all 12 elements of a thoughtful bird feeding station.

1. Foundational feeder

The main chamber holds enough seed blend for several days, and it has enough perching areas for several birds at a time, all visible from inside your home.

2. Tray feeder

The removable lid is also a tray feeder. The wooden rain ledges above the hopper feeding area are also small trays, ideal for a few nuts or peanuts in the shell. An additional small tray can be added to the front surface for additional treats.

3. Fat feeder

The rough cedar side is ideal for offering Bark Butter, or one of the hangers can hold a suet cake or cylinder feeder. You can also attach a suet cake holder to the side of the feeder.

4. Finch feeder

Just hang a finch feeder from one of the hangers.

5. Nectar, jelly, and fruit feeder

You can hang a multi-purpose oriole feeder from the hanger, place orange slices on the tray feeder lid, and put jelly in the removable small tray.

6. Snack/specialty/convenience

The tray feeder lid, ledges, and side dish can hold all sorts of snacks, including Bark Butter Bits, peanuts, and mealworms. The hanging arms conveniently suspend any type of cylinder feeder. Dozens of food and feeder combinations are possible.

7. Water

A small dish, with the drainage holes plugged, holds a small amount of water.

8. Perching branches

A metal branch or branch holder can easily be attached to the wooden sides.

9. Vertical landing spot

The feeder is made of rough cedar for a reason. Woodpeckers and nuthatches naturally land on the main wooden feeder before jumping to their chosen feeder.

10. Thoughtful feeder placement

The Outfitter can be mounted on a 4 x 4-inch pole or on a metal pole using a flange, so it can be placed in the ground or on a deck. The feeder has multiple levels, so several species can feed at the same time without conflict. All the birds feeding are visible from inside your home.

11. Multiple bird feeding stations

This can be your main bird feeding station, supplemented by smaller, specialized stations around the yard.

12. Freedom from squirrel, chipmunk, raccoon, nuisance bird, and cat problems

A baffle under the feeder and the right choice of various foods can solve most problems.

3 The Birds

Why are these birds in my backyard, and how do they find my feeders?

I T I S T H E tapestry of expected and unexpected visitors that creates daily excitement in our yards. We can divide our visitors into several groups: year-round residents, seasonal residents, irregular migrants, and spring/fall migrants. Each species has its own survival strategies and has evolved to use certain habitats at different seasons.

Chick-a-puff!
This Carolina Chickadee fluffs its downy feathers to hold more heat during a frigid winter's day.

Year-round residents

Year-round residents are those birds that can reasonably be expected to be seen or heard almost every day of the year. Just which species are resident varies from one region to the next. In Iowa, for example, a forested backyard is probably the year-round home of Northern Cardinals, Red-bellied Woodpeckers, and Black-capped Chickadees. If you travel to northern Minnesota or west to Colorado, only Black-capped Chickadees remain. If you go south to Kentucky, you still find Northern Cardinals and Red-bellied Woodpeckers, but the slightly smaller Carolina Chickadees replace Black-capped Chickadees. In Iowa, American Goldfinches are present year-round, but they are seasonal residents in Florida, occurring only during the winter.

Year-round resident birds can meet all their needs within a small local area. For instance, where cardinal populations are at their densest, a male Northern Cardinal's home range can be as small as 2.8 acres. To help you think about the size of territories, an acre is just a bit smaller than a football field without its end zones. A Red-bellied Woodpecker occupies a home range of 30 to 45 acres, though it may actively defend only about one third of it. A Black-capped Chickadee's home range averages 28 acres, but can be as small as 13 or as large 93 acres, depending on the season, the availability of food, and the bird's possible status as a "floater" moving from one flock to another.

Seasonal residents

Seasonal residents are birds that migrate between distinct summer and winter homes. For example, in much of the U.S., Dark-eyed Juncos make their home with us only in the winter, and they then travel to Canada or to higher elevations in the western mountains for nesting.

In Indiana, it is fairly predictable that as soon as the Dark-eyed Juncos have headed north in spring, the Ruby-throated Hummingbirds show up; in fall, we expect to see the first juncos in the couple of weeks after the last hummers have gone south. With the exception of year-round populations on the Pacific Coast, Southwest, and Gulf Coast, hummingbirds are seasonal residents in the U.S., migrating hundreds or thousands of miles to and from their winter homes. When the hummingbirds arrive in the spring, they nest and then gather energy for the trip south. Male Ruby-throated Hummingbirds spend only about four months in their Indiana summer home, and their true long-term residence is in tropical Central America.

Sparrows provide other examples of seasonal residents. In that same Iowa backyard with the Northern Cardinals, or more likely in a yard with a nearby shrubby field, you will see American Tree Sparrows only in the winter and Field Sparrows only in the summer. Tree sparrows tolerate much lower winter temperatures than Field Sparrows. Both species migrate south only as far as they need to find suitable habitat and food.

Irregular migrants

Many species have unpredictable migration patterns. At bird feeders, we can observe this phenomenon most commonly in the species collectively called "winter finches": Pine Siskins, Purple and Cassin's Finches, Common and Hoary Redpolls, Evening and Pine Grosbeaks, and White-winged and Red Crossbills. All of these birds breed in the forests of Canada and move south or to lower elevations only when their main food is in short supply.

In any given winter, you may have zero of these birds, or you may have dozens. When finches disperse far south of their normal winter range,

Cardinal-puff!
Cardinals also puff out their feathers to hold more heat on very cold winter days.

an event known as an "irruption," fortunate bird feeding stations become their host. Sometimes more than one species irrupts into the same region, as in the winter of 1997-1998, when Red and White Crossbills, Common Redpolls, and Evening and Pine Grosbeaks all converged on the northeastern U.S.

Common Redpolls have irrupted consistently every two or three years since about 1960. Their main food sources are spruce and birch trees, which bear a poor seed crop every other year. Their normal southern wintering limit reaches from Massachusetts west to Idaho, but in an irruption, they can extend as far south as North Carolina and Oklahoma.

Hoary Redpolls are one of the few songbirds to spend the winter in the months-long darkness above the Arctic Circle. They obviously have learned to forage in the dark! But they also have a two-year irruptive cycle, and every other winter they migrate south, though rarely as far south as their Common Redpoll cousins. Both redpoll species are attracted to nyjer seed and sunflower chips.

White-winged Crossbills can eat thousands of spruce seeds in a single day, using their unique bill to open the cone and their tongue to remove the exposed seed. However, the shape of that same bill restricts their ability to eat other seeds, making them even more dependent on conifer crops. Red Crossbills, more commonly seen year-round in southern Canada and the mountains of the western U.S., are also irruptive, moving in years of low cone production. Fortunately for us, both crossbills are perfectly able to open sunflower seeds, which will attract crossbills by the dozens if they pass through your yard.

Pine Siskins, year-round residents of southern Canada and mountainous western regions, are famous for their erratic irruptive behavior. Siskins' broad range of food sources includes conifer cones, smaller seeds of grasses and composites, and alder and birch seeds. When these food sources are low, they irrupt into the central and southern U.S. Because of their smaller bills, Pine Siskins tend to favor nyjer and sunflower chips over larger seeds.

Spring/fall migrants

Many birds pass through our yards on the journey between their winter and summer homes. Your yard, in other words, can be considered a migration stopover point. Scientists have emphasized that the habitat and food supply at these stopover points are just as important as the conditions at each end of the journey. Migration can last several weeks, and exhausted birds must restore their depleted fat stores along the way. Can you imagine driving from Florida to Michigan without stopping at any gas stations or restaurants?

Your yard can become an important link in the migration of dozens of species. Several species of migrants—such as Rose-breasted Grosbeaks, White-crowned Sparrows, and Golden-crowned Kinglets—might come to your feeders. Other birds, such as most of the warblers, find food away from your feeders as they glean cutworms, fruit, buds, beetles, and ants from your trees. Many will find rest and refuge from predators in your dense shrubs or high trees. Birdbaths and wildlife ponds are often the best way to attract these migrants; moving or dripping water is usually most immediately appealing. Many spring migrants that feast on caterpillars can be enticed to a tray of mealworms and many species of warblers are attracted to an offering of Bark Butter.

Your spring and fall migrants become someone else's seasonal residents farther north or south. For instance, Magnolia Warblers regularly winter in Central America. If you see one in the spring in Iowa, you are seeing a migrant; it will keep migrating until it reaches northern Minnesota or Canada, where it is a resident while nesting before moving south again to its winter home.

Why don't all birds migrate south for the winter?
Migration is risky business, and a high percentage of migrating birds die during the journey. If you have evolved ways of finding food and staying warm during the winter, why not just stay north? Come spring, the birds that have wintered farther to the north get to the choice nesting sites first and can take advantage of their head start to raise more than one brood of young.

Even so, many of the birds that summer in the north must migrate south simply because their food sources disappear with the change of seasons.

What would a Tree Swallow swallow if it spent the winter on its northern breeding grounds? Tree Swallow diets are 80 percent insects and spiders, mostly caught in flight. The other 20 percent is fruit, mostly bayberries. So Tree Swallows go north only for nesting, then depart before frosts kill all the flying insects. They can live on bayberries in fall or winter, but this food source is not as consistently available as insects.

Hummingbirds provide a more extreme example of the loss of food sources in winter. They fly north to raise their young, dine on flower nectar and small insects, and then head south or to temperate coastal areas where food is available all winter. You will notice that hummingbirds are very aggressive around sugar-water feeders, all out of proportion to their size. That is because the stakes are high: hummers are literally just hours away from starvation, so when they find a reliable source of food, they defend it with great gusto. This aggression seems to be even more extreme in the late summer, when they need food both for daily needs and for fuel on the long migration south.

Partial migration
Some birds migrate only as far as they need to, depending on the climate, snow cover, and food availability. For example, only the far northern populations of American Robins and Eastern Bluebirds are consistently migratory. Those populations living farther south tend to stay as far north as they can for as long as they can, and migrate south only if the winter turns out to be extremely cold, snowy, and berry-deficient. Such birds are called "partial migrants," since some individuals in a population are permanent residents in the nesting area and others migrate. In some winters, it is possible to see robins flocking by the hundreds or thousands to search for berries in even the coldest areas; the availability of food affects their survival more significantly than the temperature does.

The Magnolia Warbler is a spring/fall migrant across most of eastern North America. It breeds in Canada and the northeastern U.S. and winters in the Caribbean and Central America.

How do birds find feeders?

By sight, sound, touch, or smell?

Songbirds mostly find their food in the wild by sight, which is probably the most highly developed of the senses in most species. They constantly search through plants and foliage or scratch around in the underbrush, and some species are adept at spotting and catching flying insects.

Although it often seems that an American Robin is cocking its head to listen for a worm, it's actually just trying to get a better view. On the other hand, woodpeckers appear to actually hear insects crawling under rotten bark. Some groups, such as shorebirds and wading birds, find food by feel with their beaks or by shuffling their feet through the mud. Only a few birds, such as some of the carrion-eating vultures, find their food by smell.

Always hunting

So, songbirds are always visually hunting for their food. Perhaps a bird feeder is just another object to a bird, because they instinctively are checking everything out. What a nice surprise it must be to find a feeder full of sunflower seeds, a suet feeder full of food that does not have to be coaxed out of a wood cavity, or a hummingbird feeder with a bountiful supply of sugar-water. With patience, just about every well-stocked bird feeder will be found by birds as they check out all possible food sources. Once found by one bird, many others will follow.

Individual styles of hunting

Each species has its own particular style of looking for food, a distinctive set of behaviors often easily seen and enjoyed at our feeders.

White-breasted Nuthatches creep down tree trunks, scouring the bark for insects. If the feeder design allows for it, they cling upside down to inspect a feeder offering, grab it, and go. Often they take a sunflower seed back to a tree, lodge it in the bark, and peck it open while perching head-down. Chickadees are gleaners, looking everywhere for insects and seeds, even hanging upside down from a leaf or twig to search all surfaces. They are often the first species to come to a new feeder, where they usually grab a seed and fly to a branch to peck it open while holding it with their feet.

Chickadees, nuthatches, and titmice often travel together in small foraging flocks. This behavior lets all the birds take advantage of a food source found by any one of them, and also lets the group stay more alert to predators. Even though they flock, all of these birds tend to visit feeders only two or three at a time.

Always moving, or stay until empty

Because their food can be quite plentiful and concentrated once it is found, some seed-, bud-, and fruit-eating birds travel in large flocks at some seasons. Especially in winter, those flocks stay on a productive plant until their food is gone, while insect-eaters—whose food is more scattered, more mobile, and less abundant—must constantly keep on the move. Seed- and fruit-eating birds tend to visit feeders in flocks and stay on a bird feeder for a long time. Since this "tree" is magically replenished each day—by you, of course—the birds stay and gulp down one seed after another. Goldfinches, House Finches, Pine Siskins, Evening Grosbeaks, Northern Cardinals, and other seed-eating species may settle in at a feeder for many minutes at a time, leaving only when they are startled or forced off by a hungry flock mate.

The**Cornell**Lab of Ornithology

Which of these birds are in my yard?

A good way to find this out, of course, is to visit your local bird feeding specialty store and ask. You can also consult a wide range of internet resources. The Cornell Lab of Ornithology makes available many years' worth of data about birds at feeders all over North America, along with some very helpful resources to help you identify birds.

Birds at feeders in your area during the winter

To see the 25 birds most abundantly seen in your area, see the Project FeederWatch pages starting on page 408 or go online and explore www.feeder-watch.org.

Great Backyard Bird Count (GBBC) for birds in your area in February

For detailed information about can be seen in your area on a single February weekend, visit the Great Backyard Bird Count: gbbc.birdcount.org.

This event, organized by the Cornell Lab of Ornithology, the National Audubon Society, and Bird Studies Canada, has been sponsored by Wild Birds Unlimited from its beginning in 1998.

eBird and hotspots for birds in your area year-round

To learn about all the birds ever seen in your area or vacation destination, look at an eBird hotspot near you: ebird.org and look for "Explore Hotspots."

Tricky identifications

The Great Backyard Bird Count website offers help with such tricky identification challenges as chickadees, woodpeckers, red finches, and hawks: gbbc.birdcount.org and look for "Tricky Bird ID's."

Over 600 birds on line

And to learn about most North American birds in detail, you can go to All About Birds, another service of the Cornell Lab of Ornithology at www.allaboutbirds.org.

Phone apps

A really effective smartphone app is Merlin Bird ID by Cornell Lab of Ornithology. Merlin will ask you a few questions and then show you several possible identifications, one of which is probably the species you are trying to identify.

Other apps are comprehensive guides to the identification of birds in the field. Go to your app provider and type in "Field Guide to Birds" to call up many useful titles.

Keep a list of the birds in your yard! Go to the Feeder Birds Checklist on page 406–407

Guide to Feeder Birds

All of the approximately 180 species of common, uncommon, or regionally restricted birds that visit feeders are included in this guide; a few rare birds that may come to feeders are not treated.

Along with the photographs and range maps, there is information about what they eat and how they behave at feeders. If there is more than one species in a family, an introduction to that family is followed by detailed information about each species. Except for hawks, which are described at the end of this section, the birds are listed in more or less the conventional field guide order, which begins with waterfowl and ends with finches.

The range maps included for each species in this section of the book indicate breeding range in green and winter range in blue for North America north of Mexico. Where these ranges overlap (year-round) is indicated in purple. Migratory routes are shown in orange and areas of rare occurence are shaded yellow.

Feeder Foods
Whole corn, cracked corn, sunflower chips

■ BREEDING

■ WINTER

■ YEAR-ROUND

■ MIGRATION

■ RARE

Black neck, white cheek.

Canada Goose

Preferring to feed on grasses and other short vegetation in open fields and near bodies of water, Canada Geese have taken to residential areas, parks, business parks, and golf courses very well, and their numbers are rapidly increasing in most areas. When attracted to bird feeding stations, it is usually in the fall and winter when they turn more to grains and are eating seeds under the feeder. They find a life-long mate in their second year and each of their broods will stay with them through their first year.

Male with iridescent green head, white neck ring, gray body. Bill bright yellow. Males look similar to females in late summer.

Female plain brown and tan with iridescent blue patch on wing. Bill is patterned black and orange.

Feeder Foods
Whole corn, cracked corn, milo

BREEDING

WINTER

YEAR-ROUND

MIGRATION

RARE

Mallard

Mallards are one of the most easily recognized ducks in North America. They are not common at backyard bird feeders, but pairs sometimes visit to look for food and nesting sites. If a pair of Mallards is hanging around each day in the spring, they may attempt to nest nearby. Mallards eat a wide variety of foods throughout the year, consuming more vegetation in the spring and more grains in the fall. They may browse on seeds under a feeder, especially if there is cracked corn.

White tips on tail feathers visible when fanned.

Feeder Foods

Milo, cracked corn, sunflower, figs, berries

BREEDING

WINTER

YEAR-ROUND

MIGRATION

RARE

Olive-brown overall, bare red throat, long light-tipped tail.

Plain Chachalaca

Resident in the lower Rio Grande Valley of Texas, this large chicken-like bird spends most of its time foraging in trees for berries, leaves, buds, and seeds. It readily comes to feeders for cracked corn and milo. It is also partial to grapefruit and orange halves. Usually found in small family groups, which can merge into larger flocks and overwhelm feeders or even an entire feeding station. Named for its raucous call.

Quail, Pheasants, and Turkey

Quail are plump, talkative birds found in family groups most of the year. In some species, those groups may join with others into large flocks, or coveys. Quail have short rounded wings for explosive take-offs and quick bursts of flight to evade predators—but they prefer to walk and run, especially when they are entering backyards. They often post a sentinel to call out any danger while the rest of the covey is feeding or drinking in the open. Quail often visit feeders right after dawn and before dusk. The calls of California and Gambel's Quails are a loud, harsh *ChiCAgo*.

Western species are well suited to desert climates. They don't need water as long as green plants are available. All the same, they are attracted to water features. Quail eat a wide variety of foods at feeders, including milo, millet, cracked corn, and sunflower. They glean seeds from the ground or a ground feeder or peck at a seed block.

Ring-necked Pheasants are introduced game birds that occasionally visit feeders in large flocks. Native Wild Turkeys also visit feeders in large flocks in some areas.

Feeder Foods

Millet, cracked corn, milo, oil sunflower, sunflower chips, nyjer, oats, Bark Butter

Male with forward-drooping crest, white eyebrow, black throat, dark brown cap, white face lines, scaly nape and belly. Female is plain, with gray head and scaly belly.

■	BREEDING
■	WINTER
■	YEAR-ROUND
■	MIGRATION
■	RARE

California Quail

Fairly common in high desert, foothills, and sagebrush habitats. Diet is mostly vegetarian, but does eat beetles, caterpillars, and snails. Nests in shallow depressions that can hold up to 16 eggs, possibly laid by several mothers. Tear-shaped crest of six or more feathers. California Quail form winter coveys, normally of 20-70 birds.

BREEDING

WINTER

YEAR-ROUND

MIGRATION

RARE

Male with forward-drooping crest, white eyebrow, black throat, dark brown cap, white face lines, scaly nape and belly. Female is plain, with gray head and scaly belly.

Gambel's Quail

The desert range of the Gambel's Quail does not overlap with that of the similar California Quail. Not as scaly as the California Quail, it also has a forward-drooping "top knot." Gambel's Quail form coveys of 5 to 15 birds, at times up to 200.

BREEDING

WINTER

YEAR-ROUND

MIGRATION

RARE

Male with striped head, white eyebrow and throat, barred belly.

Female plainer with tan-patterned head.

Northern Bobwhite

An infrequent feeder visitor, usually in fall and winter. Uses open patches of loose dirt for dust bathing. Coveys are small, 5 to 15 birds. The call, *bob-WHITE*, is loud and easily recognized.

Male with vertical crest, bluish gray head and breast, reddish throat, bold white barring on sides. Female similar but slightly paler.

Male with scaly look on breast, shoulders, and belly; fluffy, white-topped crest. Female very similar, with slightly paler head and shorter crest.

Mountain Quail

These large, very secretive quail are easily overlooked, as they keep to thick brush most of the year. Their diet is mostly fruits, nuts, and seeds gleaned from the ground. They are easily identified by their distinctive head plume, which can stand straight up like an exclamation point. Mountain Quails form coveys of 10-20 birds.

Scaled Quail

Scaled Quail have a fluffy white crest that earns them the nickname "cottontop." Scaled pattern on neck and body. Often 25 to 40 birds in a covey.

BREEDING

WINTER

YEAR-ROUND

MIGRATION

RARE

BREEDING

WINTER

YEAR-ROUND

MIGRATION

RARE

Male with long tail, iridescent green head, red around eye.

Feeder Foods
Sunflower, cracked corn, millet, milo

BREEDING

WINTER

YEAR-ROUND

MIGRATION

RARE

Female pale brown with black spots, pale buff underparts.

Ring-necked Pheasant

Pheasants are long-tailed runners, the males sporting an iridescent green head. They are powerful flyers with a noisy take-off, but usually fly only when flushed, going to roost, or trying to reach fruit in a tree. They are usually found in prairies and agricultural fields, where they feed on waste grain. These large birds blend in amazingly well with the landscape. Male pheasants gather a harem of females during nesting season, which they defend vigorously against other males. In winter, pheasants gather in single-sex flocks. They may visit feeders at any time of year.

Male with black and white head, spotted sides, reddish brown chest and belly. Female mottled brown.

BREEDING

WINTER

YEAR-ROUND

MIGRATION

RARE

Montezuma Quail

A beautiful small quail with a knack for hiding. Uncommon and quiet, Montezuma Quail prefer to hide and stay very still when approached, flushing only when one is almost upon them. They visit feeders on rare occasions. Found in pairs or coveys of up to 12 birds. Male is colorful, with a clownish black and white head and spotted sides.

Large stocky bird. Male with iridescent bronze-brown body and wings with bare red and bluish head. Stiff "beard" feathers coming out of chest. Female dark brown.

Feeder Foods
Whole corn, cracked corn, white millet, milo, oil sunflower, sunflower chips, oats, safflower, Bark Butter

BREEDING

WINTER

YEAR-ROUND

MIGRATION

RARE

Wild Turkey

The Wild Turkey is found in all states but Alaska and just north of the border into Canada in a few areas. Turkeys live in large flocks, traveling on the ground by day and roosting in trees at night. Their favorite habitat is mature forests with plenty of acorns and nuts from oak, beech, and hickory. They readily fly onto tray feeders or gather on the ground for spilled seed.

Doves and Pigeons

Feeder Foods
Cracked corn, white millet, milo, oil sunflower, safflower, suet and Bark Butter (rarely)

Doves and pigeons are closely related family members and often wear out their welcome when large numbers of them dominate bird feeders to the exclusion of smaller songbirds. They have an impressive appetite, and settle in for sustained feeding sessions when food is abundant. These banquets often end with a mass retreat to a favorite roost.

Watch closely when these birds come to water: Unlike other birds, which take up one bill's worth of water at a time, doves and pigeons are able to suck up a continuous stream of water. It takes less than 20 seconds for them to consume an entire day's supply.

Mated pairs usually stay together for at least one full season. It takes both parents to provide enough food for the growing nestlings, which are fed on "crop milk," a yogurt-like secretion produced in the adults' crop.

BREEDING

WINTER

YEAR-ROUND

MIGRATION

RARE

Dark, iridescent bluish green, bluish gray, or reddish brown head and neck, with gray, brown, or black multi-colored body.

Rock Pigeon

Though not a common visitor to most suburban feeders, large numbers of this familiar bird may invade feeding stations in urban or rural areas. Many consider it a pest because of its dominance over other birds at feeders, its large appetite, and its copious droppings. See page 326 for ways to discourage Rock Pigeons from visiting your feeders. Plumage varies widely.

Dark-tipped yellow bill, white neck collar, gray body.

BREEDING
WINTER
YEAR-ROUND
MIGRATION
RARE

Band-tailed Pigeon

The Band-tailed Pigeon is the Rock Pigeon's country cousin. Instead of a city life, it prefers more remote wooded habitats, where it forages in trees for acorns, nuts, and berries. Rarely a nuisance at feeders, small flocks visit to feed on cracked corn, milo, and sunflower.

Overall gray, black collar, square tail.

BREEDING
WINTER
YEAR-ROUND
MIGRATION
RARE

Eurasian Collared-Dove

Native to Europe and Asia but released into the wild in The Bahamas in the mid-1970's, this dove has now taken up residence across most of North America. In areas with large populations of collared-doves, they can overwhelm feeders as they seek seeds and grain from the ground and at elevated feeders.

Overall pale gray with scaly appearance, rusty wing feathers visible in flight.

- BREEDING
- WINTER
- YEAR-ROUND
- MIGRATION
- RARE

Inca Dove

Small, chunky birds of Texas and the Southwest, Inca Doves appear more frequently at suburban feeders than rural ones. They move and forage together in small to large flocks. The male's courtship display is an entertaining performance of head bobbing, strutting, bowing, and tail fanning.

- BREEDING
- WINTER
- YEAR-ROUND
- MIGRATION
- RARE

Males are overall pale gray with pinkish wash on head, black-tipped orange bill, scaly neck and head, and iridescent black spots on wings. Female paler below, less pink on head and neck.

Common Ground-Dove

Tiny, only the size of a sparrow. Not as social as other doves, pairs or small flocks commonly forage on the ground around feeders.

Bonded pairs are rarely more than a dozen feet apart.

Overall grayish brown, prominent white crescent on forward part of wing, dark line on cheek. Square-tipped tail. Female similar to male.

BREEDING

WINTER

YEAR-ROUND

MIGRATION

RARE

White-winged Dove

These doves readily use elevated feeders. They seem to prefer corn, sunflower, and safflower over the small seeds that Mourning Doves routinely take. Common in desert areas where they eat saguaro and other fruits. They are often seen in large flocks as they move about the countryside.

Brown and gray plumage, small head, pointed tail with white tips. Male is slightly larger than female with a more colorful bluish crown and pink-tinged breast.

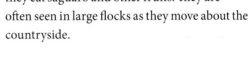

BREEDING

WINTER

YEAR-ROUND

MIGRATION

RARE

Mourning Dove

Mourning Doves' diet is 99 percent seeds, taken mostly from the ground. Amazing fliers, they are often seen making rapid direction changes. Listen for the whistling sound their wings make when they take off.

Brown and gray plumage, white-tipped square tail, red legs, yellow eye.

BREEDING

WINTER

YEAR-ROUND

MIGRATION

RARE

White-tipped Dove

Found in the Rio Grande Valley of southeastern Texas, the medium-size White-tipped Dove can be overlooked or mistaken for a White-winged Dove or the smaller Mourning Dove. The White-tipped Dove has no black on the head, no white on the wings, and a square tail. It spends most of the day on the ground, often in dense cover, foraging singly for seeds, fruits, and insects. An aggressive dove, it is rarely found in flocks, and is known to chase and harass other dove species. White-tipped Doves readily visit bird feeders for cracked corn, milo, and sunflower.

Hummingbirds

There may be no greater spectacle in the hobby of backyard bird feeding than the one you can witness at your hummingbird feeders. The aerobatic flight, buzzing wings, brilliant iridescent colors, and loud chirps of these tiny dynamos are guaranteed to provide non-stop entertainment.

Hummingbirds have a specialized tongue to lap nectar from flowers and feeders; the bill tip is flexible to let them also capture insects. They love spiders and spider eggs. Hummingbirds typically do not play well together at nectar feeders, as males defend their territory and siblings squabble. This behavior often decreases when large numbers of hummingbirds are drawn to the same feeders.

Hummingbirds are promiscuous in nature as they form no bond with their breeding partner. In most species, the male hummingbirds perform a spectacular courtship display of repetitive climbs, dips and dives. Unassisted by the male, the female builds the nest and raises the young.

Foods at Feeders
Sugar-water nectar, fruit flies drawn to rotting bananas

Hummingbirds, like this male Ruby-throated, will visit feeders throughout the day. Offer sugar-water nectar that is 1 part table sugar and 4 parts water. Keep it fresh!

Male with iridescent purple forehead, metallic green throat, black breast.

Female plain with green back and large white eye spot.

BREEDING

WINTER

YEAR-ROUND

MIGRATION

RARE

Magnificent Hummingbird

Found regularly only in the mountains of southeast Arizona. This slow-flying hummingbird probably consumes a larger percentage of insects than our other hummingbirds, but it also actively seeks out nectar feeders and flowers.

Male with green head, back, and tail, with iridescent red or reddish orange throat, grayish white underparts, black wings.

Female plain, with green back.

BREEDING

WINTER

YEAR-ROUND

MIGRATION

RARE

Ruby-throated Hummingbird

The most common spring and summer humming-bird at feeders in the East. Ruby-throated males arrive in spring before the drab olive females, and depart weeks earlier in fall. They routinely return to the exact location of last year's feeder or to their previous nest site. Ruby-throats are fearless and easily lured to hand-held feeders, or even to a pool of nectar in the palm of your hand.

Male with dark head, black chin, distinctive purple throat band. Green upperparts and whitish underparts.

Female plain, with green back.

BREEDING

WINTER

YEAR-ROUND

MIGRATION

RARE

Black-chinned Hummingbird

This western hummingbird occupies a wide range of habitats in the spring and summer, from deserts to mountain forests. Many winter along the Gulf Coast in Texas. The chin feathers are black, in the right light bordered below by a beautiful purple band.

Male with brilliant rosy-pink head and throat with small white spot behind eye. Throat gorget flares down slightly on each side. Metallic green above and dingy green below.

Female plain, with iridescent rosy patch in center of throat.

BREEDING

WINTER

YEAR-ROUND

MIGRATION

RARE

Anna's Hummingbird

Common along the Pacific Coast throughout the year, the hardy Anna's Hummingbird is spreading northward, probably in response to exotic winter-flowering plants and the year-round availability of nectar feeders. The male is known for its amazing dive display, in which it ascends over 100 feet before diving rapidly towards the female. Males sing a complex song, unusual among hummingbirds.

Male with purple crown and throat with each side of throat gorget extending downward, dark wings.

Female plain, with iridescent green upperparts, white underparts.

BREEDING

WINTER

YEAR-ROUND

MIGRATION

RARE

Costa's Hummingbird

This small hummingbird breeds in late winter and spring in desert scrub habitats in California and Arizona. After nesting, it can be found in a variety of mountain and coastal habitats, including backyards and gardens.

The deep purple on both the male's throat and crown is exclusive to this species.

Male with metallic green above with brilliant red throat, white breast and belly.

Female with speckled throat, green back, buffy sides, whitish underparts.

BREEDING

WINTER

YEAR-ROUND

MIGRATION

RARE

Broad-tailed Hummingbird

Found in the high elevations and foothills of the Rocky Mountains, the Broad-tailed Hummingbird survives cold nights by lowering its body temperature. Not many hummingbirds are easily identified by their sound, but the broad-tailed is well known for the loud, shrill buzzing trill it makes in flight. In spectacular courtship displays, males climb to great heights and dive towards a female, making a loud trilling noise all the way down and as they reascend.

Male with bright rusty face, flanks, back, and tail, iridescent reddish gold throat.

Female with green back, rusty flanks, white breast and belly, and olive-green spots on throat.

BREEDING

WINTER

YEAR-ROUND

MIGRATION

RARE

Rufous Hummingbird

One truly tough hummingbird, the Rufous is the northernmost nester (as far north as Alaska!) and one of the most belligerent defenders of feeders and flowers. A fast agile flyer, its wings beat up to 62 beats per second. In recent winters, this westerner has been found occasionally at feeders in the eastern U.S.

Male with green cap and bright rusty face, sides, and tail, with greenish back and iridescent scarlet throat gorget.

Female with greenish back, coppery sides and flanks, spotted throat.

BREEDING

WINTER

YEAR-ROUND

MIGRATION

RARE

Allen's Hummingbird

Easily confused with the virtually identical Rufous Hummingbird, the Allen's Hummingbird breeds only along the Pacific Coast from southern Oregon to southern California. The male's wings produce a loud metallic buzz in flight; territorial defense is a spectacular display that includes repeated pendulum flights and a 90-foot power dive, ending with a burst of loud metallic sound.

BREEDING

WINTER

YEAR-ROUND

MIGRATION

RARE

Male with metallic green back, distinctive streaked reddish purple gorget.

Female with buffy sides and belly, green back and throat spots.

Calliope Hummingbird

The smallest bird in the U.S. and Canada, the Calliope nests in the high mountains of the Northwest. Its round-trip migration to and from southern Mexico is over 4,000 miles, an amazing feat for a three-inch bird that weighs less than 1/10 of an ounce. Small but tough, Calliope Hummingbirds are very territorial during nesting season and chase away small and large birds including hawks! They tend to migrate north along the coast and migrate south in the interior higher elevations.

Male (above and below left) with bright reddish orange bill with dark tip, dark iridescent green body, brilliant blue throat, broad notched tail.

Female with plain green upperparts, gray underparts, white line behind eye.

BREEDING

WINTER

YEAR-ROUND

MIGRATION

RARE

Broad-billed Hummingbird

Don't look for a broad bill on the Broad-billed Hummingbird as the size difference is indistinguishable in the field. Found mostly in foothills and along streams in southeast Arizona, Broad-billed Hummingbirds forage in scattered patches of flowers and visit nectar feeders.

Woodpeckers

Feeder Foods
Suet, suet blends, Bark Butter, peanuts, tree nuts, mealworms, sunflower, sunflower chips, cracked corn, fruits, nectar

What would bird feeding be without the thrill and excitement woodpeckers bring to our yards? Once they have discovered your feeders, these bold, boisterous, and hard-working birds are likely to become the most faithful visitors. Part of the excitement lies in the sheer variety of species that can visit. No other family of feeder birds is as diverse, and a day with seven woodpecker species visiting the feeder is not out of the ordinary in many areas of North America.

Though the variety of woodpeckers can be impressive, their numbers never get out of control, as they visit feeders alone or in the company of their mate. Summer can be the busiest time of year, when many species of woodpeckers bring newly fledged youngsters to the feeders. Their clumsy antics and disheveled plumage give the kids away every time.

Woodpeckers seem to have endless adaptations to a lifestyle so punishing that most other birds would consider it a sentence of hard labor. From the top of the head to the tip of the tail, every part of a woodpecker has evolved to help it cling to hard surfaces and dig for nesting cavities and insects. The feet of all but Black-backed and American Three-toed Woodpeckers have two toes pointing forward and two back, unlike the three-and-one arrangement of most birds. The two opposing sets of toes give woodpeckers a much better grip on trees and cacti. The barbed tip of a woodpecker's tongue is very sensitive, and is used to both detect and impale insect larvae. The tongue is also coated with sticky mucus to keep prey from slipping away.

A female Northern Flicker (yellow-shafted type) about to launch from a nesting cavity.

Metallic green above, extensively pink belly, wide gray collar, red face patch. Sexes alike.

Entirely red head with black back and shoulders, large white wing patches and white underparts. Sexes alike.

Lewis's Woodpecker

The Lewis's could be called the "flycatching" woodpecker thanks to its unusual habit of taking insects right out of the air. This is its major foraging technique in summer, and unlike most other woodpeckers, it rarely digs in trees for prey. In fall and winter, Lewis's Woodpeckers cache large quantities of acorn pieces and other food in the cracks and crevices of trees. They are infrequent feeder visitors, but are known to visit for suet, peanuts, and Bark Butter.

	BREEDING
	WINTER
	YEAR-ROUND
	MIGRATION
	RARE

Red-headed Woodpecker

These striking birds with their bold black and white pattern and unmistakable solid red head are always welcome in any backyard. Unfortunately, they are sporadic feeder visitors, even where they are locally abundant. Having nearby oak trees seems to be a key as they are acorn specialists and cache them in large numbers for a reliable winter food supply. In addition to the standard woodpecker feeder fare of suet and peanuts, they can also be drawn to Bark Butter, cracked corn, and sunflower on a platform feeder.

	BREEDING
	WINTER
	YEAR-ROUND
	MIGRATION
	RARE

Black back and wings, white underparts, white eye, and red, white, and black face. Bold white patches seen in wings and rump during flight.

Black and white barred back, pale buff head and underparts. Male with scarlet cap.

Acorn Woodpecker

With its cartoon-like appearance, comic performances, and fascinating social behavior, the Acorn Woodpecker is one of the most entertaining visitors you can have in your backyard. These birds are best known for their practice of storing acorns in holes drilled into a "granary" tree. A single tree can hold 50,000 acorns! Acorn Woodpeckers also catch flying insects. They are readily attracted to suet, peanuts, Bark Butter, and tree nuts, and occasionally take sugar-water from humming-bird feeders.

Gila Woodpecker

Nesting in saguaro cacti, mesquites, or cottonwoods, this species survives on a wide-ranging diet that includes cactus fruits and flowers, insects, seeds, small lizards, and many other items. It can be drawn to your backyard with suet, oranges, and Bark Butter, but its real passion is sugar-water in hummingbird and oriole feeders.

- BREEDING
- WINTER
- YEAR-ROUND
- MIGRATION
- RARE

- BREEDING
- WINTER
- YEAR-ROUND
- MIGRATION
- RARE

Black and white barred back, pale buff underparts, golden orange nape, black tail, and golden forehead patch. Male with red cap. Golden belly hard to see.

Black and white barred back, pale buff underparts. Male with scarlet crown and nape; female with red nape. Faint red streak on belly hard to see.

Golden-fronted Woodpecker

Found in brush land and open woodland in south and central Texas and southwest Oklahoma, the Golden-fronted resembles the closely related Red-bellied Woodpecker in appearance and behavior. Named for the small forehead patch of golden feathers, this woodpecker dines on a wide variety of foods, including ants, moths, cicadas, acorns, pecans, cactus fruits, and persimmons. It visits feeders for suet blends, peanuts, Bark Butter, sunflower seeds, oranges, corn, and nectar.

Red-bellied Woodpecker

Among the most adaptable woodpeckers, Red-bellieds eat an amazing variety of natural foods. This is mirrored at feeders, where they seek out suet, sunflower seeds, Bark Butter, peanut pieces, tree nuts, corn, and many other foods. Though they favor suet, they are just as likely to use a hopper, tray, or tube feeder, and frequently scavenge food from the ground. Watch for them to make repeated visits to your feeders in the fall, when they are busy caching food for the winter.

- BREEDING
- WINTER
- YEAR-ROUND
- MIGRATION
- RARE

- BREEDING
- WINTER
- YEAR-ROUND
- MIGRATION
- RARE

Male (right) with mottled black and white back, dirty white-yellow underparts, red crown and throat, white wing stripe. Female (left) similar with white throat.

Male with mottled black and white back, white stripe on side, dirty white-yellow underparts, red crown and throat, red nape patch. Female with white chin, red throat.

Yellow-bellied Sapsucker

This sapsucker can drill up to 50 small holes an hour into a tree. When the holes fill with sap, the sapsucker returns to suck up the sap with its brush-tipped tongue as well as insects attracted to the sweet sap. The "sap wells" can be an important food source for early arriving hummingbirds. The Yellow-bellied is the most frequent of the sapsuckers to visit feeders, but it is still uncommon. It seems to be most attracted to Bark Butter, less so to suet blends. Sapsuckers are also attracted to nectar and juicy fruits.

BREEDING

WINTER

YEAR-ROUND

MIGRATION

RARE

Red-naped Sapsucker

This is the sapsucker of the Rocky Mountains, where it taps conifers and hardwood trees, especially quaking aspen, for sap. It favors aspens for nesting cavities. Once abandoned by the sapsucker, these cavities become important roosting and nesting sites for birds like the Mountain Bluebird. Like the other sapsuckers, it is not a regular visitor to feeders, but can be attracted with suet blends.

BREEDING

WINTER

YEAR-ROUND

MIGRATION

RARE

Red head, throat, and breast, black and white back, distinctive white wing stripe, dirty white-yellow underparts, white rump seen in flight.

Black overall, white head and wing patch. Male with red nape patch.

Red-breasted Sapsucker

Many other birds, mammals, and insects take advantage of the sap wells these woodpeckers drill in aspen, alder, and other trees. Rufous Hummingbirds follow sapsuckers to new wells and nest in areas with trees that are actively being tapped. Red-breasted Sapsuckers are infrequent visitors to feeders, but can be attracted with suet blends.

White-headed Woodpecker

North America's only black woodpecker with a predominantly white head. This bird is typically found in ponderosa and other large pines, as it depends heavily on their seeds as a major portion of its diet, especially in fall and winter. It forages quietly and rarely digs in trees, instead gently flaking off bark and prying open cones in search of insects and seeds. This woodpecker is most likely to visit backyards with large pines and dead trees. It will visit suet feeders and Bark Butter.

BREEDING

WINTER

YEAR-ROUND

MIGRATION

RARE

BREEDING

WINTER

YEAR-ROUND

MIGRATION

RARE

Robin-sized and long-billed, black and white overall with unspotted white outer tail feathers. Male with red nape.

Female lacks red nape.

Hairy Woodpecker

The Hairy Woodpecker is as widespread as the Downy, but it is a less frequent backyard visitor. Despite the 2-inch difference in length, it can be tough to separate these two look-alikes. A key difference is the Hairy's much longer, chisel-like bill, roughly as long as the head is wide. The Downy's short bill is less than half the width of its head.

The Hairy Woodpecker seems to enjoy a sweet drink on occasion, drinking from sapsucker wells, hummingbird feeders, and even sugar cane.

BREEDING

WINTER

YEAR-ROUND

MIGRATION

RARE

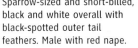
Sparrow-sized and short-billed, black and white overall with black-spotted outer tail feathers. Male with red nape.

Female lacks red nape.

Downy Woodpecker

Our smallest woodpecker, the Downy is found year-round in most of North America, except for the arid Southwest. In winter, Downy Woodpeckers flock and forage with chickadees, titmice, nuthatches, and Hairy Woodpeckers. Each member of the mixed flock relies on its companions to help find food and to provide early warning of predators.

The Downy's contrasting black and white back pattern confuses predators by breaking up the bird's shape and outline. When threatened by a hawk in your backyard, a Downy will freeze motionless on a feeder or nearby tree for up to ten minutes, undetected and safe unless it moves too soon. Attracted to a wide variety of foods, including suet blends, Bark Butter, sunflower chips, peanuts, tree nuts, and mealworms.

BREEDING

WINTER

YEAR-ROUND

MIGRATION

RARE

Barred black and white above, pale below, mostly black cheeks and white throat. Male with red crown.

Barred black and white back, light underparts, black cheeks. Male with red crown

Nuttall's Woodpecker

A California resident, Nuttall's Woodpeckers are most often found in oak woodlands, where they forage for insects and acorns. Usually probe openings and scale off bark while searching for insects. The nesting holes excavated by these woodpeckers are important to other cavity-nesting species. Nuttall's can be attracted to suet, sunflowers, and Bark Butter.

BREEDING

WINTER

YEAR-ROUND

MIGRATION

RARE

Ladder-backed Woodpecker

Closely related to the Nuttall's Woodpecker of oak woodlands, the Ladder-backed is almost exclusively a bird of deserts and other arid areas, where it feeds and nests in cacti and mesquites. Its diet is primarily insects, with some cactus fruit. This sporadic feeder visitor eats suet blends, peanuts, sunflowers, Bark Butter, and occasionally sugar-water from hummingbird feeders.

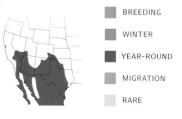

BREEDING

WINTER

YEAR-ROUND

MIGRATION

RARE

Overall tannish brown with black spots and barring, white rump and belly, black chevron on breast. Yellow-shafted males with black mustache.

Red-shafted males with red mustache; females lack mustache.

Northern Flicker

The Northern Flicker breaks the woodpecker mold. Instead of the typical black and white patterns, flickers have a tan body with black breast spots, light black barring on the back, and a black chevron on the breast. The eastern variety (Yellow-shafted) sports yellow underwings, and western birds (Red-shafted) have red underwings.

Unlike other woodpeckers, which forage primarily in trees, flickers spend much of their time foraging on the ground for ants and beetles. Often roost under porches and on rafters.

BREEDING

WINTER

YEAR-ROUND

MIGRATION

RARE

Crow-sized, black overall, bold white neck stripes. Bold white patches visible in wings during flight. Male with red mustache and completely red crest.

Female with black mustache and black forehead.

Pileated Woodpecker

One of the biggest thrills in backyard bird feeding is having a Pileated Woodpecker appear at your suet feeder. It is hard not to be awestruck when you watch this handsome crow-sized bird with its conspicuous black and white plumage and jaunty red crest at such close range.

This large woodpecker is usually heard before being seen. Despite their impressive size, Pileateds can be surprisingly tentative at feeders, and rarely come in without scouting out the area from a nearby tree. They eventually gain more confidence, but are easily spooked by any movement inside the house. They can become regular and faithful visitors, often in pairs, and even bring their young to your feeders. Upright suet feeders with a "tail prop" seem to be their preferred choice, but they are also attracted to Bark Butter, bird food cylinders, peanut pieces, and tree nuts.

BREEDING

WINTER

YEAR-ROUND

MIGRATION

RARE

Pileated Woodpecker behavior

I was fortunate to photograph this encounter between a male and female Pileated Woodpecker. The male landed while the female was dining on the feeder. She apparently fed him just as she would feed young, inserting her bill inside his. The female then left and the male took over the feeder. This happened in January, and was probably part of a ritual marking the beginning of another breeding cycle.

Escaped Exotics

Feeder Foods
Millet, milo, cracked corn, sunflower, fruits

Exotics are birds that are not native to North America but have escaped from captivity. Several species of exotic parrots, parakeets, lovebirds, and bulbuls have managed to establish breeding populations in the United States. They often gather into flocks, which can completely cover a bird feeder. The Monk Parakeet has been reported in over 20 states, but most exotic species are found in California, Texas, and Florida.

Parrots

There are over a dozen species of exotic parrots in California alone. These birds feed on the seeds, buds, leaves, and fruit of at least 34 plant species. Unlike many of the larger parrots, Monk Parakeets and lovebirds regularly visit bird feeders.

Green above, lime green below, pinkish red face, short tail.

Peach-faced Lovebird

Also known as the Rosy-faced Lovebird, this small African parrot has escaped from captivity and is now thriving in pockets around Phoenix, Arizona. Since their introduction in 1987, they do not appear to be having any negative impacts on native bird populations or habitats. Flocks of these brilliantly colored birds are easily attracted to bird feeders and fruiting trees. At feeders, they prefer shelled peanuts, papaya, and oil sunflower. A water feature or birdbath is also a major draw for these entertaining little birds.

Stocky green parrot with bright red crown and blue feathers behind the eye.

Red-crowned Parrot

Although likely endangered in its native habitat of northeastern Mexico, the Red-crowned Parrot is now found in southern California, southern Texas and in some southern Florida locations.

Not known to interfere with local native birds as they prefer to roost and nest in ornamental plants in developed areas.

Green back and belly, gray face and chest. Long tail. Blue wings visible in flight.

Monk Parakeet

Commonly seen in Miami, St. Petersburg, Houston and New Orleans, but since they are one of the few parrots that can survive frigid winters, Monk Parakeets have also established populations in New York City and Chicago. Altogether, they have been sighted in over 20 states. These natives of Argentina nest communally in large stick nests in trees and on power poles.

Flycatchers

Feeder Foods
Mealworms, Bark Butter

Members of the flycatcher family, with a natural diet that consists mainly of flying insects, are rarely drawn to feeders. However, they have been known to visit feeders with mealworms and Bark Butter. Water features and birdbaths also attract them.

· ·

Black head, chest and tail with white belly. Bobs tail.

BREEDING

WINTER

YEAR-ROUND

MIGRATION

RARE

Black Phoebe

Closely related to the Eastern Phoebe, the Black Phoebe occupies a similar niche from Texas to California. It builds its nest under bridges and overhangs and pumps its tail continuously while perched. It is almost always found near water, where there is an abundance of insects and plenty of mud for nest construction. Mated pairs stay together for as long as five years. Uncommon at feeders but has been observed eating Bark Butter.

Gray head and back, white breast and belly. Bobs tail.

Male with bright scarlet crown, neck, and belly, with brownish back, wings, and tail. Female with brown head and upperparts, white breast, scarlet blush on belly.

Eastern Phoebe

Listen for a buzzy whistled *fee-bee* and watch for a bird with a bobbing tail. The Eastern Phoebe survives mostly on insects, but it can also eat small fruits, letting it spend the winter farther north than other flycatchers. This is one of our earliest nesting species with some nest building occurring by late March. They are best known for choosing nesting sites under bridges, in barns, under porches and below the eaves on homes. The male and female are indistinguishable and are rarely seen together, even when nesting.

Vermilion Flycatcher

A spectacular flycatcher found in southwestern scrub, especially near water. Where present, it is easy to spot as it finds a perch with a good view and repeatedly flies out and back to catch insects. A rare visitor to feeders, it has been recorded at feeders with mealworms.

- BREEDING
- WINTER
- YEAR-ROUND
- MIGRATION
- RARE

- BREEDING
- WINTER
- YEAR-ROUND
- MIGRATION
- RARE

Jays, Magpie, Nutcracker, Crows, and Raven

Feeder Foods
Peanuts in the shell, peanut pieces, striped and oil sunflower, sunflower chips, suet blends, Bark Butter, Bark Butter Bits, mealworms, whole and cracked corn, orange halves, dried fruits

Bold and intelligent, these birds make their presence known with loud and distinctive calls as they take charge of the bird feeding station. Males and females look alike. They are omnivores, eating a wide variety of foods in the wild, including seeds, nuts, fruits, and road kill.

All of these birds make repeated trips to feeders to gather seeds and nuts, which they then cache in a safe spot, sometimes miles away, for later retrieval. These birds have been seen stuffing their crop with 50–100 seeds at a time. Only the Steller's and Blue Jays have crests.

Gray below, darker above, dark patch on back of head, white forehead, no crest.

BREEDING

WINTER

YEAR-ROUND

MIGRATION

RARE

Gray Jay

The Gray Jay is one of the few non-raptor species known to carry food in their feet in flight. Gray Jays store food by gluing it to high branches with their sticky saliva. This food is always available, even in the deepest snow. Mated pairs of Gray Jays live out most of their lives in a territory of less than 200 acres. Very tame, will fly to your hand for peanuts and dried fruits.

Green body, black face and throat, violet crown and cheeks, yellow underside of tail. No crest.

Overall dull blue, long dark bill, no crest.

Green Jay

The only green-colored jay; found in the U.S. only in southern Texas. Usually in small family flocks; last year's young help the parents in their next nesting attempt. Some are very tame, visiting picnic sites and feeders, while others stay well hidden. They eat a wide variety of insects, spiders, nuts, berries, fruits, and even small rodents. Orange halves, peanut butter, and sunflower seeds are a favorite at the feeders.

- BREEDING
- WINTER
- YEAR-ROUND
- MIGRATION
- RARE

Pinyon Jay

A mated pair of Pinyon Jays works together to cache food so that both members of the pair know where to find it later. In years when pinecone crops fail, Pinyon Jays engage in an irruptive migration, leaving their home territories and moving great distances in search of food. Pinyon Jays live in permanent social groups that can be 40-500 individuals, often showing up at feeders.

- BREEDING
- WINTER
- YEAR-ROUND
- MIGRATION
- RARE

Blackish front half, deep blue back half with dark crest, white eyelash. Long vertical crest.

Blue crest, black-barred tail, black necklace, bright blue, gray, and white upperparts.

Steller's Jay

Steller's Jays are birds of the evergreen forests of the western mountains and coasts. They are very bold around human habitations and campgrounds, and will seek out feeders and steal any food left out. They usually announce their presence with loud rasping calls. Fledglings are very loud, calling for food at first light. They have the broadest palate of any jays, eating a wide variety of foods. They usually visit feeders in small flocks.

Blue Jay

Blue Jays live at forest edges and in suburban yards, especially where there are oak trees. Peanuts in the shell are a favorite, since they resemble their wild favorite, acorns. Watch your feeder to see them shaking peanut shells to determine if they are full or empty. The Blue Jay is a talented mimic, giving imitations that can fool even experienced birders; its rendition of a Red-shouldered Hawk's call may be given to clear other birds from a feeder so that the jay can eat without disturbance.

BREEDING

WINTER

YEAR-ROUND

MIGRATION

RARE

BREEDING

WINTER

YEAR-ROUND

MIGRATION

RARE

Blue head, wings, and tail; white throat with blue necklace, pale forehead and shoulders, no crest.

Blue head, wings, and tail, white throat with gray underparts, no crest.

Florida Scrub-Jay

Listed as threatened under the Endangered Species Act, the Florida Scrub-Jay is found only in oak-scrub habitats of Florida. The Florida Scrub-Jay can become very tame, and will even land on you in search of a tasty handout. Florida Scrub-Jays often help raise the young of others in the flock.

California and Woodhouse's Scrub-Jays

In 2016, scientists "split" the Western Scrub-Jay into two separate species: the California Scrub-Jay and Woodhouse's Scrub-Jay. Both species are nearly identical in appearance and are very vocal, with many different calls. Mule deer sometimes let jays land on them to search for parasites. At feeders they enjoy sunflower seeds, peanuts, and Bark Butter Bits at feeders.

BREEDING

WINTER

YEAR-ROUND

MIGRATION

RARE

BREEDING

WINTER

YEAR-ROUND

MIGRATION

RARE

Light blue head, wings, and tail, grayish back and underparts, no crest.

Mexican Jay

Found year-round in flocks of 5 to 25 birds in oak woodlands of southeast Arizona, southwest New Mexico, and the Big Bend area of Texas. Mexican Jays are cooperative breeders, helping one another with just about everything to do with nesting. Their natural foods include acorns, pinyon nuts, small insects, and lizards. Observed at feeders eating peanuts and Bark Butter.

Black head and rear, white belly and wing patches, iridescent blue-green wings, long dark tail.

Black-billed Magpie

With their striking markings, long tail, and constant raucous chatter, Black-billed Magpies are hard to mistake for any other bird. They prefer grasslands and sagebrush, and often come close to buildings in search of food. They build a bulky, domed stick nest in trees.

Gray body with black wings, tail, and bill. White patches visible in wings and tail in flight.

BREEDING

WINTER

YEAR-ROUND

MIGRATION

RARE

Clark's Nutcracker

A large, stocky mountain bird, the Clark's Nutcracker makes itself known with loud calls and a flash of white in wing and tail as they fly. These birds specialize in opening pinecones, caching seeds by the thousands to supplement their diet through the winter. At feeders, they fill their crop with peanuts or Bark Butter Bits and fly away to hide them. They also enjoy mealworms, oil sunflower, and sunflower chips. The male Clark's Nutcracker is one of the few members of the crow and jay family to incubate eggs.

Large all-black body.

American Crow

American Crows are present just about everywhere except for extremely arid areas. They can show up in small groups or by the thousands. Crows make a large number of sounds, including many imitations, but are best known for the familiar caw. In flight, their wings appear to be rowing. They eat just about anything in the wild and at feeders.

Failrly large all-black body.

Large all-black body.

Fish Crow

Smaller than the American Crow. Most common in the Southeast, on coasts, in swamps, and along large rivers. The best way to identify Fish Crows is the short nasal call *cuh-uh*, unlike the *caw* of an American Crow.

Northwestern Crow

Slightly smaller than the American Crow. Common only right on the Pacific Coast, from northern Washington north. Best distinguished from American Crow by hoarser call and range.

Large, black, with long thick bill, shaggy throat feathers, wedge-shaped tail.

BREEDING

WINTER

YEAR-ROUND

MIGRATION

RARE

Common Raven

These extremely smart birds of the North and West occupy open and forested habitats. Like a stunt pilot at an air show, the Common Raven often performs rolls and somersaults in flight. It is best distinguished from crows by their size and their deep, guttural croak.

Chickadees

Feeder Foods
Oil sunflower, striped sunflower, sunflower chips, nyjer, safflower, peanut pieces, mealworms, walnuts, pecans, suet, Bark Butter, Bark Butter Bits

The dictionary definition of "cute" could just be a photo of a chickadee! Chickadees are constantly on the move, searching for food nearly every daylight minute. They stay warm during the long winter nights by roosting in small groups in cavities and temporarily lowering their body temperature to conserve calories. On cold days, they fluff out their feathers to hold more warm air next to their bodies. Chickadees are often the first birds to find new bird feeders, and are among the easiest to tame to feed from your hand. Chickadees often travel during the winter in mixed flocks with titmice, nuthatches, woodpeckers, kinglets, creepers, and others. Each of these species hunts differently, so the flock members do not compete directly for food. Once they arrive at the feeders, four or five chickadees quickly take turns at the perches, grabbing a seed and flying off to open it or peck it into bite-sized pieces. Watching closely, you can observe dominant and submissive behaviors and determine flock hierarchies. Provide perching branches, and you will get more sustained views of chickadees when they land on the perches to peck at seeds. In fall and winter, chickadees cache many of the seeds they take from the feeders for later consumption. Chickadees readily use nesting boxes.

Carolina Chickadees enjoying oil sunflower, sunflower chips and safflower from a feeder that has anti-microbial protection in the tube, perches and powder-coated metal parts.

Black cap and throat, light buffy wash on flanks.

BREEDING

WINTER

YEAR-ROUND

MIGRATION

RARE

Carolina Chickadee

The Carolina Chickadee is a year-round resident from the lower Midwest to the entire Southeast, where almost any feeding station will be visited by flocks of two to six birds. Its northern range boundary is shared with the Black-capped Chickadee where identification can be difficult. The Carolina Chickadee's mating song is four notes, *FEE-bee, FEE-bay*, and the Black-capped's is two notes, *FEE-bee*. The Carolina is slightly smaller than the Black-capped.

Black cap and throat, buffy wash on flanks.

BREEDING

WINTER

YEAR-ROUND

MIGRATION

RARE

Black-capped Chickadee

The Black-capped Chickadee is a common year-round resident of the northern half of the U.S. and nearly all of Canada and Alaska. It readily uses nesting boxes. They live in forests and on forest edges, in suburbs with mature vegetation, and in park-like settings. Where the Black-capped and Carolina Chickadees meet, the two can interbreed, making species identification impossible.

White eyebrow, black eye stripe.

BREEDING

WINTER

YEAR-ROUND

MIGRATION

RARE

Mountain Chickadee

The Mountain Chickadee is easily identified by its white eyebrow and black stripe through the eye. They prefer western mountainous habitats ranging from pinyon pine, juniper, and cottonwoods at lower elevations to ponderosa pine at mid-elevations and spruce and fir at higher elevations. One of the tamest of birds, they will land on the feeder while you are filling it and can easily be enticed to feed from your hand.

Black cap and throat, gray wash on sides.

BREEDING

WINTER

YEAR-ROUND

MIGRATION

RARE

Mexican Chickadee

Similar to the Black-capped, the Mexican Chickadee lives in the U.S. only in the Chiricahua Mountains of southeast Arizona and the Animas Mountains of southwest New Mexico, where no other chickadees occur. There is not much data on these rare visitors to feeders, but they likely eat sunflower. They have been observed feeding on Bark Butter.

Black cap and throat, chestnut back and sides.

BREEDING

WINTER

YEAR-ROUND

MIGRATION

RARE

Chestnut-backed Chickadee

This chickadee, best known for being an inhabitant of the Pacific rain forests and the mountains of northern Idaho and Alberta, can actually be seen all along the Pacific coast from central California to Alaska. Similar to Black-capped, but sports a rich chestnut-colored back and flanks. Flocks of 4 to 20 birds flit through the treetops in mixed flocks with kinglets and nuthatches. They cache seeds in the fall; like other chickadees, they use nest boxes.

Brown cap, black throat, brown sides.

BREEDING

WINTER

YEAR-ROUND

MIGRATION

RARE

Boreal Chickadee

The only chickadee with a brown cap, it lives in dense coniferous boreal forests in Canada and the northernmost U.S. It is extremely cold-tolerant, and caches spruce seeds, spiders, and insects to eat in the winter. They are very friendly and commonly use feeders, although in fewer numbers than Black-capped.

Titmice

Feeder Foods
Striped and oil sunflower, sunflower chips, safflower, peanuts in the shell, peanut pieces, mealworms, tree nuts, suet blends, Bark Butter, Bark Butter Bits

Titmice are the ventriloquist sentries of the woods. When a predator is near, titmice give a warning call that seems to fade away, presumably to trick the predator into following a phantom.

Titmice pairs stay together for a few years and protect their territory year-round. You will often see two at a time visiting feeders. You may see more than that in winter where the feeding territories of two or more pairs overlap. Otherwise, titmice often forage with chickadees, nuthatches, woodpeckers, creepers, kinglets, wrens, and bushtits. The frequent calls of titmice and chickadees keep the mixed-species flock together. You will hear them before you see them.

Titmice typically select one seed at a time from a feeder, usually the largest, and then fly off to a perch to open it with their stout bill. They have strong legs, and are one of the few species other than birds of prey to hold food with their feet. In fall and winter, they shell the seeds and hide the kernels up to 130 feet away from the feeder, remembering where each one is hidden for a later meal.

Bridled Titmouse

The Bridled Titmouse is found in the U.S. only in southeast Arizona and southwest New Mexico, where it lives in oak or oak-pine-juniper woodlands. Often travels with flocks of chickadees, vireos, nuthatches, warblers, kinglets, and creepers, and gives loud alarms calls when danger approaches.

BREEDING

WINTER

YEAR-ROUND

MIGRATION

RARE

Gray, with beautifully patterned black and white crested head. Jet black eyes.

Plain gray, with crested head. Jet black eyes.

Plain gray, with crested head. Jet black eyes.

Oak Titmouse

Plain gray with a crest. As the name suggests, it prefers oak woodlands, but also inhabits mixed oak-pine woods. Unlike other titmice that may have a mate for a few years, the Oak Titmouse mates for life and together they defend a territory all year. They are not known to join winter foraging flocks.

Juniper Titmouse

Very similar to the Oak Titmouse, the Juniper Titmouse is slightly smaller, has different calls, and rarely overlaps in range. It inhabits arid juniper-oak and juniper-pinyon woods.

BREEDING

WINTER

YEAR-ROUND

MIGRATION

RARE

BREEDING

WINTER

YEAR-ROUND

MIGRATION

RARE

Gray crest and upperparts, white belly, orangish sides, jet black eyes, black forehead.

BREEDING

WINTER

YEAR-ROUND

MIGRATION

RARE

Tufted Titmouse

Frequent feeder visitors, Tufted Titmice may become tame enough to eat seed from your hand. They are easily recognized by their song, *peter-peter-peter,* and their harsh, scolding calls.

The species' range is slowly expanding northward. At feeders, they enjoy sunflower seeds and chips, peanuts, safflower, mealworms, and Bark Butter and Bark Butter Bits.

BREEDING

WINTER

YEAR-ROUND

MIGRATION

RARE

Black crest, gray upperparts, orangish sides, jet black eyes

Black-crested Titmouse

Like a Tufted Titmouse, but with a black crest. Favors mixed oak and juniper scrub, riparian woodlands, and mesquite scrub. Attracted to sunflower seeds, peanuts, fat, and mealworms at feeders.

Dull gray with yellow head; rusty shoulder often hidden.

Small, overall gray-brown with round head, tiny bill, and long tail. Female with pale eyes, male has black eyes.

Verdin

Tiny, with a gray body and yellow head, Verdins are talkative birds often heard before being seen. They constantly chatter as they travel through the bushes and trees. Verdins flit about like chickadees, acrobatically looking for insects as they bounce from twig to twig and hang upside down. Monogamous in the breeding season, Verdins are solitary the rest of the year. Only one or two visit feeders at a time. They are very tame and fearless of humans. Look for their spherical nests, which they use as roosts all year long. They are most easily attracted to nectar in hummingbird feeders, apple and orange halves, and mealworms.

Bushtit

Flocks of up to 40 birds constantly utter short, twittering chips and calls as they travel through bushes and trees. Foraging Bushtits stretch and reach in all sorts of odd positions, often upside down like chickadees. When threatened by a predator, the entire flock immediately begins a droning trill that makes it difficult for the predator to determine the location of any single bird. They build a long sock like nest out of mosses, grasses and twigs that is held together by spider webs. Fearless around humans, flocks often visit feeders.

BREEDING

WINTER

YEAR-ROUND

MIGRATION

RARE

Feeder Foods
Nectar, apples, oranges, mealworms, Bark Butter

BREEDING

WINTER

YEAR-ROUND

MIGRATION

RARE

Feeder Foods
Oil sunflower, sunflower chips, mealworms, peanuts in the shell, peanut pieces, suet blends, Bark Butter

Nuthatches

Feeder Foods
Oil sunflower, striped sunflower, sunflower chips, safflower, hulled peanuts, mealworms, tree nuts, suet blends, Bark Butter, Bark Butter Bits.

These "upside down" birds creep headfirst down tree trunks while searching cracks and crevices for insect food. This unique feat is made possible by a long, strong hind toe with an impressively curved claw. It only takes one of these toes to keep the nuthatch safely secured to the tree. Woodpeckers would crash and burn if they tried the same maneuver!

Some nuthatches remain on their home territory all year while others move about in family groups or irrupt in large numbers to find better food sources. Bonded pairs of nuthatches rarely use the same feeder at the same time. The male is dominant, and almost always eats first. Nuthatches regularly join other species to look for food and warn off predators.

Nuthatches typically take a single sunflower seed and fly to a nearby tree, where they wedge the seed into the bark and hack it open with repeated blows of the bill. Nuthatches are also hoarders, caching seeds for later use, especially in fall and winter.

BREEDING

WINTER

YEAR-ROUND

MIGRATION

RARE

Blue-gray back, rusty underparts, bold black eye line, white eyebrow and throat, very short tail. Male with black cap, female with gray cap.

Red-breasted Nuthatch

The Red-breasted Nuthatch loves company. If you see one, you may well see a number of them foraging together. When winter food supplies are scarce in northern Canada, Red-breasted Nuthatches "irrupt" in search of food. Listen for the *yank-yank* call.

White cheeks and belly, black shoulders, blue-gray back, short tail. Male with black cap, female with grayer cap.

Brown cap, whitish underparts, slate gray back, short tail.

White-breasted Nuthatch

White-breasted Nuthatches, the largest American nuthatch, often forage together with chickadees, titmice and Downy Woodpeckers. Even so, White-breasted Nuthatches tend to be aggressive towards other birds and even their own kind while on the feeder. They usually visit the feeder one bird at a time and constantly perform wing-flicking threat displays in an attempt to scare other birds away.

BREEDING

WINTER

YEAR-ROUND

MIGRATION

RARE

Pygmy Nuthatch

This tiny bird especially favors western ponderosa pine forests and travels in small family flocks constantly moving and chattering their "rubber ducky" squeak call. They are the only bird in North America that uses three strategies to survive cold nights—sheltering in tree cavities, gathering together with family members in the cavities and reducing their body temperatures to save energy.

BREEDING

WINTER

YEAR-ROUND

MIGRATION

RARE

Brown cap, white throat, pale gray to buffy belly, blue-gray back, short tail.

Mottled brown above, whitish underparts, downcurved black bill, long tail.

Brown-headed Nuthatch

The Brown-headed Nuthatch is resident year-round in south-eastern U.S. pine forests. Usually forages in small family flocks, and in winter joins other species. Favors insects in warm months and pine seeds in the winter. One of the few birds to use tools in the search for food, using a sliver to probe and pry behind loose bark. Usually stays high in the forest canopy, but readily comes to bird feeders.

Brown Creeper

Brown Creepers are more closely related to perching birds but act like small woodpeckers. They use their tail like a woodpecker, bracing themselves against the tree trunk while looking for small insects and insect eggs. They spiral up the trunk and occasionally venture out onto branches, then fly to the base of the next tree and spiral up again. To hide from predators, they flatten themselves and freeze in place against the tree. They often forage with chickadees and nuthatches in winter. The thin, high trilling call is a good clue that they are nearby. Not regular visitors to feeders, they may venture a quick check or grab a small seed or bite of suet when no other birds are around. They are more readily attracted to Bark Butter spread on a tree trunk.

BREEDING

WINTER

YEAR-ROUND

MIGRATION

RARE

BREEDING

WINTER

YEAR-ROUND

MIGRATION

RARE

Feeder Foods
Hulled sunflower seeds, suet blends, Bark Butter

Wrens

The hide-and-seek specialists of the bird world, wrens are often heard before they are seen. These enthusiastic singers have some of the most dazzling and complex voices to be heard in our backyard. Bursting with energy and always going full speed ahead, they are truly entertaining guests at our feeders, even if their visits are often brief. Wrens always nest inside an enclosed structure, be it an elaborate self-made nest, a man-made nest box, or inside your porch or garage. Some wren species pair for life and defend their home territory year-round; other species bond only for a single nesting. Males and females are virtually identical in plumage, and they most often come to feeders singly or in pairs.

Feeder Foods
Peanut pieces, mealworms, suet blends, Bark Butter, sunflower chips

Plain brown above with barring on wings and tail, dirty white belly, pinkish gray legs.

BREEDING

WINTER

YEAR-ROUND

MIGRATION

RARE

House Wren

This noisy wren of summer loves our birdhouses, but visits feeders only irregularly. House Wrens are a mixed blessing in a yard, as they can be aggressive to other cavity-nesting birds and have even been known to destroy their eggs and young. But they are fun to watch and add charming bursts of bubbling song to the sounds of summer. They are most attracted to mealworms and Bark Butter.

Warm rusty brown above, tan below, with bold white eyebrow.

Carolina Wren

The Carolina Wren is the most common wren you will attract to your feeders in the eastern U.S. If you are successful, this large, colorful species will reward you year-round with its delightful antics and loud song, *teakettle-teakettle!* Carolina Wrens pair for life and travel everywhere together. They often nest in unusual places, including hanging plant baskets and in old shoes in garages.

Gray brown above, dirty white below, white eyebrow, long tail flicked sideways.

Bewick's Wren

A medium-size wren similar to the Carolina Wren, but with a longer tail and no buffy orange on the underparts. Often flicks tail sideways. Unlike the Carolina Wren, the Bewick's is not a faithful feeder visitor. Most of its feeder activity is in the winter months, when it visits alone or occasionally in pairs. Bark Butter and suet blends are the best foods.

Rusty cap, white eyebrow, brown stipe through eye; streaked brown and white above, heavily spotted breast, long barred tail.

BREEDING

WINTER

YEAR-ROUND

MIGRATION

RARE

Cactus Wren

The largest wren in North America, the bold and fearless Cactus Wren lives up to its size. These residents of southwestern deserts are usually seen in pairs, and show little fear of people, spending much of the day exploring and probing everything around your house and yard. Often seen on a conspicuous perch in trees or cacti. A true desert species, the Cactus Wren can survive without any free water; its diet of insects, fruit pulp, and seeds provides all needed moisture.

Kinglets

Feeder Foods
Suet blends, Bark Butter, mealworms, peanut pieces, sunflower chips

Kinglets are tinier than chickadees, yet just as active. They are insect specialists even in winter, gleaning prey from tree branches and buds. Found at feeders only during migration and in winter, they return to the same wintering areas each year. They often join chickadee, titmouse, and nuthatch flocks at feeders or in the search for wild food. They recognize the alarm call of chickadees and halt their activity, remaining still, until the all-clear is sounded. They frequently flick or quiver their wings while foraging or eating at feeders, Ruby-crowns more emphatically than Golden-crowns.

Tiny olive-gray, wing-flicking bird. Black and white striped face with golden crown stripe.

Tiny olive-gray, wing-flicking bird. White bar on dark wing, white eye ring. Ruby crown stripe.

Golden-crowned Kinglet

Hardier than the Ruby-crowned, Golden-crowned Kinglets winter farther north. They are more often found in small groups and mixed-species flocks. Easily identified by their series of high-pitched *tsee* notes. The orange patch in the male's golden crown is often hidden, but is clearly displayed by agitated birds.

Ruby-crowned Kinglet

Constantly in motion and frequently singing its loud, high-pitched twittering and melodic song. The male's ruby crown is visible only when the crest is raised. Usually seen one at a time at feeders.

BREEDING
WINTER
YEAR-ROUND
MIGRATION
RARE

BREEDING
WINTER
YEAR-ROUND
MIGRATION
RARE

Bluebirds

Bluebirds truly bring happiness and joy to the backyard. First you hear their gentle song, and then you see one or both of the pair sitting up high on an exposed branch, on a fence post or wire, or in the outer twigs of a small tree. Bluebirds search for food among the branches and on the ground. Eastern and Western Bluebirds live where there are plentiful perches, along edges of woods and in open areas. Mountain Bluebirds hover while searching for insects and are less dependent on perches. Amazingly, Eastern Bluebirds are known to be able to see insects up to 50 yards away. Look for the male bringing construction materials to the nest, which is actually built by the female alone.

Eastern Bluebird numbers had seriously declined by the 1960s, but since then have recovered thanks to the efforts of organizations such as the North American Bluebird Society and others that encourage the building and monitoring of bluebird boxes and trails. If bluebirds nesting in your area face competition from House Sparrows, place two nest boxes about 20 yards apart; the House Sparrows usually defend only one box, and you may have better luck with bluebirds in the other.

Bluebirds will come to any feeder that holds their favorite foods, but are often fed in feeders that have clear plastic sides with bluebird-size holes on the sides that only bluebird and smaller birds can enter.

Feeder Foods
Mealworms, Bark Butter, Bark Butter Bits, suet, peanut pieces, sunflower chips, raisins, currants, grapes

Male cobalt-blue with white belly, rusty red throat, breast, and neck.

Female paler. Juvenile with blue wings and spotted breast.

- BREEDING
- WINTER
- YEAR-ROUND
- MIGRATION
- RARE

Eastern Bluebird

Eastern Bluebirds have become very tame in backyards in the last 20 years, where they come to feeders as pairs, winter flocks, or families with fledglings. Mealworms are their favorite food, but they also enjoy Bark Butter and Bark Butter Bits.

Look for a behavior called perch hunting, where they hunt from a low branch, then drop quickly onto insect prey on the ground and then return to their perch.

Male with dark blue back, head, and throat; rusty red breast and sides. Female paler. Juvenile with blue wings and spotted breast.

Male sky-blue with whitish belly, breast, and neck. Female paler. Juvenile grayish with spotted breast.

Western Bluebird

Western Bluebirds favor open pine and oak woodlands and forest and farmland edges. Migration is more likely to higher or lower altitudes than long distance. The male's blue and red colors are deeper than the Eastern Bluebird's, often making the bird look dark overall. Typically a perch hunter, but also catches insects in the air and hovers to eat berries. Commonly seen on fences and telephone lines. Readily uses nest boxes.

Mountain Bluebird

Preferring more open country than the other bluebirds, Mountain Bluebirds have no red feathers at all, just sky-blue backs and whitish bellies. They perch and hover to hunt ground and flying insects and also eat many berries including juniper and elderberries. Often identified by being the only medium-size bird on fences and phone lines that has graceful flight patterns as it launches from perches.

BREEDING

WINTER

YEAR-ROUND

MIGRATION

RARE

BREEDING

WINTER

YEAR-ROUND

MIGRATION

RARE

Thrushes

Feeder Foods
Varies by species: mealworms, raisins, currants, grapes, Bark Butter, Bark Butter Bits, suet, peanut pieces, sunflower chips, millet and cracked corn

If you see a medium-size, plump bird with a medium-length tail hopping through the underbrush or low brances, it is likely to be a thrush. A red breast makes it a robin, and an orange belly and black neck band make it a Varied Thrush. If it has a plain brown or gray back and a slightly or highly spotted breast, it is one of the woodland thrushes. Thrush diets vary from earthworms and other insects in the summer to mainly fruits and berries in the winter. Other than the bluebirds, thrushes are unpredictable visitors to feeders, sometimes common and sometimes completely absent. Robins are the easiest to entice with mealworms, fruit, and suet nuggets, while the smaller, browner woodland thrushes are sometimes attracted to Bark Butter on tree trunks and feeders during migration or nesting times.

Indistinct spots, warm brown upperparts, plain face.

Veery

The Veery's haunting, reedy, descending song is most conspicuous at dusk on the breeding grounds. It has fewer and less distinct breast spots than the other woodland thrushes. This rare visitor to feeders has been observed eating Bark Butter.

BREEDING

WINTER

YEAR-ROUND

MIGRATION

RARE

Grayish brown back, small black spots on breast.

Gray-cheeked Thrush

Seen mostly on its spring migration to northern Canada and Alaska breeding grounds, the Gray-cheeked Thrush is plain grayish brown above, with small but distinct spots on the white breast. Few are familiar with its reedy song, as it rarely sings on migration. This rare visitor to feeders has been observed eating Bark Butter.

BREEDING

WINTER

YEAR-ROUND

MIGRATION

RARE

Swainson's Thrush

Feeding higher in the forest canopy than other thrushes, the Swainson's Thrush is most easily detected by its flute-like song with an upward spiral. Often seen hovering to glean insects from branches, and flycatches more than other thrushes. Rarely seen at feeders, but has been observed eating Bark Butter.

Olive-brown upperparts, heavily spotted buffy breast, buffy eye ring.

Hermit Thrush

If you see a thrush quickly raise and slowly lower its rusty tail, it is probably a Hermit Thrush. Sings a beautiful two-parted warble. Similar to the Wood Thrush, but with an olive-brown back and head and more lightly spotted breast, the Hermit Thrush is the only woodland thrush to commonly winter in the eastern and southern U.S. Comes infrequently to Bark Butter, suet, mealworms, and water.

Brown back, lightly spotted white breast, rusty tail, pale eye ring.

Wood Thrush

The Wood Thrush is the most likely of the woodland thrushes to nest in suburban yards and neighborhood forests. My wife, Nancy, names the Wood Thrush as her favorite bird, its beautiful flute-like song heard at dusk and dawn in the nesting season. The large spots on its breast and sides are darker and more extensive than in any other thrush. Not common at bird feeders, but has been observed eating Bark Butter on trees, and will also use birdbaths and water features.

Bright rusty cinnamon head and back, white breast covered with dark spots.

American Robin

The American Robin is the most widespread and commonly seen thrush in North America. Though many migrate, robins are present all year long in most of the U.S. The "first robin of spring" might actually be the "last robin of fall." The diet changes from insects, worms, and soft fruits in the summer to berries and tree seeds, such as juniper, viburnum, sumac, and hawthorn in the winter. You can often see the male tending the fledglings while the female is incubating a second brood in their grass, twig, and mud nest. Robins often ignore offerings at the feeder, but are sometimes attracted to mealworms, fruits, and fats, especially during blizzards or extreme cold. Robins are active users of birdbaths and water features.

BREEDING

WINTER

YEAR-ROUND

MIGRATION

RARE

Male with brick-red breast, dark gray upperparts.

Female paler than male.

Juvenile with speckled breast.

Varied Thrush

It is easier to hear the Varied Thrush's haunting, buzzing-bell whistle than it is to see this strikingly beautiful bird. Feeders can draw it out of the deep branches and ground clutter it frequents. On rare occasions, it strays as far east as New England, typically lingering at a feeder for a few days. Eats Bark Butter, suet, mealworms, fruit, cracked corn, and millet.

BREEDING

WINTER

YEAR-ROUND

MIGRATION

RARE

Robin sized. Male with orange throat, belly and wing bars; black breast-band and eyestripe. Female paler.

Catbird, Thrashers, and Mockingbird

Feeder Foods
Fruits, Bark Butter, mealworms, suet, sunflower chips

These birds are famous for their vocal prowess. They love to sing loud and long, giving amazingly complex songs that often mimic a wide variety of natural and man-made sounds. At feeders, which they visit singly or in pairs, they range from bold and almost tame to skulking and painfully shy.

The thrashers are ground-feeding specialists that spend most of their time searching beneath feeders for seeds, fruits, and insects. As a group, they are known for their tenacious defense of their home territory; they form monogamous pair bonds, in some species lasting for several years.

Overall dark gray, black cap, rusty undertail.

BREEDING

WINTER

YEAR-ROUND

MIGRATION

RARE

Gray Catbird

Catbirds are secretive, medium-size songbirds that dart into the bushes when approached, but their distinctive cat-like mewing always gives them away. High-quality backyard habitat with lots of cover is a key to attracting them. They can be quite tame when feeding, and are becoming more common visitors to backyard feeders. They seem to be especially attracted to Bark Butter. Catbirds' natural diet is over 50 percent berries, so they also enjoy raisins and currants that have been plumped up by soaking in water.

Large; grayish brown overall with faint spots on breast, long downcurved black bill, long tail, bright yellow eye.

BREEDING

WINTER

YEAR-ROUND

MIGRATION

RARE

Curve-billed Thrasher

Often staying in the same territory for its entire life, this southwestern thrasher inhabits a broad range of dry habitats, and does well around houses and farms. Listen for the *whit-wheet* call. Always a little skittish, they quickly retreat to cover when disturbed or frightened. Curve-billed Thrashers usually visit feeders singly or in pairs, and are often seen foraging on the ground. They eat grains such as milo, millet, and cracked corn, in addition to Bark Butter, mealworms, fruit, suet and sunflower chips.

Rusty brown above, brown spots on white breast, white wing bars, yellow eyes, slightly downcurved bill, long tail.

BREEDING

WINTER

YEAR-ROUND

MIGRATION

RARE

Brown Thrasher

The only thrasher east of Texas. Dense shrubbery and adequate undergrowth are a must to lure this ground-feeding specialist to your feeders. The highly varied song is often heard before the thrasher is seen. Brown Thrashers will come out in the open to forage under feeders as long as a quick retreat to good cover is available. They thrash and sweep the ground with the strong bill, flipping through the leaf litter and probing the soil for food. Brown Thrashers can be antagonistic at feeders, but rarely chase away your regular visitors for more than a short time.

Deeply downcurved bill, overall gray-brown, white throat, long tail.

California Thrasher

A secretive resident of chaparral in California, this shy, plain bird with a strikingly downcurved bill seems to prefer walking to flying. When it does take to the air, its graceless flight rarely takes it very far. Mated pairs stay together for extended periods, and strongly defend their home territory throughout the year. An occasional feeder visitor, it forages mainly on the ground, but will visit platforms for grains including milo and millet.

Deeply downcurved bill, gray-brown overall, white throat, orange-brown under tail.

Crissal Thrasher

A bird of low scrubby vegetation and dry washes, the Crissal Thrasher is less likely to be seen at feeders than the other thrashers; when it does visit, it is often in the early morning. Always energetic, it walks, runs, and hops beneath dense brush, and rarely flies even when threatened. Like the other thrashers, it forages under feeders for seeds and insects.

Gray head and back, whitish underparts, long tail. White wing bars become bold white wing patches in flight.

- BREEDING
- WINTER
- YEAR-ROUND
- MIGRATION
- RARE

Northern Mockingbird

Truly a mixed blessing in your backyard. Mockingbirds are incredibly beautiful singers, but they vocalize at all hours of day and night, and their territorial behavior can be taken too far, intimidating your regular feeder visitors. To keep Northern Mockingbirds from becoming bullies, create a feeding area just for them. Place this second set of feeders as far away from your other feeders as possible, and fill them with goodies such as suet, mealworms, grapes, cranberries, dried fruit mixes, and raisins. The mockingbirds will be attracted to this food and usually abandon the attempt to defend both feeding areas at once.

Waxwings

Feeder Foods

Raisins, currants, apples, Bark Butter

Can you imagine having waxwings as regular visitors to your feeders? These strikingly handsome birds travel in flocks, and although they rarely visit feeders, they are an impressive sight when they do.

If they are already active in the trees and shrubs around your home, you may be able to entice them to raisins, currants, and apples placed on a platform or tray feeder. If those foods fail to gain their attention, the next ploy is to fill a birdbath and spread Bark Butter on a tree trunk. In summer, insects are added to their diet. Watch for waxwings flying out from a high exposed perch to catch insects on the wing.

Overall tannish brown, with brown crest, black mask and throat, yellow-tipped tail; rusty beneath tail, and white, yellow, and red spots on wings.

Tannish brown head and breast, gray wings and tail, brown crest, yellow belly, black mask and chin, red tips on wing feathers, yellow-tipped tail.

Bohemian Waxwing

Bohemian Waxwings are the larger, more northerly cousin of the Cedar Waxwing. They share many of the same habits and behaviors, including being gluttonous fruit eaters. They are capable of consuming more than two times their own weight in fruit each day. They are rare feeder visitors.

Cedar Waxwing

The name "waxwing" refers to the red tips on some of the wing feathers, which look as if they were dipped in red wax. The "cedar" part comes from the species' fondness for cedar berries. Highly social, Cedar Waxwings can be found in flocks throughout North America. This is one of the last birds to nest each summer, delaying breeding until an abundance of insects and ripe fruit is available to feed their young.

BREEDING

WINTER

YEAR-ROUND

MIGRATION

RARE

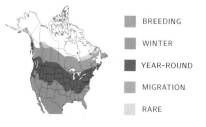

BREEDING

WINTER

YEAR-ROUND

MIGRATION

RARE

Warblers

It is very exciting to attract an uncommon bird to your feeders. Warblers provide that opportunity. They are colorful, lively, and strongly seasonal.

The widest variety of warblers passes through our yards during migration, while a few will stay to nest in your neighborhood.. Moving water is the best way to draw them in for closer views. The best foods to attract them to your feeders imitate their mainstay diet of insects. Offer mealworms, suet, and Bark Butter. Bark Butter has attracted a number of warbler species that are not normally found at feeders; spread it on tree trunks or crumble it on tray feeders.

Most warblers winter in the tropics, where insect populations are higher and more reliable. But there are a few "winter warbler" species that brave the cold. These birds add high-calorie waxy berries and fruits to their daily menu. Depending on the species, other foods may include sap, insect honeydew, nectar of winter-flowering plants, and pine and other seeds.

Most winter warblers are found low in small trees, bushes, and vines, or even on the ground. Often they are alone or with a companion. Some loosely associate with mixed-species feeding flocks.

Feeder Foods
Bark Butter, suet, mealworms, sunflower chips, nectar

Plain olive to yellowish. Faint eye line, broken eye ring, sharply pointed bill.

Orange-crowned Warbler

The Orange-crowned Warbler is a plain warbler that rarely displays its orange crown. More common in the West than the East, it often feeds closer to the ground than other warblers, usually in dense shrubbery or other vegetation. Orange-crowneds often join mixed flocks in winter.

BREEDING

WINTER

YEAR-ROUND

MIGRATION

RARE

Palm Warbler

The Palm Warbler is a tail-bobber with a rufous cap that often feeds on the ground in weedy or brushy fields. They eat seeds in winter, and may take sunflower chips at feeders. Small groups can be found wintering in the Southeast, especially near the coast.

BREEDING

WINTER

YEAR-ROUND

MIGRATION

RARE

Rusty cap, yellow eyebrow, yellow undertail. Paler in winter.

BREEDING

WINTER

YEAR-ROUND

MIGRATION

RARE

Other Warblers

These species of warbler have all been observed eating Bark Butter: Ovenbird, Nashville Warbler, Northern Parula, Magnolia Warbler, Yellow Warbler, Black-throated Blue Warbler.

BREEDING

WINTER

YEAR-ROUND

MIGRATION

RARE

Breeding male "Audubon's" with yellow throat, cap, rump, and sides. Female and winter male paler.

"Myrtle" breeding male with black mask and white throat. Yellow patches on cap, rump and sides. Female and winter male paler.

Yellow-rumped Warbler

Yellow-rumped Warblers are our hardiest and most widespread winter warbler, sometimes found as far north as the Pacific Northwest and New England. They eat berries and fruits in winter, especially bayberry and wax myrtle.

Yellow-rumpeds used to be considered two separate species: The yellow-throated "Audubon's" is found more in the West, the white-throated "Myrtle" more in the East. They visit feeders alone or in small flocks.

Male with yellow stripes surrounding black cheek patch; black cap and throat; Yellow chest with white belly, two white wing bars.

Female paler.

Townsend's Warbler

The beautiful Townsend's Warbler spends the winter on the Pacific Coast and locally in the Southwest. Its main winter foods are insects and

insect honeydew. Townsend's Warblers occasionally venture to bird feeders, where they eat suet, mealworms, and Bark Butter.

Bright yellow throat, black and white face, white belly.

Yellow-throated Warbler

Yellow-throated Warblers have a large breeding range in the Midwest to the Southeast, but in winter are found on the Gulf Coast and Florida. They usually hunt for insects high in palm and pine trees or even under eaves. They share their habitat with the Pine Warbler, but their longer bill can reach insects in pinecones and needle clusters that the Pine Warbler can't. Fairly common visitor to suet blends and Bark Butter.

▇ BREEDING

▇ WINTER

▇ YEAR-ROUND

▇ MIGRATION

▇ RARE

Male with yellowish chest with olive back, two white wing bars on gray wings, thick bill. Females paler.

Pine Warbler

Named for its favorite tree, the stocky Pine Warbler prefers pure or mixed pine forests in the nesting season and in winter. Pine Warblers wedge pine seeds into bark crevices and break them open with their heavy bill. Seen at feeders more often in winter, they usually visit one or two at a time, and are one of the few warblers to feed on sunflower seeds. Also attracted to Bark Butter.

▇ BREEDING

▇ WINTER

▇ YEAR-ROUND

▇ MIGRATION

▇ RARE

Male with bright yellow head; black throat and nape. Grayish back with two wing bars. Female duller.

Hermit Warbler

A fairly common resident of the tops of coniferous trees on the Pacific coast and in mountain areas, it is not often seen as easily as it is heard. However, it is attracted to Bark Butter and can be quite tame during its frequent visits. Uncommon winter resident of Oregon and California coast.

▇ BREEDING

▇ WINTER

▇ YEAR-ROUND

▇ MIGRATION

▇ RARE

Towhees

Feeder Foods
Sunflower chips, oil sunflower, Bark Butter, millet, peanut pieces, suet dough, cracked corn, milo

Towhees are often heard before they are seen. These shy birds spend much of their time noisily scratching for food in dead leaves beneath dense brush. They use a hop-and-scratch foraging method, jumping forward with head and tail up while kicking backwards to uncover food. They use this technique on the forest floor and under feeders, even when seed is already clearly visible. Towhees usually visit the feeder singly or in small groups of two to four birds. Even though they are relatively large birds, they are often shy at feeders, giving the smaller birds lots of space.

Overall grayish with greenish yellow tail and wings, rusty crown, white throat.

Male with black head, red eye, rusty sides, white belly, white spots on back and wings. Female browner.

Green-tailed Towhee

Unlike the other five U.S. towhee species, the Green-tailed Towhee is completely migratory. Green-taileds are secretive birds that spend much of their time noisily scratching for food in dead leaves beneath dense brush. In the West, if you see a medium-size songbird on the ground with a rusty crown and white throat, it could well be a Green-tailed Towhee.

Spotted Towhee

Usually heard before seen. Listen for the variable but distinctive song, *drink-drink-drink-teee!* and other loud trills. When the robin-sized Spotted Towhees are visible, their striking black head and red eye makes identification easy. Spotted Towhees are fairly skittish when in the open, and at feeders they are quick to dart back to cover if they see movement inside your home.

BREEDING
WINTER
YEAR-ROUND
MIGRATION
RARE

BREEDING
WINTER
YEAR-ROUND
MIGRATION
RARE

Male with black head and back, with rusty sides and white belly.

Female paler brown.

BREEDING
WINTER
YEAR-ROUND
MIGRATION
RARE

Eastern Towhee

Eastern Towhees are among the more skittish members of their family, but they are definitely around if you hear their cheerful *drink your teee!* They quickly head to cover at the slightest disturbance. They can be very faithful feeder visitors week after week, or infrequent drop-ins in spring and fall. Most Eastern Towhees have red eyes, but the resident population of Florida and southern Georgia has light yellow eyes.

Rusty cap and undertail.

Clean breast with central dark spot.

BREEDING
WINTER
YEAR-ROUND
MIGRATION
RARE

Canyon Towhee

Rather than the typical towhee hop-and-scratch, Canyon Towhees prefer to just pick up food they find while walking around. They are plain gray brown and easily overlooked in arid, scrubby habitat. Canyon Towhees are uncommon feeder visitors, seen in pairs that mate for life.

Gray overall, streaked throat, rusty undertail.

BREEDING

WINTER

YEAR-ROUND

MIGRATION

RARE

California Towhee

California Towhees are birds of arid scrub and chaparral in California and Oregon. Fairly common feeder visitors, they usually arrive in life-long mated pairs. When moving through the brush or when the pair is separated, they give loud 2-second call to stay connected. They prefer millet on the ground or low trays, and have been observed eating Bark Butter.

Overall brown with black face, pale bill, rufous undertail.

BREEDING

WINTER

YEAR-ROUND

MIGRATION

RARE

Abert's Towhee

The Abert's Towhee occupies one of the smallest ranges of any species, occurring in the U.S. only in Arizona and small parts of California, Nevada, Utah, and New Mexico. Abert's Towhees average two successful broods a year despite their hot and dry environment, but it may take as many as six nesting attempts to produce those two broods. An uncommon feeder visitor, usually seen as mated pairs.

Sparrows

Sparrows are all around us, from seashores to mountain ranges and from the Arctic tundra to the Mexican border. At first glance, they all appear to be a bunch of small brown birds. In fact, some birders refer to them as LBJ's, little brown jobs. However, a closer look reveals distinctive, often beautiful plumages and unique behaviors. Most sparrows are found in pairs during the nesting season and in flocks during migration and winter. They frequent bird feeders year-round, but visit in greater numbers in winter, when their diet is more heavily seed-based. Sparrows prefer to be grounded: Sprinkle some seed on the ground or on a ground-feeding platform, and they are happy to browse. They like to have some cover nearby so that they can pop out, eat some food, and pop back in. They also visit water features to drink and bathe.

Watch how quickly sparrows grab food at feeders. They either pick up a seed and roll it around in their mouth to remove the husk, or they immediately swallow it, filling their crop so they can remove the husk later in the comfortable shelter of bushes or a brush pile.

Feeder Foods
Millet, oil sunflower, sunflower chips, cracked corn, nyjer, peanut pieces, Bark Butter, Bark Butter Bits

White-crowned sparrows are among the beautiful but often ignored sparrows that visit our yards and feeders.

Rusty crown, white throat, edged by dark throat stripes.

Rusty cap, rusty eye line, bicolored bill, dark breast spot.

Rufous-crowned Sparrow

Not a common feeder visitor, but have been known to feed on Bark Butter. Habitat is one of the best clues to this plain-looking sparrow. They prefer brushy, rocky slopes of hills and canyons as well as open grassy or scrubby ground. They prefer to run from cover to cover rather then fly. Usually secretive in pairs; not in flocks. Best bet to see one is when the male is perched in the open singing.

American Tree Sparrow

Mainly winter visitors to feeders, The American Tree Sparrow arrives in small flocks that search the ground for various seeds and grains. When the ground is snow covered, American Tree Sparrows have been observed to fly around a weed plant, using their wings to dislodge its seeds onto the snow below for easy retrieval. Preferring low fat weed and feeder seeds in the winter, they must eat large amounts every day to have enough energy to make it through the long winter nights.

BREEDING

WINTER

YEAR-ROUND

MIGRATION

RARE

BREEDING

WINTER

YEAR-ROUND

MIGRATION

RARE

Rusty cap, black eye line. Eyebrow white in summer, buffy in winter.

Pale head, pink bill, white eye ring.

Chipping Sparrow

Most birds molt their body plumage once or twice a year, but the Chipping Sparrow may also replace the feathers of its face and throat up to six times over that same period. In breeding plumage, the cap is bright rusty, and there is a black line through the eye. Look for mated pairs or small flocks in the summer on the ground or on feeders seeking sunflower and millet and, on occasion, Bark Butter.

Field Sparrow

This sparrow is more fond of overgrown fields with scattered bushes and tall grass than of suburbs. They often flutter to the top of a grass stalk and then ride it to the ground to eat the seeds. Males usually return to breed in the same territory each year, while females normally select a new territory and male. Males sing vigorously until they find a mate, and only occasionally thereafter. The song is an accelerating series of descending notes, reminiscent of a ping-pong ball settling on a table.

BREEDING

WINTER

YEAR-ROUND

MIGRATION

RARE

BREEDING

WINTER

YEAR-ROUND

MIGRATION

RARE

Boldly patterned chestnut, white, and black head; dark spot on white breast.

Dark head, black throat, white eyebrow and mustache.

Lark Sparrow

A very conspicuously colored sparrow with a quail-like head pattern. The tail's unique white border is conspicuous in flight. Often found in pairs or small flocks walking (rather than hopping like many sparrows) on fields, lawns, and parks with nearby trees or bushes. An occasional feeder visitor. Lark Sparrows often perch in the open on fence posts, wires, and treetops.

Black-throated Sparrow

Black-throated Sparrows are found in pairs or small groups in open, arid habitats. They can be heard calling to one another with two notes then a quick buzz as they feed. Generally tame and easily viewed. Not a common feeder visitor, as they do not take very well to suburban areas, but they are known to feed on Bark Butter.

- BREEDING
- WINTER
- YEAR-ROUND
- MIGRATION
- RARE

- BREEDING
- WINTER
- YEAR-ROUND
- MIGRATION
- RARE

Rusty rump, tail, wings, and streaks.

Heavily streaked head, breast, and flanks; sketchy central spot on breast.

Fox Sparrow

Fox Sparrows are named for their reddish rump, tail, wings, and breast streaks. Pacific Coast birds are more brownish overall. These large sparrows are ground foragers that double-scratch with their feet in search of food. Fox Sparrows feed in winter in small groups of two to four birds, usually on the edges of mixed sparrow flocks.

Song Sparrow

The most common and widespread sparrow native to North America. Males have up to 20 different songs, which they sing throughout the year from an exposed perch. On spring mornings, they may sing a song every eight seconds, adding up to over 2,300 songs a day. They forage beneath dense undergrowth using the double-scratch technique, kicking at debris while sweeping both feet quickly back along the ground. Rarely feed in flocks. They visit water features to drink and bathe.

BREEDING

WINTER

YEAR-ROUND

MIGRATION

RARE

BREEDING

WINTER

YEAR-ROUND

MIGRATION

RARE

Finely streaked buffy breast, whitish belly, buffy eye ring; crown often raised.

White eye ring, white outer tail feathers.

Lincoln's Sparrow

Most often seen during migration, the crisply streaked Lincoln's Sparrow may come into yards to feed under bird feeding stations. Like warblers, Lincoln's Sparrows occasionally forage for insects at the tips of branches. Usually seen alone or in small groups.

Vesper Sparrow

A fairly common grassland bird in the western half of North America, Vesper Sparrows occasionally visit the ground beneath feeders to eat millet and sunflower chips. These streaked brown sparrows are distinguished by their white outer tail feathers, most easily seen in flight, and their white eye ring. Listen for its song mostly in the evening.

BREEDING

WINTER

YEAR-ROUND

MIGRATION

RARE

BREEDING

WINTER

YEAR-ROUND

MIGRATION

RARE

Breeding adult with black cap with golden-yellow crown stripe.

Breeding adult with black cap, face, and bib. Large pink bill, black streaks on white breast, plain grayish cheeks.

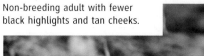

Non-breeding adult with fewer black highlights and tan cheeks.

Winter adult brown.

Golden-crowned Sparrow

Meet "Weary Willie," so nicknamed for its tired-sounding, melancholy song. Golden-crowneds spend about eight months on the wintering grounds along the West Coast, where they form flocks of up to 25 birds. They are very loyal to their wintering areas and are regular feeder visitors.

Harris's Sparrow

Harris's Sparrows return each winter to wooded or brushy habitats on the Great Plains. Their loyalty runs so deep that they stop off at the same bird feeders on their fall and spring migration. They are the only songbird that breeds exclusively in Canada. Harris's Sparrows form small flocks of two to five birds, and also join mixed sparrow flocks. The most dominant birds have the largest black bibs.

BREEDING

WINTER

YEAR-ROUND

MIGRATION

RARE

BREEDING

WINTER

YEAR-ROUND

MIGRATION

RARE

White and black striped head, clear throat and breast; bill yellow, orange, or pink.

White throat, yellow lores, dark bill, white or tan head stripes.

White-crowned Sparrow

Common feeder visitors over much of North America, White-crowned Sparrows are only in the U.S. during migration and winter, except for a few populations in the Rockies and on the Pacific coast. Prefer open/brushy areas with low bushes and twigs. Prefer low platform feeders. Usually visits feeders in flocks of two to eight birds.

White-throated Sparrow

White-throated Sparrows are likely to return to the same winter territories each year. Watch for them feeding on the ground, flipping leaves aside with their bill or scratching at the leaf litter with a series of quick kicks. Individual White-throated Sparrows have either white or tan stripes on their heads; the color does not indicate sex, but white-striped birds are more dominant. They usually arrive at feeders in flocks of four to six. Listen for their distinctive song, *Ol'-Sam-Peabody-Peabody*.

BREEDING

WINTER

YEAR-ROUND

MIGRATION

RARE

BREEDING

WINTER

YEAR-ROUND

MIGRATION

RARE

Male with gray cap, rusty nape, white cheek, black throat and bib. Female brown, with pale stripe behind the eye.

Rusty crown, black spot on white cheek, black chin.

House Sparrow

Although they look similar, House Sparrows are not very closely related to North American sparrows. One of the most abundant and widespread birds in the world, they are extremely adaptable. Native to Eurasia and North Africa, they have followed people to all of the continents except Antarctica. Introduced here in the 1900s, they occupy habitats as demanding as Death Valley and the high peaks of the Rocky Mountains. No matter the location, they are rarely found far from humans.

Eurasian Tree Sparrow

Introduced to the Midwest in the nineteenth century, this species has still not dispersed very far. Found in small flocks, Eurasian Tree Sparrows are still uncommon and local in northeast Missouri, southwest Illinois, and southeast Iowa. Similar to its relative the House Sparrow, except that both sexes of this species have a distinctly rusty crown.

BREEDING

WINTER

YEAR-ROUND

MIGRATION

RARE

BREEDING

WINTER

YEAR-ROUND

MIGRATION

RARE

Dark-eyed Juncos

The most common winter bird at many feeders, Dark-eyed Juncos are often called "snowbirds," and many people believe that their return from the northern breeding grounds signals the return of cold and snowy weather. Juncos' white bellies and dark backs inspired the nineteenth-century nature writer Wilson Flagg to describe them as "leaden skies above, snow below."

Juncos spend the entire winter in flocks of 6 to 20 birds, which return to the same ten-acre area each year. Flocks are usually larger in rural areas. Each winter flock has a dominance hierarchy with adult males at the top, followed by juvenile males and adult females, and young females at the bottom. You can often see individuals challenge the status of others with aggressive lunges and tail flicking. To avoid the competition, many female juncos migrate earlier and go farther south than most males. Male juncos spend the winter farther north, reducing the distance they must cover in spring to arrive first on prime breeding territories.

You can attract juncos to your yard with a seed blend containing millet and hulled sunflower seeds. They will also clean up any nyjer that falls to the ground. Juncos will sometimes eat pieces of suet blends or dough, and will also take crumbled Bark Butter Bits from a platform.

The Dark-eyed Junco comprises many distinct populations, which can be broken down into six "types" based on color and geographic range. They all have white outer tail feathers that can be seen as they flick them at flock mates or fly away from a feeder. Each type has its own breeding range, but especially in the West, several types flock together in winter. In winters in Colorado, I often see three or four distinguishable types of Dark-eyed Junco beneath the feeders at the same time. Here we will detail each of the 6 "types" of Dark-eyed Juncos.

Juncos are almost always seen on the ground or in low bushes and scrub. Look for the flash of white on each side of the tail as a small grayish to dark songbird flies in spurts from one low area to another.

BREEDING

WINTER

YEAR-ROUND

MIGRATION

RARE

Male with gray head, back and sides. Female paler, with brownish tones.

"Slate-colored" Junco

The most widespread "type" of Dark-eyed Junco. While Slate-colored Juncos breeding in northern North America migrate, populations in the western and eastern highlands and mountains are sedentary, remaining in more or less the same area year-round. Adult males are darkest.

BREEDING

WINTER

YEAR-ROUND

MIGRATION

RARE

Pale gray upperparts and breast, two faint white wing bars.

"White-winged" Junco

Breeding in the Black Hills of South Dakota and Wyoming and on the Nebraska Pine Ridge, this largest of the Dark-eyed Juncos migrates south into Colorado and New Mexico for the winter. It has more white in the tail than the other juncos.

Male with dark hood, rusty back and sides. Female with grayish hood.

BREEDING

WINTER

YEAR-ROUND

MIGRATION

RARE

"Oregon" Junco

Male Oregon Juncos have a distinct black hood and rusty back and sides. Juncos of this type are widespread year-round in the West, favoring higher elevations in the summer. A familiar feeder visitor.

Males with gray hood, reddish-brown back and pinkish sides. Females are paler.

BREEDING

WINTER

YEAR-ROUND

MIGRATION

RARE

"Pink-sided" Junco

Gray-hooded, with pinkish sides and darker brown back, the Pink-sided Junco breeds in the north-central Rockies and winters widely on the western Great Plains and in the Southwest. Often seen at feeders and on the ground nearby.

Gray head and sides, reddish brown back. Pink bill, with black between bill and eye.

BREEDING

WINTER

YEAR-ROUND

MIGRATION

RARE

"Gray-headed" Junco

This junco is uniformly gray with a neatly defined reddish brown back; the gray belly shades into white under the tail. Breeds in the southern Rockies and winters in the Southwest. The sexes are similar to one another.

Gray head and sides, reddish brown back, whitish throat, bill dark gray above and dull pinkish below. Black between bill and eye.

BREEDING

WINTER

YEAR-ROUND

MIGRATION

RARE

"Red-backed" Junco

The Red-backed Junco is similar to the Gray-headed Junco, but is found only in Arizona, New Mexico, and west Texas. This is the only Dark-eyed Junco with a largely grayish bill; all others have pinkish bills.

Cardinals

There are two cardinals in North America, the Northern Cardinal and the Pyrrhuloxia. Both are mostly non-migratory and can be attracted to feeders all year long. Cardinals have long crests, conical bills, and bright male plumages. The calls and songs of the two species are similar, and the songs can be hard to distinguish where their ranges overlap.

• •

Female gray to soft brown, with crest and red highlights. Downcurved yellow bill.

Male brilliant red face, crest, front of body, wings and tail. Downcurved yellow bill.

BREEDING

WINTER

YEAR-ROUND

MIGRATION

RARE

Pyrrhuloxia

Often called the "desert cardinal," the Pyrrhuloxia lives in dry brush in southwest Texas, Arizona, and New Mexico. Can be seen during their short flights between patches of brushy shrubs or when males sing from exposed perch. The upper bill curves down, while in the Northern Cardinal the upper bill has a straight edge. Pyrrhuloxias prefer hedgerows, woodlands, and suburban yards. Winter flocks travel widely in search of seeds.

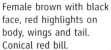

Female brown with black face, red highlights on body, wings and tail. Conical red bill.

Male scarlet with distinct crest, conical red bill, all-black face. Young birds with dark bill; young males mottled red and brown.

BREEDING

WINTER

YEAR-ROUND

MIGRATION

RARE

Northern Cardinal

The beautiful Northern Cardinal is one of the most common and popular birds in eastern North America; it has been named the official bird of seven states. Widespread east of the Rocky Mountains, it also has a limited distribution in the deserts of the Southwest. This is one of the 10 most frequently seen birds at feeders in its range. The male's bright scarlet body and black face contrast with the subtle but equally beautiful browns of the female. In late summer, cardinals sometimes lose all of their head feathers at once, exposing its dark blue-black skin. This abnormal molt, its causes unknown, ends with the regrowth of the feathers before winter. The Northern Cardinal is one of rather few birds in which the female also sings, and if you listen carefully, you might hear a mated pair sing a duet. Fledglings have dark bills. Even though cardinals are so commonly seen at feeders, they are also one of the shyest birds, and fly away quickly if they see humans nearby or through a window.

Feeder Foods

Oil and striped sunflower,
sunflower chips, safflower,
Bark Butter, Bark Butter
Bits, suet dough, cracked
corn, fruits

Grosbeaks

Grosbeaks are well named, as the word means "large bill." The Rose-breasted, Blue, and Black-headed Grosbeaks are closely related to cardinals and buntings, while the Evening and Pine

Grosbeaks are members of the finch family. To make identification more convenient, this guide treats all the grosbeaks together.

BREEDING

WINTER

YEAR-ROUND

MIGRATION

RARE

Female overall brown with light belly below streaked chest, strong tan eye-stripe. Pale, conical bill.

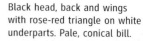

Black head, back and wings with rose-red triangle on white underparts. Pale, conical bill.

Rose-breasted Grosbeak

Wow, what a beautiful bird! First you notice the bright red triangle on the breast, then you see the black tuxedo of head, back, and wings, accented by a white belly and bill. Wow! In my Indiana yard, we count on these beauties to show up reliably in the first week of May, with an occasional nesting pair staying all summer. They favor the edges of deciduous and mixed forests, and readily come to feeders. This is one of the few birds to sing right from the nest. Both male and female raise the young. They are attracted to sunflower and safflower seeds, Bark Butter and suet dough.

Female with striped head, dark back, buffy belly.

Male with black head and back, orange belly and neck band, and striking white wing patches in flight. Both sexes have conical gray bills.

Young male is a pale version of adult male, but with distinct eye-stripe.

BREEDING

WINTER

YEAR-ROUND

MIGRATION

RARE

Black-headed Grosbeak

These western birds prefer wooded foothills and woodlands along rivers and streams. They are most often seen flying around in the low underbrush and scrub, except when males are singing their beautiful songs from high perches. Both males and females incubate and feed the young. They eat wild seeds, insects, and berries, but mated pairs readily come to feeders for sunflower seeds and Bark Butter Bits.

Female brown. Large bill is grayish above, light below.

Male with dark blue body with reddish brown wing bars, large gray bill.

Blue Grosbeak

Blue Grosbeaks favor old fields and grasslands with scattered flowering plants, bushes, and small trees. Often seen perching on fences and wires. The males look like big, fat Indigo Buntings with brownish wings; the females are plain brown with buffy wing bars. Widespread but not common in most areas, these birds are infrequent feeder visitors, eating sunflower seeds, Bark Butter, and millet.

Female paler than male with yellow-orange highlights on head and tail.

Dark bill large but not massive. Male with reddish body, dark wings and white wing bars. Bill has slight overbite.

Pine Grosbeak

Large, plump, and colorful, the Pine Grosbeak is a bird of the far North and Rocky Mountains, but migrates south in years with poor conifer and fruit crops. Usually in flocks of 5 to 30 birds, they seek out sunflower seeds at feeders or dine on the berries of crabapples, red cedar, and mountain ash. Pine Grosbeaks are very tame, and usually continue to feed even if you come close.

Female pale grayish-brown with black and white wings and tail. Both sexes with large pale to light green bill.

Male with yellow body, black head with yellow eyebrow, black wings and tail with white wing patches.

BREEDING

WINTER

YEAR-ROUND

MIGRATION

RARE

Evening Grosbeak

What a treat when a flock of Evening Grosbeaks shows up, announced by sweet chirping as they swoop in, white wing patches flashing, to look for sunflower seeds. They prefer large platforms or long perches for feeding, but beware: each bird can eat dozens of seeds in a few minutes. This is one of the few birds whose bill is capable of crushing wild cherry pits. They also eat buds and seeds, especially maple, but switch to mostly insects in the summer. They have an appetite for salt in the winter, so you might put some out on a platform to keep them off the salted roads.

Buntings

Feeder Foods
Sunflower chips, nyjer, millet, cracked corn, Bark Butter, Bark Butter Bits

The Indigo, Painted and Lazuli Buntings are sparrow-sized birds related to cardinals, grosbeaks, and tanagers. The slightly larger Snow Bunting is related to the longspurs.

Their diet consists mostly of small seeds in the winter, with the addition of insects in the spring and summer.

Winter nonbreeding birds most often seen in U.S. Small orange bill, white-and-orange head with crown stripe. White breast with warm brown highlights.

BREEDING

WINTER

YEAR-ROUND

MIGRATION

RARE

Breeding birds with white head and underparts, dark wings and distinctive white wing patches in flight.

Snow Bunting

Common on winter cornfields, grasslands, and lakeshores, Snow Buntings are not frequent feeder visitors. If you see a flock in a nearby field, offer cracked corn and millet near or on the ground.

Male with blue head and darker bluish back and wings, reddish breast, and white belly and wing bars.

Female plain, with buffy breast and pale wing bars.

BREEDING

WINTER

YEAR-ROUND

MIGRATION

RARE

Lazuli Bunting

Beautiful Lazuli Buntings are common in spring and summer in a wide range of scrubby habitats in the West. Usually only one to four at a time visit feeders. Listen closely and you can tell that each male has its own unique song. Will eat sunflower chips, nyjer, and millet.

Male blue all over with darker wings.

Female plain light brown with whitish throat. Blusih tail.

BREEDING

WINTER

YEAR-ROUND

MIGRATION

RARE

Indigo Bunting

The male is a beautiful rich blue, often looking nearly black in the shade; the color is visible only when sunlight striking the feathers is reflected as blue. Wintering in Central America and the Caribbean, in spring and summer these birds are often seen visiting finch feeders with nyjer, fine sunflower chips, millet, or a combination of the three. They have also been observed eating Bark Butter. Usually seen in groups of two to four singing their lively song up to 200 times per hour. They live in thickets along edges of fields and woods, and often perch on exposed branches.

Male with blue head with red underparts, yellow and green back.

Female distinctive green above, paler or slightly yellow below.

BREEDING

WINTER

YEAR-ROUND

MIGRATION

RARE

Painted Bunting

Our most colorful songbird, the male Painted Bunting starts with a blue head, followed by yellow, green, and brown on the shoulders and wings, and finishes with a bright red throat, belly, and rump. The female is a plain light green all over, with a thin white eye ring. Painted Buntings spend the breeding season in brushy areas near grassy fields, or in open pine and palmetto forests. Attracted to finch feeders with millet, fine chips, and nyjer; they have also been observed eating Bark Butter. Usually seen one to three at a time.

Blackbirds and Starling

Feeder Foods

Cracked corn, milo, millet, sunflower chips, peanut pieces, suet blends, Bark Butter, Bark Butter Bits, mealworms

Blackbirds are medium to large songbirds with pointed bills. The males range from completely dark to black with colorful red, yellow, or brown highlights. Up close and in bright light, the black feathers show beautiful iridescence. Females are usually brownish, some streaked. Often seen in huge flocks numbering in the hundreds or thousands. These birds eat mostly insects during breeding season and grains and fruits at other times.

Breeding summer birds are overall iridescent purplish-green, with pale spots on back and yellow bill.

Winter birds have purplish-green feathers, but covered with bright white to buffy spots, bill pale to dark.

Juvenile dull brown.

BREEDING

WINTER

YEAR-ROUND

MIGRATION

RARE

European Starling

This aggressive introduced species is found all across North America wherever people live. The European Starling nests in just about any cavity, and competes with woodpeckers, bluebirds, and other native species for nesting sites. Starlings feed and roost in huge flocks. Look for the short tail and translucent wing feathers in flight. Greatest numbers usually arrive in the backyard in winter, with dozens competing for space on the feeder and on the ground. The body feathers of winter birds have white spots at the tips, which wear away during the winter and eventually disappear. European Starlings really like peanuts, whether in pieces or mixed into suet and seed blends. They also eat milo, cracked corn, oil sunflower, sunflower chips, millet, mealworms, and Bark Butter. Look closely and you will see the "gaping" behavior, in which a feeding bird repeatedly and quickly opens its bill while going through the bird food looking for the best seeds.

Male black all over, with red and yellow shoulder patches.

Female streaky brown with buffy throat.

BREEDING

WINTER

YEAR-ROUND

MIGRATION

RARE

Red-winged Blackbird

A very common bird of marshes, scrubby pastures, and roadsides. Flashing his red and yellow shoulder patches while perched, flying, or walking on the ground, the male does his best to make sure everyone knows he is in charge of his territory. The females keep a low profile during breeding season. Flocks can be seen at feeders as they migrate and during the winter, but in the nesting season, only one or two of these territorial birds will be present at feeders. They eat millet, cracked corn, sunflower chips, and Bark Butter.

Breeding male (left) glossy black with pale eye. Rusty feather highlights in winter. Nonbreeding bird (below) with extensive rusty plumage.

Male black with bright yellow head and neat white wing patch. Female blackish with yellow face and breast.

Yellow-headed Blackbird

A bird of western prairie and marshland, most often seen breeding in cattails, foraging in old fields, or wintering in agricultural fields in the Southwest. Slightly larger than the Red-winged Blackbird, Yellow-headeds are distinctive with their bright yellow heads on black bodies. Not common at feeders, but can arrive in large flocks where they do visit. They eat millet, cracked corn, and sunflower chips.

Rusty Blackbird

Seen in most of the eastern U.S. only during migration and winter, the medium-size Rusty Blackbird is rapidly declining for unknown reasons. This blackbird is splattered with rusty feather edges, most of which wear off as spring arrives. Rusties prefer moist habitats such as bogs, beaver ponds, and swamps. They often join mixed flocks with other blackbirds. They eat cracked corn, and have been observed eating Bark butter.

BREEDING

WINTER

YEAR-ROUND

MIGRATION

RARE

BREEDING

WINTER

YEAR-ROUND

MIGRATION

RARE

Male glossy black with green and blue highlights and yellow eye.

Female unstreaked light brown with dark eye.

Male glossy black with dark bluish iridescence on head and shoulders. Female browner and less iridescent.

Brewer's Blackbird

This common, mostly western blackbird is smaller and shorter-tailed than grackles. Small numbers seen together in breeding season, but can migrate in huge flocks. Beautiful shimmering black feathers with shades of green and dark blue in full sun. Flocks rise and fall in unison, and often circle and flutter as they land. They eat cracked corn, and have been observed eating Bark Butter.

Common Grackle

Very common in large flocks in the non-breeding season. Medium-large with fairly long tails, which males fold into a "V" in the their display flight. Flocks are very bossy at feeders, and can be very aggressive towards other birds. They are sometimes considered an agricultural pest. The flight is fairly direct, without conspicuous undulation. At the feeders, they enjoy cracked corn, milo, peanuts, sunflowers, mealworms, and Bark Butter.

- BREEDING
- WINTER
- YEAR-ROUND
- MIGRATION
- RARE

- BREEDING
- WINTER
- YEAR-ROUND
- MIGRATION
- RARE

Tail about half of bird's total length. Male black with bluish iridescence. Female smaller, overall rich brown with darker wings.

Male dark purple to blue iridescent black with pale yellow eye.

Female smaller, with rich brown body and darker wings.

Boat-tailed Grackle

The Boat-tailed Grackle is a large blackbird, slightly smaller than the Great-tailed but much larger than the Common. Males defend breeding harems of several females. In the wild they eat just about anything, but at feeders they prefer milo, millet, and cracked corn, and have been observed eating Bark Butter. Only share range with Great-tailed Grackle on the western Gulf Coast.

Great-tailed Grackle

Much larger than the Common Grackle, with a much longer tail. The females are noticeably smaller than the males and rich brown. Both have a pale yellow eye. Males often pose with the head pointing straight up, or look all blustery, with tail feathers going everywhere. They are mostly resident in their range, but gather by the hundreds of thousands in southern Texas in winter. Prefers cracked corn and milo at feeders.

- BREEDING
- WINTER
- YEAR-ROUND
- MIGRATION
- RARE

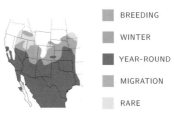

- BREEDING
- WINTER
- YEAR-ROUND
- MIGRATION
- RARE

Male with brown head on glossy black body.

Female plain brown.

BREEDING

WINTER

YEAR-ROUND

MIGRATION

RARE

Brown-headed Cowbird

A small blackbird found over most of North America, the Brown-headed Cowbird is common in open fields, small woods, and forest edges. Males display with heads-up postures and inflated feathers. Once you learn his liquid gurgling song, you will always know cowbirds are present. Look for the brown head and black body; the short conical bill is unlike the longer, pointed bills of other blackbirds. Female cowbirds lay their eggs in other birds' nests, and the foster parents raise the chicks. Prefer milo, millet, cracked corn, peanut pieces, and sunflower chips at the feeders.

Orioles

Many of us dream of having an oriole take up residence in our yard or neighborhood. To behold a brilliantly colored male flashing from branch to branch, while serenading us with its uplifting whistles, is cause for celebration! In their tropical winter range, orioles feed on fruit and nectar, and they bring an affinity for those foods with them on their springtime return to North America.

Attract orioles with orange slices, grape jelly, and nectar feeders. In some areas, they visit only during migration, but in other areas they can be present all summer. Orioles construct some of the most amazingly complicated nests of any bird. A gourd-shaped pouch hanging from the tip of a thin branch, these nests are skillfully woven out of hundreds of fibers—one strand at a time. You can increase the odds of having a pair nest in your yard by providing six-inch or shorter pieces of natural fiber string and yarn. A suet cage makes a great holder.

Male Baltimore Orioles dining on oranges and jelly.

BREEDING

WINTER

YEAR-ROUND

MIGRATION

RARE

Male with orange or orange-yellow hood, back, and belly; black mask, throat, wings, and tail.

Female plain olive on back, yellow underparts.

Hooded Oriole

What this oriole lacks in vocal talent, it makes up for it with its beautiful yellow-orange to orange-hooded head and black mask and throat.

A breeding resident of the Southwest and south Texas, Hooded Orioles particularly like to nest in tall palm trees, using fibers from the fronds to weave the nest.

Male with black head, back, wings, and tail; lemon-yellow below, yellow shoulder patch.

Female duller with plain grayish green head; black speckled breast; two white wing bars.

BREEDING

WINTER

YEAR-ROUND

MIGRATION

RARE

Scott's Oriole

It's hard to miss the beautiful black and lemon-yellow Scott's Oriole, a summer and occasionally year-round resident of the Southwest, where it readily visits nectar feeders. It is largely a yucca plant specialist, feeding on yucca nectar and weaving its nest out of fibers pulled from dead yucca leaves.

Male with black head, wings, and tail; chestnut underparts.

Female with bright yellow throat and belly, dull olive back and tail.

BREEDING

WINTER

YEAR-ROUND

MIGRATION

RARE

Orchard Oriole

The smallest of the North American orioles, the striking chestnut-colored male and the drabber olive-yellow female are common summer residents east of the Rocky Mountains. These orioles live in fairly open park-like habitats near lakes, rivers, and marshes, often several nesting pairs in close proximity. They usually stay amazingly well hidden, but can be drawn into the open with orange slices, grape jelly, mealworms, and nectar feeders.

Male with black crown and back. Orange cheek with black eye line, bright orange breast and body.

Female dull yellows and browns.

BREEDING

WINTER

YEAR-ROUND

MIGRATION

RARE

Bullock's Oriole

A western species fond of tall trees near water, the male Bullock's Oriole is mostly black on the upperparts and orange below, with a distinct black eye stripe. Both males and females sing, but their songs are slightly different; the female may sing more often.

Once the nesting season begins in earnest, these and other oriole species turn to insects for the major portion of their diet; this is the best time to add mealworms to your feeding station.

Male with black hood, wings, and tail; bright orange breast and body.

Female drab and much less vibrant version of the male's coloration. Lacks solid black hood and back.

BREEDING

WINTER

YEAR-ROUND

MIGRATION

RARE

Baltimore Oriole

Out of nine possible U.S. species, the Baltimore (east) and Bullock's (west) are the most widespread orioles to raise their families near to us. In past times the Baltimore was exclusively a three month summer visitor, but in recent decades they have become a year-round resident in parts of the south and along the eastern seaboard. Overall, they remain primarily a migratory species, so be sure to place your feeders out well in advance of their expected arrival time. In addition to the regular oriole fare of nectar, oranges, and mealworms, both Baltimore and Bullock's are attracted to suet blends with fruit and to Bark Butter and Bark Butter Bits.

Finches

Feeder Foods
Sunflower seeds, kernels and fine chips, nyjer, safflower, Bark Butter

The Finch family of birds is one of the most common and popular group of birds that visit our feeders. Consisting of small to medium-size songbirds that live in a wide range of habitats and regions, they tend to be fast, undulating flyers that gather in flocks and often roam irregularly depending on annual weather and food sources. The males and females have different plumages and often have very noticeable courtship displays such as wing fluttering and begging that we can see in our backyards. They are monogamous and usually very territorial around the nest. Primarily seed-eaters their bills are adapted to crack seeds open.

Gray head with black forehead, brownish body with pink on wings and flanks. Black and pink plumage paler in females.

BREEDING

WINTER

YEAR-ROUND

MIGRATION

RARE

Gray-crowned Rosy-Finch

Birds of western mountain tundra, Gray-crowned Rosy-Finches migrate to lower elevations in the winter, arriving in flocks that can number in the hundreds. They like open areas, where they peck around on the ground. When a large flock lifts off, you can hear them from inside your house. Very distinctive, with gray head, black forehead, and light conical bill in first winter that turns dark in breeding season. Highly variable, with six geographic races recognized. They enjoy sunflower seeds, chips, and nyjer, preferring platforms and other feeders with lots of room for landing.

Black body, gray head patch, much pink on wings and belly.

BREEDING

WINTER

YEAR-ROUND

MIGRATION

RARE

Black Rosy-Finch

Similar to Gray-crowned, but body is distinctly grayish to black. Birds of the high central Rocky Mountains, large winter flocks visit feeders to eat sunflower seeds, chips, and millet. Interestingly, winter flocks have been observed roosting at night in caves, barns, and mine shafts.

Brown head limited gray, brown body with pink on wings and belly.

BREEDING

WINTER

YEAR-ROUND

MIGRATION

RARE

Brown-capped Rosy-Finch

The Brown-capped Rosy-Finch is restricted almost entirely to Colorado and northern New Mexico at any season. The absence of distinct gray on the head distinguishes this bird. Brown-cappeds arrive at feeders in winter, often in flocks with the other rosy-finches.

Males with orange-red face, chest and rump with brown streaks on back and belly.

Female plain with brown streaks.

BREEDING

WINTER

YEAR-ROUND

MIGRATION

RARE

House Finch

The male House Finch varies in color from orangey red to orangey yellow, depending on region and diet. The females are brown-streaked with no face markings. The House Finch was originally restricted to dry, open or brushy habitats in the western U.S.; it was introduced to the East in 1940, and is now common there as well, though rarely seen far from human habitation. House Finches arrive in flocks; vegetarians, they consume large quantities of sunflower, safflower, and nyjer seeds. House Finches can contract an eye disease called avian conjunctivitis, which reduced their numbers in the East by about 50 percent in the mid-1990s.

Male raspberry-red colored with brown-streaked wings and tail.

Female streaked brown below, with strong face markings.

BREEDING

WINTER

YEAR-ROUND

MIGRATION

RARE

Purple Finch

Purple Finches are actually more raspberry-red than purple. The males have little or no streaking on the breast. This is one species in which the female can be easier to identify: her strong facial markings, with light stripes above and below the eye, isolate the strikingly dark cheeks. Purple Finches are an irruptive species, traveling south every other winter or so when food supplies are low. Their strong bills can crush oil sunflower seeds, but they also eat nyjer and some millet.

Male rosy-red overall with whitish belly. Slight crest.

Female with sharply defined streaks on underparts and patterned brown on face and back.

BREEDING

WINTER

YEAR-ROUND

MIGRATION

RARE

Cassin's Finch

A bird of the western mountains, the Cassin's Finch is similar to the House and Purple Finches. The male is distinguished by its rosy color, with little streaking below and a slightly crested head.

The female has brown upperparts and sharply streaked white underparts. Like House Finches, Cassin's Finches arrive in flocks and jostle for position on the platform or perches.

Male reddish overall with brown wings and tail.

Female with yellowish highlights on body. No wing bars.

BREEDING

WINTER

YEAR-ROUND

MIGRATION

RARE

Red Crossbill

The Red Crossbill has eight different forms that exhibit great variation in bill, body size and calls. The larger billed varieties are able to open larger pine cones, while the smaller billed varieties tend to harvest smaller cones such as spruces, firs and hemlocks. The amazing bill is truly crossed at the tips and enables this bird to specialize in opening cones of evergreens and extracting the seed. Small or large flocks will always be seen in habitats with plenty of these cones. They can easily open sunflower and safflower seeds at the feeder.

Male pinkish to deep red, white wing bars on black wings.

Female with yellowish highlights on body. White wing bars on darker wings.

BREEDING

WINTER

YEAR-ROUND

MIGRATION

RARE

White-winged Crossbill

Actually, just the wing bars are white, but they contrast strongly with the rest of the black wing. Thin, distinctively crossed bills let White-winged Crossbills specialize on spruce and larch cones. Small to large flocks visit feeders or land on roadways to eat salt.

Male with red cap and reddish throat and chest; black face with pale bill.

Female with red cap, black face with pale bill.

Common Redpoll

Common Redpolls are hardy northern finches that migrate south every other year or so, when food sources are sparse. They travel in busy flocks that can be hundreds of birds with lots of activity, chatter and then rapid movement to the next food source. Common Redpolls are among the hardiest of birds, surviving temperatures as low as -65° F. They prefer smaller seeds such as nyjer, sunflower chips, and small oil sunflower.

Red cap and pale bill, pale overall with little streaking or color on flanks.

Females with small red crown and generally darker and streakier than males.

Hoary Redpoll

The Hoary Redpoll breeds even farther north than the Common Redpoll, but can also be seen migrating south every two years or so, sometimes in flocks with Common Redpolls. Identification can be challenging, but look for an extremely pale redpoll with whiter underparts and a bulkier or fluffier appearance.

Brown streaks, buff to yellow wing bars, pointed bill. Yellow in wings and tail easily seen in flight.

Immature male and female less yellow.

BREEDING

WINTER

YEAR-ROUND

MIGRATION

RARE

Pine Siskin

These brown-streaked birds might at first be confused with female House Finches, but the thin, pointed bill and yellow wing markings quickly distinguish them from other finches. Very common in some winters and completely absent in others, Pine Siskins are nomadic, moving north and south or east and west every couple of years, when seed supplies are short in their breeding range. Easily identified once you learn to recognize the harsh rising *zreeee* and constant chatter of a flock.

Male upperparts all black, or greenish with black cap, wings, and tail.

Female paler, with pale wing bars on darker wings.

BREEDING

WINTER

YEAR-ROUND

MIGRATION

RARE

Lesser Goldfinch

The Lesser Goldfinch has both a green-backed and a black-backed form. The green-backed is seen mostly in the Southwest and on the Pacific Coast, while the black-backed is more frequent in the Rockies and Texas. It is possible, though, to see both on the same feeder, as I sometimes do in northern Colorado. The Lesser Goldfinch arrives in flocks, at times with other finches, and fights for position on the finch feeder or nearby branches. Look for the prominent white wing patch as birds fly to and from feeders.

Male with dark face, yellow breast and wings.

Female pale gray-brown with some yellow in wings.

BREEDING

WINTER

YEAR-ROUND

MIGRATION

RARE

Lawrence's Goldfinch

This handsome finch is commonly seen in the breeding season in the open woodlands of California; it winters irregularly eastward to Arizona and New Mexico. If you see yellow on the breast and wings and a dark face, you are seeing a Lawrence's Goldfinch. This species travels in flocks and eats seeds in open fields. Generally only a few come to feeders in the summer, while larger flocks may arrive in the winter.

Breeding male with bright yellow body, black wings and cap.

Nonbreedng male and female plain brownish-yellow body with wing bars on darker wings.

American Goldfinch

A fortunately common bird across all of the U.S. and southern Canada, this beautiful finch molts its body feathers in the fall and spring. So, not only do the sexes differ in plumage, the males especially differ from summer to winter and are hard to distinguish from the females in the winter. American Goldfinches are only seen in the southern states in the winter, so their brightest colors are not often seen in these states. These acrobatic seed-eating birds of old fields will readily visit your feeders full of Nyjer and sunflower and will also be attracted to your garden plantings of purple coneflower and other composite flowers. Often visiting in large flocks, especially in the winter. Look closely for other finches mixed in with the flock such as Pine Siskins, Lesser Goldfinches, House Finches, redpolls, and Purple Finches.

Hawks

Of all the hawks that live in North America, there are only two that commonly hunt birds in backyards and near bird feeders. The smaller Sharp-shinned and larger Cooper's Hawks are members of the genus *Accipiter* and are equipped to fly fast with quick maneuvering through branches or as attacking birds on the ground.

Small hawk with gray hood, back and wings with patterned rusty-brown chest. Bottom of banded tail square. Juveniles brownish with vertically-streaked chests. Females much larger than males.

Sharp-shinned Hawk

A small hawk at only 11 inches, these can be distinguished from Cooper's Hawks mainly by their size, their small head and bill and the flatness of their tail tip. They are very talented at pursuing birds through tangles and understory and tend to pursue smaller birds than the more powerful Cooper's.

Adults and juveniles similar to Sharp-shinned but is a much larger bird. Bottom of banded tail rounded.

Cooper's Hawk

Cooper's Hawks are medium-sized hawks at about 16 inches long. These talented bird-hunting hawks will often keep an eye on local feeders and then swoop in low with a "flap-flap-glide" pattern hoping to surprise and startle the flock. They will often target mid-sized birds such as doves and starlings as they are slower flyers and easier to grab with their talons. The juveniles have vertical brown streaks on their chest with brown backs while adults will have tight horizontal reddish barring on their chests with gray crowns and backs. Both have a banded tail that is rounded at tip.

BREEDING

WINTER

YEAR-ROUND

MIGRATION

RARE

BREEDING

WINTER

YEAR-ROUND

MIGRATION

RARE

4 The Foods

I F YOU LOOK at the bird food aisle in a store or study the selections at an online outlet, it can all seem very complicated. Which foods should you offer? Fortunately, it is simple to make good choices once you know which foods work in your yard and give you the best value for your dollar. Unless you have a reason to serve foods separately, create or buy a good blend, which will bring a wider variety of birds to your feeders.

Foundational feeder blends

With a foundational blend based on sunflowers to target sunflower-eating birds:

1. Add more white millet for more ground-feeding birds such as juncos and sparrows.

2. Add more peanuts for more perching birds such as woodpeckers, jays, chickadees, and titmice.

Your foundational feeder should dispense large quantities of the most effective foods. In Chapter 1, you learned which foods work best in your yard: all of those foods are probably on the following list of ingredients I recommend for a foundational feeder blend.

Main ingredients

Mix these ingredients in proportions suitable to your region, the season, and the number of millet- and peanut-eating birds:

1. Oil sunflower

2. Sunflower chips

3. Peanut pieces

4. White millet

5. Hulled white millet

Special additions: for extra benefit at different seasons:

6. Safflower

7. Striped sunflower

8. Bark Butter Bits or suet nuggets

9. Tree nuts

10. Dried fruit

11. Dried mealworms

12. Calcium

These same eleven foods and calcium as an additive, should also be the main ingredients in bird food cylinders and cakes offered in foundational feeders.

Avoid

You should stay away from the following foods in buying or creating a foundational feeder blend.

1. Nyjer

2. Cracked corn (no more than 15%)

3. Milo (sorghum)

4. Wheat

5. Oats

6. Canary seed

7. Other grains

Nyjer belongs in a finch feeder on its own or blended with fine sunflower chips. Turn to page 215 for more details.

Cracked corn is fairly attractive to many birds, some of which are often considered undesirable, such as European Starlings, grackles, Rock Pigeons, and House Sparrows. Admittedly, there are birds that you want to attract that do like cracked corn, such as Northern Cardinals, jays, Dark-eyed Juncos, and native sparrows. The good news is that your foundational feeder blend of oil sunflower and millet already attracts those beautiful birds, but is less appealing to starlings and House Sparrows. If you add cracked corn, my advice is to keep it less than 15 percent of the total blend.

Milo is preferred by only a very few birds, for the most part in the southwestern U.S. In other areas, it should be avoided in foundational feeder blends.

Wheat, oats, canary seed, and other grains are often added to wild bird mixes, but they are rarely eaten. These ingredients are a waste of your bird feeding dollar.

Tray feeder blends

You can always use the same blend in your tray feeder and in your foundational feeder. If you place a tray near the ground, use a blend with lots of millet for ground-feeding birds. This is where you can add a bit of cracked corn—but not more than 15 percent, or it might go uneaten. Again, back off of the cracked corn if you are attracting birds you consider undesirable.

Of course, you can use the tray feeder for much more than seed blends. You might offer fats such as suet nuggets, fresh and dried fruit, and other snack foods.

No-mess blends

After many years of sunflower shells all over the deck and below the feeders, I finally switched to no-mess seed blends. What a difference! If you use no-mess ingredients such as sunflower chips, peanut pieces, and hulled white millet, you will avoid piles of shells under the feeders or on the deck.

With additions such as tree nuts, dried fruits, dried insects, and calcium, you can broaden the appeal to even more birds, and still have a no-mess blend.

Bird food preference chart

A better understanding of all the possible foods will let you make good decisions about when to add, change, or delete foods from your blends and when to use a food by itself.

This chart shows species or groups of birds and their *preferences* among 19 bird foods. It does not list every food eaten by every bird, but instead highlights *preferred* foods.

Birds might eat a seed when it is the only thing offered, but won't touch it if a preferred food is also available. Pine Siskins will eat oil sunflower, nyjer, and sunflower chips, but when all three are offered, they take the nyjer and chips and hardly touch the oil sunflower.

Food	Cardinals	Grosbeaks	Jays & Nutcracker	Woodpeckers	Carolina Wren	Cactus Wren	Goldfinches	Pine Siskin	Purple Finch	House Finch	Redpolls	Chickadees	Titmice	Nuthatches	Bushtits	Bluebirds	Orioles
Oil sunflower	•	•	•	•			•	•	•	•	•	•	•	•			
Striped sunflower	•	•	•	•							•	•	•				
Sunflower chips	•	•	•	•	•		•	•	•	•	•	•	•	•		•	
Safflower	•	•							•	•		•	•	•			
Nyjer							•	•	•	•	•	•					
Peanuts in shell			•	•									•				
Peanut pieces	•	•	•	•	•							•	•	•	•		
Mealworms				•	•	•						•	•	•		•	•
Suet products				•	•	•								•			
Bark Butter/PB mix	•	•	•	•	•	•						•	•	•	•	•	•
White millet																	
Corn kernels																	
Cracked corn			•														
Milo																	
Wheat																	
Oats																	
Fruits				•												•	•
Jelly																	•
Nectar				•													•

The chart does not include red millet, as birds that eat red millet also eat, and prefer, white millet.

After studying this chart, you will conclude that oil sunflower, sunflower chips, safflower, white millet, and peanut pieces do the heavy lifting as the basis for your foundational feeder blends. The other foods have great usefulness for "target birds" when offered alone on a tray or in a feeder.

Fruit, jelly and nectar definitely attract specific birds and safflower is a great addition for varying the diet as well as being relatively unappealing to squirrels and blackbirds.

No birds prefer wheat or oats over other foods.

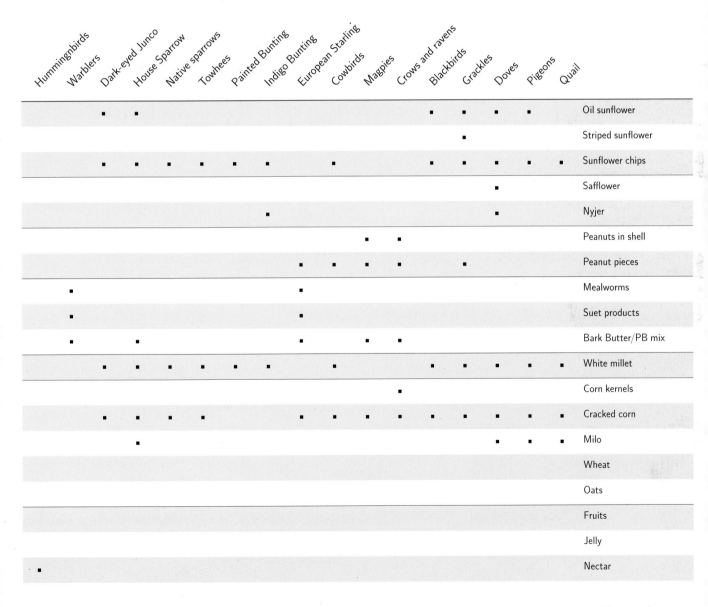

Food	Hummingbirds	Warblers	Dark-eyed Junco	House Sparrow	Native sparrows	Towhees	Painted Bunting	Indigo Bunting	European Starling	Cowbirds	Magpies	Crows and ravens	Blackbirds	Grackles	Doves	Pigeons	Quail
Oil sunflower			•	•									•	•	•	•	
Striped sunflower														•			
Sunflower chips			•	•	•	•	•	•		•			•	•	•	•	•
Safflower															•		
Nyjer								•							•		
Peanuts in shell											•	•					
Peanut pieces									•	•	•	•		•			
Mealworms		•							•								
Suet products		•							•								
Bark Butter/PB mix		•		•					•		•	•					
White millet			•	•	•	•	•			•			•	•	•	•	•
Corn kernels												•					
Cracked corn			•	•	•	•			•	•	•	•	•	•	•	•	•
Milo				•											•	•	•
Wheat																	
Oats																	
Fruits																	
Jelly																	
Nectar	•																

What natural foods does bird food mimic?

Seeds, nuts, fruits, berries, insects in all life stages, flower nectar, sap, and leaf and flower buds are among the natural foods available to birds seasonally or year-round, and the food in our feeders should resemble those natural sources.

Birds have evolved their size, bills, tongues, feet, eyesight, dexterity, metabolism, and behavior to take advantage of wild food resources. Ground-feeding birds such as Dark-eyed Juncos and other sparrows eat vast quantities of weed seeds, including smartweed, ragweed, foxtail, pigweed, and knotweed. At your feeders, these birds prefer millet, cracked corn, and other grains similarly high in carbohydrates. Since their natural foods are very low in fats and proteins, they must eat constantly to get all the nutrition they need.

Perching and tree-dwelling songbirds that find most of their food above the ground seek out foods with a balance of fats, proteins, and carbohydrates. These birds prefer sunflower seeds, nyjer, peanuts, and fats.

Guide to the foods we offer at our feeders

Sunflower seeds: the main course

Sunflower seeds are the favorite at feeders in all parts of North America, and the major component of top-quality blends. The loose seed blend you put in your foundational feeder will have lots of sunflower along with smaller quantities of other ingredients such as white millet and peanuts. Sunflower is usually the major ingredient in blends used for bird food cylinders and cakes.

Mimics what natural food?

Sunflower seeds mimic the seeds of trees including pine, hemlock, spruce, fir, maple, elm, sweetgum, and beech, plus flower seeds of all sizes, of course including the 60-plus wild sunflower species.

Types

Two kinds of sunflower seeds are used for feeding birds: oil sunflower and striped sunflower. Oil sunflower is the main variety used now, as it is preferred by the birds, has higher oil content, and is usually less expensive.

Sunflower seeds without the shells are called kernels, chips, hulled, or hearts; they are all the same product but different sizes. Most sunflower chips are produced as a by-product when striped sunflowers are processed for food-grade products, which use only the best whole kernels. The smaller pieces are screened out to become medium and fine chips for the birds.

Oil sunflower (far left), striped sunflower (near left), and sunflower chips (below right).

OIL SUNFLOWER
▶ 40% fat ▶ 16% protein ▶ 20% carbohydrates
▶ calories/100g: 517

Sometimes called black oil sunflower. Almost all seed-eating birds prefer oil to striped sunflower. This is the best of all seeds in the shell, attracting the greatest variety of small and large birds. Oil sunflower has 50 percent more calories per pound than striped sunflower, its smaller shells make less mess, and it is typically less expensive than striped sunflower. Another reason birds like oil sunflower: the thin shell is easier to crack open than striped sunflower.

Premium oil sunflower
Premium oil sunflower is the same seed but screened to be at least 99 percent pure, which means that only 1 percent can be sticks, stems, or other foreign matter. Standard oil sunflower is 98 percent pure; the difference can be quite noticeable, because standard oil sunflower has twice as many sticks and stems. This can make a difference in keeping feeders, especially tube feeders, from becoming clogged.

STRIPED SUNFLOWER
▶ 26% fat ▶ 15% protein ▶ 18% carbohydrates;
▶ calories/100g: 356

Sometimes called medium-dark or black striped sunflower, this larger seed was the sunflower used

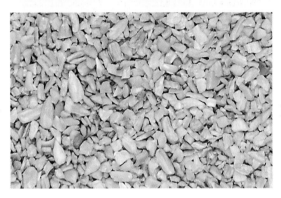

for feeding birds until oil sunflower was developed in the 1970s. I have found that Tufted Titmice, Blue Jays, and Red-bellied Woodpeckers, when given a choice, slightly prefer striped sunflower to oil sunflower. However, they heartily feast on oil sunflower when it is the only sunflower offered.

SUNFLOWER CHIPS
▶ 50% fat ▶ 19% protein ▶ 24% carbohydrates
▶ calories/100g: 592

Whole kernels and medium chips are the sizes most commonly used alone or in blends. Fine chips are often used in finch feeders, alone or in a blend with nyjer, to feed goldfinches and other small-billed birds. An advantage of chips is that they leave no mess beneath the feeder. They are highly preferred by the birds because they are easier to eat than seeds in their shells.

Like any seed removed from its shell, hulled

A male Northern Cardinal easily opens a sunflower seed with its strong, conical bill.

sunflower is more apt to spoil or gum up in wet or humid conditions. Offer chips only in low-capacity feeders designed to keep the seed dry or in feeders with a very high level of bird activity. Because sunflower shells are known to kill or stunt plants, sunflower chips, having no shells, are excellent in feeders near flower or vegetable beds.

How do birds eat sunflower seeds?

Sunflower-loving birds split sunflower seeds, pound them open, or swallow them whole. Large-billed birds like cardinals, grosbeaks, and crossbills skillfully split the seed to extract the meat. Oddly, sunflower seed is the favorite seed of many smaller birds with smaller bills, which have other ways to extract the meat. Chickadees and titmice hold a seed in their toes and pound it open. Nuthatches wedge it into a bark crevice. Larger birds such as Mourning Doves often don't bother splitting a sunflower: they just swallow it whole and let their muscular gizzards grind it up.

Nutritional benefit

All types of sunflower seeds are high in protein and fat. Oil sunflower has a bit more protein than striped, but it also has a whopping 50 percent more fat content, because it was bred to be pressed for sunflower oil. Sunflower chips have the highest calorie count per weight of all common bird foods, slightly higher than peanuts.

Feeders

Hoppers, tubes, trays, window feeders, and small-bird-only feeders all work well with sunflower seed, alone or in blends.

Safflower: a special addition and the problem solver

That darn squirrel! Those pesky blackbirds and starlings! I want more cardinals!

A white or whitish seed similar in size to oil sunflower, safflower contains similar amounts of fat, protein, and calories. It is an excellent problem-solver when used alone in a feeder, because while blackbirds, European Starlings, and many squirrels do not seem to like it, Northern Cardinals, chickadees, House Finches, Tufted Titmice, and many other sunflower-loving birds do. Safflower is typically more expensive than oil sunflower; however, it is economical in the sense that squirrels and undesirable birds are not eating it.

How to introduce safflower

Sometimes you put safflower in your feeder and nothing happens—no birds. In this case, you need to introduce safflower to the birds. Prepare a fifty-fifty mix of safflower and sunflower or any good foundational feeder blend. After a week or two, the cardinals will be well acquainted with the safflower and you can go to 100 percent safflower in your feeder.

Mimics what natural food?

Safflower seeds mimic the same wild foods as sunflower seeds.

Types

Safflower

▶ 38% fat ▶ 16% protein ▶ 34% carbohydrates
▶ calories/100g: 517

Several varieties of safflower are grown, but they all go by the name "safflower" when they hit the retail stores. The seed's bright white color varies from crop to crop, and some might show brown coloration from frost damage, but the nutritional value is still just fine.

Safflower Fact

It is believed that one reason grackles and European Starlings tend to not eat safflower is that their bills are not built for cracking open seeds of this size with such hard shells. It is also thought that squirrels eat safflower less readily than other seeds because of its bitter taste. Chipmunks, though, seem to love safflower. I've seen them fill their cheeks with safflower seeds and take the food down to their underground storage chambers. I have to assume they actually like it, or they are in for a long winter's surprise of bitter-tasting seeds.

NutraSaff
► 47% fat ► 20% protein ► unknown % carbs
► calories/100g: unknown

Sometimes called "golden safflower" for its brownish color, NutraSaff, a variety developed by Safflower Technologies International, has advantages and disadvantages. It has 15 percent more oil, 25 percent more protein, and 30 percent more fat than regular safflower. Organic and chemical-free, it has a 40-percent thinner shell, so it is easier to crack open and eat.

It does seem to live up to the claim that birds really like it better. Observations by staff, store owners, and customers at Wild Birds Unlimited show that Carolina Chickadees absolutely love it.

Because this variety produces only 70 percent of the yield of regular safflowers, it costs more. Although there are claims that squirrels do not like it, our own experience is that they will eat it; it may not be the problem solver that regular safflower is.

NutraSaff is very popular with many birds and has excellent nutrition, but results differ as to whether it solves squirrel and blackbird problems.

How do birds eat safflower seeds?

Birds eat safflower in the same ways as sunflower. They crack it open, pound it open, or swallow it whole.

Nutritional benefit

Regular safflower is nearly identical to oil sunflower in oil and protein content, but it has 70 percent more carbohydrates. It is a good addition to blends, because it contributes a variety of nutritional components not found in sunflower.

Feeders

Safflower can be offered in any kind of feeder, and it is especially appropriate for your foundational feeder, window feeders, or deck feeders to discourage blackbirds and squirrels. Just remember that you don't need to use safflower in a squirrel-proof feeder.

White millet is preferred over red millet for blends (left), and hulled white millet (right) is preferred in no-mess blends.

Millet: the best small seed

For Dark-eyed Juncos in the winter, Chipping Sparrows in the summer, and many other ground-foraging birds year-round, millet is an excellent treat. It's also a featured ingredient in a foundational feeder's seed blend.

White proso millet, a shiny round seed, is the best small seed to include in blends or to offer alone. Such beautiful birds as Dark-eyed Juncos and White-crowned Sparrows and Painted Buntings are attracted to millet. It is preferred by doves when offered on the ground or in trays. White millet is grown in the U.S. mostly for wild and domestic bird food and livestock feed, but in much of the rest of the world it is grown for human consumption. None of the other grains, such as milo, wheat, and canary seed, are as attractive to birds as white millet, so look for blends that have white millet and none of those other grains.

Mimics what natural food?

Millet is a grain that mimics small native flower and weed seeds such as ragweed, buckwheat, bristlegrass, crabgrass, violet, smartweed, chickweed, pigweed, panicgrass, knotweed, and dock. These wild seeds are eaten by birds right from the plant or after they have fallen to the ground.

Types

White proso millet

White millet, as it is commonly called, is preferred over red proso millet. It is usually not entirely white, but has a cream or yellow tinge. A popular choice for feeding the birds, it is relatively low in cost and high in attractiveness.

Red proso millet

Reddish and slightly smaller than white millet, red proso millet is eaten by the same birds as white millet, but is not preferred if both are present. It should not be confused with red milo (the size of a bb pellet), which is generally considered a filler.

Hulled white millet

Hulled white millet is used alone or in blends that are truly no-mess, with zero shells to pile up on the feeder or on the ground. Beware of blends advertised as no-mess that include millet with shells.

How do birds eat millet seeds?

Millet is eaten whole by doves and cracked open by smaller birds such as sparrows. Close inspection after a flock leaves shows that only the empty shells are left.

Millet Facts
Millet can be grown in hot, dry areas that do not support thirstier crops. Hulled millet is becoming more popular among humans in North America and Europe as a healthy alternative to other grains, and is included in gluten-free diets.

Nutritional benefit

▶ 4% fat ▶ 11% protein ▶ 73% carbohydrates
▶ calories/100g: 378

Millet is a typical grain, with almost no fat, just a bit of protein, and lots of carbohydrates. In fact, carbohydrates are 73 percent of the seeds.

Feeders

Millet is best offered in hoppers and trays or on the dry ground. In a hopper, it should be a small percentage of the blend; sunflower-eating birds will kick aside millet as they seek out the sunflowers. I designed the Wild Birds Unlimited Classic hopper feeder with that in mind: the millet in the seed blend is knocked out of the feeder onto the ground through an opening on the perch sides. Tube feeders are not recommended for millet blends, because the sunflower will be eaten first, leaving the millet. Sunflower-eating birds then leave the feeder alone, and millet-eating birds are on the ground without food. The few exceptions include Lazuli, Indigo, and Painted Buntings, which prefer white millet from tube feeders. In this case, offer millet alone or in a blend with just a bit of sunflower or nyjer.

Given a choice, use white millet instead of red millet.

Nyjer: goldfinches' favorite

Per-chick-oree, per-chick-oree—or it might be easier to remember *po-ta-to-chip*. What a welcome call to hear in our yards! American Goldfinches give this call as they fly over in their undulating pattern. If you offer nyjer, you have a great chance to attract these beautiful birds and other finches to your feeders.

Though it is sometimes called "thistle," this seed does not come from native or invasive thistles, but from a plant named *Guizotia abyssinica*.

It was called "thistle" by 1970s marketers to emphasize its attractiveness to goldfinches, which are very fond of the seeds of true thistles. Unlike some true thistles, nyjer—a member of the aster family, with pretty yellow flowers—does not spread as a noxious weed. Its original common name was "niger" seed, and as it was unfortunately easy to mispronounce, the Wild Bird Feeding Industry created a new spelling that is easy to correctly pronounce. Nyjer is a registered trademark of the Wild Bird Feeding Industry and is used with permission from the WBFI.

Most nyjer is grown in Ethiopia and India, where it is processed into oil for cooking and lighting. Because nyjer must be imported to North America, it is relatively high-priced and sometimes in short supply. Before it is distributed in North America, nyjer is treated with dry or steam heat to sterilize any noxious weed seeds that might be a threat to agriculture. Processing does not always sterilize the nyjer seed itself, which can grow and flower underneath feeders if given enough moisture, sunlight, and the very long growing season it requires.

Nyjer has a thin shell and is vulnerable to spoiling in the tube if moisture is present. Finches are picky eaters, and seem to prefer fresh seed. You should replace it every three or four weeks if it is not being eaten. If the seed in the tube gets moldy, clean out the tube and sterilize it with a 10-percent bleach and water solution. Rinse it thoroughly, and let it dry completely before refilling it. Stored in a cool dry place, nyjer can stay fresh for up to two years. You can test the seed for freshness by pounding it with a hammer on newspaper. If oil squishes out, it should still be fresh.

Nyjer is a tiny, shiny black seed best offered in special finch feeders.

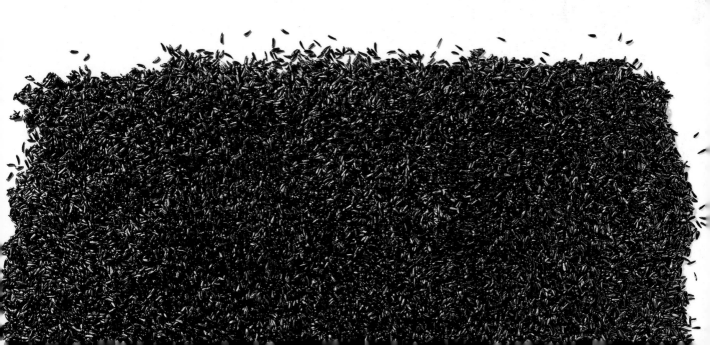

Nyjer fact
Recently developed short-season varieties are now being grown in the U.S. and Canada.

Mimics what natural food?

Nyjer mimics weedy flowers with small seeds such as native thistles, goldenrod, and ragweed, all of which goldfinches seek out in open fields.

Types

There is only one species of nyjer seed.

How do birds eat nyjer seeds?

Goldfinches split the shell, extract the meat, and drop the shell. It may seem as though all the nyjer has been tossed on the ground, but a close look shows that only the empty shells remain. Whole seeds dropped to the ground are readily eaten by doves, Dark-eyed Juncos, and other sparrows.

Nutritional benefit

▶ 38% fat ▶ 21% protein ▶ 13% carbohydrates;
▶ calories/100g: 478

Nyjer is a highly nutritious food, with high oil content and a good proportion of protein and carbohydrates.

Feeders

Nyjer is typically fed to smaller birds in finch feeders, also called tube feeders, with very small feeding ports to prevent unwanted species with larger bills from eating the food and to keep the seed from spilling out of the feeder. Nyjer is also offered in metal mesh tube feeders or finch socks. Finches can eat from the horizontal perch or cling to the side of the mesh feeders. House Finches sometimes bully goldfinches off the feeders, so finch feeder have been developed with the holes below the perches: goldfinches can hang upside down, but House Finches have trouble.

Beautiful yellow Nyjer flowers.

Peanuts

When I need lots of energy for a long morning run, I spread some peanut butter on a banana, and I am good to go for miles. Birds constantly seek out high-energy foods, and peanuts are one of the highest-calorie foods they can find, second only to sunflower chips.

Peanuts are fed to birds in a variety of forms, including peanuts in the shell, shelled peanuts, peanut pieces, and peanut hearts. Runner peanuts are the main variety used for bird food and peanut butter, while the larger Virginia peanuts and smaller Spanish peanuts, usually saved for human treats, are occasionally available.

I recommend offering roasted, unsalted peanuts. As we don't know how much salt songbirds can use or how easily they eliminate excess salt, it is best to choose unsalted. If you do occasionally offer salted peanuts, just make sure there is plenty of water nearby.

In damp seasons, feed only as many peanuts as can be eaten quickly, since aspergillus molds might grow on moist peanuts and produce the poison aflatoxin. If you see a black mold, you should toss all the peanuts into your trash can and thoroughly clean the feeder with a 10-percent bleach and water solution.

Mimics what natural food?

Peanuts, in or out of the shell, most closely mimic many species of acorns and pine nuts. Several species of birds, especially jays and magpies, cache great numbers of acorns all over forests and fields, and they also cache peanuts.

Types

Peanuts in the shell

Peanuts in the shell are typically offered to jays and other corvids such as Clark's Nutcrackers. Titmice and woodpeckers also enjoy peanuts in the shell as they are able to peck through the shell. Place peanuts in the shell on platform feeders or other feeders designed for such food.

Peanut pieces

Peanuts without the shell are called peanut kernels, peanut rejects, peanut splits, peanut pieces, or peanut seconds. I like to call them all peanut pieces. In size, peanut pieces can be wholes, halves, pieces, or diced. The size of the pieces will determine the type of feeder to use; see the Feeders section below. Peanut pieces attract titmice, chickadees, jays, woodpeckers, and many other birds.

Peanut hearts

Peanut hearts are the embryos of the peanut, which are removed in making peanut butter. They are not as attractive to most birds as shelled peanuts, but they seem to be extremely appealing to European Starlings. I recommend sunflower chips or peanut pieces over peanut hearts as a no-mess, no-waste seed.

How do birds eat peanuts?

Peanuts in the shell are a formidable challenge, and only a few birds have the beak strength to open them. Blue Jays, Tufted Titmice, and many woodpeckers can crack holes in the shells. Titmice just love peanuts: they give it all they have to crack the shell and are quite successful at this endeavor.

Peanut fact
Peanuts have been a popular food for birds in the United Kingdom for decades, but were not widely used in North America until the 1990s. Even birds that do not normally eat nuts in the wild go for peanuts: I have seen Dark-eyed Juncos and American Robins feasting on tiny pieces that fell from a feeder onto the ground.

Jays really like peanuts in the shell; they put on quite a show as they clean out a feeder in a few minutes or hours. Instead of eating them all right away, jays often cache peanuts for later retrieval—fortunately, they have great memories. Chickadees cache half a peanut at a time, while magpies stuff their entire gullet with peanut pieces before flying off to hide their treasure. Larger birds can swallow peanut meats whole and let their gizzard do the work of mashing them down to size, while smaller birds like chickadees and titmice hold the peanut in their feet and peck it into smaller bites. Nuthatches wedge peanuts into grooves in bark before hammering them into smaller pieces, all the while clinging head-down on the tree. Woodpeckers also break peanuts up before eating them.

In some areas such as the prairies, local wild birds prefer mostly smaller diced peanuts, while not too far away in the Rocky Mountain foothills, they prefer whole halves. It likely depends on how many jays and similar birds are present, because jays like the larger pieces.

Nutritional benefit

▶ 49% fat ▶ 26% protein ▶ 19% carbohydrates
▶ calories/100g: 581

Peanuts are full of nutrition and energy. They are among the feeder foods with the most calories by weight.

Feeders

You have many feeder options for peanuts in the shell, but they all have in common a mesh that is small enough to hold in the peanuts but large enough the birds can pull them out. These feeders can be tubes, squares, and wreathes and are made of many materials. Peanut pieces can fit into similar mesh feeders but with smaller mesh. Both types of peanuts can easily be offered on a tray feeder, where they disappear very quickly.

Peanuts are a common ingredient in high-quality foundational blends, suet cakes, and bird food cylinders.

Peanuts are available with or without their shell and can be offered alone or as an ingredient in blends, suets and cylinders.

Fat and suet

Fat feeders are the third element in your thoughtful bird feeding station—and with good reason. The most consistent patrons of suet and fat products are woodpeckers, but many other insect-eaters are attracted to fats. Many of what we think of as "seed-eating" birds, such as chickadees and nuthatches, eat mostly insects in the summer and seeds in the winter. These birds visit both seed and fat feeders all year.

With a 94-percent fat content, pure suet is a very desirable high-energy food. The best suet for bird feeding is high-quality rendered beef kidney fat. Rendering kills bacteria and removes moisture. This gives suet a higher melting point and protects it from spoiling. Unrendered suet goes rancid quickly, and should be offered only on freezing winter days.

Types

Pure suet

Pure rendered suet cakes or tubs are not as commonly offered as suet blend products. Pure fat is not preferred by birds, and the nutrition it offers is not as complete as that provided by suet blends. One benefit of pure suet is that squirrels and European Starlings generally avoid it, preferring suet blends with other ingredients.

Suet blends

Suet cakes are more properly called "suet blend cakes" as there is usually more "blend" ingredients than suet tallow in the cake. Adding ingredients to high-quality suet and other fat products increases protein content and more closely approximates the nutritional value of insects. Roasted peanut pieces, peanut butter, almonds, pecans, and sunflower hearts add proteins and additional fats, while cracked corn, corn meal, and oats add carbohydrates.

So, I categorize suet blend cakes into three categories: Low Protein, Medium Protein and High Protein. The more protein added—such as peanuts, nuts, and dried insects—the higher the quality and more the product will cost. High Protein suet blend cakes will have a nice percentage of protein for the birds' diet. These higher protein suets usually have higher fat content as well, so these are the most nutritious products you can offer your birds.

Low protein suet blend cakes, the least expensive, have a very high percentage of low-cost high-carbohydrate grains and seeds such as cracked corn, milo, millet, and wheat, with very little protein. These low protein suets may have less suet as well in order to keep the price low; suet is more expensive than the added grains.

I recommend buying suet blend cakes with high levels of added protein ingredients. These offer the best nutrition for your birds.

Fats fact

Any suet product that does not require refrigeration is usually made of rendered beef kidney suet . After rendering, suet is solid at room temperature and stable for many months without refrigeration. Raw suet must be refrigerated, and should be offered to the birds only in subfreezing weather.

Fruit suet blend cakes

Adding real fruit to suet increases both its price and its appeal to fruit-eating birds. If the label mentions fruit or the product is called "orange suet" (or another name including fruit), read the label carefully; often, that "fruit" is artificially colored and flavored juice, and no actual fruit has been added. Look for fruit suet that lists real dried fruit such as raisins, cherries, papaya, or blueberries among its ingredients.

No-melt suet/suet dough

Regular suet products become soft and melt at 100°F in the shade and much lower if in the sun. No-melt products such as no-melt suet dough have a higher melting point of 115°F and are very useful when feeding suet in the summer in high-temperature environments. The higher melting point is achieved by adding substantial amounts of ingredients such as corn meal and roasted peanuts into the suet tallow. The higher-quality no-melt

Hot pepper
Oddly, I have seen Northern Cardinals and Rose-breasted Grosbeaks very attracted to hot pepper suet dough when they normally leave suet blend cakes alone.

products are first made into a soft dough texture and then pressed into the tray instead of poured into the tray, which might lead to separation of the ingredients during cooling.

Hot pepper suet/suet dough

Suet with hot pepper powder or oil added is used mostly to deter squirrels and raccoons. Birds appear to show no adverse reaction to the hot pepper, while the mammals are more like us and don't like their mouths to be on fire. Apparently there have been no laboratory tests, but years of outdoor use show that these products perform as desired with no known harm to the birds. It is wise to wear gloves and not wipe your eyes after handling these products—and to make your own decision as to whether this product performs as needed. For further discussion, go to page 242.

Suet plugs

Suet plugs inserted into a feeder log are meant to reproduce the natural feeding situation of a woodpecker on a tree trunk.

Suet balls

About 2 inches in diameter, suet balls can be placed in unique feeders designed for the balls. The feeders shoud have good places for the birds to land.

Suet recipes

Homemade suet mixtures and puddings are some of the most popular wild bird foods. Many recipes can be found online, and most of them work just fine. They usually combine suet, corn meal, peanut butter, and other ingredients such as rolled oats and wheat flour. If you opt to use raw suet from the butcher, you must render it to kill bacteria and mold. Boil the suet in a pan, and add the ingredients as it cools but before it hardens.

Suet nuggets

Suet nuggets are pea-sized chunks made of finely-ground corn, roasted peanuts, suet, and other ingredients such as raisins, oats, hot pepper, and soy oil. They can be offered alone in a tray or added to loose seed blends and bird food cylinders. They attract woodpeckers and other fat-loving birds to your foundational, tray, or specialty feeders. Jim's Birdacious Bark Butter Bits is an example of suet nuggets.

Jim's Birdacious Bark Butter Bits are very popular with the birds and can be offered alone or added to blends.

A female Downy Woodpecker finds it very natural to eat Jim's Birdacious Bark Butter on a tree trunk.

Jim's Birdacious Bark Butter

After making suet puddings for many years, I came up with a secret recipe using pure rendered suet. Adding specially determined quantities of corn meal and peanut butter produced the best pudding I had ever used. It had the consistency of soft dough, sticky enough to stick to the tree bark but not to the fork I used to apply it. This was perfect for the birds, because they could grab a bite-sized chunk and fly away to eat it or offer it to their nestlings and fledglings.

Even the shy Brown Creepers, which would not come to any other fat or suet, came to this food. Bark Butter was attracting many other birds that were not coming to my suet feeders, including Gray Catbirds, Northern Mockingbirds, and even Northern Cardinals. This stuff was hot!

I took my formula to our Wild Birds Unlimited suet producer to see if they could replicate it. It is one thing to make it in your kitchen and quite another to make it in mass quantities in a factory. After three years of failed effort, we almost gave up. The factory manager asked for one more chance— and got it right. The last attempt produced the perfect consistency and was even more appealing to the birds than my original. We also added powdered calcium as a nutrient. We called it Jim's Birdacious Bark Butter, and after several years in the market it is now eaten by more species than any other bird food in the world: at the time of writing, over 140 species of birds have been seen eating Bark Butter. (To see this list, go to BarkButter.com.)

It is easiest to apply Bark Butter with the back side of a fork. Leave grooves in it so it looks like a peanut butter cookie.

Jim's Birdacious Bark Butter in a Tub
Spread this no-mess food on trees or feeders.

Jim's Birdacious Bark Butter Brick
Place this in suet-cake feeders.

Jim's Birdacious Bark Butter Plugs
Use this in plug feeders.

Jim's Birdacious Bark Butter Bits
Offer Bark Butter Bits on trays, in peanut feeders, and in foundational seed blends to attract woodpeckers and other fat-loving birds.

Suets and fats mimic what natural food?

Suet and other fats are most desirable to birds that eat insects in their various life stages. Most woodpeckers seek wood-boring larvae as well as adult beetles, spiders, ants, and other insects, and they are highly attracted to suet and fat products. Many birds have wild diets composed of both animal and plant foods and will eat a combination of seeds, nuts and fats at feeders. Birds such as chickadees, jays and crows have been seen picking pieces of fat off of animal carcasses, so suet mimics real animal fat for these birds.

How do birds eat suets and fats?

Available in endlessly creative styles, suet feeders either provide a perch or expect the birds to cling to the mesh holding the suet. Some provide a "tail prop" beneath the feeder to let woodpeckers brace themselves while they grab the mesh with their feet. Many birds swallow the suet on the feeder, but others grab a chunk and finish it elsewhere.

Nutritional benefit

Suet by itself is 94 percent fat, but it is mostly offered as a blend with ingredients that add proteins, other types of fats, and carbohydrates. I suggest you offer suet in the winter with a more complete diet of high-protein ingredients like peanuts, tree nuts, sunflowers, and dried insects. If your summers are cool, you can offer a suet blend, but if your temperatures become extremely hot, you should switch to suet dough products that won't melt but do offer protein and real fruit pieces.

Bark Butter Birds

Overall, 140 species have been observed feeding on Bark Butter and/or Bark Butter Bits. These two pages feature just 20 species—the full list is available at barkbutter.com.

1. Red-bellied Woodpecker
2. Brown Creeper
3. Northern Cardinal
4. Carolina Chickadee and Downy Woodpecker
5. Pileated Woodpecker
6. Blue Jay
7. Northern Flicker
8. Cedar Waxwings
9. Clark's Nutcracker
10. Carolina Wren
11. Yellow-rumped (Myrtle) Warbler
12. Red-breasted Nuthatch
13. Downy Woodpecker
14. Townsend's Warbler
15. Woodhouse's Scrub Jay
16. Hermit Warbler
17. Scarlet Tanager
18. Nuttall's Woodpecker
19. Yellow-bellied Sapsucker

11

13

14

12

15

16

17

18

19

Mealworms

Mealworms are the larvae of non-flying beetles of the species Tenebrio molitor. You can grow these at home or buy them ready to go into the feeders. Being live insects, they sure do mimic natural insects better than a suet cake, but they tend to be wiped out pretty quickly. Most folks offer mealworms as a short-term treat with other fat products providing fat the rest of the day.

Some birds, including bluebirds, survive mainly on insects in the summer and switch to berries such as dogwood, holly, juniper, and hackberry in the winter. With their high protein and fat content, mealworms must be a welcome supplement to bluebirds' high-carbohydrate winter diet of berries. Year-round insect eaters such as woodpeckers and wrens also welcome these live treats. Of course, omnivorous birds like chickadees, titmice, and nuthatches gobble them down, sometimes having to make a difficult choice between peanuts, sunflower, suet, or mealworms. But watch out: European Starlings love them, too.

Types

Live mealworms
▶ 22% fat ▶ 18% protein ▶ 2.5% carbs ▶ calories/100g: 122 (approx. from various sources)

Live mealworms come in various sizes, but are usually sold as medium or large. They range from ½ inch to 1 inch in length.

Dried mealworms
▶ 32% fat ▶ 49% protein ▶ 6.9% carbs ▶ calories/100g. 471 (approx. from various sources)

Live mealworms are preferred to dried mealworms. However, dried mealworms are easily added to other foods, and are an important part of new school bird feeding (see page 27).

Live mealworms are very attractive to insect-eating birds.

Other insect products

Other insect products are harder to find and generally more expensive: waxworms, alive or dried; dried crickets; dried silkworms or canned soft-bodied silkworms; and canned soft-bodied caterpillars. Wild birds don't seem to like these enough to justify the extra expense.

Mimics what natural food?

Mealworms mimic…worms! Well, not really. More accurately, they mimic wild insect larvae, not earthworms.

How do birds eat mealworms?

They fly in to the feeder, grab one, and eat it on the spot or fly off to finish it. Sometimes you will see a bluebird stuffing its mouth with mealworms before taking them back to its nest or fledglings. A dozen or more bluebirds may visit the mealworm feeder at once, while other birds like titmice come in one at a time, grab, and fly.

Nutritional benefit

Insect eaters readily eat this live treat, which is 22 percent fat, 18 percent protein and contains minerals such as potassium and phosphorus.

Feeders

Mealworms are one of the snack foods in your thoughtful bird feeding station, and can be offered in a tray feeder with slippery sides that the little crawler's cannot scale. These feeders are often made of plastic or glass, or a combination of metal, glass, and plastic.

Only seeds, only insects, or both?

Some birds, such as American Goldfinches, eat mostly seeds year-round. Their flocking behavior and constant movement from field to field enable them to find food and avoid predators. Carolina Wrens rarely eat seeds in the wild and can live entirely off insects year-round. Other birds are omnivores, eating a combination of seeds, insects, fruits, nuts, and flower and leaf buds; their primary food might change with the seasons. Chickadees eat both seeds and insects year-round, mostly seeds in the winter and mostly insects in the summer.

Dried mealworms by themselves generally are not as attractive as live mealworms, but are a good addition to high-quality foundational blends and cylinders and can be mixed in with spreadable suets like Bark Butter.

Tree nuts

As you can imagine, nuts are very attractive to many forest-dwelling birds, from woodpeckers to titmice. Also squirrels! Pecans and walnuts are classic favorites, but this category also includes many other nuts that work just as well, though they may not be native to your area.

Types

Tree nuts include walnuts, pecans, cashews, pistachios, hazelnuts, hickory, Brazil nuts, and pine nuts. Nuts that do not meet the standards for human consumption are often sold as bird food.

Mimics what natural food?

This is an easy one: they mimic themselves. And acorns.

How do birds eat tree nuts?

Whole pecans, walnuts, and similar nuts can be opened in nature only by squirrels, so these are always commercially offered as pieces out of the shell. If you offer half-broken walnuts and pecans, the birds will pick the nuts out from the shells. Tree nuts are readily eaten by chickadees, titmice, nuthatches, jays, and woodpeckers, right on the spot or taken away to peck into smaller pieces.

Nutritional benefit

Tree nuts vary in nutrition, but they all have balanced quantities of fats, proteins, and carbohydrates. Pecans have 72 percent fats, 9 percent protein, 14 percent carbohydrates, and 17 percent more calories by weight than peanuts. Walnuts contain 64 percent fats, 14 percent protein and 4 percent carbohydrates, while almonds have 50 percent fats, 21 percent proteins, and 21 percent carbohydrates.

Feeders

Tree nuts can be offered alone as a snack on tray feeders, added to seed or suet blends instead of or in addition to peanut pieces, or packed into bird food cylinders and cakes.

Tree nut fact
Approximately 99 percent of the walnuts used in the U.S. and 75 percent of the walnuts used worldwide are grown in California.

Adult female or immature Rufous Hummingbird enjoying, and protecting, its source of sugar-water nectar.

Nectar

Hummingbirds and orioles are the most commonly seen nectar-drinking birds in our yards, and they love the simple sugar-water solutions we provide in feeders. When they aren't at our feeders, hummingbirds are busy drinking nectar from flowers and catching small insects, and they usually have a belly full of tiny flies, gnats, spiders, and aphids. Orioles eat many spiders and insects in the wild, including caterpillars, beetles, and ants. They also eat fruits such as mulberry, cherry, and elderberry, and they drink nectar from certain flowers. They too can be attracted to sugar-water solutions, which mimic flower nectar and perhaps the juice in fruits.

There is an ongoing debate about the percentage of sugar and the types of sugar to be used in feeders. Some argue that because some wildflower nectar has a concentration higher than the usually recommended 4:1, our sugar-water solution should, too. My recommendation is to use the Cornell Lab of Ornithology's formula of 4 parts water to 1 part table sugar (sucrose).

Nutritional benefit

Sugar-water nectar is 20 percent carbohydrate with zero fat or protein. It serves to provide quick energy for high activity levels.

Nectar formula: 4 parts water to 1 part table sugar (sucrose)

That's about 2 heaping tablespoons of sugar to 1 cup of water, or 1 cup (8 ounces) of sugar to 1 quart (32 ounces) of water.

Mix a large quantity by dissolving the sugar in warm water, and refrigerate the extra. It is unnecessary to boil water from most domestic supplies, but if you do, boil the water first, let it cool, and then add the sugar. If you mix the water and sugar first, boiling will change the concentration.

I find it easiest to make a quart solution of nectar and store it in the refrigerator. In a 32 ounce container, such as this Nectar Bottle, first add 32 ounces of water, then add 1 cup of table sugar to make a perfect 1:4 sugar-water solution.

Feeders

Hundreds of feeders are available for offering sugar-water nectar to hummingbirds and orioles. Many are very practical in functionality and looks, while others are extremely beautiful or whimsical. No matter what kind you use, I suggest that you find one that does not leak and is easy to fill and clean. Also make sure that visiting hummingbirds will be visible: some feeders block the view if the birds come to the nectar port away from your window.

Sugar-water considerations:

▶ Never add red food color or buy a commercial mix with red color. Feeders with red parts or other bright flower colors will attract the hummers. Flower nectar is colorless, and we do not want to add artificial colors to the hummers' diet.

▶ Never use honey to make sugar-water. It spoils too easily, and fermented honey may encourage a potentially fatal fungus that grows on hummingbird tongues. Never use fruit juices, sport drinks, or any other source of sugary water.

▶ Never use a ready-to-use liquid with artificial preservatives such as sodium benzoate. We don't know their effects on hummingbirds.

▶ It is unnecessary to add vitamins, minerals, and electrolytes to the nectar. All of these nutrients are already present in the birds' natural diet, which includes large quantities of insects.

▶ Keep it fresh. Put your feeder in a shady spot, and replace it every two to three days. In sunny spots and on very warm days, replace it every day.

▶ Consider FeederFresh Nectar Defender. This product from Sapphire Labs keeps hummingbird nectar fresh for several weeks by adding a trace of micronutrient copper. The product is safe, with a copper level lower than that in diets formulated for captive hummingbirds; the copper serves as both a micronutrient and a spoilage inhibitor. I have always thought that one of the greatest dangers to hummingbirds at our feeders is spoiled nectar, and I fear that spoiled nectar is quite common. I have used this product, and believe that it is an excellent additive for keeping nectar fresh. This is the only additive I recommend for hummingbird nectar.

▶ Keep an eye out for winter hummingbirds. Hummingbirds are tougher than we thought, and some regularly winter along the Gulf and northwestern Pacific Coasts and inland. Fourteen species of hummingbirds have been recorded spending the winter in the U.S. Winter hummers need an unfrozen nectar source to survive cold temperatures, rain, and snow. Continue using a 4:1 sugar solution, and in freezing weather, heat the feeder occasionally by using electric heat tape, setting the feeder in a shallow birdbath with a heater, or placing a 150-watt incandescent outdoor floodlight about 12 inches below the feeder.

Fruits, berries, and jelly

Adding fruit feeders to your yard can attract many birds that might not otherwise come to feeders. Fruits as a category include just about any fruit and berry available, but only a few are truly convenient to add to bird food blends as dried fruit or on a tray feeder as fresh fruit.

 Many birds that eat fruit and berries in the wild will come to feeders for fresh or dried fruit, berries, and melon. Apple, plum, orange, and cantaloupe pieces are favorites of orioles, Northern Mockingbirds, American Robins, and Gray Catbirds. Some people have found that the fruit flies attracted to rotting bananas are a great feast for agile hummingbirds. Jams and jellies are very attractive to orioles, resembling thick sap or mashed fruit.

In most regions, fruits are not as popular as seeds, nuts, and fats, so offer them sparingly until you determine the right kind and amount to offer.

Types

Fresh fruit

It is fun to test just about any kind of fruit that happens to be in your kitchen or about to become a kitchen scrap. Apples, oranges, pears, blueberries, bananas, grapes, cherries, and currants can be offered fresh on a tray feeder.

Cut the fruit into small pieces, or open it up so the birds can get to the juicy insides. Because fresh fruit spoils quickly, offer it in small quantities or only in chilly weather. In late summer, beware of bees, yellowjackets, and hornets; they find fresh fruit quickly, so it should be avoided at that season.

Dried fruit

A great bet for a year-round offering is dried fruit such as raisins, currants, cranberries, blueberries, or papaya. However, even dried fruits degrade quickly into a messy glob in summer, and they also attract yellowjackets, so offer them sparingly and in the shade.

Jelly

 Jelly is highly sought after by orioles—once they find it. Jelly can be offered alone or in combination with orange slices and sugar-water. Many other birds, such as Yellow-rumped Warblers, Gray Catbirds, American Robins, and Northern Mockingbirds, also visit jelly.

Most well-known manufacturers use high-fructose corn syrup to sweeten their basic line of jellies; their higher-end lines generally use sucrose. The effects of high-fructose corn syrup on the appetite and digestive systems of birds are unknown, so you need to make your own choice of which product to use. As an alternative, there is a brand named BirdBerry Jelly created specifically for wild birds; it is made with real fruit juice, sugar, and pectin.

All jellies and jams have 50 to 60 percent sugar content, a percentage higher than just about anything in nature. For instance, natural grape juice contains 15 percent sugar, and most flower nectars range from 12 to 30 percent sugars. Since jelly has such a high sugar content, there is some debate about whether an unlimited jelly supply is good for the birds. One argument is that orioles might like it too much and rely on this food source to the neglect of their natural diet of insects, fruits, and nectar. Pay attention to whether orioles at your feeders are feeding jelly to their young instead of insects, the natural diet of fledglings. When oriole fledglings arrive at our feeders, it is a good idea to offer mealworms and real fruit instead of jelly.

Northern Oriole dining on grape jam on a feeder that also provides sugar-water nectar and orange slices.

Fruit and berry fact
The Northern Mockingbird's diet consists of nearly equal amounts of fruits and arthropods (insects and spiders). The fruits include grapes, apples, barberries, hawthorn, elderberries, and rose hips.

Orange-lovers
Red-bellied Woodpecker
Northern Mockingbird
Gray Catbird
Brown Thrasher
Scarlet Tanager
Rose-breasted Grosbeak
Baltimore Oriole
Orchard Oriole
Gray Catbird
Western Tanager
Hooded Oriole
Bullock's Oriole

Grape-lovers
Northern Mockingbird
Gray Catbird
Eastern Bluebird
American Robin
Cedar Waxwing
Scarlet Tanager
Eastern Towhee
Rose-breasted Grosbeak
House Finch
Acorn Woodpecker
Western Bluebird
American Robin
Western Tanager
Spotted Towhee
Black-headed Grosbeak
House Finch

Rasin-lovers
Northern Mockingbird
Gray Catbird
Eastern Bluebird
Cedar Waxwing
Northern Mockingbird
Western Bluebird
Cedar Waxwing

Offering only a small amount of jelly at a time in a small dish can help keep the birds' bodies from contacting the jelly, which can smear feathers and be difficult to clean off. There are reports of small birds getting stuck in large open pans of jelly. I recommend offering jelly in small containers, in amounts that are eaten rapidly and gone by the end of each day. That way, you can clean the container daily, fill it with fresh jelly, and prevent any accidents.

Beware of offering fruits and dried fruits late in the summer or in extremely hot areas, as the fruit can rot quickly and can also attract yellow jackets.

Mimics what natural food?

This is an easy one: Fruits mimic themselves or native fruits and berries, including wild grapes, black cherries, viburnums, hawthorns, raspberries, and mulberries. And don't forget that birds love berries from vines such as poison ivy and Virginia creeper.

How do birds eat fruits?

Bite-size pieces of fresh fruits are easy to eat, but dried fruits might take a bit of work: if the fruit is too large, birds will hold it to peck off manageable chunks.

Nutritional benefit

Jellies and jams contain only carbohydrates, with sugar being about 50 to 60 percent of their weight. Jelly (and nectar) should be only one part of a diet that also includes sliced fruits, mealworms, and natural foods.

Feeders

Sliced fruit can be offered on tray feeders or in one of the many hanging feeders designed for the purpose. Jelly should be offered in small bowls or in the small indentations on the top of nectar feeders.

Skewering a branch with an orange half may quickly attract a number of types of birds, including Baltimore Orioles in the East.

Corn

Corn is a common bird food with both good and bad attributes. It can be fed to birds and wildlife as cracked corn, whole kernels, or ear corn. Cracked corn is attractive to such beautiful birds as Northern Cardinals and Red-bellied Woodpeckers, but it also attracts House Sparrows, blackbirds, European Starlings, and Rock Pigeons. For that reason, I don't offer it at my feeders.

Types

Cracked corn

Corn is best offered as fine or medium cracked corn, since smaller birds have a difficult time cracking the whole kernel. It is typically used in blends rather than by itself. Where European Starlings, blackbirds, crows, and House Sparrows are not a problem, this low-cost food can be used to attract doves, Northern Cardinals, jays, and a few woodpeckers. Sometimes cracked corn is offered on a tray at a distance from foundational feeders so that the sparrows, starlings, and doves will gorge themselves on the low-cost food rather than flying up to the feeder with the best blend.

Cracked corn deteriorates quickly in wet weather or high humidity. It should be stored in a cool, dry place, and offered in low-capacity feeders. If any mold appears, remove the food and clean the feeder thoroughly with a 10-percent bleach solution. If a blend contains more than about 15 percent cracked corn, some of the corn will go to waste if the other ingredients are more popular. To keep the price down, commercial mixes often contain large percentages of cracked corn and milo, so read the label carefully.

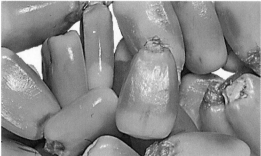

Whole corn kernels

Whole kernels are offered to ducks, geese, Wild Turkeys, pheasants, and large seed-eating birds such as jays. "Wildlife blends" with a high percentage of whole corn kernels are ideal for feeding both larger birds and squirrels.

Ear corn

Ideal for feeding squirrels and jays, ear corn can be provided in specially designed feeders . This can be an effective way to lure squirrels and jays away from bird feeders.

Mimics what natural food?

Cracked corn most closely mimics small, high-carbohydrate wildflower and grass seeds. The birds that eat cracked corn have natural diets high in these types of seeds.

Corn fact
Humans have found over 3,500 uses for corn products, among them the production of high-fructose corn syrup. One bushel of corn can produce enough syrup to sweeten 325 cans of soda.

Ear corn attached to a tree trunk is an ideal way to feed squirrels like this hungry Fox Squirrel.

How do birds eat corn?

Northern Cardinals and finches with specialized beaks can manipulate cracked corn in their beak and crack it even smaller. Smaller birds pick out sizes they can swallow whole, while larger birds can swallow larger pieces and let their gizzards do the work of mashing them down to size.

Nutritional benefit

▶ 5% fat ▶ 9% protein ▶ 74% carbohydrates
▶ calories/100g: 478

A typical grain, corn is high in carbohydrates and very low in fats and proteins. It has about 60 percent of the calories as the same weight of sunflower chips. This can be important on extremely cold winter nights: to keep warm, birds need to eat 50 percent more corn than sunflower chips to get the equivalent energy stores. I recommend oil sunflower, peanuts, sunflower chips, and fat products for winter days, all of which have a high calorie content per gram.

Feeders

Cracked corn is usually offered at tray feeders, alone or in a blend. When offered in hopper and tube feeders, it is usually not eaten as readily as the other ingredients, so it tends to clog up the feeder. Since it is susceptible to molding when wet, it needs to be offered carefully, with uneaten remnants promptly cleaned out. Ear corn is usually stuck on a large nail or screw and made available to squirrels. Whole kernel or cracked corn is often thrown on dry ground or placed on ground trays for ducks and wildlife.

Common fillers in "Wild Bird Mixes"

Milo

Milo is one of the most common ingredients in wild bird mixes. I call milo a filler because it is added solely to fill up the bag; it has little or no value to the birds. With the exception of a few birds in the southwestern U.S., such as Gambel's Quail and Curve-billed Thrashers, birds generally do not eat it. Milo, also known as sorghum, is a common livestock feed, and is an important food for people in much of the world. But most wild birds just don't like it. When you put a wild bird mix with milo into a hopper or tube feeder, the milo will be scratched, pecked, or tossed onto the ground, where it often rots. Even worse, milo on damp ground can grow hazardous mold and bacteria.

Milo is sometimes included in suet blends. If cracked and rolled and then added in *small* quantities, it might be eaten by suet-eating birds, and it does contribute carbohydrates to the diet. Beware of when it is added as whole seeds and in large quantities as it just fills space, is ignored by the birds and wasted.

Consider any money wasted that is spent on fillers such as milo, wheat, and oats. It is also a waste of valuable agricultural resources to grow, harvest, distribute, and sell a product that does not do what it is sold to do.

Wheat

Wheat is another food added to fill the bag with cheap ingredients. Very few birds choose wheat even when it is offered on its own. Wheat and wheat products are sometimes added to suet blends; if small quantities are used, wheat can add carbohydrate nutrition.

Oats

Very few birds other than European Starlings and grackles eat oats or oat groats. There is no reason for oats to be offered, alone or in blends. Rolled oats or processed oats are sometimes used in homemade suet and peanut butter puddings or in commercial suet blend cakes. If not used in excess, they can contribute to nutritional quality.

Canary seed

This should be a good food for ground-feeding birds, because it has much higher protein and fat content than the other grains favored by these birds. But since white millet is preferred over canary seed and is much less expensive, that is the food of choice for ground-feeders.

Other grains

Buckwheat, flax, and rice should be considered fillers. The birds do not eat them, and they are added only to keep the price of wild bird mixes low.

Milo is a common ingredient in wild bird mixes, often making up 50 to 90 percent of the seeds. It is added to greatly lower the price but generally goes to waste as it is preferred by very few birds. Milo should be avoided in all foundational blends.

There is a difference in bird foods

I have been hoping for 35 years that the wild bird food industry would change its ways and sell only blends with ingredients that the birds actually eat. Recently I visited a large feed store that supplies all kinds of pet, horse, chicken, and wild bird foods. The bird food aisle had a few small bags of fairly decent blends, but it was clear from the size of the stacks that most of the blends sold were "Wild Bird Mix."

One bag had zero percent of the foods that local birds would eat, such as the one pictured below. You can see the large quantity of milo in this blend, plus a fair amount of wheat kernels and a bit of cracked corn. There is some white millet and a few sunflower seeds, so I would say that at least 80 percent of this mix will be scratched out of the feeder onto the ground as the birds seek out the sunflower and millet. The milo and wheat will either to go to waste or only be eaten by starlings and pigeons.

Another selection was one dollar more because it contained about 5 percent oil sunflower. I discuss how to read the ingredients list on a bag of bird seed in Chapter 9, but for now, let's say that it is "buyer beware" in the bird seed aisle of feed, hardware, and big box stores.

I feel very strongly about this, and have repeatedly heard from my customers that they bought bird seed at a store where they also picked up pet supplies because it was convenient and "cheap." They came back to buy seed at my store because the "cheap" and convenient seed from the other store had been ignored in the feeder or scratched to the ground and wasted.

From your kitchen

I do not put out very many kitchen scraps, but older books often provide information about the kind of scraps that birds like. Much of the following comes from John V. Dennis's 1975 *A Complete Guide to Bird Feeding*.

Fruit and melons
It is a good idea to put out fruit scraps or slightly overripe fruits such as grapes, apples, pears, and oranges. Baked apples can appeal to bluebirds. Be careful with melon as it can go bad quickly and attracts yellowjackets and hornets.

Melon and squash seeds
Save and dry all of your cantaloupe, watermelon, squash, and pumpkin seeds. Many sunflower-eating birds will come to them, including chickadees, titmice, Northern Cardinals, grosbeaks, jays, and towhees. Pumpkin seeds are sold in stores as squirrel food and sometimes added to blends for cardinals and grosbeaks.

Popcorn
Popped popcorn appeals to jays, chickadees, and crows. It can be strung with cranberries and hung on evergreens as a decorative Christmas treat.

Meat
Meat scraps should be offered only cooked; options include meaty bones, bacon bits and rind, and bits of hot dogs and hamburgers. You may or may not like the birds that meat attracts, and since this food also attracts vermin, you should offer only small quantities that can be eaten quickly. The birds attracted to meat include chickadees, titmice, European Starlings, jays, crows, magpies, gulls, and hawks.

Potatoes
Cooked potatoes—boiled, fried, or mashed—have their bird fans. The birds that eat everything, such as European Starlings, jays, crows, grackles, and Gray Catbirds, have been known to enjoy this offering. Even the Brown Creeper has been reported to enjoy small bits of boiled potato.

Animal fat
This includes suet, lard, grease, and bacon fat, all of which should be boiled and screened for impurities. Put these sterilized fats on dried bagels or other baked goods, especially in winter. Be aware that high odor fat will bring just about any meat-eating animal to your back door.

White bread
As many of us know, many birds love white bread. Offer it only sparingly, as it is not the greatest in terms of nutrition.

Cornbread
If you must feed bread, feed cornbread. It is much more nutritious than white bread.

Baked goods crumbs
These can be offered alone or added to suet puddings.

Cheese
Shredded American and other cheeses are a favorite of Carolina Wrens, European Starlings, American Robins, and Downy Woodpeckers.

Cream cheese
Cream cheese has been reported to attract White-breasted Nuthatches.

Dog food and biscuits
Jays, Carolina Wrens, European Starlings, and grackles like all kinds of dog food, including canned, dry, and soft extruded pieces. Soak biscuits in water.

Eggs
Eggs are very popular—boiled, fried, or scrambled—with jays, Gray Catbirds, Northern Mockingbirds, European Starlings, and grackles.

Eggshells
Birds always need calcium, but especially at nesting time. Eggshells should be offered only after being boiled or baked for 20 minutes to kill bacteria. Break the shells into small pieces, or grind them up and add them to suet puddings.

Fried fish
Oddly, fried fish is known to attract Gray Catbirds, and is probably also appealing to gulls, crows, and a few cats and rodents.

Rice
Cooked rice is sometimes eaten by Northern Bobwhites, doves, European Starlings, meadowlarks, blackbirds, orioles, and many sparrows and finches.

This high-quality bird food cylinder is feeding Carolina Chickadees, an American Goldfinch, and a Downy Woodpecker all at the same time. Before cylinders were available, it might take three feeders to attract these species: a sunflower feeder; a finch feeder; and a suet blend cake feeder.

Bird food cylinders and cakes

When I talk about new school bird feeding, I am definitely talking about bird food cylinders. (See page 27). Because they bring so many things together, cylinders have broken new bird feeding ground. They can be used as a foundational food or as a snack . They can be made of one type of seed or food or be a high-quality blend that includes every major food group: seeds, fats, nuts, fruit, dried mealworms, and added calcium.

Cylinders can target a specific group of birds, or they can have something for everyone, a place where insect specialists, seed eaters, and ground-dwelling and perching birds all eat at the same feeder. Instead of having three feeders—one

for sunflower and millet birds, one for finches, and one for woodpeckers—you can put out a single cylinder with all three of these birds' favorite foods.

For almost every loose seed and blend available, there is a corresponding bird food cylinder. The cylinders are held together with a natural gelatin binder that stands up to light rain; I recommend a roof to shelter the cylinder in heavy rain and snow. Suet cylinders are also available and are processed to harden to just the right firmness so that they hold their shape yet remain attractive to the birds.

Cylinders generally come in three sizes: small, medium, and large. The small cylinders are what we call Stackables, and are used as described in

Chapter 1. The medium cylinder is most commonly selected for general feeding, and the large cylinder is for extended foundational feeding or for feeding while you are away from home.

Seed cakes have been around for many years. The bird seed bells offered at grocery, hardware, and garden stores introduced many people to bird feeding. In the early years, most bells were made of low-cost food with little sunflower. Good-quality bells are available now, and they work just fine.

Later, the bell concept was changed into bird food cakes, squares or rectangles that fit into wire cages. These cakes work very well if they are made of high-quality ingredients, but they still have their limitations. Mostly, I don't use these cakes because you need a different cage for every size of cake and I don't like the appearance of these large cages. Another consideration: at 8 inches across, these cakes tend to hide birds eating on the back. My favorite bird seed cake is the small 6- to 8-ounce size that fits into suet cages. This way, I can use the same feeder for suet blend cakes or seed cakes.

Because all cylinders have a hole up the center, you can buy a single feeder to be used with any type or size of cylinder. The curve of the cylinder provides a view around the sides, and only a small part is hidden from view, making nearly every feeding bird visible even on large cylinders.

There are many reasons to include bird food cylinders in your thoughtful bird feeding station.

▶ Convenience: easy to carry to feeders and to install.

▶ Tidy: can be put on the feeder with no spillage.

▶ No-mess: options include foods with no shells.

▶ Long-lasting: four-pound cylinders last for days or weeks.

▶ Lightweight: easy to buy and carry.

▶ Minimal storage space: take up less room than loose seed.

▶ More birdwatching time for each seed eaten: It takes longer to peck food off the cylinder, so you get to watch each bird longer.

▶ Every major food group—seeds, nuts, fats, fruits, and insects—can be included in a single cylinder, which means that a wide variety of species will be attracted.

▶ Bark Butter can be smeared on the cylinder to provide extra fat.

▶ The birds love them!

Here you see a Carolina Wren (left), who mostly eats insects, and an American Goldfinch (right), who mostly eats seeds, dining together on a high quality no-mess bird food cylinder.

Fun foods by shape, ingredients, and season

Who knew that bird food could be fun? Take the bird food cylinder and cake idea, put it together with creativity and craftsmanship, and revel in bird food that is beautiful, fun, and very much liked by the birds. Bird food can be shaped into limitless creations: songbirds, snowmen, penguins, owls, cats, raccoons, wreaths, Santa Clauses, stars, trees, hearts, chalets, cottages, bird houses, and of course, gingerbread men. With these shapes and ornaments, not only are you looking out the window at beautiful birds, you are looking out at festive handcrafted creations that can be enjoyed at holidays and year-round.

You can create a Christmas tree for the birds with small bird food ornaments, or hang a bird food wreath that looks fantastic and also is functional.

You can buy pine cones covered with bird seed—or create your own feeders with pine cones, dried bagel halves, using peanut butter or Bark Butter as a base to hold the seeds and nuts.

Tufted Titmice and an immature male Downy Woodpecker (left) enjoy owl-shaped and decorated bird food balls. Female Downy Woodpecker and a White-breasted Nuthatch (right) enjoy a no-mess cylinder shaped and decorated like a raccoon. The fruit decorations can bring in other birds as well.

Cat and mouse made of sunflower chips, safflower and peanuts (above far left) attracts a Carolina Chickadee and a Downy Woodpecker; a wreath made of sunflowers, pecans, and peanuts (above middle) attracts a Steller's Jay; a large pine cone covered with fine sunflower chips and a few red millets (above right) attracts American Goldfinches and a House Finch; and a snowman made of sunflower chips, safflower and peanuts (bottom left) attracts a Tufted Titmouse.

Bird food additives

Since wild birds do not depend on our food offerings for their entire diet, we do not need to provide the complete nutritional array of fats, proteins, carbohydrates, vitamins, and minerals. There are, however, a few additives that can benefit the birds or the hobbyist.

Calcium

Imagine being a small songbird and producing an egg a day for six days straight, as chickadees often do. Whew, that's a lot of calcium in all those eggshells! A study by Andre Dondt at the Cornell Lab of Ornithology determined that female birds must have a source of daily calcium during egg-laying, because they do not store enough for their needs. Blue Jays may hoard calcium in the fall. The study recommended that calcium be provided at platform feeders and on the ground.

Calcium is usually offered in commercial foods as oyster shell grit or limestone dust. Both are finely ground and easily consumed by small songbirds. At home, you can add oyster grit or sterilized eggshells (see page 237) to seed blends, suet, and peanut butter recipes.

At Wild Birds Unlimited, we have developed several foods that offer calcium, mostly in the form of limestone dust. Our blends with calcium can be offered seasonally as "nesting blends" or year-round for general nutrition. We also include calcium as a year-round nutrient in Jim's Birdacious Bark Butter products.

Grit

Birds don't have teeth, but they do have a gizzard they fill with grit to grind up all those seeds they eat. Birds can find natural sources of grit, but they also benefit from our efforts to help them. Grit in the form of oyster shell comes with a bonus: while it is grinding down seeds in the gizzard, it slowly dissolves and becomes a source of calcium.

Salt

Redpolls, Pine Siskins, crossbills, goldfinches, Purple Finches, rosy-finches, grosbeaks, House Sparrows, crows, doves, and Hairy and Downy Woodpeckers all have a craving for salt. Some winter visitors to the northern U.S., such as Horned Larks and Snow Buntings, are often seen along the side of roads pecking at salt, a dangerous way to fulfill a craving.

The most interesting way to offer salt is described by John V. Dennis in his book A Complete Guide to Bird Feeding. He suggests pouring a saline solution over a stump or piece of wood until crystals form.

If you offer salt in any form—on a stump, loose in a dish, or on salted peanuts—be sure to offer plenty of water year-round.

Hot pepper/capsaicin

The use of hot pepper/capsaicin products in bird food has been the subject of debate.

▶ Does it discourage squirrels?

▶ Is it safe for the birds?

▶ Is it safe for hobbyists?

Warning!
All hot pepper, capsaicin and cayenne products are highly irritating to human eyes, noses, and skin. Wear gloves and safety glasses, and avoid unprotected contact with hot pepper bird food and the feeders that contain this food. Keep food and feeders out of the reach of children!

At the end of the discussion of these three questions, I share with you how I approach the use of hot pepper products.

Does it work to discourage squirrels?

Hot peppers contain a compound called capsaicin, which comes in all levels of "heat." Capsaicin is added to wild bird foods as a powder or oil, mainly to deter squirrels, raccoons, and other mammals. It is clear that many birds will eat bird food with hot pepper products on them and that squirrels will avoid it.

One of the few tests of hot pepper bird seed was conducted in 2000 by scientists at Cornell. They confirmed that capsaicin-coated seed worked against gray squirrels, and that capsaicin-treated seed still appealed to wild birds. There were more bird visits to the feeders because the squirrels spent less time there. This study also showed that capsaicin-treated seed did not discourage eastern chipmunks, which filled their pouches and left to store the food. It was suggested that their fur-lined cheek pouches protected the chipmunks from the heat caused by the hot pepper seed.

Is it safe for birds to eat hot pepper food?

In mammals, capsaicin from hot peppers interacts with a specific receptor protein called VR1 (vannilloid receptor 1) found on nerve endings and evokes sensations of burning and pain. Scientist have isolated the VR1 receptor in birds and found that capsaicin does not bind to it, thus it does not produce a painful sensation. Capsaicin alone does not irritate or damage tissue in the mouth, eyes or digestive tract of birds. In fact, several species of birds and wild peppers have evolved a symbiotic (mutually beneficial) relationship, in which the birds consume the pepper's fruits and then go on to disperse the seeds. Turkeys, Curve-billed Thrashers, Northern Cardinals, Northern Mockingbirds, Gila Woodpeckers, Cedar

This pair of female (left) and male (right) Downy Woodpeckers are happily dining on a hot pepper seed blend cylinder.

Waxwings, Elegant Trogons, Great Kiskadees, Tropical Kingbirds, and Hepatic Tanagers have all been documented eating the fruits of different capsicum species in the wild.

Capsaicin-treated bird food has been on the market for over 15 years, and its anecdotal track record is remarkably unblemished. There are virtually no reports by ornithologists or hobbyists of the use of this food resulting in declines in feeder bird populations or causing the birds health problems. Although the anecdotal evidence to date strongly suggests that birds are unharmed by capsaicin-treated foods, there is still no empirical data proving that capsaicin is safe for all feeder birds.

A Carolina Chickadee (left) and Downy Woodpecker (right) share a hot pepper no-melt suet cylinder.

Is it safe for hobbyists to offer hot pepper foods?

Capsaicin is added as a ground powder or as liquid oil. Both coat the seed, and both coat the feeders that hold the seed. The powder has potentially greater danger than oil for humans at the time of filling the feeders as it is more easily separated from the seed by wind and may blow onto the hobbyist. The oil may have more danger to humans long-term as it will soak into wooden products and is not as easily hosed off of plastic and metal surfaces. The danger to hobbyists may not be at the time of filling the feeders (if they are wearing rubber gloves), but might come later as feeders with residual surface hot pepper are unsuspectingly handled without gloves. If eyes, noses or lips are rubbed, then a reaction to the hot pepper could range from mild to severe.

Hot pepper can be added to suet products, bird food cakes, and cylinders. I have always felt that these are the safest use of hot pepper for humans, as these "bind" the hot pepper. It cannot be blown into our eyes, and I feel that these products leave less residual oil or powder on our fingers and feeders than loose seed with hot pepper.

With all of these concerns about hot pepper products, here is what I do

▶ I use safflower seed as the first option. It works very well against squirrels without irritating birds, wild mammals, or humans. It attracts most sunflower-loving birds, and has the additional benefit of being unattractive to blackbirds. However, chipmunks like safflower.

▶ I use squirrel-baffling deterrents. There are many ways to keep squirrels and raccoons off your feeders that also work against chipmunks. If you use one of the methods in Chapter 7 (see page 298), you can deter all three without using hot pepper.

▶ When feeders and food are placed in certain trees, on decks, or near windowsills, it may be difficult to keep squirrels, raccoons, and chipmunks away. In these situations, suets, cylinders, or cakes with hot pepper may be a good solution. I use only products that bind the hot pepper tightly, such as suet cakes, suet dough cylinders, and bird food cylinders and cakes.

Anti-moisture additives

One of the unavoidable challenges in feeding birds is the weather. Rain, snow, and humidity are always affecting your feeders and dampening the food. Moisture can clump seed, reduce its attractiveness, and worst of all, create an environment for mold. Mold can grow in any feeder that retains moisture for very long, and is a real problem in extended rain or hot, humid weather.

Because some molds and their toxins are unhealthy for birds and humans, we should always keep food and feeders as dry and fresh as possible. The most likely feeders to get moldy are nyjer tube feeders, which tend to concentrate moisture in the bottom and are difficult to ventilate. The food in the bottom 3 or 4 inches of these tubes gets moist, clumps up, and then becomes moldy. It is difficult to clean out and certainly is not good for the birds. Remember: Any feeder food can get moldy in the right conditions.

We can put drains, screens, perforated metal, and ventilation into feeders and keep refilling the food, but those actions cannot completely solve the problem. I know of only one product that helps: FeederFresh. This granular, bird-safe moisture trap can be added to bird food or placed in the bottom of feeders. It is a sand-like product similar to a sponge with micro-porous spaces to absorb liquid; it does not swell when it absorbs moisture. The birds generally recognize this product as not food and toss it aside. If they do ingest it, it is similar to the sand that birds ingest as grit, and thus is not only harmless but helps the birds digest food. This product should be replaced every one to four weeks, depending on rainfall and humidity.

If mold grows on feeder surfaces or on food, throw the food into a trash can, then scrub the feeder with soapy water and sterilize it with a 10-percent bleach in water solution.

Vitamins and minerals

With cage birds, we know exactly which species we are feeding. Since we provide 100 percent of a captive bird's diet, we need to offer complete nutrition, including supplements.

But the wild birds at our feeders range from those that normally eat only insects to those that normally eat only vegetable matter, with all combinations in between, making it impossible to identify the proper supplements for all of our feathered visitors. In addition, the wild birds in your yard or local forest get only a portion of their food from feeders. With these facts in mind, I have never felt it was important or necessary to fortify wild bird food with vitamins and minerals (calcium being the exception).

You may see bird food products with supplemental vitamins A, D3, E, B12, B5 (pantothenic acid), and B3 (niacin), and minerals in the form of potassium iodide, sodium bicarbonate, sodium chloride, choline chloride, ferrous sulfate, magnesium sulfate, manganous oxide, zinc oxide, copper sulphate, copper oxide, cobalt carbonate, dicalcium phosphate, and sodium selenite, to name just a few.

Many of these vitamins and minerals are already in the seeds and grains in bird food and are also found in natural food sources. For instance, sunflower seeds contain vitamins A, C, E, thiamin (B1), riboflavin (B2), niacin (B3), pantothenic acid (B5), B6, and folate (B9), as well as calcium, iron, magnesium, phosphorus, potassium, sodium, zinc, and many other minerals.

Millet contains vitamins E, K, thiamin (B1), riboflavin (B2), niacin (B3), pantothenic acid (B5), B6, and folate (B9), as well as calcium, iron, magnesium, phosphorus, potassium, sodium, zinc, and many other minerals.

Unsalted dry-roasted peanuts contain vitamins B6, E, thiamin (B1), riboflavin (B2), niacin (B3), pantothenic acid (B5), and folate (B9), as well as calcium, iron, magnesium, phosphorus, potassium, sodium, zinc, and many other minerals.

Acorns are a major wild food for jays and many woodpeckers. Acorns contain vitamins A, thiamin (B1), riboflavin (B2), niacin (B3), B6, B12, and folate as well as calcium, iron, magnesium, phosphorus, potassium and zinc.

With the exception of calcium, which is recommended by Andre Dondt of the Cornell Lab of Ornithology, I do not believe you need to add any kind of vitamin or mineral supplements to bird food, including nectar and sugar-water solutions for hummingbirds and orioles.

5 The feeders

W ITH THOUSANDS OF feeders available, how do you make the right choices?

Let's think about the purpose of the feeder and then decide which one will work for us. After an overview of the feeders appropriate to a thoughtful bird feeding station, we'll assess the qualities of each feeder type. Armed with this information, you'll be a knowledgeable shopper.

Feeder choices: The first six elements of a thoughtful bird feeding station

1. **Foundational feeder**
2. **Tray feeder**
3. **Fat feeder**
4. **Finch feeder**
5. **Nectar, jelly, and fruit feeders**
6. **Snack/specialty/convenience feeders**

Element 1. Foundational feeders

Every complete bird feeding station needs a foundational feeder—one that holds a blend attractive to 80 percent of the local seed- and nut-eating birds, can feed many birds at one time, and has the capacity for four or more days of food. The exceptions are stations on small balconies or apartment and condominium decks, where a smaller feeding presence is necessary.

Pages 247 to 250 feature a few of the many feeders that can play the role of a foundational feeder.

Gazebo or very large hopper on post

You turn to gazebos when you want to feed the birds and decorate your yard with bird feeder eye candy. Although these are the most expensive feeders, they can be an important part of a well-designed landscaping plan. That plan should have a few focal points for the eyes, and feeders like this bring a landscape to life just as much as a beautiful fountain, a curved brick path, or an enticing bench does. A gazebo with a hopper is a fabulous foundational feeder. Without a hopper, it is a fancy tray, which may not work well as a foundational feeder.

Make sure that feeders of this sort are easily cleaned, or empty shells and droppings may pile up.

Hopper

This is the classic feeder with a chamber for seed, a roof, and ledges for perches. It can be suspended or be mounted on a pole. Any large hopper feeder works as a foundational feeder.

Decorative gazebo feeders (top) combine functionality with beauty and are an important element in your landscaping plan. The classic hopper feeder (bottom) is always a great choice for a foundational feeder.

Mesh hopper

These foundational feeders are made of mesh that is the right size to hold the seed but large enough that birds can land anywhere and pull it out.

Tube feeder

A large-capacity hanging tube works very well as a foundational feeder. Variations include a feeder with three tubes, letting you feed loose blends or nyjer seed. You can also add a tray.

Large mesh hopper nyjer feeder (top left); large mesh oil-sunflower feeder (top right).

An extra-large tube feeder (bottom left) can be hung or pole-mounted; a three-tube feeder (bottom right) allows several seeds or blends to be offered.

Large capacity hanging squirrel-proof feeder (top far left), hanging squirrel-proof feeder (bottom left); bird food cylinder (top middle); medium-sized decorative feeder, (top far right), large decorative feeder (bottom right).

Squirrel-proof feeder

Large squirrel-proof feeders work very well as foundational feeders. They hold lots of food, feed lots of birds, and keep the squirrels off.

Bird food cylinder

Bird food cylinders work very well as foundational feeders. They can last up to two weeks, even with a constant stream of visiting birds.

Decorative feeder

Mid- to large-size decorative feeders can work as foundational feeders, and are a pleasant landscaping accent if you do not have the budget or space for a gazebo feeder.

I use this feeder to keep my birds fed for up to four weeks when I am traveling.

Timed-release feeder

These hoppers release a few ounces of seed every few hours. These can be excellent feeders for keeping the birds fed at your home or a remote location while you are away.

Feeders should do more than just hold food

Many feeders can get the basic job done: They hold bird seed, the birds can perch on them, and you can see the birds. However, some don't really meet the birds' needs—or yours. They might be hard to land on, or it might be hard to get to the seed, or they might fail to keep the seed dry, letting mold grow. From your point of view, the feeder might be hard to open and fill, especially while wearing gloves. It might have parts that get lost in the snow, or be difficult to clean. The good news: You can choose feeders that avoid all these problems.

Element 2. Tray feeders

Trays come in all different sizes and styles. They can have four legs, be mounted on a post, or be added to tube feeders. They might come with a roof or be open to the elements. They can also be designed as fanciful accents that mimic natural items such as leaves and shells.

Small trays (see next page) come in all styles, some of them more of a shallow dish than a platform. These are great for individual birds, but they are not large enough to let you see lots of interaction between birds. Small trays can be added to foundational feeder setups or used on balconies, decks, and windows to feed seeds, mealworms and a variety of snacks.

Hanging trays (top left and right); tray on post with roof (bottom far left); tray added to tube feeder (bottom middle); large tray on post below feeder to catch seeds (above middle); large tray on legs (bottom right).

A small side dish with roof can be added to poles (top left); even a mealworm feeder can be pretty and be used for many different snacks (top right); a small tray for mealworms (bottom left); small trays can hold a variety of snacks (bottom right).

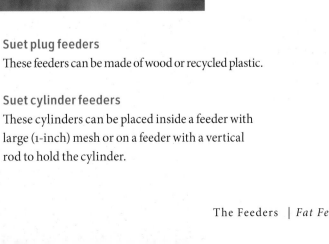

Tail-prop suet blend cake feeder (top far left); suet cage mounted on a pole (top middle); a suet plug feeder can be natural wood or recycled plastic (top right); suet dough cylinder feeder (bottom left); suet dough cylinder with perch (bottom right).

Element 3. Fat feeders

Suet cake feeders
Suet cakes can be provided in simple wire cages or in "tail-prop" feeders, suspended or post-mounted.

Suet plug feeders
These feeders can be made of wood or recycled plastic.

Suet cylinder feeders
These cylinders can be placed inside a feeder with large (1-inch) mesh or on a feeder with a vertical rod to hold the cylinder.

Suet ball feeder (top left); tree as Bark Butter feeder (top middle), hanging Bark Butter feeder (top right); hanging Bark Butter feeder (bottom left); tray for Bark Butter Bits (bottom middle); mesh feeder holds Bark Butter Bits (bottom right).

Suet ball feeder
Suet balls can fit into a variety of feeder designs.

Bark butter feeder
You can spread Jim's Birdacious Bark Butter on a tree trunk or branch, or it can be offered on a feeder.

Bark Butter Bits feeder
A mesh tube or tray is the usual feeder for these nuggets, but any hopper or tube feeder can offer Bark Butter Bits when they are mixed with a good blend.

Tube feeder with anti-microbial protection in all metal and plastic parts and E-Z Clean bottom (top left), finch tube with E-Z Clean bottom (top right); metal mesh finch feeder (bottom left); nylon mesh sock bottom right).

Element 4. Finch feeders

Available in all sizes, finch feeders can be plastic tubes with small holes and perches, mesh tubes without perches, or nylon mesh "socks."

Hanging hummingbird feeder (top left); pole-mounted hummingbird feeder (top right); window-mounted feeder with suction cups (bottom left); small hanging feeder (bottom right).

Element 5. Nectar, jelly, and fruit feeders

Hummingbird nectar feeders can be hung, post-mounted, or secured to a window with suction cups. Some are very decorative, adding beauty to the garden even when the hummers are not feeding. Oriole feeders (see page 258) serve such foods as sugar-water, fruit, jelly, and mealworms, separately or in combination.

Hanging hummingbird feeder with larger capacity and dome for shade to keep nectar cool (top left); decorative glass feeder (top right); glass and wood combination feeder (bottom left); pottery feeders can be beautiful, but dripping nectar may occur (bottom right).

Copper fruit feeder (top left); copper and glass jelly feeder (top right); plastic nectar, fruit, and jelly feeder (bottom left); nectar oriole feeder (middle right); covered fruit and jelly feeder (bottom right).

Element 6. Snack/specialty/ convenience feeders

Bluebird feeders

These feeders offer mealworms, suet nuggets, Bark Butter Bits, nutmeats, sunflower chips, and dried fruit in a hopper designed to exclude larger birds such as European Starlings. Bluebirds can see through the feeder's transparent sides; they go through the hole on the end to get to the food.

Sometimes they have to be shown how to use the feeder: you can place some food on the ledge right below the hole, and when that food is gone, the birds should find the entrance. A dome-covered tray with a mesh protector can accomplish the same result.

Mealworm feeders

Available in many styles and shapes, these need to have slick walls, drainage, and a place for the birds to land.

Covered mealworm feeder (top left); mealworm feeder with hole sized just right for bluebirds (top right); small dish on side of pole (bottom left); glass dish on small pole (bottom middle); hanging glass dish holds mealworms with slick sides (bottom right).

Whole peanut feeder (top left); metal mesh tube for peanut pieces (top right); whole peanut wreath-shaped feeder (bottom left); Downy Woodpeckers often peck hole in peanut shell while still in feeder (bottom right).

Whole peanut feeders
Whole peanuts can be offered in a mesh tube, a spiral wreath, or a tray of any size.

Peanut pieces feeders
Peanut pieces can be served in a mesh tube or bound into a bird food cylinder. There are decorative peanut feeders, too.

Feeders should suit your lifestyle and personality

Your feeding station should match your lifestyle. Where do you spend the most time watching the action at the feeders? Are you there every day to put food on a tray, or do you need the food to last a week between fillings? If the feeder is at your vacation cabin, you might want a timed-release feeder that can offer a few ounces every day and keep the birds coming until your next visit.

Your personality can be reflected in your bird feeding station, too. You might like to have feeders that are colorful, uniquely shaped, and scattered haphazardly all over your yard. Or you might want a well-ordered feeding station that adheres strictly to your landscape plan. Whatever your style, there are feeders that can help express your personality.

Decorative peanut pieces feeder (top left); peanut and tree nuts bird food cylinder feeder (bottom left); fun decorative peanut pieces feeder (right).

Only small birds can cling to this feeder (top left); small birds can land on this globe feeder even when it is slightly spinning (top right). With the dome lowered on this feeder (below left) only small birds, such as this Chestnut-backed Chickadee may land and feed; an added cage to a tube feeder (bottom right) creates a barrier for larger birds.

Small-bird-only feeders

These entertaining feeders work very well to exclude large birds. They can be placed in small areas such as balconies and small patios, or hung from windows with suction-cup hangers.

A combination hopper and Bark Butter feeder (top left) is very comfortable for woodpeckers as they hang on the tree while approaching and feeding. This combination works as a hanging feeder (top right), too. A plexiglass window on the backside (inset) shows the food level.

Woodpecker feeders

Hung or mounted on a tree, these feeders are filled with a seed blend with lots of peanuts and tree nuts, and sometimes sunflower seeds or Bark Butter Bits. Some have a rough, bark-like surface for spreading Bark Butter.

Cylinder and cake feeders

Cylinders of all types and sizes can be hung on any feeder with a rod to go through the center of the cylinder. Seed cakes require a mesh cage.

Simple bird food cylinder feeder (bottom left); bird food cake mesh feeder (bottom right).

A corny seat (top left) makes a comfy spot for feeding; squirrels have to open the lid for the goodies with this feeder (top right); this hinged feeder is made of metal (bottom left); this squirrel might go for a spin on this carousel feeder (bottom right).

Squirrel feeders

Some attach to trees, and others hang from poles or branches. There are entertaining variants with bouncing wires, spinning rods, and secret compartments.

Window feeders

I really like window feeders, because you can sit quietly several inches away to get an incredibly close look at the birds. They are great for introducing children to nature.

Window feeders can be open trays or hoppers.

They are secured with suction cups or tension rods, and can even be integrated into double-hung windows. Suction-cup hangers can turn any small feeder into a window feeder. I often use a bracket with a suction cup to hold a hummingbird feeder.

Window panorama feeder (top left); nectar feeder with a suction-cup hanger (bottom left); suction-cup feeder with dome (right).

A peanut feeder shaped like a black bear (top right); makes sense—a sunflower seed feeder shaped like a sunflower (bottom left); a stained-glass cardinal is pretty even when no birds are feeding (bottom middle); a candy cane-shaped sunflower feeder celebrates the holidays (bottom right).

Fun and whimsical feeders

There is no limit to the fun when creativity, art, and craftsmanship combine to create whimsical feeders in the shape of mansions, barns, covered bridges, cats, dogs, or even birds. Some incorporate rustic or modern architectural elements. It is important for the feeder to be safe for the birds and easy to fill and clean. Use water-soluble paints and stains, and leave no sharp nails or staples exposed.

Feeder Combinations

We can always add different feeders to poles with multiple arms, but some feeders already have multiple types built in.

Loose seed hopper and suet blend feeder combo (top left); mealworm and suet plug feeder combo (top right); bird food cylinder and Bark Butter feeder combo (bottom left); three trays and a tube feeder combo (bottom middle); tray and bird food cylinder combo (bottom right).

Roofs keep foods in trays dry (top left); weather domes keep peanuts dry (top middle) and keep rain from diluting nectar solution (top right).

A wire cage will keep squirrels and large birds off tube feeders (bottom left), small hanging trays, and ground-feeding trays (bottom right).

Feeder accessories

Roofs for trays
Adding a roof to a tray feeder can keep moisture off the food. Clear roofs let in more light for viewing the birds.

Weather domes
Add a plastic dome to keep moisture out of tube feeders in very rainy or snowy conditions.

Squirrel and large-bird cages
Add a cage that lets small birds in but keeps most squirrels and large birds out.

Ant problem-solvers for nectar feeders

If your nectar feeder does not have an ant moat built in, then you can add one above it.

You can also add an ant moat to the top of the WBU pole system and mount the hummingbird feeder above it.

If your feeder is on a pole, you can keep ants from climbing up the pole with a product called Nectar Fortress™. Apply a small bead of gel around the circumference of the pole, and the gel keeps the ants from climbing any further.

Ant moat built into pole; decorative hanging ant-moats (top inset); Nectar Fortress applied to pole (bottom inset).

What to look for in features and construction quality

The best way to advise you is to review the design features we consider when designing and manufacturing Wild Birds Unlimited feeders. My team of naturalists, product specialists, manufacturers and I have designed, tested, and redesigned many feeders over 30-plus years, all the while keeping aesthetics, functionality, and longevity in mind. Other manufacturers also make fine feeders, and you will find many features shared by all high-quality feeders.

To help you make good feeder choices, in the text that follows I detail one type each of tray, hopper, tube, hummingbird, and fat feeders. You may want to take a copy of these pages with you when you go feeder shopping.

Overall design features

Appearance
I think feeders should be aesthetically pleasing, either in the simplicity of their functional design or in the beauty of their overall appearance.

Visibility of birds
Choose feeders that give the best visibility of the birds no matter where they land. The idea is to see the birds on the feeder. Unfortunately, many designs offer views of birds only on one side of the feeder, with birds on the back invisible to the observer. Naturally, more birds tend to land on the side of the feeder away from the window, so the joy of seeing birds is greatly reduced.

Functional design features

Easy to fill
Feeders should be easy to fill, with no need to take them apart to get to the food chamber. Ideally, lids are on an easily opened hinge or attached wire so that the feeder can be filled without having to remove any parts or set them on the ground: any parts that have to be removed from a feeder will eventually be lost.

Easy to fill even in sub-freezing weather
It should be quick and easy to fill the feeder even with gloves on. It should be easy to open the feeder after a storm has coated it with ice, one of the most important times to feed the birds.

Feeds birds even in blizzard conditions
I want the food in my feeders to be available to the birds even in a blizzard or ice storm. Snow usually blows from one direction and covers up the feeding areas or holes on that side of the feeder, so it is important that food be available on the downwind side during a storm.

Easy to see seed level
Ideally, you can see the level of food in the feeder from inside your home. At 3:00 on a very cold afternoon, a low food level will hopefully encourage you to go outside and fill the feeder so that there is food late in the day and first thing in the morning. Or if you see that the feeder is full, you can relax and stay inside to enjoy the show.

A female Northern Cardinal (opposite) is visible to the hobbyist while perched on a quality hopper feeder that kept the seed dry during the snow fall and snow melt.

Keeps food dry

Rain and snow can get into any feeder, so it must have good drainage to ensure that there is never any standing water and good ventilation to let wind and sun dry the feeder and its contents.

Easy to clean

The easier it is to open the feeders and remove their floors and bottoms, the quicker and more effective the cleaning. In designing feeders, I consider the cleaning that should occur at each refill, the deeper cleaning that should be done every month, and the even deeper quarterly cleaning with a 10 percent bleach solution. Every time I fill a feeder, if there has been any kind of moisture from rain, snow, mist, or humidity, I clean out all leftover seed. At least every month, I spray down the feeders with a hose to remove droppings and old seeds. At least four times a year, feeders need to be taken apart and deep-cleaned with a bleach solution.

Good flow to the last seed

Seed diverters should deliver all food to the feeder openings so that every last seed is eaten. Uneaten seeds tend to gather moisture and get moldy or encourage squirrels to start chewing to get to the last seeds.

Self-cleaning by wind or bird activity

Hopper feeders tend to gather empty shells that have been dropped by birds like cardinals and House Finches. Some feeders, like my Classic WBU Hopper feeder, are designed so that the wind blows the empty shells out a side opening. Actively feeding and interacting birds will scratch out empty shells.

Able to withstand a fall

You will drop your feeders, so they had better be able to handle a few falls.

Ease of mounting or hanging

It should be easy to mount your feeders on a pole or to hang them from a hook. Even if mounted on a pole, they should be easy to remove for filling and cleaning. It is easier to hang feeders with a stiff wire or hook that does not collapse as you raise the feeder.

Comfortable perches

Birds should be comfortable on the perches and perching areas, with perches of the proper thickness and length for the bird's toes to grip. Hopper roofs should be far enough above the perching area for larger birds like cardinals to comfortably perch and dine as seen on page 270.

Squirrel-tolerant or squirrel-proof

I don't like it when squirrels destroy feeders, so I think all feeders should be either squirrel-tolerant or squirrel-proof. Squirrel-tolerant means that squirrels can eat from the feeder but cannot destroy it. Squirrel-proof means that the squirrels cannot eat the food and cannot destroy the feeder when they try.

Special features

Some feeders have features that add value to the hobbyist.

High-quality materials

Materials such as recycled plastic boards add strength and longevity, while other materials can add functionality, such as protection from squirrel attacks. Classic wooden or plastic hoppers built with screws instead of nails or short staples will last longest. High-quality roof hinges create a better seal from rain and increase longevity, as they do not rust. Perforated screen floors can be made from many materials, ranging from plastic to powder-coated metal, with corresponding differences in strength and longevity.

"Green" materials good for the environment
Recycled plastic boards and sustainably harvested western red cedar and eastern white pine are examples of green materials.

Health of birds and humans
Many of these design elements contribute to cleanliness, which keeps the feeding station healthy for birds and hobbyists. Stains and paints should be water-soluble, without any harmful components such as lead, and with zero Volatile Organic Compounds (VOC) off-gassing. Some feeders have anti-microbial protection built into the plastic parts and powder-coated paint.

Made in the USA or Canada
Many feeders are manufactured overseas, while others are manufactured in the U.S. and Canada. You get to decide whether that is important to you.

Warranty
Feeders come with warranties and guarantees that range from nothing at all to lifetime replacement of damaged or missing parts or the entire feeder.

Avoid feeders that:

▶ Hide most of the birds on the back, as most land on the side away from your window.

▶ Are difficult to clean or do not come apart.

▶ Are uncomfortable for birds to perch on.

▶ Are dangerous in any way to the birds, posing a risk of getting heads or feet caught in openings, etc.

▶ Are made of poor-quality materials that will not stand up to harsh weather. You will be buying another one very soon.

▶ Are difficult to hang or mount on a pole.

▶ Are difficult to fill, especially with gloves on.

▶ Have areas where seed is out of the birds' reach. Leftover seed will probably spoil.

▶ Can be easily destroyed by squirrels or raccoons.

A large tray (above) can catch seed from hopper feeder for "tidy dining" and can also hold a variety of snacks and foods for a diverse offering.

The Wild Birds Unlimited tray (left) is made of recycled plastic boards with removable perforated metal bottoms with anti-microbial protection. A cage (right) can be added to keep squirrels and large birds out of food and legs mounted to attract ground-feeding birds.

Tray feeder

This large tray has features worth looking for in any size or style of tray. Trays must be very easy to clean: birds leave their droppings in the tray, and any uneaten food gets wet. A removable bottom is a very helpful feature on a pole-mounted tray, while a hanging tray can easily be tipped over for cleaning. A removable perforated, powder-coated metal tray with anti-microbial protection is an added quality feature.

Overall design elements

▶ **Appearance** Simple yet efficient, with materials, colors, and design to match any other feeders on the same pole.

▶ **Visibility of birds** All birds are visible as they feed.

Functional design elements

▶ **Easy to fill even in sub-freezing weather** Just pour it in!

▶ **Feeds birds even in blizzard conditions** Will fill up with snow unless it has a roof. However, this will be the most active of your feeders as soon as the storm is over and you have refilled it.

▶ **Easy to see seed level** All seed is visible.

▶ **Keeps food dry** Food will get rain or snow on it, so you must refresh it or add a roof to keep food dry. Removable mesh bottom makes it easy to dispose of shells. The metal mesh floor provides drainage and ventilation.

▶ **Easy to clean** Easily taken apart to be sprayed, scrubbed, or soaked.

▶ **Good flow to the last seed** All food is visible and available to the birds.

▶ **Self-cleaning by wind or bird activity** Deep trays are not self-cleaning, making a removable floor advisable.

▶ **Ease of mounting or hanging** Can be mounted at any height on a pole or on the top of a pole.

▶ **Comfortable perches** Thick vertical sides provide comfortable perches.

▶ **Squirrel-tolerant** Squirrels can reach every seed, so they have no need to destroy the feeder.

▶ **Accessories**

Flanges for mounting on poles.

Roofs for pole-mounted versions.

Legs for ground-level feeding.

Cages to keep out squirrels and large birds

▶ **High-quality materials**

Western red cedar, ¾ inch thick, with bird-safe wood stains.

Recycled plastic, ⅝ inch thick, withstands any weather short of tornados and hurricanes.

Able to withstand a fall of at least 15 feet.

All-screw construction. No nails or staples to loosen or pull out.

▶ **Metal screen floor** Rust-proof powder-coated perforated metal with anti-microbial protection.

▶ **"Green" materials good for the environment**

Recycled plastic board version manufactured from recycled milk jugs and bottles.

▶ **Made in the USA** All wood and recycled plastic components are manufactured in the U.S.

▶ **Warranty** Satisfaction guaranteed.

▶ **Health of Birds and Humans**

Easy cleaning.

Anti-microbial protection in removable metal floor.

This is a good foundational feeder (top) that can feed lots of birds such as this flock of House Finches. A wire insert can discourage large birds such as these White-winged Doves (left). A removable perforated bottom with anti-microbial protection (right) is visible above the board where a flange can be attached for pole mounting.

Classic hopper feeder

This is a long list of features, but it took me 10 years of selling and thinking about bird feeders to come up with this design. And then it took another 15 years of use and innovation, along with the help of my team and our manufacturers, to improve the materials and functionality.

Overall design elements

▶ **Appearance** Asthetically pleasing with 3 identical angles, curved hopper sides, overhanging roof, and decorative chickadee stamp. Matches other available feeders in style and color.

▶ **Visibility of birds** Face the end of the feeder towards the window, and all birds on both sides are visible, thanks to curved sides and angled perch. No invisible feeding areas.

Functional design elements

▶ **Easy to fill even in sub-freezing weather** Hinged roof stays open while filling, both pole-mounted and hanging.

▶ **Feeds birds even in blizzard conditions** If one side faces into the wind, the other side will still be open for business.

▶ **Easy to see seed level** Clear plexiglass sides.

▶ **Keeps food dry**

   Roof overhangs to protect food from rain and melting snow.

   Metal screen floor improves drainage and is removable for easy cleaning.

▶ **Easy to clean** Easiily taken apart to be sprayed, scrubbed, or soaked

▶ **Good flow to the last seed** Seed diverter on hopper floor ensures good seed flow.

▶ **Self-cleaning by wind or bird activity** Empty shells can be blown off feeder by wind or bird activity.

▶ **Able to withstand a fall** Solid construction with thick materials. Plastic board version can withstand fall of 20 feet.

▶ **Ease of mounting or hanging** Bottom area for pole flange and pre-drilled holes on sides for optional hanging wire.

▶ **Comfortable perches** Thick, angled perches are correct distance from hopper for comfort of birds both small and large.

▶ **Squirrel-tolerant** Squirrels can reach every seed, so do not destroy feeder.

▶ **Feeds at two levels** Gap on each side of perches allows foundational blend to include millet, which is scratched to the ground through the gaps.

▶ **Accessories**

   Anti-pigeon insert to discourage large birds.

   Hanging wire.

   Metal pole-mounting flange.

▶ **High-quality materials**

   Western red cedar ¾ inch thick, bird-safe wood stains.

   Recycled plastic ⅝ inch thick, withstands all weather.

   short of tornados and hurricanes.

▶ **All-screw construction** No nails or staples to loosen or pull out.

▶ **Roof hinge** Rust-proof piano hinge runs along entire length of roof and keeps out rain and moisture.

▶ **Metal screen floor** Rust-proof powder-coated perforated metal.

▶ **"Green" materials good for the environment**

   Recycled plastic board version manufactured from recycled milk jugs and bottles.

▶ **Made in the USA** All wood and recycled plastic components manufactured in the U.S.

▶ **Warranty** Satisfaction guaranteed.

▶ **Health**

   Easy cleaning.

   Anti-microbial protection in removable metal floor.

A foundational seed blend works well in this seed tube (top left), where you can see the seed diverter in the bottom making every seed available. This finch feeder (top right) still had port holes available during and after the snow storm. Seed diverters are visible delivering every seed to bottom port holes. A weather dome (center right) may be added to keep food dry. An optional tray (bottom right) with anti-microbial protection incorporated may be added for extra feeding oppurtunites.

EcoClean tube feeder

This is another example of the considerable thought my staff and the manufacturer put into every feature of every feeder.

Overall design elements

▶ **Appearance** Very aesthetically pleasing as it is functional, yet blends into the landscape.

▶ **Visibility of birds** All birds are visible on perches or on optional tray as tube spins.

▶ **Easy-open bottom** Base is easily removed for cleaning.

▶ **Anti-microbial protection** Incorporates anti-microbial protection in all important areas of bird and seed contact.

▶ **Feeds in snowy conditions** Half or more of feeding areas remain available in snowy or icy conditions.

Functional design elements

▶ **Easy to fill** Hinged lid is easy to lift open and stays attached while filling.

▶ **Easy to fill even in sub-freezing weather** Easily opened while wearing gloves. Freezing rain can be cracked off or thawed to lift lid.

▶ **Feeds birds even in blizzard conditions** Half of ports are usually available even if blowing snow has closed up the others.

▶ **Easy to see seed level** Clear tube.

▶ **Keeps food dry**

Top of seed port diverts water from seed chamber.

Seed diverter in bottom has holes for drainage and air circulation.

▶ **Easy to clean**

Two buttons make bottom easily removable so entire tube can be cleaned with hose and brushes.

Strong construction can withstand pressure washers.

▶ **Good flow to the last seed** Seed diverter in bottom of tube delivers every seed to bottom holes.

▶ **Self-cleaning by wind or bird activity** Shells are dropped to the ground and the seed in tube stays clean.

▶ **Able to withstand a fall** I drop these feeders from a second-story balcony all the time without any damage.

▶ **Ease of mounting or hanging** Metal wire hanger is stiff, so it is easy to reach hanging hook. Bottom has threads for mounting on pole.

▶ **Comfortable perches** Vinyl-covered perches.

▶ **Squirrel-tolerant** Metal lid, seed ports, perches, and bottom protect plastic tube from squirrel damage.

▶ **Feeds at two levels** Birds can feed from perches or optional tray.

▶ **Accessories**

Domed rainguard.

Various trays, some with anti-microbial protection.

▶ **High-quality materials**

Polycarbonate plastic withstands heat, cold, sun, and rain.

Powder-coated metal parts. Rust-proof. Hanging wire and perches are stainless steel.

▶ **Made in the USA** All metal and plastic components manufactured in the U.S.

▶ **Warranty** Lifetime warranty.

▶ **Health of birds and humans**

Easy cleaning.

Anti-microbial protection in tube, perch covers, seed diverter, and black powder-coated metal parts.

Hummingbird feeder

Hummingbird feeders should work for the birds and for the hobbyist. The feeder should be bright red or some other bright color to attract hummingbirds. Never add red or any other colors to sugar-water nectar solutions. Nothing should block the view of hummers using the ports away from the viewer. It is very important that hummingbird feeders can be easily cleaned with soap and water by hand or, better yet, in the dishwasher. They should be drip-free to avoid making a mess, wasting sugar-water, and attracting yellowjackets and ants. Ants will climb a great distance to get to the nectar and can often fit through the ports, so a built-in ant moat is a benefit.

Overall design elements

▶ **Appearance** Simple, unobtrusive design looks great even when no birds are present.

▶ **Visibility of birds** Nothing blocks the view of any of the birds, perched or hovering.

▶ **Highly visible to birds** Entire lid is bright red and easy to spot.

Functional design elements

▶ **Does not leak** With sipping holes placed above the nectar, the feeder does not leak.

▶ **Ant moat incorporated** Ants will not swim across the moat . The ant moat has overflow drains so that it cannot spill over and dilute the nectar when it rains.

▶ **Easy to fill** Simple two-piece construction. The lid pops off easily and the bottom sits flat.

▶ **Easy to see nectar level** Transparent nectar chamber also allows hobbyist to watch hummingbird tongue lap up nectar.

▶ **Nectar recipe printed inside lid** Makes it easy to remember the correct 4 to 1 formula.

▶ **Easy to clean** Comes apart easily, and all parts can be cleaned by hand or in dishwasher.

▶ **All nectar is available** Distance from feeding hole to bottom of feeder is less than the combined length of the hummingbird's bill and tongue.

▶ **Able to withstand a fall** I drop these from a second-story balcony all the time without any damage to the feeder.

▶ **Ease of hanging or mounting** Metal wire hanger is easy to hang anywhere. The bottom has an opening to mount on pole.

▶ **Comfortable perches** High perching ring is at comfortable angle for the birds and gives viewers a good look.

▶ **Keeps rain out of nectar** The raised flower ports divert water from the nectar chamber.

▶ **Accessories**

Optional inserts decrease yellowjackets' ability to enter chamber.

Rainguard dome for extra protection.

Suction-cup hanger for mounting on windows.

Tiny brushes to clean out drinking holes.

▶ **High-quality materials**

Polycarbonate plastic. Very strong, withstands heat, cold, sun, and rain. Dishwasher safe.

▶ **Made in the USA** All plastic and metal components manufactured in the U.S.

▶ **Warranty** Lifetime warranty.

▶ **Health of birds and humans** Easy to clean by hand or in dishwasher.

Tail-prop suet feeder

Suet feeders should be comfortable for birds to cling to, easy to fill, and easy to clean. "Tail-prop" designs let woodpeckers maintain their natural clinging style, reproducing how they cling to a tree using their feet and tail as a three-point stance.

Overall design elements

▶ **Appearance** Simple design and colors blend into landscape. Matches other available feeders in style and color.

▶ **Visibility of birds** If you leave suet cakes in plastic tub, birds feed from only one side.

Functional design elements

▶ **Easy to fill** Lid easily slides up the hanging wire.

▶ **Easy to fill even in sub-freezing weather** Easily filled with gloves on in the worst weather.

▶ **Feeds birds even in blizzard conditions** Half or more of the feeding areas remain available in snowy or icy conditions.

▶ **Easy to see remaining suet level** All the suet is visible.

▶ **Keeps food dry** Not as important with fats, but food still needs to be kept fresh in damp conditions.

▶ **Easy to clean** Comes apart easily to be cleaned by hand or in dishwasher.

▶ **All suet is available** All the suet is reachable by woodpeckers.

▶ **Able to withstand a fall** I drop these from a second-story balcony all the time without any damage to the feeder.

▶ **Ease of hanging** Stiff metal wire hanger is easy to hang anywhere.

▶ **Comfortable perching** Tail prop is used by a woodpecker as if it were a real tree trunk.

▶ **Vinyl-covered wire mesh** Vinyl covering protects bills and eyes from any sharp points on mesh.

▶ **Accessories**

  Cages to prevent squirrels and large birds from getting access to food.

  Weather domes to keep moisture and snow off feeder.

▶ **High-quality materials** Recycled plastic and metal screws withstands heat, cold, sun, and rain. Won't fade, rot, crack, or warp.

▶ **Made in the USA** All plastic components manufactured in the U.S.

▶ **Warranty** Limited lifetime warranty.

▶ **Health of birds and humans** Easy cleaning.

A double suet cake feeder (left) held together with long metal screws is just the right size for this male Pileated Woodpecker. A single suet cake (right) works well for smaller woodpeckers such as this male Downy Woodpecker.

6 Poles and Hangers

No MATTER WHERE you want your feeders, there is generally a way to put them exactly where you want them. This chapter shows how to choose the hangers and poles you will use to get your feeders in the right place.

▶ Hanging from tree branch

▶ Hanging from pole

▶ Mounted on top of pole

▶ Deck setups

▶ Tree trunk/wall-mounted

▶ Window-mounted

A tree hook (left) can suspend the feeder at the right level for you to fill the feeder and view the birds. A reach extender (right) can help you access out of reach hanging areas.

Hanging feeders from a tree branch

Tree branches are a highly preferred location for the birds. They can fly in, land in the tree, check out the feeders, look for predators, and chat with all their flock as they take turns flying to the feeders. They can then quickly return to the tree to finish pecking at their sunflower seed or peanut. If a hawk cruises overhead, smaller birds can quickly find cover in the branches and hide until the coast is clear. Hanging your feeders from a horizontal tree branch is one of the easiest, quickest, and least costly ways to start bird feeding. Throw a rope or a chain over a branch and put a hook on the bottom, and you are good to go. This works out just fine in many situations.

Safely getting the right height

Tree branches are not always within easy reach. You might risk climbing a ladder, or you might want to avoid that entirely. The easiest way to suspend a feeder from a tree branch is with a long metal hanger, sometimes called a tree hook. These hangers come in lengths from 12 inches to 6 feet, and have a large hook at the top and a small hook at the bottom. The large hook goes over the branch, and you simply hang your feeder from the small hook. A reach extender can also help you put the tree hook over the branch or get the feeder onto the bottom hook.

In general, a feeder suspended from a 3-foot or longer tree hook, under a dome baffle, 8 feet from the tree trunk and at least 4 feet above the ground, is the very best combination. The feeder is safe from squirrels, and it can easily be reached to be filled. Because the rigid tree hook makes it harder than a loose chain to pull the feeder up into the tree, it will also be fairly safe from raccoons.

Tie it off

If you still have trouble with raccoons lifting the feeder to the branch, tie the top of the tree hook to the branch so it cannot be lifted off.

Pulley systems

A homemade pulley system (top) works great, seen here at a local nature center. Hanging plant pulleys (bottom) can also be used for raising and lowering bird feeders.

Homemade horizontal pulley systems can work in some situations. The idea is to hang feeders between two trees in a way that makes it difficult for a squirrel to reach them. Sometimes plastic tubes are placed on each side of the feeder to make it impossible for the squirrel to walk along the wire. Old LP records with that handy hole in the middle can be strung on the wire, too. All situations are different, and this is pretty much a job for the hobbyist who likes to cruise the hardware store for ropes, pulleys, and tree mounts—and knows how to safely use a drill while standing on a ladder.

Hanging plant pulleys, used to lower a basket of flowers for watering, can also help keep feeders in places where squirrels can't reach them, such as under eaves. These pulley systems make it easy to bring the feeder down for refilling.

Hanging feeders on poles: basic and pole systems

There are many ways to hang feeders from poles, with shepherd crook poles being the most common. Many other clever ways exist, but the best way to put your feeders exactly where you want them is to use a shepherd's crook pole, which looks just like the shepherd crooks that Little Bo Peep carries around in the nursery rhyme.

There are two main types of shepherd crooks: basic poles and pole systems.

Basic poles

These are ready to go into the ground and hang a feeder, but they don't offer many options. Basic poles may or may not come with an attached stabilizer, which usually doubles as an easy way to push it into the ground. It may or may not be easy to add a squirrel baffle. Basic poles are the least expensive,

and can work well when the options offered by a pole system are unnecessary. The illustration show this option in its typical pose—leaning.

Pole systems

These have many options, including stabilizers to keep them straight, variable heights, extra arms, side trays, and an array of baffles and decorative finials. They can even hold a hopper feeder on top. Pole systems usually come in sections, with the bottom section ending in an auger for screwing into the ground. You can start with one or two hanging arms and then build up to as many as seven or eight feeders on one pole.

Basic pole options often lean over time (left). Pole systems (right) are designed to stay straight and have many options for mounting and hanging feeders, perching branches and critter-proofing.

Pole Systems: Why I think they are so great

Wild Birds Unlimited Advanced Pole System
In the late 1990s, I worked with Joe Holscher of Holscher Products and our staffs to design a pole system that would stand up straight and offer dozens of options for creating a bird feeding station. We ultimately patented the Wild Birds Unlimited Advanced Pole System.

Joe Holscher and Jim Carpenter, co-inventors of the Wild Birds Unlimited Advanced Pole System.

The base unit is a 4-foot pole with an auger at the base.

Insert a screwdriver into the hole.

Twist the base into the ground, making sure to keep it straight.

Add the stabilizer to the base.

Add the stabilizer and jump on it to drive the stabilizer arms flush with the ground.

Add extra pole lengths as needed, with the button lock holding them in place.

You can choose an even longer baffle to keep raccoons off and then add feeders for a basic two-feeder station. You can start with two feeders, then add more feeders as desired (shown in the images below) with four, five or nine feeders on one pole with some hanging and some attached to the pole.

The nine feeders shown below are:

► Finch feeder

► Seed blend tube feeder

► Peanut feeder

► Suet cake cage

► Side dish tray

► Cylinder feeder

► Bark Butter spot

► Large tray feeder

► Hummingbird feeder

Slip on a squirrel baffle, mount the double shepherd's crook arm, and top it off with a decorative finial.

Feeders on top of poles

A simple hopper feeder on a pole connected with a metal flange works well.

Basic hopper pole

Basic poles usually come as one post or in sections for easier packaging and shipping. They will include a metal or plastic flange to connect a feeder to the post, or the top may fit into a hole in the feeder's bottom. They might have an auger or pointed base to make it easier to twist or pound the bottom section into the ground. It is easy to add a squirrel baffle; slip the baffle down over the top of the pole before you mount the feeder flange. The heavier-duty poles sometimes come with a "ground sleeve" that can be embedded in concrete, essential for keeping heavy feeder and pole combinations straight in wet or sandy soil.

Pole system for hopper feeders

Similar to shepherd's crook systems, a hopper pole top can be one of the options in a system. In the Wild Birds Unlimited Advanced Pole System, all of the options are the same as in the shepherd's crook pole systems but instead of a finial, you place the hopper on top. The same 4-foot base with built-in auger is placed in the ground. Then a feeder flange is attached to a 2-foot extension for a hopper feeder. For a tray, the 4-foot base may be high enough. With the system, many options are available to add below the feeder, such as a center-mounted tray, perching branches, side dishes, and any type of baffle. Hanging arms also can be placed on the pole below the feeder, so hanging tube feeders can be on the same pole.

With a pole system, hundreds of options exist for mounting a hopper on top and then adding other feeders or accessories.

The best way to install a heavy feeder, such as this gazebo (above), is a 4 x 4-inch PVC (left) or wooden post (right). The posts use metal bases with an auger that twists deeply into the ground for strength and stability.

Wood or PVC post for heavy feeders

For the largest feeders, a 4-by-4-inch wooden or PVC post is best, with a special flange to hold the feeder on top. The post is placed into a 24-inch hole dug with a posthole digger.

For lighter and medium-weight feeders, it is not necessary to use concrete in the hole. You can line the bottom 4 inches of the hole with loose gravel, put the pole in the center of the hole, and fill the hole with gravel while using a level to keep the pole straight.

For feeders that are heavier than 20 pounds when filled, you should use concrete to reinforce the pole. This is a two-person job. Again, dig a 24-inch hole, fill the bottom 4 inches with loose gravel, install the 4-by-4-inch pole, and, using a level to keep the pole straight, pour concrete all around the post. Leave about 4 inches of space at the top of the hole to fill in with gravel or soil once the concrete has hardened.

There is an easier way to install a 4-by-4-inch post. Wild bird specialty stores commonly carry an 18-inch auger that can be twisted into the ground. The post is inserted into the metal collar and screwed in tight. A similar product is found in hardware stores, but it has to be pounded into the ground.

A basic deck pole (left) with a tube feeder and a raccon-proofed deck set-up with a hopper feeder (right).

Feeders on decks

Deck-mounted feeders face special challenges

Not all decks are the same, so different feeder mounts are needed for different decks. You can find mounts that work with wood or metal railings and with top boards that are vertical or horizontal.

The feeders should hang in such a way that they are easy to reach and fill, but shells and droppings do not fall onto the deck.

Squirrel- and raccoon-proof systems on decks are a whole different game than on feeder poles in the ground. Basically, the squirrels and raccoons are starting from the height of the deck railing, so the challenge is to use an effective baffle while keeping all the feeders within reach. Since I mostly feed birds with feeders on my second-floor deck, I have solutions! For full details on two raccoon-proof setups, turn to page 318.

Always use a very steady stepladder when changing and filling feeders on a deck.

Basic deck poles

These include both the pole and the mounting flange. Even though they do not offer optional additions, basic poles and flanges work well for finch, mealworm, and nectar feeders where squirrels and raccoons are not a problem.

Deck pole system with fancy look (above) and additional metal perching branch. Using a steady step ladder (right) is essential when working with feeders on second floor decks.

Deck mounts for vertical wooden top rail (above left); deck mount for vertical deck support post to keep scattered food and bird droppings from hitting deck surfaces (above right). Easy attach horizontal deck mount (below left) with simple screw-in tightener; very strong horizontal deck mount (bottom right).

Deck-mounting systems

These systems give you the widest options for mounting several feeders on one mounting bracket and for deterring wildlife. The components are usually sold separately, so you can choose the mount that works best for your deck and then the poles that will create the bird feeding station you want. You can add hangers, baffles, and accessories. First, figure out how to mount the base support for the pole and then build your station from there. These systems also work great for building fake trees out of dead branches to provide perches and vertical landing spots.

Male Downy Woodpecker (left) and male Hairy Woodpecker (right) both enjoy a tree-mounted feeder that has food in the hopper and Bark Butter on the surface.

Feeders on trees, fences, and walls

Some feeders are designed to be placed directly on a tree, fence, or wall. In these cases, just screw the feeder into the tree. It is also easy to put a feeder on a fence or a wall. Many hangers are available, ranging in design from simple to ornamental. They work best where there are no squirrel or raccoon problems or if you offer only foods that don't attract unwanted wildlife. Good options include nectar and mealworm feeders, squirrel-tolerant feeders, or feeders with safflower, which squirrels do not like. Most hanging squirrel-proof feeders need to be 18 to 24 inches from the fence, or the squirrel will pull them over sideways and defeat the mechanism.

This feeder, attached to a window with three suction cups, gives the birds two perches to land on and is easily filled by slipping the hopper out of the roof section.

Window feeders

One of my favorite places to mount a feeder is on a window with suction cups. No other feeder brings the birds to within inches of your face for an intimate bird-watching experience.

There are hundreds of designs of feeders that serve this purpose.

7 Critter Solutions

FREE FOOD JUST sitting there. Easy pickings! Any creature that can fly, jump, climb, reach, or drop onto the feeder can enjoy a free buffet. And why not? Finding food in the wild is hard work.

A bird feeding station with a huge supply of yummy foods attracts all sorts of animals. Hopefully your station attracts plenty of the birds you enjoy, but it almost certainly hosts other visitors that you just don't want to see. They might eat all the food and keep your desired birds off the feeders and they might even destroy your feeders.

There is usually a solution to most critter problems. Many work really well, while others may not be 100 percent effective but still at least reduce the problem. Sometimes you simply have to stop feeding until the problem goes away. Sometimes I learn to live with the problem and decide maybe it isn't as bad as I originally thought. For instance, I have learned that House Sparrows come to the feeders at my office no matter what I do, but I have also learned that they do not stay all day. With a diverse buffet in several feeders, the Northern Cardinals, chickadees, and woodpeckers have plenty of time to visit. And when the House Sparrows are there, it is actually quite interesting to watch their behavior in the flock as they fly to and from the feeders.

Squirrels, squirrels, squirrels!

The critter that gets the most attention is our friendly backyard squirrel—with good reason. They really want to eat that free food. And they are smart, agile, and persistent. Whole books and hundreds of articles have been written about how to keep squirrels off your feeders. Fortunately, there are solutions that work in most cases, so read on, and good luck!

Gray and fox squirrels

If you live in the U.S. or Canada east of the Rocky Mountains and you have trees, you probably have eastern gray or eastern fox squirrels in your yard. In most places, you probably have only the one or the other; where their ranges overlap, they often prefer different habitats. There are typically only gray squirrels in New Jersey, most of New York, and New England.

The smaller gray squirrel has a whitish belly, a silvery gray coat, and white-tipped tail hairs. In spite of its name, this species varies in color from black to gray to red. The larger fox squirrel typically has rusty brown fur, a tan or orange belly with no white areas, and a fluffy tail with rust-tipped guard hairs. There are also a few color variations of the fox squirrel in certain regions with black or silver fur. Both species are incredible athletes, and exhibit great persistence and patience as they try to find a way to eat the food at your feeders.

The gray squirrel (top) has a white belly, while the fox squirrel (bottom) has a tan or orange belly.

Red squirrels

The red squirrel is diurnal (out during the day), while both the northern flying squirrel and southern flying squirrel (right) is nocturnal (only out at night).

The small red squirrel, sometimes called piney or pine squirrel, is found over most of Canada and in the U.S. is found in the Northeast , upper Midwest, Smokey Mountains and Rocky Mountains. They usually prefer conifer or mixed hardwood forests. Only slightly larger than some chipmunks, red squirrels are about half the size of a gray squirrel. The coat is reddish or reddish gray with a white belly. They are very athletic, and can jump sideways distances that their larger cousins just can't cover. They may occur in the same forests as fox and gray squirrels, but are very protective of their territories. If a squirrel is living in your attic, odds are it is a red squirrel.

Flying squirrels

There are two species of flying squirrels in North America: the southern and the northern. These chipmunk-size squirrels are nocturnal, communal, and much more common than is known simply because they come out only at night. They don't actually fly but glide on membranes of skin between their legs.

I always thought flying squirrels should live in my woods but didn't see them until 20 years had passed. After finally seeing them come to my feeders after dark and learning their chirping call, I recognized it as a familiar sound from late evening walks with the dogs. I feel it is a special treat to have flying squirrels glide in for dinner!

Ground squirrels and chipmunks

"Ground squirrels" is a very numerous and diverse group with the larger ones being marmots, groundhogs, and prairie dogs; the smallest being chipmunks; and the medium size usually called ground squirrels. In the Colorado foothills, you might see Least Chipmunks, Golden-mantled Ground Squirrels and Rock Squirrels all in the same habitat—and they are all interested in your bird food. Out east, the eastern chipmunk is likely the only ground squirrel to be interested in your bird food (with an occasional groundhog!). Ground squirrels usually stuff their cheek pouches full of seeds and nuts, and then return to their underground dens to store the seed.

Every bird feeding hobbyist has a different opinion about these cute little critters or #@&*% varmints. Some folks enjoy feeding them, and some make it a life crusade to keep them off the feeders. Either way, there is likely a solution that gives you exactly what you desire.

Golden-mantled Ground Squirrels and Least Chipmunks both eagerly fill up on bird food from a feeder (left) or on the ground (top right). An eastern chipmunk (bottom right) is a common visitor in the eastern U.S. and southern Canada.

A golden-mantled ground squirrel (left) with cheeks stuffed full of sunflower chips and peanuts.

There are three kinds of feeders in this world: squirrel-bait, squirrel-tolerant, and squirrel-proof.

A typical "squirrel-bait" feeder (above). After one day, the squirrel opened the roof filling port and its weight separated the bottom from the plastic hopper. Typical squirrel-chewed damage (right) to a "squirrel-bait" feeder.

Squirrel-bait feeders

This is a very large group of feeders, most made of plastic or thin wood, that a squirrel can easily chew through or rip apart to get to the seeds. Usually inexpensive, these feeders might feed birds just fine, but they won't last long if a squirrel or raccoon hops on them and starts chewing or ripping to eat the last remaining seeds in the hopper.

Where a squirrel can reach the feeder, a squirrel-tolerant or squirrel-proof feeder is the way to go.

Squirrel-tolerant feeders

Squirrels can eat from these feeders but cannot destroy them. The designers have protected the vulnerable areas of the feeder with metal coverings so squirrels and raccoons cannot chew through. In tube feeders, this means the seed ports, lids, bottoms, perches, and hanging wires are all metal. Some feeders are entirely made of metal parts.

Another squirrel-tolerant feature can be incorporated into wooden or recycled-plastic hopper feeders. If the feeder is designed so that the squirrel can reach the remaining seeds in a nearly empty hopper, it has no reason to destroy the feeder. Even without metal protection, these feeders can be called squirrel-tolerant. Trays are squirrel-tolerant by definition: there is no reason for a squirrel to chew on anything to get to the food.

Squirrel-proof feeders

I mean it! Yes, we joke about squirrels being so smart that no feeder can confound them, but the truth is that there are 100-percent squirrel-proof feeders out there. There might be "rules," such as they cannot be too close to a pole or window sill because then the squirrel just pulls the feeder over and defeats the mechanism. When these feeders are hung or mounted according to instructions, they work very well.

Squirrel-proof feeders: beating the unbeatable

Feeder designers use nine strategies to make feeders squirrel-proof yet still available to birds:

1. Fat squirrel closes off food source

2. Fat squirrel bends perch

3. No handholds

4. Spinning class

5. ZZZZap 'em!

6. Jail-bird exclusion cages

7. Roll 'em over

8. Slip-and-slide domes

9. Timed and tolerant

The Eliminator squirrel-proof feeder from Wild Birds Unlimited feeds the birds, but the squirrel's weight shuts down the feeding ports. It is protected with metal or extremely durable plastic parts wherever a squirrel is likely to chew to access the food.

1. Fat squirrel closes off food source

There are two main types of this method, used in tube or hopper feeders.

In tube feeders, spring-loaded perches are connected to a shroud that drops and closes off all the food ports when the squirrel puts weight on the perches.

When the squirrel retreats, the springs pull the perches and shroud back up, and the food is again accessible to the birds. Wild Birds Unlimited, Brome Bird Care, and Perky-Pet Products, among

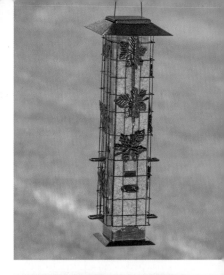

others, have feeders using this method.

In some hopper feeders, the horizontal perch is spring-loaded or counter-weighted, with a similar effect. When the squirrel sits or puts weight on the perch, the perch lowers to bring an attached cover down over the food offering. Woodlink Products, among others, offers this type of feeder.

In both cases, the entire feeder is squirrel-proof, with all-metal parts, metal protecting plastic areas, super-tough resin, or slick surfaces in the tube or roof that prevent traction.

Both of these types usually have the capability to keep large birds such as Rock Pigeons and grackles off the feeder, too. The more expensive feeders

have a more sensitive "dial" and the less expensive have a few pre-sets for the spring tension. For instance, pigeons weigh 9 ounces, grackles weigh 4 ounces, Northern Cardinals weigh 2 ounces, and chickadees weigh 0.4 ounces. The spring tension can be adjusted to account for these weight differences.

When hanging a squirrel-proof feeder off of a pole system that does not have a squirrel baffle, you will want to use a hanging arm with extra length. This puts the feeder a few inches farther from the pole, so that even if a squirrel can reach the feeder ring or perches, it closes off the mechanism as it pulls the feeder to the pole.

Fundamentals from Wild Birds Unlimited (top left); Brome Squirrel-buster Peanut Feeder (top middle);Perky-Pet Squirrel-Be-Gone (top right); Woodlink Red Bird's Choice (bottom left; Woodlink Reflective RD Vista (bottom middle); demonstrating that the squirrel-proof mechanism will still work if the feeder is on a longer arm (bottom right).

2. Fat squirrel bends perch

This is a simpler solution, where the weight of the squirrel collapses a spring-loaded or counter-balanced perch, leaving it nothing to hold onto. The squirrel falls off, and the perch flips back into position to welcome the next songbird. The key here is that the rest of the feeder has no surfaces for the squirrel to grab. Droll Yankees and Woodlink Products, among others, sell feeders using this strategy.

With strategy number two, the food port is not closed down, but the squirrel has no place to hang onto as the perches collapse. Woodlink's "The Bouncer" (left) and Droll Yankees Dipper (middle) and Tipper (right) all employ this strategy.

3. No handholds

These feeders have been engineered to remove any "handholds" but the perches themselves. With no moving parts, these feeders, represented by the Classic Feeder by Birds Choice, are the simplest squirrel-proof designs. The hanging versions have a wide, tall, and slick plastic seed chamber above the perches; they might also include a weather guard as further protection from squirrels and large birds. The pole-mounted version has the same slick tube that is too wide to grab onto, plus a metal stovepipe baffle below the perches.

With strategy three, it is very hard for squirrels to jump and hang onto the perches, so these feeders can be very successful.

Strategy number four, Spinning Class, is entertaining while keeping the food just for the birds.

4. Spinning class

Otherwise similar to any large tube feeder, the Droll Yankees Flipper has a battery-operated motor that, when it senses a squirrel on a perch, starts the squirrel's education in spinning class. The circular perch starts spinning and keeps spinning until the squirrel drops off. Eventually squirrels learn their lesson and give up. This is perhaps the most entertaining of the squirrel-proof feeders. You do have to remember to charge the battery, and the feeder is out of service during the recharge. Because of the electronics, battery, and moving parts, it is the most likely of all squirrel-proof feeders to need warranty service. But with all that entertainment, many people just love this feeder.

5. ZZZZap 'em!

These feeders teach the squirrels that the food is definitely not for them. The Wild Bill's Squirrel-free Bird Feeder has several sizes that can be hung or pole-mounted. When the squirrel jumps on the feeder and touches two contact points, it completes a circuit and receives a mild shock. The shock does not harm the squirrel; it is very mild and will shut itself off after three seconds. Birds are not able to touch the two contacts at once, and the hard scales of their feet, unlike squirrel toes, do not complete the circuit. One disadvantage is that you cannot hang the feeder from a shepherd's crook, because it is recommended that it be placed at least 4 feet away from a pole or tree trunk. You cannot hang it from a metal hook, either, unless it is properly insulated. Always remember to turn the feeder off when filling or moving it! The nine volt batteries need to be regularly replaced. Another model, the Squirrel-boss, has a remote control that allows you to decide if the squirrel gets to eat or is encouraged to depart. This feeder needs weekly charging with an AC adapter.

A light electric shock is one of the strategies to keep squirrels off of feeders by Squirrel-Boss (left) and Wild Bills (right).

Looking like a feeder inside a jail, these feeders keep the squirrels out and let smaller birds in. Available from Woodlink (top left and right), and Wild Birds Unlimited (bottom).

6. Jail-bird exclusion cages

Put the feeder in jail so the squirrels can't get in! Smaller birds can enter and leave any time they like.

The key to these feeders is that all exposed parts are metal; otherwise, the frustrated squirrel would just chew them up. Large birds cannot use these,

which might be an advantage unless you would like jays and doves to visit. Wild Birds Unlimited, Duncraft ,and Woodlink have representative products in this class. The suet cage in a cage is designed by Wild Birds Unlimited to feed woodpeckers without European Starlings and squirrels. Small woodpeckers go in through the sides, while larger woodpeckers can hang on from beneath or sides.

7. Roll 'em over!

There are few feeders similar to this design by Rollerfeeder, perhaps because it is somewhat hard for the birds to locate the food. However, this feeder does keep squirrels off the food, and it provides entertainment while you watch them try to figure it out. The central rod is an axis that holds the food chamber secure but allows the outer shell to roll over if a squirrel puts any weight on it. This feeder might also be a good one where there are raccoon problems.

8. Slip-and-slide domes

All of the previously discussed squirrel-proof feeders are safe from attacks from below, above and sideways when mounted as directed. The slip-and-slide domes are generally squirrel-proof only from above; sideways attacks can successfully make it to the trays. These feeders are more effective with perches than with trays. The large dome is very effective, though, when hung properly. Arundale Products and Droll Yankees offer products in this category.

9. Timed and tolerant

OK, this AutoFeeder by Wingscapes is not totally squirrel-proof, but it is squirrel-tolerant because it can't be destroyed by the squirrel. An effective weapon in the squirrel wars, it offers only a small amount of food at a time. If the squirrel is there when the food is released, it gets some seeds; if not, then the birds get the food. Now if the squirrel learns the times…well, then it is just another squirrel-tolerant feeder. This feeder is a favorite of mine for keeping the birds fed when I go on vacation.

Squirrel-bait and squirrel-tolerant feeders can be made squirrel-proof—with help

With the right combination of baffles, feeder placment, and food choices, just about any feeder can be made squirrel-proof. Squirrel-bait and squirrel-tolerant feeders are most easily protected from attacks from above or below, but are more difficult to protect from sideways jumps. To be perfectly safe from athletically inclined squirrels, hang or post-mount these feeders 8 to 12 feet away from anything that gives the squirrel a height advantage, including tree trunks, fences, lawn chairs, deck railings, and window sills. Eight feet works for fat fox squirrels; you'll probably need 12 feet for red squirrels.

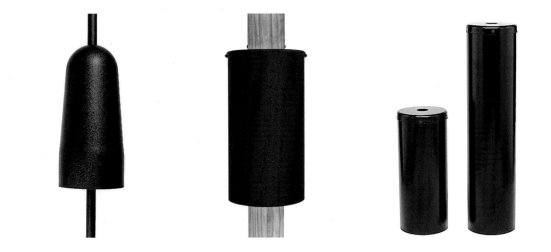

A chipmunk is "baffled" by this stovepipe baffle (above). All of the food in these squirrel-tolerant feeders (below) are protected from squirrels and chipmunks since the only access to the feeders is to climb the pole from the ground. Various stovepipe baffles are available (right), depending on the size of the metal or wooden pole. Longer baffles are more effective against raccoons.

Attack from below

There are several ways to keep squirrels from climbing poles. Well, you can't stop them from climbing poles; you can only stop them from climbing all the way to your feeders.

Stovepipe baffles

The best way to protect feeders on poles is to use stovepipe baffles, making sure the top of the baffle is at least 4 feet above the ground. These baffles have proven themselves over many decades of use.

The squirrel ascends a skinny pole, and all of a sudden it is faced with a 6- to 10-inch floppy stovepipe. It tries to wrap its arms around it, but the baffle is just too wide and too slick. The squirrel tries to squeeze up inside the stovepipe and hopes for the best, but—no luck—the top is solid metal. The squirrel jumps to the ground and studies the situation. Surely there is a solution!

This same baffle works for chipmunks, ground squirrels, and raccoons. Raccoon baffles are longer, at 23 inches, so the raccoon can't reach up and grab the pole above the stovepipe. Any feeder is safe above this baffle as long as squirrels cannot jump sideways or drop from a tree or roof to the feeders. These baffles basically last forever and have no batteries to replace, nothing to break, nothing that needs fixing. They are my favorite pole baffle.

Cone-shaped baffles

These have proven to be effective because they not only stop the critter's climb but also are floppy if the squirrel does try to get around them. These range in size from 14 to 22 inches, with the widest being the most effective. I recommend at least 17 inches to be safe.

Zap 'em

Another way to stop the squirrel from climbing is to place a device around the pole that gives a static pulse when touched. One such device, called the Tough Bird Feeder Guard, fits poles up to 1 inch. The feeder and pole are safe to touch at all times even when the unit is turned on. When a squirrel runs across the contact strips it delivers a little shock similar to touching a door knob in the winter time. It's an entirely safe and humane way to keep squirrels off your feeder.

Greased pole (not recommended)

An old technique is to smear petroleum jelly all over the pole. This certainly works, and is good for watching some entertaining efforts by the squirrel, but it has drawbacks, and I do not recommend it. For one, it is temporary and has to be constantly applied. But this is the bigger concern: I don't believe petroleum jelly is an easy material for the squirrel to remove from its fur, and this could endanger the squirrel when it needs its coat to be in good condition for the winter. The same goes for birds; they sometimes land on the pole below the feeder and could get totally slimed. They cannot properly clean petroleum jelly out of their feathers as they preen, clean, and realign them for proper insulation. It's best to find other solutions.

Slinky-type spring

Some people have had luck hanging a Slinky toy or similar spring below their feeders, with the pole up the center of the slinky.

Attack from above

Many methods have been used through the years to protect hanging feeders from squirrel attacks. Some hobbyists have used old vinyl LP records that squirrels could not navigate around. Every kind of dome has been tried, with various results. Basically, the idea is to create a barrier that is wide enough to keep the squirrel from holding onto the hanging chain or wire and doing a quick flop down onto the feeder.

Domes

There are dozens of versions that will work when hung above the feeder. The widest domes work the best, while the smaller, 12-inch domes are more appropriately called weather domes, as they offer better protection from rain than from squirrels. 15 inches across or larger is recommended if the dome

is to work as a squirrel baffle.

Hanging domes differ from pole baffles in several ways. If a pole baffle can keep a squirrel from climbing up a pole, every type and any number of feeders above the baffle are protected. A dome can usually protect only one feeder. Since every feeder is different in width and length, the ability of the dome to do its job differs with every feeder placed beneath it.

Tippy domes don't work as well as domes with stiff rods. For instance, when a small feeder is tucked up inside a dome, it is most definitely protected from a squirrel. However, if a wide hopper feeder is hung under that same dome, the squirrel can still tip the dome and slip down onto the feeder. If a tube feeder has a large tray, then the tray may be visible to a squirrel when it tips the dome, and with a quick flip, it is on the tray.

Tippy domes can work well or poorly, depending on the situation.

Here is how you can tell if a dome will work. Hang the feeder under the dome, holding the dome's top hook in your hand and close to the ground. Look down at the dome, and tip it like a squirrel would; if you see any part of the feeder or feeder tray sticking out, then assume that squirrels can get around that dome.

The domes that work best have a length of stiff rod above or below the dome. The rods make it more difficult for the squirrel to tip the dome, but even if they do, the feeder stays more completely under the dome. Wild Birds Unlimited has an 18-inch dome with a 6-inch rod that works in this manner. The rod can be placed above the dome for small feeders and below the dome for larger feeders. Droll Yankees sells a 15-inch dome that is very deep, so it works well for small feeders tucked up inside, or, with the adjustable hanging rod below the dome, it a can protect tube feeders without a tray. Small feeders such as suet cages can be protected easily if they are hung directly beneath the dome.

This dome might work on this tube and tray (above, far left), but it would work best without the tray. This dome (middle) rests on top of the tube and is very effective as the tray cannot be reached by the squirrel. This dome (right) might work on this hopper, but an agile squirrel might flip on to the tiny bit of exposed roof when the baffle is tipped.

This dome works well, but an agile squirrel might be able to tip it and jump on the tray.

Many tubes are not sold with a built-in exclusion cage, but you can retrofit most feeders. This option allows you to either use or not use the cage. For instance, I would take off the cage and add a tray when Rose-breasted Grosbeaks are migrating through Indiana as they could not fit through the mesh of the cage.

Retrofitting with exclusion cages

Another option that works well in some situations is to put your feeder in jail. There are many cages of all sizes and dimensions to protect feeders from squirrels and large birds. Wild Birds Unlimited has many On-Guard cages that can be used to retrofit feeders to be squirrel-proof and large-bird-proof.

Twirl that squirrel!

Bird Quest's Twirl-a-Squirrel (shown above) is a clever device that replaces baffles for feeders up to 10 pounds. It hangs above the feeder, and when it senses the weight of a squirrel, it spins the entire feeder and twirls the squirrel right off. Given its cost and the need for battery maintenance, this device might work best in situations where hanging domes don't work, such as near a window sill, a deck railing, or a tree trunk.

Squirrels are attracted to ears of corn, whether hanging, mounted on the side of a tree, or on an amusing feeder that twirls or bounces.

Give squirrels their own feeders

You may not want to feed the squirrels, but sometimes it makes sense to give them a feeder or two of their own. If you feed the squirrels at a distance from your foundational and specialty feeders, they just might stay away long enough to give the birds squirrel-free meals for a while. Wildlife blends with lots of whole corn kernels, peanuts in the shell, and sunflower can be used on a tray feeder for this purpose. Corn on the cob works well, too, and can often be fed in amusing ways. If you put the corncob on a Squngee (a squirrel bungee cord), the animal will get one kernel with each springy ride. Put the cobs at the end of a twirling device, so the squirrel has to twirl to get its reward. Watch a squirrel learn how to open a box and grab a peanut or go inside a large transparent jar to find its food. There are many feeders that feed the squirrels while entertaining us.

Feed foods squirrels don't like

Squirrels love sunflowers and nuts most of all. The number 1 food they do not like—though birds do—is safflower, and that is my number 1 recommendation for feeders that cannot be squirrel-proofed.

Squirrels don't usually have any interest in nyjer, millet, or plain suet cakes. I have seen them chew through finch tubes in search of sunflower seeds and then leave when they find only nyjer. They just don't seem to pay any attention to millet—too small to mess with? And you would think they would like suet, but mostly they like the other ingredients in suet blends, such as peanuts or corn meal. Plain suet? Not so much. Another food they leave alone is mealworms.

Offer safflower, nyjer, millet, plain suet, and mealworms, and you should have very few squirrel problems.

Raccoons in the pantry?

Raccoons, especially with their babies, are really cute—until they destroy your feeders. Keeping them out of your feeders can be easy or difficult, depending on the situation.

Baffled poles easily solve raccoon problems

If you put all your feeders on a pole, you can follow the same advice as for squirrels. If you use the longer stovepipe baffle, your problem is solved.

Hanging feeders from a tree branch without raccoon problems

One option is to baffle an entire tree. Raccoons do not jump from tree to tree like squirrels, so you can baffle an isolated tree by placing 24 inches of aluminum flashing around the trunk. I learned to use this technique to protect my Barred Owl box from raccoons.

If you are hanging feeders from a tree branch, raccoons are a bigger challenge simply because they are stronger than squirrels. Instead of sliding down the chain or wire, they haul the feeder up to the branch. It's best to use a tree hook instead of a chain or rope to hang your feeders as feeders on tree hooks are very hard to haul up. The longer the tree hook, the more effective it is. A hanging dome at the bottom of the tree hook provides extra protection. In addition to being hard to haul up to the branch, the slippery metal hook is also difficult to climb back up, so raccoons usually choose not to slide down in the first place.

Feeding on your deck?

This is the most challenging raccoon-proofing situation. Because the raccoon starts its attack on top of the deck railing, the usual strategies for feeders on poles do not work. But in the nearly 30 years I have been feeding birds on a second-story deck in a forest, this challenge has become one of my specialties.

My two favorite methods both use the same overall strategies:

▶ Use a raccoon baffle on a tall pole, with the top of the baffle at least 3 ½ feet above the deck railing.

▶ The bottom of feeders hanging near the deck rail must be at least 3 feet from the deck railing, just beyond the grasp of most raccoons.

▶ Ensure that feeders hang at least 2 feet out from the deck so raccoons cannot reach them.

▶ Make it easy to reach feeders for filling.

Method 1: Extended raised arm above raccoon-proof pole

A raccoon cannot climb a 4-foot pole mounted to the deck railing or upright if it has a raccoon baffle placed as high as possible. To place the feeder higher and to make sure it hangs away from the deck, an extended deck arm is added to the top of the 4-foot pole. To bring the feeder down to where you can reach it, add an 18-inch tree hook to the hook on the end of the extended pole. The feeder hangs way out from the deck, but can easily be pulled over to the deck for easy filling. This simple setup will hold one feeder, but additional arms and feeders can be added above the baffle. Then you can add a finial for a decorative touch and a metal branch as a landing perch and place to hang

hummingbird feeders. You can hang either squirrel-tolerant or squirrel-proof feeders from this setup, depending on your goals.

A simple raccoon-proof deck set-up.

I have as many as ten feeders on this set-up depending on the season.

Method 2: Large double-baffled cross-pole
(For expert installation only on a second story or higher)
This method allows for a large number of feeders on a deck while preventing raccoon mayhem. Two upright poles are connected at the top by a horizontal. Each vertical pole has a raccoon baffle, with its top at least 4 feet above the deck railing. All the feeders are hung from the cross pole and any extra hanger arms. You can add accessories such as metal and real perching branches and vertical landing spots. After the large hickory tree in the photo blew over in a high wind, I added tree perching branches to the deck railing on each side; most of the birds land on these before flying to the feeders. The bottom of every feeder needs to be a minimum of 3 feet above the deck railing: otherwise, the raccoons can reach up and yank a feeder off its hook. Some of the feeders in the photo are hanging lower than usual, as I added them during the day to feed more birds after the snow.

Warning: If you mount this on a second-story or higher deck, be careful as you reach from a ladder over the abyss. You must always be secure of your footing and balance, or you may fall. Use Method 1 if you have any uncertainty about installing this setup.

I successfully used Method 1 for 20 years, but Method 2 is my current favorite on the deck. All the feeders and all the birds are easily visible from my windows.

Caught in the act!

I determined the feeders' correct distance above the deck rail by using a game cam. The smart little guys could not get around the baffles, but from the deck rail they could reach the lowest feeder's perch ring and pull it off its hook. The feeders they could not reach were at least 36 inches above the deck rail. 1. Hey, look at all that food! 2. How do we get to it? 3. Just climb up this pole, I think. 4. Can't climb the pole, let's see if I can grab the feeder. 5. I've got this! 6. Oops, got the feeder but we both took a little trip to the ground. 7. Can't grab these—must be at least 3 feet from the deck rail!

Other critter problems

Chipmunks

Chipmunks are seriously cute, but they can cause two problems. They eat lots of seed, and they burrow under foundations and sidewalks. They don't usually eat the seed at the feeder, but stuff their mouth pouches to take the food into their burrows for later consumption. To keep them from eating your seed, follow all of the advice about squirrels (see page 304).

Also, keep food off the ground so that you do not make it easy for them to gather it on the ground. Make sure that all feeders have a tray underneath to catch any seed.

Rats

Bird feeders are rarely to blame for attracting rats to an area. Rats are more likely to be attracted by odors from pet waste, outdoor pet food bowls, inadequate garbage containers, compost bins, barbecue grills, vegetable garden waste, or unharvested fruits and nuts.

Good practices to avoid feeding rats are very similar to the advice for chipmunks. Keep rats off the feeders the same way as squirrels, and keep food off the ground. Do not use filler-filled "wild bird mixes" that will be scratched onto the ground. Use high-quality blends that will all be eaten at the feeder or taken elsewhere and consumed. Offer only foods that will not spill or drop to the ground in any significant amount, such as suet cakes and suet cylinders, seed and nut cylinders, mealworms, and fruit—all in a squirrel-proof setup. If food spills onto the ground, rake it up. Store all food in tightly sealed metal or heavy chew-proof plastic containers.

In addition, keep all household and kitchen trash in closed metal containers, keep all dog droppings cleaned up, feed pets indoors, clean barbecue grills after each use, and rake up all nuts and fruits that fall from trees and bushes.

Black bears

Black bears have become quite numerous in the last 30 years, and it is estimated that there are now 300,000 in 40 U.S. states and that many again in Canada. Naturally shy of humans, they usually live separate lives even when their habitat is close to civilization.

It is possible to have bears living nearby and never see one in your yard. However, that could change if the bears experience a lack of natural food, a population increase or they discover a buffet provided by one of your neighbors. Bears know an easy meal when they see one, and in addition to unsecured garbage, greasy barbecue grills, fruit trees, and outdoor pet food bowls, bird feeders are an easy target.

If bears live close to you, you have several choices:

1. Remove all bird feeders when the bears are active, which in many areas means no bird feeders between April 1 and November 30. Check with local wildlife officials to determine when black bears are active in your region. All laws pertaining to bears must be respected. It is illegal to feed bears in some areas. If a bear grows accustomed to human offerings, wildlife officials may need to kill it, so it does the bears no favors to feed them, intentionally or unintentionally. Unfortunately, the saying "A fed bear is a dead bear" is true.

2. If you feed birds during active bear season, bring in your feeders every night, leaving no food on the ground. Also make sure that you bring in all pet food and that your outdoor grills are clean. This works very well in most yards because bears are nocturnal—but if bears visit during the day, you will probably have to remove your feeders.

3. Do as the beekeepers do. Bears have a sweet tooth and can destroy many hives in just one night. Many wildlife agencies recommend electric fences to safeguard beehives. Such electric fences would also work for bird feeding stations. An online search for "electric fences for bee hives" will take you to resources

that offer advice and a few commercial sites that sell electric fences. It is important to read and follow all instructions for the safe and proper use of this equipment.

4. Hang bird feeders out of the reach of bears, and catch any seed that may scatter by adding large trays under the feeders. The bottom of a feeder needs to be at least 10 feet above the ground. Various pulley systems or extremely strong poles can keep the feeders high enough. Such a system can cost several hundred dollars and use 600 pounds of concrete to stabilize the pole.

Bears can wreck havoc with bird feeders and poles. If bears are in your area, follow the four strategies in the text and/ or contact state wildlife officials for advice.

Deer

Deer are similar to squirrels in the sense that some people like to feed them and others don't. White-tailed and mule deer do quite fine in the wild, but sometimes find our feeders quite to their liking.

I do not recommend feeding corn or hay to deer in the winter; it does not duplicate the natural foods they eat in the wild, and it can endanger their health. The Maine Department of Inland Fisheries and Wildlife warns that because deer stomachs develop a very specific stomach microfauna in the winter, offering them anything but their normal winter diet of woody browse can actually lead to illness or even starvation. Just because deer will accept food from humans in winter does not mean that it is an appropriate diet.

Feeding deer brings them too close to the dangers of roads and domestic dogs, and can encourage disease and a loss of their fear of people. If you want to help deer in a blizzard, the best thing you can do is cut down aspens or maples so the deer can munch on the branches.

There are many foods available for deer, including compacted blocks and loose food in bags. Some of these might be safe to feed in certain situations and at certain times of year. It is best to check local and state regulations governing the feeding of deer at different seasons. New York, for instance, legally prohibits feeding deer, hoping in that way to limit the spread of chronic wasting disease.

Keeping deer out of bird feeders

There are several strategies to keep deer from eating bird seed from feeders.

1. Height. Deer can reach up to about 6 feet, so hanging your feeders higher is one way to solve the problem. Pole systems like the Advanced Pole System at Wild Birds Unlimited allow extra poles to be added to reach the necessary height. Another option: You can use a hanging plant pulley system to put your feeders up high, then lower them for filling.

2. Timing. Deer are mostly nocturnal, so bring the feeders in at night.

3. Fences. Use the same type of fence that keeps deer out of your garden.

4. Repellents. There are all kinds of repellents on the market to keep deer out of your yard and garden. You can find liquids and powders that repel with scent, taste, or both. The scent is often putrid eggs, which resembles that of dead animals, and the taste repellent is often a form of hot pepper or capsaicin. Blood meal is a common ingredient. Some of these work fairly well and are worth a try, especially since fences can be expensive and unsightly.

5. Motion-activated sprayers. These are a really good idea when the temperature is above freezing. When the device detects a deer, it shoots an intense spray of water and makes noises to scare it away. If you use one of these, your feeders don't have to be on high poles. They also work against cats, rabbits, geese, and even Great Blue Herons at your garden pond.

Too many blackbirds, European Starlings, Rock Pigeons, House Sparrows

I can find something interesting to observe in any bird that visits my feeders. I actually find it really interesting to watch European Starlings and House Sparrows feed and interact at the feeders—for about 10 minutes. Then it's time for Northern Cardinals and chickadees! While everyone has their opinion, I will call these birds "nuisance" birds, as that is what many hobbyists consider them.

Fortunately, there are ways to design your bird feeding station to favor certain birds and discourage others. I say "favor" because most solutions have shades of gray, and when it comes to unwanted birds at the feeder, words like "decrease," "discourage," and "encourage" are more accurate than "control," "solve," or "eliminate."

There are several strategies to avoid feeding certain birds.

1. Weight

2. Size

3. Feeder choice

4. Food choices

5. Feeder placement

6. Give them their own feeder

The Eliminator from Wild Birds Unlimited has settings that allow larger and/or several birds to feed such as this Red-bellied Woodpecker and Carolina Chickadee. Or, you can set it so that larger birds close down the seed ports.

1. Weight

The squirrel-proof feeders that shut down the food source when a fat squirrel lands on it also work to keep large birds out. Usually there is a setting on the feeder that allows smaller songbirds up to Northern Cardinal size and keeps out Mourning Doves, European Starlings, Rock Pigeons, and other larger birds. It might take some experimentation to get the right setting, and you might choose a setting that allows one starling but not two, which might be just fine as then you could also have at least two or three cardinals on the perch at the same time.

This feeder feeds woodpeckers up to Red-bellied Woodpecker size, but European Starlings cannot reach the food.

2. Size

There are several ways to keep large burds out by size.

Mesh cages

The same cages used to keep out squirrels will keep out large nuisance birds. Unfortunately, 1½-inch mesh will also prevent Northern Cardinals, Red-bellied Woodpeckers, and other pretty birds from feeding, so this becomes a feeder for small birds. A larger 2-inch mesh lets the cardinals in, but it also admits European Starlings. Some suet feeders have been carefully designed to allow Red-bellied Woodpeckers to reach the food even though they don't fit through the mesh; starlings do not fit through the mesh, either, and their head and bill are built differently from the woodpecker's, so they cannot reach the food. But oh, how they try!

Adjustable domes

When a dome or tray cover is lowered to within an inch or two of the feeder, only small birds can get in. To keep starlings from the mealworms, this dome can be lowered until only smaller birds can fly up under dome and reach the tray.

This Dinner Bell feeder from Wild Birds Unlimited has an adjustable sliding roof that can be lowered to keep out large birds.

Perch size

If you cut finch feeder perches down to ½ inch, the goldfinches can still hold on with two feet, but House Finches and House Sparrows, which are fatter, can fit only one foot onto the perch, and so cannot feed for long.

Perch above hole

Some finch feeders have the food hole below the perch. Goldfinches can hang upside down, but House Finches have difficulty.

No perch

Eliminate perches on seed tubes. Small birds land on the seed ports just fine, while larger birds can hang on to the port for only a short time and thus eat less food.

Starling-resistant suet feeders decrease the amount of food that European Starlings eat since the starlings don't like to hang upside down while woodpeckers do it with ease.

3. Feeder choice

Starling-resistant suet feeders
These suet feeders force all the birds to approach the food from beneath. Woodpeckers can easily hang on with their strong feet and tail, but European Starlings can manage for only a short while, thus eating less and giving the woodpeckers more time on the feeder.

Feeders with smaller food ports
Trays and hopper feeders can make it too easy for large numbers of House Sparrows, European Starlings, and Rock Pigeons to eat lots of food very quickly. Use only tube feeders, which have smaller food openings and fewer places to perch.

4. Food choices

Don't offer grains
Study the chart on pages 206–207. Don't offer foods such as cracked corn and millet that are favorites of House Sparrows, European Starlings, Rock Pigeons, grackles, and blackbirds. Feed sunflower seeds in the shell or, if you go no-mess with sunflower chips, offer them only in tube feeders, where it is more difficult to eat quickly and scratch food onto the ground. Sometimes it works to offer only larger, harder-shelled sunflower seed, which is harder for sparrows and starlings to open. High-quality blends that contain no millet or cracked corn can be offered in tube feeders.

Offer only safflower
Instead of sunflower seed, offer only safflower seed. Blackbirds, grackles, and starlings do not seem to like this seed and will leave it alone. As a bonus, squirrels do not like safflower, either.

Offer only nyjer in a finch feeder
At a minimum, if you have had no luck discouraging the nuisance birds, keep feeding the finches as this can be done without any problems.

Offer only pure rendered suet
European Starlings like the other ingredients in suet-blend cakes more than the suet. Offer only pure rendered suet cakes; the starlings often ignore them.

Starlings will eat cracked corn and milo on the ground and may leave your sunflower feeders alone. Only feed cracked corn in dry conditions as it might grow toxic mold when wet.

5. Feeder placement

Depending on your yard, certain areas might favor European Starlings, blackbirds, House Sparrows, and Rock Pigeons over birds that like different habitat. Move your feeders around, and see if it makes a difference whether your feeder is surrounded by open lawn or is near bushes and trees.

6. Give them their own feeder

Sometimes, you can feed the good stuff to your favored birds in one set of feeders and then feed cracked corn to the flocking pesky birds. Offer cracked corn or milo on a tray or on dry ground; it does work to at least feed these guys with food that costs less and might give the sunflower fans a better chance at your Foundational Feeders or other feeders.

Northern Mockingbirds can become very protective of "their" feeders. This mockingbird kept all other birds off this feeder even though it could not fit through the cage to eat the food.

Bird bullies

Sometimes even a really pretty bird dominates a feeder. Northern Mockingbirds do it, hummingbirds do it, Blue Jays do it. Some mockingbirds are pushy only seasonally when their hormones are telling them to be protective of their territory at all costs. Others just seem to bully other birds all the time, whether they are actually eating a lot of the seed themselves or not. It's their feeder!

Hummingbirds are well known for fighting at feeders, a behavior evolved to protect scarce flower resources. Even though our feeders have plenty of sugar-water for all, hummingbirds continue to squabble.

The best way to solve this problem is to have several feeders in different places, ideally out of sight of each other. If a feeder is being fought over in the backyard, put a second feeder in the front yard and maybe a third and fourth on each side of the house. The territorial bird can't be at all the feeders at the same time, so other birds can feed without being chased off. Besides solving the problem, you get to see more birds overall!

Hawk-safe bird feeding

A mature Cooper's Hawk perched on a feeder pole (top) and an immature Cooper's Hawk (below) with prey.

I know that hawks occasionally catch a bird that was a guest at one of my feeders, and I don't like seeing it. However, I also know that these hawks need to eat, and that their specialty is catching birds. But does it have to be "my" cardinal? As the New Jersey Audubon Society's website reminds us so well, we do not cause birds' death by offering them food and bringing them to our yards; we just make it more likely that we will witness the act of predation.

Sad but true. But why make it easy? If hawks are a problem at your feeders, you have a few choices. Stop feeding: Sometimes stopping for a few days or a few weeks is a good idea if the hawk is hanging out every day and regularly catching birds. When the feeder birds are gone, the hawk will leave.

Don't stop feeding, but follow feeder placement guidelines: Hawks can cause window strikes, as they seem to learn that they can fly past a feeder and startle the birds into hitting the glass hard enough to be injured or stunned. Place feeders either within 3 feet of the window or more than 10 feet from the glass. Birds close to the window will probably not hurt themselves if startled, and birds farther out usually have time to make a quick turn if they are flushed towards the building.

Provide clear views and cover: Provide perching branches to give the birds a place to assess what is going on before coming in to the feeders. The perches will sometimes be used by the hawks, too, but at least they will be very visible. You can also provide stacks of branches or a thicket where the birds can retreat and hawks cannot follow.

Appreciate the hawks: In reality, I immensely appreciate a close-up view of a wild hawk. Though the hawks that come to your feeders are specialized hunters, only a small percentage of their attempts to capture a bird are successful. The hawks that most frequently come to feeders are Cooper's Hawks and Sharp-shinned Hawks. The larger Red-tailed Hawks and smaller American Kestrels can also be seen, but less often. Any of these birds up close is a magnificent sight. Enjoy the hawks for what they are, what they accomplish, and the important role they play in nature.

Cat-safe bird feeding

Feral and other outdoor cats are one of the greatest dangers to native birds and other wildlife. American Bird Conservancy estimates that cats kill approximately 2.4 billion birds a year in the U.S. ABC sponsors a Cats Indoors program to try to reduce that number. Cats are very skilled at sneaking up on birds on the ground or at low feeders. Here are a few things you can do to decrease the likelihood of a cat killing birds at your feeders.

Keep your cat inside

And ask your neighbors to do so, too. Since neighbors don't always agree about outdoor cats and there are other feral cats, further precautions may be in order.

Feeder placement and fencing

Place feeders 10 feet from low bushes or other cover. A cat in the open has less chance than one hiding in the bushes to sneak up successfully.

Place a low fence around the feeders. The fencing should have mesh large enough for birds to fly through but small enough that cats must jump over. I would suggest a 3 x 3-inch or 4 x 4-inch mesh so that larger birds such as doves can escape, too. When a cat has to pounce by jumping over a fence, the birds on the ground have a microsecond's advantage and can fly away directly through the fence. Many varieties of garden fencing will work for this purpose.

Test deterrents

There are a few sprays, plastic spikes, and ultrasonic devices that claim to repel cats. I have had good luck with the CatStop ultrasonic device. These devices might be effective for you, and they are worth a try if you have a repeat offender.

Try motion-activated sprayers

These work on cats as well as on deer; cats really hate to get sprayed with water, and if it happens to them often enough, they might just leave your feeder birds and garden alone. Some sprayers need to be attached to a garden hose, while others come with their own water tank. The angle of spray can usually be adjusted from very narrow to 360°. These can only be used in above-freezing conditions.

Keep your cats indoor and your feeders will keep them entertained.

8 Situations and Solutions

Besides unwanted birds and other animals at the feeders, there can be other difficult situations at your feeding stations and in your yard, including a lack of birds, messiness around the feeders, window strikes, woodpecker damage to your home, and orphaned or sick birds.

Additionally, bird feeders at certain locations, such as hospice care or apartment complexes, require that thoughtful consideration be given to visibility, ease of filling, and cleanliness.

At the feeders or nearby

New feeder, no birds

What's up with this? I bought a feeder and filled it with seed, but it just sat there for weeks without any customers.

That's why we call them "wild" birds. They don't always do what we want them to do, including finding a new feeder full of seed. It is quite normal for the birds to take a while to find it—sometimes a couple of days, sometimes many weeks.

If it is the first feeder in your yard and there are no neighbors feeding birds for miles around, then it is likely that yours is the first feeder the local birds have seen in their short lives. If you put up a new feeder within two feet of an active bird feeding station, there will be birds on the new one in minutes. Your situation is probably somewhere between those two scenarios. After you get the first bird on your feeder, the rest will follow.

A feeder full of seed but with no birds is a sad but hopefully temporary situation.

Fortunately, there are ways to reduce the time it takes for a new feeder to be found.

1. **Visibility of the feeder** If the feeder is hidden under your eaves or is a window feeder, it is very hard for the birds to see. A window feeder is not the best first feeder in a yard. Make sure the feeder is visible by putting it out in the open on a pole.

2. **Location of the feeder** Place it where birds are hanging out. If your feeder is near trees, bushes, vines, and hedgerows, the birds usually come out to see what it is, find a free meal, and keep returning.

3. **Visibility of the seed** Sometimes you have to offer seed on a tray first; then they will find your hopper or tube feeder. Any old board will do, or invest in a nice tray, as every bird feeding station should have a tray feeder. You'll find more details on pages 16–17 and 251–252.

4. **Slowly move the feeders closer to your home** If the spot favored by your birds is not near your home, your feeders should start out near their current hangout. Then slowly move the feeders to your preferred location. Study the instructions for incorporating the 12 Elements of a Thoughtful Bird Feeding Station starting on page 28. The birds will soon come to your feeders even if they normally hang out farther away. Recently, I was frustrated when the Mountain Chickadees I could hear nearby

were not coming to our feeders. I put No-Mess Blend in several feeders out in the ponderosa pines and junipers where they were hanging out. They found those feeders, and once they had been emptied, the chickadees quickly came in to the feeders near the house.

5. **Longer perches** Sometimes Northern Cardinals don't use tube feeders at first, so I attach extension perches made from real tree branches. If you attach 6- to 8-inch branches to several perches, the cardinals will be much more comfortable landing to feed. Once they start eating at the feeder, you can remove the branches and the birds will use the shorter perches.

Yard on steep slope

Anywhere there are hills or mountains, there will be yards with steep slopes. If you have a deck where you want the feeders, follow the recommendations on pages 293 to 295. If you don't have a deck, there are other solutions.

1. **Use really tall poles** At times, I have used poles that extend up to 15 feet to get feeders up to a second floor where there are no decks. Usually these are Purple Martin house poles that have the option to put a wooden feeder flange on top and can be lowered to fill the feeders. These need to be installed in a post-hole and secured with concrete.

2. **Use window feeders** Sometimes you just can't get a pole high enough, so install a window feeder instead. You can choose feeders with suction cups, feeders mounted on a spring-loaded tension rod, or feeders incorporated into a double-hung window.

3. **Use a wall hanger** Install a hanging arm on the outside of your house that can swing around to lock in front of your window.

New yard in subdivision with few trees

Many homes have been built in what used to be cornfields or grasslands, and there just aren't any trees other than the newly planted ones. After 10 years, there will be some great habitat for the birds, but the first few years are a bit lean. Here are some ideas.

1. **Start planting** Choose plants that are native to your region. The birds will show up.

2. **Don't offer food for birds that are not there** This may not be a good yard for suet cakes, because there are no woodpeckers—unless you are near a forest. You can attract birds that like open spaces, such as goldfinches, sparrows, doves, Dark-eyed Juncos, and American Robins.

3. **Change your offering as your habitat grows** Birds such as Northern Mockingbirds, jays, and hummingbirds like at least a bit of shrubby cover and flower gardens. From this point on, experiment with different foods and feeders to keep increasing the number of birds your station attracts.

It is common for finch feeders to have periods of inactivity. If that happens for two or three weeks, you must replace the nyjer and clean the feeder.

Seasonally low activity

Every region has times of the year when activity at the feeders is slow. These periods often come around at the same time each year, as happens in the fall in the southeastern U.S. states. You cannot change this, but you can react to it and be Seasonally Savvy (see page 36).

For instance, fall is a slow time at feeders in many areas because of all the wild food that is available. There might be millions of acorns ripe for the taking, and the jays and certain woodpeckers will be spending their time caching them for later consumption. Even so, there are some things you can do to have active feeders.

1. **Double up** Pay attention to which birds are still coming, and double up on feeders offering the foods they are eating. If the woodpeckers are not coming in, maybe the goldfinches are. Put out twice as many goldfinch feeders.

2. **Experiment with new foods on a tray**
   This is a good time to offer a small amount of many different foods. There might be resident or migratory birds in your area that will come to your feeders if they have a large offering of food choices.

3. **If nothing works, decrease the portions**
   Sometimes you just have to serve less—you do not want uneaten food lying around to spoil.

No snow or no cold weather

In regions that normally have long, cold, or snowy winters, it can happen that a stretch of a few weeks or even an entire winter is warmer or drier than normal, and the visits of the birds will decrease or stop altogether. When it is cold, birds need more calories each day to survive, so they eat more. When it warms up, they just don't need as much food. If there is little or no snow cover, natural foods are more easily accessible on the ground or in the trees. To keep birds active at your feeders during these times, just follow the same advice as for the annual periods of slow activity.

No goldfinches at feeders

Check the range map in Chapter 3 on page 202 to see if you have American Goldfinches in your area in summer. Even if you do, they might ignore your finch feeders.

Goldfinches are flocking birds that move from field to field in search of seeds they can eat on mature flowering plants or on the ground. Even if you see goldfinches at your feeders every day, you may not be seeing the same individuals; one flock spends time at your feeders, and after it departs, another entirely different flock shows up. You never know the difference, because it looks like all the same birds. In fact, though, 75 or 100 different goldfinches may visit over the course of a day.

Sometimes a few weeks go by without a flock. At this point, any goldfinches that do arrive will probably turn up their beaks at your seed because it is not fresh. They are very picky eaters and like their food to be very fresh with no sign of being spoiled. They could visit without you even knowing they were there. So, if goldfinches are not showing up at your feeders, have patience for a week or two; then throw away all the food in the feeders, clean the feeders with a 10 percent bleach solution to kill all mold, and put fresh food in them. Eventually, the finches will return and gobble up all the fresh seed in your clean feeders.

In wet seasons, shake the finch tube every time you fill it. If it seems to be getting wet or if you notice that it holds moisture in the bottom, replace it with a tube that keeps rain out more effectively and has a seed diverter with drain holes; the seed diverter should deliver all the seed to a port so that none goes uneaten. Use FeederFresh granules to help keep the seed dry.

Messy under feeder

Old school bird feeding always has a big mess under the feeders. (Not sure what old school bird feeding is? See page 27.) The empty shells of straight sunflower seeds and millet will make a mess. "Wild bird mixes" with fillers that get scratched onto the ground will definitely make a mess. Worse, these seeds will eventually spoil and create a health hazard for birds and humans.

Tidy dining solutions
New school bird feeding uses a combination of strategies to create a tidy bird feeding area. It starts with no-mess or less-mess foods that include no-mess seed blends, bird food cylinders, suet blend cakes and cylinders, mealworms, Bark Butter, and other foods that have no shells and leave no mess behind. No-mess blends are not scattered as much as others, since birds can find their preferred food easily.

When you combine a good food choice with feeders that do not easily let food fall to the ground, the area below your feeders can remain very tidy. Some hopper feeders come with a large tray to catch food and to serve as another feeding level.

Messy on deck

There are two kinds of messes on decks: bird food shells and bird droppings. Tidy dining solutions (below) will mostly eliminate the first problem but you will always have to deal with a few droppings. The best solution is to use pole and hanging systems that hang or place the feeders away from your deck and deck railing so that spilled seeds, seed shells and droppings land on the ground instead of your deck.

Birds at deck feeders usually fly away and defecate in your yard, but they occasionally sit on the deck railing or fly over to do a little "whitewashing." As needed, I spray off the railings and floor boards, and the deck is good to go. During long winters with lots of snow and freezing temperatures, there is usually a day or two above freezing. I take advantage of the thaw to bring out the hose

One tidy dining solution is to put a large tray below the feeder. On tube feeders (right), attach a large tray to catch any food spilled out of the port holes.

A decal from Droll Yankees (top) looks like a spider web, which birds naturally avoid. Window Alert produces nature image cut-outs that do not block your view but have an ultraviolet coating that is visible to birds. American Bird Conservancy has developed a line of 3-inch foggy tape that can be applied to windows in strips or blocks and Whispering Windows makes bird and nature decals to break up the reflection.

Reflective mylar ribbons attached at the top of a wndow frame will help prevent bird strikes.

and scrub brush.

I have two scrub brushes, one marked for the birdbath and one marked for the feeders and deck, and I never switch their use. The goal is to keep the birdbath water as fresh as possible. Blast out the bath water and any droppings with your hose, then finish the cleaning with your birdbath brush. Not perfectly sterile, but better than cleaning out the bath with the same brush you just used to clean droppings off your deck and feeders. At least every 3 months, soak both brushes in a 10 percent bleach solution to sterilize them.

Window strikes

Birds coming and going to your feeders rarely fly into windows. They hit the windows mostly when they are panicked or during territorial chases. Occasionally, a local or migrating bird will not recognize a window and mistake the reflection of the sky or yard for safe passage. As discussed on page 68, your feeders should be either within 3 feet of the window or more than 10 feet away to decrease window strikes. Even if your feeders are correctly placed, you may need to help the birds by putting something on your window to decrease the reflection. Go to abcbirds.org for a detailed discussion of solutions.

1. **Put window feeders on the window** This messes up the reflection and shows birds that they cannot fly any farther.

2. **Sun catchers** Put stained-glass and prism reflectors on the inside of the window to make the window look unsafe to fly through.

3. **Hang a loose screen or netting a few inches from the window** Birds that hit this screen bounce right off uninjured.

4. **Use mylar ribbons** You can put six streaming bands of mylar ribbon on each window, and they move with the wind, reflecting sunlight. Also check out Bird Crash Preventer that places monofilament lines in front of the window.

5. **Stick decals to the windows' exterior surfaces** These clever designs are usually very effective. Follow the instructions carefully to space the decals correctly.

6. **Try sprays** WindowAlert provides UV liquid sprays that add UV protection to the entire window.

7. **Try films** CollidEscape one-way film is applied to the window making the window visible to the birds without blocking the view from inside.

Fighting reflection in window

Hormones do crazy things to birds, and one thing they inspire is territorial fighting. (Hmm, what other species does that?) In the spring, you will see birds fighting their own reflection in house windows and car mirrors, apparently believing that they are disputing territory with a rival. Many species do this, including Northern Cardinals, bluebirds, and American Robins.

If one window is getting most of the action, you can try to solve the problem by removing or reducing the reflection with one of the methods suggested for avoiding window strikes. I have covered an entire window with soap film, which is easily washed off once the bird's hormones are no longer raging.

If a bird is doing battle at every window in your house, the most practical solution may be to just be patient for a week or two and wait out the hormone surge.

Woodpecker damage

Generally, woodpeckers peck at buildings for one of three reasons: to attract a mate or proclaim territory, to seek insects or other food, or to create a nest cavity. Buildings sided with grooved plywood, tongue-in-groove cedar, or shakes, and painted or stained in earth tones, have the most problems. If you have cedar siding, it is a good idea to seal up all the vertical grooves to prevent insect intrusions.

Clapboards and non-wood siding suffer the least woodpecker damage, as do houses painted in bright colors.

Woodpecker damage can be extensive and expensive to fix. It is a violation of federal law to kill these birds, so the only way to respond is to try one of the deterrents below. Be sure to begin as soon as you first notice woodpecker activity.

Cedar-sided homes are perhaps the most susceptible to woodpecker damage.

Feed the woodpeckers

If they are after food, give them a snack of suet blend cakes, or smear Bark Butter on a nearby tree. Make sure they have other drumming trees. Leave dead trees up if they do not pose a safety risk.

Put up a nesting box

If woodpeckers are excavating a nesting hole in your home, put a nesting box in a nearby tree and hope they move into it.

Exclude them

Hang a roll of screen or hardware cloth over the affected area and for some distance all around it. Tack it down in a way they cannot go behind it and still do damage or get caught.

Scare the woodpecker

Garden hose This might work if you can sneak up on the bird.

Attack Spider My favorite woodpecker-scare device is the Birds-Away Attack Spider. This crazy device actually works. When a woodpecker pecks on the house, this animated spider drops 18 inches while making an awful noise and then crawls back up the string to be ready for the next time.

Mylar ribbons These reflect light and blow in the wind, and are one of the most effective ways to prevent woodpecker damage and window strikes.

Balloons, rubber snakes, owl silhouettes These items and others might be worth a try, but are not usually very effective.

After the above damage was repaired, the Attack Spider actually scared the woodpeckers away and no further damage was done.

Be safe!
If the damaged area is high up, I recommend playing it safe and hiring a professional who is used to working on tall ladders—try a handyman, gutter cleaner, or pest control specialist.

Plastic woodpeckers

Recently, I heard about a very large home in a deep woods that had a problem with woodpeckers pecking on 44 architectural columns, which were actually covered in a stiff foam substance. The woodpeckers seemed to enjoy pecking large holes in the foam and repairs were expensive. The home owner hung a plastic woodpecker on 40 of the columns and solved the problem—but only on the columns with a woodpecker. They quickly bought four more woodpeckers and the damage stopped.

Bad-tasting sprays and paints

Bad-tasting spray Ropel is a vile-tasting substance that can be sprayed on. Absent any data about the results, I always say that this is likely to work 50 percent of the time at best.

Bad-tasting paint A vile-tasting paint named BeakGuard from Stuc-O-Flex International, Inc. is distributed at stucoflex.com. It is sold by the gallon and is painted onto surfaces that need protecting. It claims a 70-percent success rate. I like the recommended antidote if you accidentally get some in your mouth: chocolate! But seriously, use all precautions to avoid needing the chocolate.

Control carpenter bees

Woodpeckers will find the holes carpenter bees have dug into weathered wood. It's easy pickings for the woodpecker to peck a hole about the width of your finger to get to the larvae or overwintering adults. If you control the bees, you control the damage.

Finding an orphaned bird

Caring for an orphaned or injured bird and should be left to people who know how to do it right. Follow these steps to decide what to do, or download instructions from the National Wildlife Rehabilitators Association or the Cornell Lab of Ornithology to determine your next step.

Step 1: To rescue or not?

Most baby birds do not need rescuing. Fledglings might be on the ground because they are learning to fly. By "rescuing" them, you interfere with the course of nature.

Many baby birds, such as Blue Jays and American Robins, leave the nests when they are still clumsy and unable to take care of themselves. Keep yourself out of view, and watch for at least two or three hours to see whether a parent returns. If neither adult comes back, you might have found an orphaned bird.

Step 2: What's next?

If the bird is not in danger from predators, leave it on the ground. If you can find the nest, you can return the bird to it. Birds cannot detect the scent of humans, so the parents will not reject the baby bird if you touch it. Many mammals, however, can pick up your scent, which makes it easier for cats, raccoons, and other predators to find the young bird by following your scent.

Step 3: Call a wildlife rehabilitator

If you are pretty sure you have found an orphaned bird, call a professional wildlife rehabilitator. You are prohibited by federal law from having any wild bird—even an orphan—in your possession unless you are a licensed rehabilitator. The National Wildlife Rehabilitators Association, The Humane Society of the United States, and other sources such as your state department of natural resources have good websites that can help you find a licensed wildlife rehabilitator near you.

Step 4: While you wait...

If you must care temporarily for an orphaned bird, it's important to keep it indoors and warm in a small box or enclosure with ventilation holes.

Create a nest-like environment so the bird can nuzzle next to something soft and rest its head. Use paper towels or a soft cloth. Do not use grass clippings, which could be damp and cold. Do not attempt to feed the bird unless advised to do so by a professional rehabilitator.

National Wildlife Rehabilitators Association
www.nwrawildlife.org
General information and links to rehabilitators.

Cornell Lab of Ornithology
www.birds.cornell.edu/AllAboutBirds/faq/master_folder/attracting/challenges/orphaned
Information about orphaned birds.

Humane Society of the United States
www.humanesociety.org/animals/resources/tips/find-a-wildlife-rehabilitator

Searching online
Your state or provincial department of natural resources usually has a list of licensed rehabilitators, most likely available online at the department website. You can also use a search term such as "wildlife rehabilitator" in your state.

Finding an injured bird

A bird that has hit a window may recover quickly or, if it has gone into shock, take a few hours. Prop it up with a soft towel in a dark, aerated box. Do not try to give it any food or water. Check on it every 30 minutes or so.

If it is ready to fly, release it near trees or bushes so it does not have far to go. If it is not recovering, call a local licensed wildlife rehabilitator for help; it is illegal to possess or attempt to rehabilitate wild birds without a license. See the resources listed on page 341.

Finding a sick bird

A sick bird usually behaves differently from the other birds. It might be very slow, perch in one place, puff up even when it is not cold, or have weepy, crusty eyes. It may not fly when approached. Here is advice from the Cornell Lab of Ornithology's FeederWatch website (www.feeder-watch.org):

Only veterinarians or federally licensed wildlife rehabilitators can legally treat wild birds. If you see a bird that appears to be compromised in some way, perhaps due to sickness or injury, do not try to care for the bird yourself. It is illegal for you to possess most wild birds unless you are under the direction of someone licensed for their care.

If a sick bird comes to your feeder, minimize the risk of infecting other birds by cleaning your feeder area thoroughly. If you see several sick birds, take down all your feeders for at least a week to give the birds a chance to disperse. Remember that prevention is the key to avoiding the spread of disease. Regularly clean your feeders even when there are no signs of disease.

Weather situations

Every region and season is different in regards to weather. However, we do know that Seattle has lots of rain, Duluth has lots of snow, Houston has lots of humidity, and Phoenix is blazing hot. There are some solutions and strategies to deal with these.

Lots of rain?

To keep food from getting too wet and clumping or even spoiling, put all tube and finch feeders under a weather guard at least 12 inches in diameter. Even better, use a squirrel-proof dome 15 inches or wider to protect from angled rain. Many tray and hopper feeders can also be protected by a roof or dome. Rain will still be blown into the feeder, so make sure that the feeder and tray have good drainage.

When using no-mess blends in rainy weather, provide one day's supply at a time. Without shells, the starch in the seeds will become gummy, and clumped seeds will be unable to drop to the seed ports; the food will be hard for the birds to get to and difficult for you to clean out. Use larger sunflower kernels rather than fine chips, which quickly clump. Peanuts can spoil rapidly and grow toxic mold, so be especially careful to keep peanuts and blends with peanuts fresh. You can also use FeederFresh granules to absorb moisture.

Lots of humidity

The same advice of setting out only small quantities at a time holds in areas with extreme humidity, which will also cause fine sunflower chips to clump. It is also important to use feeders designed to provide ventilation to the seed chamber. For instance, the Wild Birds Unlimited Eliminator squirrel-proof feeder has vents through which humidity and warm air can escape, while fresh air enters through the seed ports.

Even with good ventilation, it is still wise to reduce the amount of food offered at any one time and to add FeederFresh to absorb moisture.

Lots of snow and freezing rain

Whenever it snows, I often hear, "I wish you could fill my feeder for me!" If you feed birds in a cold climate, your number one consideration is to place the feeders where you can easily get to them even through many feet of snow. Another goal is for the feeders to protect the food from snow, so overhanging roofs and domes are important in snowy areas. Sideways-blowing snow will get into the feeders, and you may just have to clean them out the morning after the blizzard.

I want to be able to fill my feeders while wearing gloves. When you buy a feeder, remember that you may be using it when it is −20°F. If you have to take a feeder apart to fill it, all that snow will just be waiting to swallow up any parts your gloved hands drop.

Some feeders handle freezing rain well, but others have to be brought inside to thaw out.

Lots of wind

An occasional big wind can empty feeders but is not a big deal. This is a bigger problem in areas with constant strong winds. For example, the wind

A high quality tube feeder usually has at least one or two ports open after a snow storm. Also, a well-designed top can be easily removed with gloves.

will blow seed right out of a wooden hopper with openings on both sides, so a central seed diverter is the first thing to look for when you are buying a feeder like that. If the winds are very strong, close off one of the hopper sides so that only the down-wind feeding area remains accessible. The same can be done with seed tube feeders: closing half of the holes with tape will slow down the loss of wind-blown seed. Trays with shallow sides should be used in windy areas only for heavier foods like peanuts or suet nuggets.

Really hot temperatures

Be sure to offer fresh water, which will attract many species to your yard and then to your feeders. Provide a mister for your hummingbirds. Have shady spots beneath a variety of plants. Use only no-melt suet dough products. Use feeders with good ventilation. Protect the food from humidity and thunderstorms.

Hobbyists in special living situations

For the elderly in their own homes

Watching birds at the feeders can be a great source of joy for elderly people . Everything should be done to make it easy to store the food, fill the feeders, and watch the birds from the house. If seed is purchased in bags heavier than 20 pounds, make sure it can be transferred to smaller containers for carrying to the feeders. To avoid meal moth infestations, don't keep bird food in the house. Buy only as much as will be used up quickly.

The feeders should be within 3 feet of the window for easy viewing; they should be easy to walk to and reach so that they can be conveniently filled even in rainy or snowy weather. The feeders should be easy to open, with no loose parts to remove. The lids should be on hinges or attached to the feeders with wires.

Bird food cylinders are an especially good choice. The small cylinders feed great numbers of birds over an extended time, and they can easily be kept in the refrigerator or freezer. They are easy to carry and to place on the feeders.

At retirement centers

Bird feeding offers the same benefits to the elderly living in retirement or nursing homes—except that the joy might be even greater, because watching the birds can bring deep joy to someone who has lost aspects of their own freedoms due to health issues.

Elderly nursing home residents may not be able to attend to the feeders themselves, so the goal is to make it easy for the staff. A foundational feeder that holds enough food for many days is an excellent choice; otherwise, the feeders will likely stay empty when the staff is busy with other duties. This foundational feeder can be a large hopper or a large bird food cylinder; consider a timed-release feeder that can provide food for weeks without refilling. Squirrel-proof it to the desires of the resident and/or staff as they might actually enjoy feeding the squirrels.

Stress centers

I have been involved for many years in delivering bird seed to a local stress and rehabilitation center. This is a tough time in the residents' lives, when they are very focused on their own progress, and it is a great joy and diversion for them to look out the windows at the beauty and antics of wild birds. It can be very inspiring to watch the birds surviving in a tough world with all the odds against them.

It is also a benefit for the residents to have the job of filling the feeders, which gives them a reason to go outside. And to fill the hours, it can be fun to learn to identify birds and make a list of the species visiting the feeders.

Hospice care

Hospice care attends not only to the patient's illness and pain, but also to the spiritual and emotional needs of the patient and the family. Many relatives of hospice patients have said their loved one asked for a bird feeding station as part of their hospice environment. At that difficult time, watching the birds at the feeders provided a special connection to nature for the patient. It also provides a distraction and conversation topic different from the usual more serious discussions. Watching the birds helped relax all visitors as they spent time with the patient. However grand or small a bird feeding station you might find room for, it is a welcome addition to the hospice stay.

During vacation or at vacation homes

When the feeders go empty, it is not so much a problem for the birds as for the hobbyist. The birds are OK, as they know how to survive by using natural sources of food. However, when you come home, it might take a while for the birds to discover that you refilled the feeders. In the winter, it is also possible that a deadly blizzard or ice storm blew in while you were gone—and that is the one time that your feeders really can help the birds.

The best thing is to have a supply of food that will last while you are away. Large hoppers can hold food for a week or so; longer periods call for a different strategy. I use two that work well.

1. I use a timed-release feeder that holds about 8 pounds of bird food blend

I can set how many seconds of food drop, up to eight times a day. So I set it to drop out four seconds of food in the early morning and four seconds in the early afternoon. That's about 8 ounces per day or ½ pound, so 8 pounds of food lasts 16 days. Birds check it out all day long even when empty. When I return from vacation, I fill up all my feeders, and the bird feeding station is back in business very quickly.

2. At the same time, I put out large bird food cylinders that last 10 to 14 days.

Whichever method you use, be sure to offer all the major food groups, including fats, nuts, and food for goldfinches. In the wet season, I add a bit of FeederFresh to absorb moisture.

The same strategies you use at home can also work at your vacation home, so you can watch the birds at your feeders the day you arrive.

Apartments and condominiums

First, you have to follow the rules of your residence association. If bird feeding is allowed, it is wise to keep it as compact as possible so as not to intrude into other residents' space. Also be sure that your feeders don't create a mess, or other residents and the maintenance crew will complain. The poles should be in flower beds or in a place that is easy to mow around. Most important of all, don't create a situation where pest animals visit; the other residents might understandably unite to outlaw bird feeding.

If you feed on a balcony, it is important that no mess hits the floors below. Use no-mess foods in small tube feeders, with trays to keep food from falling to the ground. Bark Butter, Bark Butter Bits, and suet blend cakes are good choices because they do not make any messes below and the birds usually grab a bite or nugget and fly away. Peanut feeders should hold the peanuts securely until the bird pulls them out. Bird food cylinders are a good choice to attract a wide variety of birds; put the cylinder in a feeder with a tray to catch any food knocked off. Mealworms work well for mess-free feeding on balconies and small patios. Unfortunately, a finch feeder with nyjer is messy for a balcony, so finches may need to be fed sunflower chips instead. Drip-free nectar feeders are fabulous on balconies, as they don't make any mess at all.

Buying and storing bird food 9

Reasons to buy bird food in a specialty shop

A S THE FOUNDER of what has become the largest franchise system of specialty bird feeding stores, I am a bit biased about where you should buy your supplies. But I believe that people will find greater joy in their hobby if they have a store partner with a serious stake in the same hobby. I always enjoy my hobbies more when I buy my products from a store that has sales associates as passionate as I am.

In our Wild Birds Unlimited stores our mission is, "We Bring People and Nature Together….and We Do It with Excellence!" Our goal is to have fabulous products on the shelves and to provide a high-energy customer experience in the store and when our products are used at home. The most important measure of success is our customers' opinion.

. . . .

The specialty store difference

Freshness
Our distribution system ensures freshness. We restock our bird food every week or two in freshly blended batches, and it never sits for long periods in a warehouse.

Locally specific blends
Each franchise store owner/manager decides which blends will work best in their area, seasonally and year-round.

Variety of food
Where else can you buy, in one trip, the very best blends and individual seeds, bird food cylinders, mealworms, suet cakes, and Bark Butter—and find the best bird feeders and pole systems when you need them?

Variety of feeders
We carefully select the products we carry based on how well they actually work, most of them with lifetime guarantees.

Competitive prices
Believe it or not, the prices in specialty bird feeding shops are very competitive if you compare the same quality foods on a price per pound basis.

Pole systems that put feeders where you want them
These systems can also turn squirrel-tolerant and squirrel-bait feeders into squirrel-proof versions.

Bird and bird feeding advice
We know which birds are active at the feeders today, and can help you choose the feeders and foods that will work in your yard.

Customer service
We are there to help you with your purchase decision or just talk about the birds. What other retailer carries your bags of bird seed out to your car?

Customer experience
From the moment you arrive to when your car is filled with your purchase, your experience will be special.

A gathering of like-minded hobbyists
In our specialty store, you will meet and share bird feeding experiences with other folks enjoying the hobby.

In a big box store, some products are good quality, some are poor quality. How do you know which is which and whether a product will serve your needs?

Shop like a pro at any store

Since most bird food is not purchased in a specialty store, here is advice on how to be a very savvy buyer when shopping at a "big box" retail outlet or anywhere else. In non-specialty stores, you can find some decent seed blends, but most of the tonnage sold is very poor quality. In most big-box stores, the majority of seed mixes are trying to hit a very low price point and are not intended to be anything other than cheap. These mixes are not intended to help you enjoy the birds more or to give you a good value, because most of the seed is wasted or attracts birds you don't want to attract.

You will always have a better experience when you buy seed that the desired birds actually eat, and you will get the most for your dollar when all the food is eaten instead of scratched onto the ground. The most expensive bird food is the bird food you waste.

Think about the 12 Elements of a Thoughtful Bird Feeding Station (see page 28) and the food recommended for your foundational feeder. The main foods in a foundational feeder blend should be various combinations of oil sunflower, sunflower chips, white millet, hulled millet, and peanuts. Oil Sunflower is the most attractive seed, so the presence or absence of millet and peanuts influences the type of birds the blend will attract. Ingredients such as striped sunflower, safflower, fruit, and calcium can also be added.

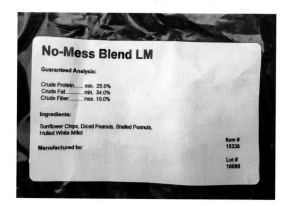

No-Mess Blend LM

Guaranteed Analysis:

Crude Protein...... min. 25.0%
Crude Fat............ min. 34.0%
Crude Fiber......... max. 10.0%

Ingredients:

Sunflower Chips, Diced Peanuts, Shelled Peanuts,
Hulled White Millet

Manufactured by:

Item #
15336

Lot #
16090

Reading labels

Many bird food bags have pictures of Northern Cardinals, chickadees, and finches, and labels that tell you about all the beautiful birds attracted to the contents. Unfortunately, there is often very little food inside the bag for Northern Cardinals, chickadees, or finches—or for most of the other birds you want to attract.

The ingredients are always listed in descending order by weight. If milo is listed first, it is the majority ingredient. If sunflower is listed last, there is very little in the mix.

Remember this as you read labels: A mix that claims to attract all the sunflower-eating birds might contain only 1 percent sunflower.

When comparing prices, also note the weight of the bag. Many bags are actually 17 pounds instead of 20, so you will need to do some math to compare per-pound prices. The good blends in larger stores are often available only in 7- or 8-pound bags. Those small bags are usually much more expensive per pound than the 20-pound bags at a specialty store.

Locally selected vs. regional blends

There is a difference in blends that claim to be regional blends. In my 300-store Wild Birds Unlimited system, the blends are locally selected by each store manager based on their knowledge of the local birds, including residents, migrants, and seasonal residents. In contrast, bird seed blends named "Northeast" or "Southwest" by national suppliers cannot be tailored to the specific birds of a given city; those multi-state regions are just too big for "regional" to have any meaning. Even worse, one company that promotes its regional blends lists the same ingredients in the same order for all of its regions. Buyer beware!

Fragrances

Songbirds don't find their food by smelling it; they find it by sight. If a bag of bird food has a strong fruity fragrance, that fragrance was added to fool you into thinking that this food is superior because it has fruit of some sort in it. I have seen decent blends that actually had real fruit but still added a fruity fragrance for no reason. I would not buy any food with fragrance. I personally would not like to eat perfume, so why would the birds? Bird food should have the good smell of seeds, peanuts, and other natural ingredients, not cheap perfume.

How to read labels on bird food bags

Here are some representative wild bird mixes, their ingredients and their claims. When you learn to read the labels, you are prepared to buy the right food at any store you shop.

• •

Poor-quality mixes

The very worst mixes usually make no claims at all, but if the manufacturer adds even a few sunflowers, the label might grandiosely state "For most wild birds." Many poor-quality seed mixes have names such as Outdoor Bird Mix, All-Purpose Seed Mix, or Premium Wild Bird Feed. These names have no connection to quality.

Sometimes manufacturers will offer a hint that they have included cheap fillers, in labels reading something like Value Blend Select, Best Buy, or Economy Mix. These are generally very inexpensive, but most of the ingredients will end up on the ground uneaten, or will be eaten only by the European Starlings, House Sparrows, and Rock Pigeons they attract.

(less than the calcium carbonate), and I estimate the white millet, which will feed juncos and other sparrows, at about 15%. A few cardinals, jays, sparrows, and blackbirds will eat cracked corn, but much of it will be scratched to the ground with the milo, where it may get dangerously moldy in wet or humid conditions. The calcium carbonate is a good addition, but because it is applied to the shells of the seeds, sunflower and millet-eating birds—which remove the shells—won't get to consume much of it.

Good foundational feeder blend? Not even close. Not a good mix for any purpose.

Sample poor-quality mix 2

Ingredients Milo, white proso millet, wheat, sunflower seed, calcium carbonate

My analysis With milo listed first and in a truly large quantity, this is a very poor mix. A quick look shows very little millet or sunflower. The wheat will be entirely ignored. Most of this mix will be scratched to the ground as birds seek out the

Sample poor-quality mix 1

Ingredients Milo, cracked corn, white millet, calcium carbonate, sunflower seed

My analysis Sunflower seed is about 1% of the total

tiny amounts of sunflower and millet. Again, the calcium carbonate is a nice addition, but will not be easily consumed.

Good foundational feeder blend? Not even close. Not a good mix for any purpose.

Medium-quality mixes

Sample medium-quality mix

Ingredients Millet, sunflower, cracked corn, milo, peanuts, safflower, calcium carbonate, wheat, artificial cherry flavor

My analysis This counts as a medium-quality blend because its majority ingredient is millet, with a decent percentage of sunflowers and a bit of safflower and peanuts. Less milo and wheat are used as fillers than in the poor-quality mixes. This mix will work better in hopper feeders than the poor-quality mixes, but the cracked corn, milo, and wheat will mostly be scratched onto the ground. The strong artificial cherry flavor is a mysterious addition. It has no benefit at all, and the smell actually gagged me when I opened the bag.

Good foundational feeder blend? No, because most of the seeds are millet, cracked corn, milo, and wheat. It might be all right for feeding on a tray, where the birds can pick out the seeds they prefer, but even then, 40 to 50% could go to waste.

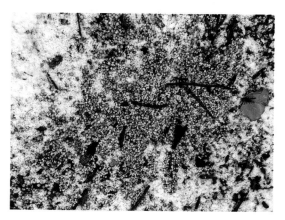

Both of the above mixes will go mostly untouched or be scratched out onto the ground. Once on the ground, if not eaten by doves, pigeons, or rodents, seeds can get dangerously moldy.

Excellent-quality blends

I will share what I consider examples of the very best seed blends by looking at the Wild Birds Unlimited blends. They are formulated for precise purposes, for example, to serve as a ground-feeding blend or a foundational blend. There is no such thing here as good, better, or best; each blend is excellent for its intended purpose. The price of each is determined by its ingredients. When shopping for blends from any manufacturer, use the following as examples of what to look for.

Excellent-quality foundational feeder blend with shells

Brand name Wild Birds Unlimited Choice Blend

Ingredients Oil sunflower, medium sunflower chips, shelled peanuts, safflower, striped sunflower

My analysis This blend has only the good stuff, with a high proportion of sunflowers for the sunflower-loving birds. The peanuts add protein and fats to the diet of chickadees, titmice, and jays, and also attract woodpeckers and other peanut-lovers. The safflower and striped sunflower increase the blend's appeal to birds such as Blue Jays and titmice, and adds variety to the diets of sunflower-loving birds.

Good foundational feeder blend? Yes. This is a great blend for tube feeders and hoppers of all types.

Excellent-quality ground-feeding birds blend

Brand name Wild Birds Unlimited Select Blend

Ingredients White millet, oil sunflower, cracked corn

My analysis White millet is the favorite seed of ground-feeding birds. The oil sunflower and cracked corn takes care of the Northern Cardinals and other birds that like those seeds and also like to feed on or near the ground. This blend has no milo, wheat, or other grain fillers to be wasted. The cracked corn percentage is acceptable low. There are no added vitamins or minerals, as they are unnecessary.

Good foundational feeder blend No. It is intended for feeding on the ground or on a low tray, in dry conditions.

A high quality ground-feeding blend will have a small amount of cracked corn and sunflower and a majority of white millet. It should be offered in a low tray feeder or on dry ground.

Excellent-quality foundational feeder blends with no mess

Brand name Wild Birds Unlimited No-Mess Blend LM

Ingredients Medium sunflower chips, diced shelled peanuts, shelled peanuts, hulled white millet

My analysis This low-millet (LM) no-mess blend also has only the good stuff, and none of the seeds have shells. If a blend's label lists millet but does not say "hulled white millet," then it is not 100 percent no-mess.

Good foundational feeder blend? Yes. And no mess!

Brand name Wild Birds Unlimited No-Mess Blend NM

Ingredients Medium sunflower chips, chopped tree nuts, shelled peanuts

My analysis This excellent no-mess blend is mostly sunflower chips, with a heavy proportion of tree

nuts and peanuts. The NM means "no millet." Even without hulled millet, this blend will feed millet-eating birds, because they will eat smaller sunflower chips.

Good foundational feeder blend? Yes. And no mess!

Brand name Wild Birds Unlimited No-Mess Blend Plus

Ingredients Medium sunflower chips, shelled peanuts, chopped tree nuts, Bark Butter Bits, cherries, cranberries, calcium carbonate

My analysis This "Plus" blend has bonus ingredients in addition to sunflower chips, tree nuts, and peanuts. It also has Bark Butter Bits to add extra fat and to attract woodpeckers and includes two types of real dried fruit to attract fruit-eaters. The calcium carbonate is attached to the foods, not to the shells, and thus will be consumed. There are no other added vitamins or minerals, as they are unnecessary. Definitely no added fragrance!

Good foundational feeder blend? Yes. This blend has something for everyone. And no mess!

If a blend says it has fruit, you should actually be able to see the fruit pieces.

A large cylinder (left) with high quality ingredients attracts a wide variety of birds, as does a smaller no-mess cylinder (right).

Bird food cylinders

Brand name Wild Birds Unlimited Cranberry Fare Bird Food Cylinder

Ingredients Pecans, sunflower chips, peanuts, safflower, oil sunflower, cranberries

My analysis This very high-quality bird food cylinder is considered a "less-mess" blend because it has only a few sunflower seeds with shells. With pecans as the highest percentage ingredient, followed by all the good seeds and cranberries, this is an excellent all-round blend, and the extra-large cylinder will last a long time.

Good foundational feeder blend? Yes. As good as they get.

Brand name Wild Birds Unlimited No-Mess Cylinder

Ingredients Sunflower chips, peanuts, tree nuts, cherries

My analysis This is a very high-quality no-mess cylinder. It has lots of sunflower chips, peanuts, and tree nuts, and it also contains cherries to attract fruit-eaters. No artificial fruit flavoring!

Good foundational feeder blend? Yes. As good as they get. And no mess!

Buying suet blend cakes and doughs

Suet blend cakes come with many fancy packages, names, claims, and price points. The claims are often misleading, and just about any suet product can claim to be "high-energy" or "premium." If you learn to read the labels, you can make good choices and decide if you are getting good value for your money.

With suet blend cakes and doughs, it is important to study both the ingredients list and the guaranteed analysis information. The guaranteed analysis statement is required on all bird food products and lists the percent of crude protein, crude fat and crude fiber in the product.

Although the guaranteed analysis uses terms like "minimum" and "maximum," and the actual contents are likely higher or lower than the number given, the guaranteed analysis on each package does give fairly accurate guidance on the level of fat and protein in the product.

Suet blend cakes

The point of suet-blend cakes is to add fat and protein to the diet of suet-eaters. It is difficult to judge a suet cake's quality just by looking at it. What you can't see is that the least expensive cakes have a high proportion of grain, which is inexpensive and adds little protein. The most expensive and highest-quality suet blend cakes often have a higher amount of suet than the lower quality cakes and will have high protein ingredients added such as peanuts, peanut butter, and sunflower chips.

Milk or oats might seem odd additions to a suet cake. But oats, milk, and peanuts are sometimes combined into small, entirely edible pellets, which can be added to the suet cake as a price-stabilizing ingredient.

Except for calcium, no minerals or vitamins add any value to suet products.

Low-protein (min. 4%) examples

1. **Ingredients** Rendered beef suet, corn, milo, wheat, millet, sunflower seeds
Guaranteed analysis Crude protein, min. 4%; crude fat, min. 30%; crude fiber, max. 12%

2. **Ingredients** Rendered beef suet, corn, white millet, oats, milk, sunflower meal
Guaranteed analysis Crude protein, min. 4%; crude fat, min. 30%; crude fiber, max. 12%

My analysis Low-protein suet blends have a high quantity of grains and very little to no peanuts or sunflower. Corn is usually listed as the second ingredient, followed by other low-protein grains such as milo, wheat, and millet. There might be a few sunflower seeds, but they will be in the shell to keep the cost down. There are usually no peanuts, as they are more expensive than grains. These low-cost suets generally have less actual suet than higher-cost suet cakes. These suets are both the least expensive and the least useful in adding fat and protein to woodpecker and other insect-eating birds' diets.

Medium-protein (min. 6%) examples

1. **Ingredients** Rendered beef suet, cracked corn, millet, peanuts, cashews, sunflower seeds
guaranteed analysis: crude protein, min. 6%; crude fat, min. 35%; crude fiber, max. 12%

Suet blend cake or suet dough cake?
There are two main types of suet cakes: suet blend cakes are best for cold to mild weather as they can melt in extreme heat conditions; suet dough cakes have a high melting point and are the best to use in hot weather.

2. ingredients Rendered beef suet, cracked corn, chopped peanuts

Guaranteed analysis Crude protein, min. 6%; crude fat, min. 35%; crude fiber, max. 12%

My analysis Medium-protein suet blends contain mostly grains, but also have some protein foods such as peanuts, nuts, and sunflowers. Corn is often listed as the second ingredient, with peanuts as the third or fourth ingredient. Other nuts or sunflower seeds (in shell) might be added. These medium-protein suets will be mid-priced and have better protein than low-protein suets.

High-protein (min. 8% to 22%) examples

1. Ingredients Rendered beef suet, chopped peanuts, peanut butter

Guaranteed analysis Crude protein, min. 12%; crude fat, min. 40%; crude fiber, max. 6%

2. Ingredients Rendered beef suet, raisins, chopped peanuts, chopped almonds, white millet, red millet, cracked corn

Guaranteed analysis Crude protein, min. 12%; crude fat, min. 40%; crude fiber, max. 6%

3. Ingredients Rendered beef suet, roasted peanuts, oats, cranberries, corn, milk, almonds, brazil nuts, cashews, pecans, walnuts

Guaranteed analysis Crude protein, min. 22%; crude fat, min. 35%; crude fiber, max. 12%

My analysis Comparing the labels, you can see that these products have higher minimum protein, higher minimum crude fat and in some cases lower maximum fiber. These high-protein products have some form of peanuts as the second ingredient (or third, if raisins are second), and if any grains are added, the quantity is not significant. These high-protein blends have the costliest ingredients yet will be the most advantageous in adding fat and protein to the diets of insect-eating birds.

Low-protein vs. high-protein fruit suet cakes

I decided to analyze a couple of fruit suet blend cakes by melting them down and weighing the suet and additional ingredients. One was a low-cost, low-protein (min. 4%), low-fat (min. 30%) cake claiming to be a "cherry" suet. One was a higher-cost, high-protein (min. 8%), high-fat (min. 40%) cake claiming to be full of nuts and fruit. Here are the results.

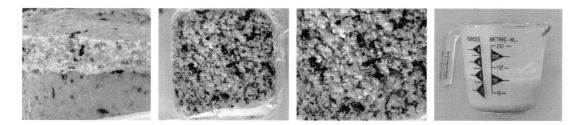

Low-protein, low-fat fruit suet cake

The low-protein (min. 4%) "cherry" suet cake weighed 11.25 oz. Its ingredients were, in order of weight: rendered beef suet, corn, milo, wheat, sunflower seeds, millet, and artificial cherry flavor. There were no actual cherries. It contained 3.65 oz. of suet and 7.60 oz. of other ingredients. Suet made up 32% of the total weight.

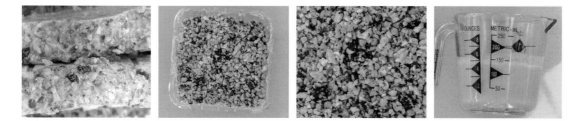

High-protein, high-fat fruit suet cake

The high-protein (min. 8%) suet weighed 11.00 oz. Its ingredients were, in order of weight: rendered beef suet, roasted peanuts, raisins, oats, corn, milk, and blueberries. It contained 4.7 oz. of suet and 6.3 oz. of other ingredients. Suet made up 42% of the total weight.

My analysis

The low-protein "cherry" suet had no fruit (just artificial cherry flavoring); its name is a marketing gimmick. It had a lower percentage of suet than the high-protein fruit suet, a high proportion of cheap grains (corn, milo, and wheat) as fillers to keep the price low, and no protein sources such as peanuts. This suet blend cake is targeted to a price point, not its attractiveness to woodpeckers and other suet-eating birds. Calling it a "cherry" suet appeals to the human desire to help and attract fruit-eating birds, but this suet does not follow through with the ingredients that would actually accomplish it.

The high-protein fruit suet had real fruit (raisins and cranberries), 30% more suet, and a high proportion of peanuts for protein. This fruit suet cake provided the promised fruit and a high level of fat and protein. It serves the purpose for which it is intended.

Ultimately, you get what you pay for in suet blend cakes, just as you do in foundational blends for your feeders. The food is worth the higher cost if it is formulated for its intended purpose, with no fillers but ingredients selected to add attractiveness and protein.

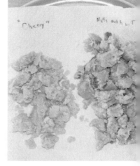

Another way to look at the amount of suet in each cake.

No-melt suet doughs
All high protein examples (above) with corn as first ingredient, roasted peanuts as second ingredient, and rendered beef suet as third ingredient. One example (middle) has cranberries and tree nuts, and another (far right) has hot pepper.

No-melt suet doughs

To give them their higher melting point, suet doughs contain a higher proportion of corn and other ingredients, with rendered beef suet usually the third ingredient. Corn meal or very fine cracked corn, a necessary ingredient in any no-melt product, is more readily eaten by most species as part of a suet dough than as loose seed.

Low-protein (7%) example

Ingredients Corn, sunflower meal, rendered beef suet, oats, sunflower hearts, soy oil

Guaranteed analysis Crude protein, min. 7%; crude fat, min. 35%; crude fiber, max. 8%

My analysis The low-protein suet doughs have no peanuts in them, making them the least expensive.

Medium-protein (9%) example

Ingredients Roasted peanuts, corn, rendered beef suet, calcium carbonate, oats, raisins, soy oil, blueberries

Guaranteed analysis Crude protein, min. 9%; crude fat, min. 25%; crude fiber, max. 4%

My analysis This medium-protein option has peanuts as the first ingredient, but still not enough to provide as much protein as the high-protein suet doughs. Medium-protein doughs are usually priced in the mid-range.

High-protein (12%) examples

1. Ingredients Corn, roasted peanuts, rendered beef suet, sweet corn, oats, soy oil, almonds, Brazil nuts, cashews, pecans, walnuts

Guaranteed analysis Crude protein, min. 12%; crude fat, min. 20%; crude fiber, max. 4%

2. Ingredients Peanuts, corn, rendered beef suet, oats, soy oil

Guaranteed analysis crude protein, min. 12%; crude fat, min. 20%; crude fiber, max. 4%

3. Ingredients Corn, roasted peanuts, rendered beef suet, plus

Vitamins A, D, E, Niacin, B2, Pyridoxine HCL, Thiamine Mononitrate, Calcium Pantothenate (vitamin B5) K, Folic Acid, Biotin, B12
minerals: Calcium Magnesium Oxide, Ferrous Sulphate, Zinc Oxide, Manganese Oxide, Copper Oxide, Calcium Iodate, Cobalt Carbonate

Guaranteed analysis Crude protein, min. 12%; crude fat, min. 40%; crude fiber, max. 10%

My analysis These high-protein examples have good quantities of peanuts as the first or second ingredient, accounting for their high protein levels. Birds such as woodpeckers that prefer insects, sunflower, and peanuts are more attracted to these suet doughs than to those with a high proportion of grains. The third example is a high-quality suet dough with added vitamins and minerals, none of which (except for calcium) I think is necessary for wild birds. High-protein suet doughs, with their higher-cost ingredients, are the most expensive.

Storing bird food

Once you have bought all your bird food and suet products, what do you do with them when you get home? I think about this a lot, and have some solutions that work very well. Bird food can be stored for up to a year if done properly.

Given that I bring home a wide variety of foods, some in fairly large quantities, here are my goals and my strategies.

No rodents

Everything is kept in chew-proof containers made of metal or very strong plastic. This deters mice, rats, squirrels, and raccoons. The larger the critter, the greater the need for metal containers.

No moisture

Bird seed must be kept dry or it will spoil and grow mold. If you see any mold or if the seed smells wrong, throw it away, and clean out the container with a 10-percent bleach solution.

No Indian meal moths or grain weevils

To avoid hatching meal moths or other insects, keep bird seed in as cool a place as possible outside of the house, such as your garage or porch. Do not buy more than you can use up in several weeks. Bird seed is more likely to attract insects in the summer heat, so this is when you must keep it cool and use it up quickly. I often put small bird seed bags and bird food cylinders in the freezer during the summer.

If you notice any webs or larvae, immediately remove the bag or container and isolate it from the rest of your seed; if the trash is your only means of disposal, wrap the seed up in a large plastic bag and throw it away. I throw buggy seed on the ground in the woods, where the birds eat all the insects. Then I wash out all the containers with a spray hose and use a 10-percent bleach solution to kill the remaining eggs. After rinsing and drying the containers, they're ready for fresh seed. Never use pesticides near your bird seed.

Constant rotation

The bags should be easily rotated so that all seed is used up within a few weeks. Do not pour new bird seed on top of old seed in a container.

Large multi-purpose chew-proof storage closets

These store all sorts of big and little bags of seed, peanuts, suets, and cylinders.

Smaller carry-to-feeder containers

Typically 1- or 5-gallon-sized, these are filled with a smaller amount of seed that can be easily carried to the feeders such as nyjer and peanuts. These containers can also be used to carry miscellaneous items and foods such as seed scoops, mealworms, Bark Butter and its spreading fork, suet cakes and bird food cylinders out to the feeding station. After filling all the feeders, the container can be used to bring back empty wrappers and suet containers for recycling or disposal.

My storage cabinet in the garage is the main storage for my various bird foods (top left). I use 1- to 5-gallon handled metal or plastic storage containers for extra storage and to carry the food out to the feeders (top middle and right). I use a scoop designed to fill tube feeders without spillage (bottom left).

My bird food storage setup

I have two storage areas for my bird food, feeders, and extra feeders and poles. One is in the garage and the other is on my deck near the feeders. The garage keeps the food cool in the summer and everything accessible in the winter. I also have a "bird feeding shed" on my deck, where I keep smaller quantities of food in containers along with cleaning supplies, extra poles, hangers, and seasonal feeders.

Storage cabinet in garage

In the garage, I use a two-shelf plastic storage cabinet that has proven to be mouse-proof. This is where all 20-pound bags, bird food cylinders, suet cakes, peanut pieces, peanut-in-the-shell bags, Bark Butter tubs, and Bark Butter Bits bags are stored.

5-gallon handled and stackable containers for storage and refills

I have four 5-gallon containers to carry the food to the feeders. I split most 20-pound bags by pouring half into one of these buckets and putting the rest into the cabinet. This way, it is easy to carry the

seed to the feeders, and there is room in the bucket on top of the seed to add items such as suet cakes, cylinders, and Bark Butter. I might have No-Mess Blend in one bucket, safflower in another, and TreeNutty Plus Blend in another. The fourth bucket might be empty so that I can put all kinds of things in it to carry to the feeders. These buckets stack nicely and don't take up much room. Of course, metal cans of all sizes work great to store seed and keep it safe from hungry wildlife.

1-gallon containers for nyjer and peanuts

I use 1-gallon containers to carry nyjer seed and peanut pieces to the feeders. The spout makes it easy to pour food into a finch tube or peanut tube.?

Good 1- to 6-gallon storage containers are available from various suppliers. I look for containers that stack and have a carrying handle.

Scoops for pouring into the feeders

I use two different scoops, usually depending on which one has not been misplaced. I often use metal coffee cans and also use the commercially-made plastic scoops that have the skinny tube on the bottom that easily fill tube feeders.

Indian meal moth control

You will know you have Indian meal moths living in your home or garage when you see small grayish-brown moths with 5/8-inch wingspans flying around. These are the annoying adults, which do little harm other than laying more eggs. Their presence is a good indication that there is an infestation. Modern food processing and packaging science does a good job of eliminating this pest, but cannot get rid of it entirely.

If moths are present, you will find the webs, larvae, and pupae in grain and cereal products, nuts, dried fruit, dried soups, herbs, peanuts in or out of the shell, and bird food. If you see adults, you need to find the infested food, immediately seal it up in a plastic bag, and dispose of it in the trash. Potentially infested food items are those that have been in the storage area for a long time in loose or thin wrappers. The moths may have come in on the infested foods or another food. Thoroughly clean the area with household cleaning products. Do not use any pesticides. Any food that passes inspection should be kept in tightly closed containers until there is no more evidence of moths.

Freeze it to kill it. If I do not plan to use bird food for a while, I place it in the freezer for at least three days to kill any eggs, larvae, or pupae that might be developing in it. The food needs to be kept in a sealed container after that to guard against re-infestation. If I detect just a few webs in the bird food, I feed it to the birds immediately, then thoroughly clean the area where the food was stored.

Be especially vigilant in summer. The hotter season is the most likely time for grain moths. In summer, the bird food has been in storage for nearly nine months since harvest, and heat can encourage any eggs present to hatch. Ideally, bird food should be stored at a temperature no higher than 65°F.

You can use pheromone traps to determine if you have meal moths. The Pantry Pest Trap by Safer is one example. I place these traps in my pantry and bird food storage areas to monitor the presence of the moths. Pheromones attract only male moths, so even though the sticky surface is full of trapped moths, you have not trapped any of the egg-laying females. You still need to find and remove the infestation.

Bird feeding shed on my deck
This all-purpose outdoor shed (above) makes it really easy to keep my deck feeders full and clean and to vary the feeders as needed.

Bird food shopping list

Foundational feeder blend for hoppers and tubes

▶ With shells. Various combinations of oil sunflower, safflower, white millet, peanuts

▶ No-mess. Various combinations of sunflower chips, peanuts, hulled white millet

Extra ingredients: Tree nuts, striped sunflower, calcium, dried fruit, Bark Butter Bits, suet nuggets, dried mealworms

Bird food cylinder

▶ 1 ¾ or 4 ¼ pounds of various combinations of the foods listed above.

Tray feeder blends (for trays low to the ground)

▶ Mostly white millet with some oil sunflower and a bit of cracked corn.

▶ Wildlife blends with whole peanuts, whole kernel corn and sunflowers.

Tray feeder snacks (for trays on a pole)

Use your foundational feeder blend or the following treats:

▶ Peanuts pieces

▶ Peanuts in the shell

▶ Bark Butter Bits

▶ Suet nuggets

▶ Dried mealworms

▶ Dried fruit

▶ Blend for woodpeckers (lots of tree nuts, peanuts, and some fruit)

Fat feeder foods

▶ Suet blend cakes

▶ Suet dough cakes

▶ Suet dough cylinders

▶ Bark Butter

▶ Bark Butter Bits

▶ Bark Butter Brick

▶ Suet plugs

Finch feeder

- ▶ Nyjer
- ▶ Finch blend
- ▶ FeederFresh to absorb moisture

Nectar, jelly, and fruit

- ▶ 5-pound bag of table sugar to make own nectar
- ▶ Nectar solution in stores
  - ▶ Buy powdered made from sucrose, the preferred hummingbird sugar. Small amounts of fructose and glucose are ok.
  - ▶ Should not have any red food coloring, vitamins, minerals, or preservatives (except for Nectar Defender).
- ▶ FeederFresh Nectar Defender
  - • Micro-nutrient copper solution for long nectar life is the only preservative I would recommend.
- ▶ Jelly
  - • ideally without high-fructose corn syrup, artificial flavors, artificial colors, or preservatives.
- ▶ Fruits including oranges, apples, raisins, and dried fruits.

Snack/specialty/convenience foods for various feeders

- ▶ Peanuts in the shell
- ▶ Peanut pieces
- ▶ Tree nuts
- ▶ Bark Butter Bits
- ▶ Live mealworms
- ▶ Dried mealworms
- ▶ Bird food cylinders and cakes
- ▶ Wildlife blends
- ▶ Woodpecker blends
- ▶ Ears of corn

Problem-solving

- ▶ Safflower (No squirrels or blackbirds)
- ▶ Hot pepper suet or suet dough
- ▶ Hot pepper bird food cylinder

10 Common-sense bird feeding hygiene

IF YOU LOVE watching birds, then you're obligated to provide a safe habitat with fresh food and water. Birds can contract several diseases at a bird feeding station, so it is your responsibility to practice proper hygiene. Follow these general guidelines to help your birds stay safe and healthy.

Many types of birds bathe frequently to keep cool in warm weather and to keep their feathers clean and free from dust and parasites. It is an important responsibility of all bird feeding hobbyists to keep your bird bath water fresh and your feeders clean.

▶ Provide multiple feeding stations in different areas of your yard. When birds crowd the feeders, they can become stressed and more vulnerable to disease.

▶ Clean your feeders every four weeks, or more often if droppings have accumulated or mold is visible. Use a 10 percent bleach solution to disinfect all feeder parts.

▶ Choose feeders that keep food as fresh and dry as possible, even in rainy and snowy conditions. If food does get wet, replace it.

▶ Scatter seed on the ground in small quantities and only if the ground is dry.

▶ Regularly clean the area beneath your feeders by disposing of hulls and uneaten seeds. To avoid the mess, use no-mess feeding solutions.

▶ Move feeders periodically to lessen the concentration of bird droppings.

▶ In birdbaths, provide fresh water every four to five days, more often if droppings, mosquito larvae, or algae are present.

▶ Always wash your hands after filling or cleaning your feeders.

Wild bird diseases

There are four principal diseases birds transmit or contract at bird feeders: mycoplasmal conjunctivitis, avian pox, salmonellosis, and aspergillosis. Excellent internet sources with further information are provided by the Cornell Laboratory of Ornithology (www.birds.cornell.edu) and the National Wildlife Heath Center (www.nwhc.usgs.gov).

Mycoplasmal conjunctivitis

Mostly contracted by House Finches, this disease is caused by the microorganism Mycoplasma gallisepticum and is transmitted by direct contact, airborne droplets, or dust. Known as "finch eye disease," it is an infection of the eye membranes, which become red, swollen, and crusty and may close over the eye entirely. Further information about this disease can be found at www.birds.cornell.edu , then search for "finch eye disease."

▶ If you see a bird with this disease, immediately wash the feeders with a 10-percent bleach solution. Recycled milk-jug plastic feeders are easier to keep clean than wooden feeders with cracks and crevices.

▶ Space feeders out to discourage overcrowding.

▶ Keep the ground cleaned up under bird feeders so that droppings do not accumulate, and move feeders periodically.

Avian pox

This disease, caused by several strains of avipoxvirus, causes wart-like growths around birds' eyes, at the base of the bill, or on their legs and feet. When they are near the eyes, the growths can be mistaken for conjunctivitis. Avian pox is transmitted by biting insects, contaminated food or water, or direct contact with infected birds or surfaces.

▶ If you see a bird with this disease, immediately wash the feeders and birdbaths with a 10-percent bleach solution.

▶ Space feeders out to discourage overcrowding. Stop offering water for a week or two.

▶ Keep the ground cleaned up under bird feeders so that droppings do not accumulate, and move feeders periodically.

Salmonellosis

This disease can arise when warm weather encourages bacterial growth around bird feeders. It is most noticeable in Pine Siskins and American Goldfinches. The salmonella bacteria spreads when healthy birds eat food contaminated with the droppings of infected birds. Affected birds are lethargic and puffed up.

▶ If you see a bird with the disease, immediately wash the feeders and birdbaths with a 10-percent bleach solution.

▶ Stop feeding for at least one week.

▶ Do not use tray or platform feeders or birdbaths if diseased birds are present.

▶ Wear gloves to clean feeders, and do not handle dead birds.

▶ Keep the ground cleaned up under bird feeders so that droppings do not accumulate, and move feeders periodically.

Aspergillosis

The aspergillus fungus (mold) grows on damp seed and other debris beneath feeders. Birds that inhale the spores can contract bronchitis and pneumonia.

▶ Keep the ground cleaned up under bird feeders so that bird seed does not accumulate, and move feeders periodically.

▶ Use trays to catch seed before it hits the ground, and use no-mess foods that are entirely eaten.

▶ Offer only fresh food free of molds or moisture.

Cleaning tools

I have the "tools of the trade" ready to clean my feeders whenever they need it.

The most useful tools are an outdoor faucet, hose, and hose nozzle. The quickest clean-up of my deck comes when I spray off the feeders, birdbath, and deck rail and finish the job with scrub brushes.

Every two to three months, the feeders need a deeper cleaning to sterilize them from any germs that might have collected. For that I have a large rubber bucket, bottle of bleach, brushes, and rubber gloves. I make a 10 percent bleach solution, soak the feeders for about 15 minutes, then hose and scrub the feeders until all the yuck and bleach residue are gone.

I have one brush for feeders and one for the birdbath. The goal is to keep the birdbath water as fresh as possible instead of using a brush that just cleaned droppings off a feeder.

Before I soak the feeders, I pull out my power sprayer and blast all the feeder surfaces so that the bleach will work best. I also use the power sprayer on the deck floor and deck railing. It has a cool attachment that cleans deck floors very nicely.

A power sprayer (opposite top left and right) along with a scrubbing brush works well to clean to clean out tubes and other surfaces. Notice the tube feeder (opposite left middle) has an easily removed bottom. I use a brush designated only for the bird bath (opposite bottom left). I keep handy a soaking bucket, bleach, brushes and rubber gloves for cleaning the feeders and deck (opposite bottom right).

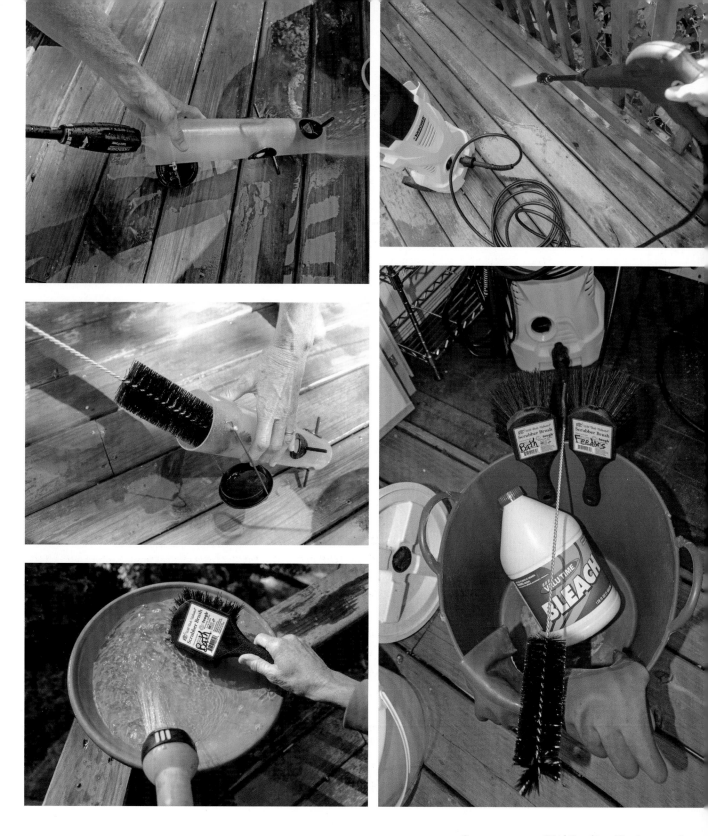

Fun bird feeding activities

THERE ARE MANY fun activities that bird feeding hobbyists can participate in that will expand their interactions with the birds and the bird watching community.

▶ Hand-feed the birds in one day.

▶ Observe birds closely with the right binoculars.

▶ Learn detailed bird identification with paper and digital field guides.

▶ Photograph birds on feeders and in the landscape

▶ Bring kids and nature together

▶ Watch birds when you are not home

▶ Get involved with Citizen Science

Hand-feed the birds in one day

Have you ever felt the breeze from a chickadee's wings? Heard the soft *yank-yank* call of a Red-breasted Nuthatch from inches away? One of the greatest joys for people of all ages is feeding birds from the hand. I will share a simple technique that I have used for 30 years and that anyone can follow with success. You can have a bird landing on your hand with only a few minutes of effort over a single day.

You do not need to stand still for long periods or gradually move closer. There are no routines, and it does not take days for the birds to get used to you. Once the birds are eating out of your hand, you can have birds feeding out of the hands of everyone in your family within minutes. All you have to do is act just like me—a dummy!

Some species are more likely to land on your hand than others. If you have chickadees, nuthatches, titmice, bluebirds, redpolls, Carolina Wrens, or hummingbirds coming to feeders, you are good to go. It is much more challenging to entice House Finches, goldfinches, and Blue Jays, but it can be done. In certain areas of Florida, the Florida Scrub-Jay readily comes to the hand. In Canada and the mountains of the western U.S., Gray Jays can become very tame. Clark's Nutcrackers can be persuaded, too, after a while. Other birds that have been reported coming to food in the hand are Pine Warbler, various hummingbirds, Carolina Wren, Evening Grosbeak, Pine Grosbeak, Chipping Sparrow, Gray Catbird, Northern Cardinal, Boat-tailed Grackle, and House Sparrow. The complete list is no doubt much longer.

American Goldfinches (opposite page) are not easily enticed to the hand (or hat) but can be with my technique and your patience. Amazingly, I could hear them cracking open the nyjer seeds and could watch them removing the outer skin from sunflower chips.

Nine A.M.

Place a dummy near the feeders and with food in in its glove so that the birds become accustomed to the dummy's presence.

1. **Feeders need to be active.** It is best to pick a time of year or time of day when your feeders are very active. Regardless of overall activity, certain birds like chickadees and nuthatches can be lured to the hand even when they are the only ones at the feeders.

2. **Put a dummy in a chair out by the feeders.** I use a hooded jacket or a jacket and brimmed hat as the basis for the whole technique. Stuff the jacket with pillows, and place the hat on the dummy.

3. **Pose your stand-in.** Prop the dummy's arm up near the feeders or rest it on the chair arm. Use a glove to simulate your hand.

4. **Put food in the glove.** Put sunflower seeds, sunflower chips, peanuts, or peanut pieces in the glove. Your dummy is ready to feed the birds.

One P.M.

5. **Reduce the birds' choices.** Remove all the feeders except for the one closest to the glove.

6. **Keep them interested.** Keep the feeder and the glove full of food. The birds should be eating out of the glove by now as if it were a little tray feeder.

Two P.M.

7. **Redirect the birds.** Remove all the food from the feeder, but keep the feeder in the same place. The birds will land on the feeder and then go to the glove when they see the food on it.

8. **Keep food in the glove.** Now the only place to get food is the glove.

Three P.M.

9. **Take the place of the dummy.** Put on the same or a similar jacket. If it has a hood, use it. Put on the dummy's hat and gloves and wear sunglasses. Just be quick about the exchange

10. **Sit very quietly.** Keep your gloved hand with food in the same place as the dummy's glove. Do not talk, open your mouth, or move your eyes too much. You may smile when a bird lands on or near your hand. Try not to jump for joy, even though you will feel like it!?

Three-fifteen P.M.

11. **Take off the glove.** Once a few birds have repeatedly eaten out of your gloved hand, it is time to take off the glove. They will land right on your hand, and might land on your shoulder and hat. Congratulations, you've done it!

Become the dummy! After the birds eat from the gloved hand for a while, remove the glove and enjoy!

You can easily switch place with family and friends so they can enjoy the experience, as I did with our daughter Casey.

Mealworms were used to entice this Brown-headed nuthatch.

Three-thirty P.M.

12. Share the fun with others. It is now easy for other family members or friends to experience birds eating out of their hand. All they have to do is take your place by quickly putting on the same jacket, hat, and sunglasses, and then sitting quietly with their hand full of food. The birds will land within minutes to grab a bite. There will be smiles!

This is a very meaningful experience for most people, one that they will remember for the rest of their lives. It is a good time to take a moment to appreciate the tiny bird—its beauty, its personality, its almost imperceptible weight, and its incredible survival skills. It is an opportunity to think deeply about the natural world that has just trusted you enough to land on your hand. Think about how we share the same habitat with these amazing creatures and how we must remember to provide for their needs as well as ours when we create a backyard sanctuary. It is a time for joy!

Variations
Carolina Wren
Start by offering mealworms in a small bowl. When the birds are active on the glove, put some mealworms on your jacket front, and the birds will hop all over you.

Pine Warbler
They can be enticed to take mealworms from a cup or directly out of your hand.

Brown-headed Nuthatch
Try offering mealworms from your hand.

Hummingbirds
Use a hummingbird feeder with a flat red top, hung inches away from the arm of a lawn chair. Plug up all the nectar holes with small sticks except for one hole near the chair. You can use the dummy technique, but some hummingbirds will let you sit in the chair yourself from the very beginning.

After the hummingbirds have gotten used to you and are using the only nectar hole, hold your index finger close to the perch. Soon, you may place your finger right on top of the perch. The birds will land on your finger and take a drink.

Goldfinches
(See sequence at the bottom of the next page). Instead of using a blend of sunflowers and peanuts, I used a finch feeder tube filled with nyjer. I also had a tray full of sunflower chips above my knees. This way, lots of goldfinches could land on the perch or tray and choose their food.

I used the dummy for about 30 minutes, then took its place. The finches, which included both American and Lesser Goldfinches, were wary at first, but after about ten minutes started to come in without any apparent worries.

I very slowly moved my hand to the perches, and the finches started landing on my finger. At the tray, they landed on my open hand for sunflower chips.

Not only was it amazing to be hand-feeding goldfinches, but I also got to watch their feeding techniques at close range. I could hear them make munching sounds as they opened each nyjer seed. Watching them this close, I could see them work the little black seed around with their tongue, and in just a second or two they had the meat separated from the shell. They swallowed the meat and dropped the shell. To eat sunflower chips, they removed the thin clear membrane, then reduced each kernel to a smaller size before swallowing it.

Hummingbirds are fairly easily enticed to a hand-held source of sugar-water, such as this male Costa's Hummingbird (left). I often plug up all the feeding ports in a hummingbird feeder except for one, and they will then land on my finger as a perch to feed from that port.

It takes a real dummy (below) to entice goldfinches to perch on your hand while they dine!

Take photos

Have someone take photographs and videos of your experience. To take photos of myself, I put a camera with a short zoom lens on a tripod, manually focused on the exact spot where my hand was, and used a remote trigger in my free hand. You can also hand-hold a small camera or phone camera to take an image of the birds on your other hand.

Getting "the" shot

To get a "selfie" of a Mountain Chickadee landing on my hand, I did the following:

▶ After removing all feeders but one hopper and observing that the chickadee was active on that feeder, I was able to stand by the feeder, place my hand on the landing perch and the chickadee immediately landed on my fingers for some sunflower chips.

▶ I then removed the feeder and using the hanger as a guide, tested a few shots to make sure I knew exactly where to put my hand so the chickadee would be properly focused. I also re-aimed the camera for a better background and to remove the hanger.

▶ I changed into a black jacket and struck a pose; when the chickadee landed, I triggered the camera's wireless remote with my left hand. *Ta-da!*

Choose the right binocular

Even when the birds are on your feeders, they are still tiny little creatures, and you cannot clearly see all the details. I pick up my binoculars all the time when watching birds out my windows, sometimes just to get a better look at the incredible beauty of bird such as a Lazuli Bunting. Sometimes I want to make sure whether I am seeing Pine Siskins, House Finches, or Cassin's Finches—or all three. What's that out in the bushes? Is that an Oregon or a Pink-sided Dark-eyed Junco? Was that flash of copper a Rufous Hummingbird? You really need good binoculars near your window, ready to be pressed into service.

Better binoculars really do make for better viewing of birds, but there is a limit to what you need for looking at birds from inside your house or from your deck. If you buy a medium-priced pair, in the range of $250 to $500, you will have binoculars that are also good enough to take into the field to watch birds or to use at sporting events. Binoculars in this price range can last a lifetime. If you buy an inexpensive pair, in the $50 to $100 range, you will have a binocular that magnifies and provides a quick view, but it will be frustrating to use in the field for very long and you will probably wind up replacing it at some point.

My simple advice

Go to your local bird feeding specialty store or camera store, and try out several binoculars. Please buy them in that store rather than going online. The store has worked to deserve your business by carrying the inventory and sharing the knowledge to help you pick the right binocular.

Start with 8 x 40 or 8 x 42 binoculars, pronounced "eight by forty" or "eight by forty-two," in the $500 range. Then work your way down to lower-priced models. The 8 x 40 is a standard size that works well for just about anyone for just about any purpose. The numbers mean that the image in the binocular is magnified eight times and that the large front lens has a diameter of 40 millimeters, which is wide enough to let in plenty of light.

If you wear glasses, keep your glasses on. The first question you should ask is about eye relief, the extent of which the binocular's eyecups twist down or roll back to let you wear your eyeglasses. Look for at least 15 millimeters of eye relief.

Next, learn how to use the diopter to accommodate any difference in focus between your two eyes. Without making this adjustment, one eye might be in focus and the other one blurry. Learning about eye relief and diopter adjustment alone will be worth your trip to the store.

Play with the focusing mechanism, and see which binoculars give you a sharp, crisp view most easily and most quickly.

See how close to your feet you can focus. If you can focus down to 6 feet with one pair but only as close as 12 feet with another, ask yourself how close you expect to be to most of the birds you're watching.

Look into a dark corner with each pair, and you will see that the nicer binoculars distinguish items in low light better than the less expensive ones do. Higher-priced binoculars have better lens coatings to let more light reach your eyes.

Check out the field of view, a measurement of how wide the image is at a distance of 1000 feet. A wide field of view is important for watching flying birds, but it may not be necessary if you are looking at perching birds in your yard.

Enjoy the birds even more with a good pair of binoculars!

Other things to consider

Do you want a full-sized or compact binocular? Consider weight, but also think about how you will use the binocular. Most compact binoculars have a narrow field of view and work best in the yard, on hikes, or at sporting events. Because compact binoculars have a smaller objective lens, they cannot provide the crisp high-resolution views of subjects in poor light delivered by larger models.

The 8x magnification should work just fine. Buy a 10x only if you have very steady hands or expect to look mostly at faraway subjects such as shorebirds. Choose a 6x if you are looking mostly at very close subjects, or if your hands are unsteady at 8x.

How do the binoculars feel in your hands? Comfort is important when you're using your binoculars for a long period of time. Some binoculars are waterproof and fog-proof. Will you be using them out in the rain or high humidity, or will you be subjecting them to rapid temperature changes, such as when you move quickly between indoor and outdoor settings?

How durable are the binoculars, and what kind of warranty do they have? Make sure you're getting a warranty appropriate to your situation.

The only routine maintenance binoculars need is ensuring that the lenses are clean. Dirty glass reduces the amount of light that can come through the binocular, making the images less clear. Dirt can even destroy lens coatings over time. When you are not using your binoculars, keep the lens caps on and store them in their case.

Field guides: paper and digital

In this book, we have provided photographs and range maps for more than 180 species of bird that commonly, or less commonly, visit feeders. Hopefully this will help you identify your backyard birds. Many other fine field guides, digital apps, and posters are available to teach you how to identify all of the birds that live in or visit North America.

An excellent, full-size print guide to the birds of North America will have details on over 750 birds and include information about the different appearances of the various ages, sexes, races, and regional variations of each species.

There are many excellent guides to choose from, including Peterson, Sibley, Kaufman, National Geographic, Crossley ID, Stokes and Golden Guides.

One new photographic field guide is the *Smithsonian Field Guide to the Birds of North America* by Ted Floyd. It is the first comprehensive guide to include a DVD of 587 downloadable birdsongs and vocalizations. Another recently published guide is *The New Birder's Guide to Birds of North America* by Bill Thompson III, designed to introduce new hobbyists to 300 of the most common birds.

Field guides covering the birds of a single state or region are also available, including the American Birding Association series published by Scott & Nix and the Adventure Publications series authored by Stan Tekiela.

Smartphone and tablet apps are also useful, since they allow you to find a bird by shape, family, name, or region; most include recordings of songs and calls. Two of the best mobile apps are "Audubon Birds Pro" and "iBird Pro Guide to Birds." The Cornell Lab of Ornithology's "Merlin" is a very clever app: You answer five simple questions, and this app helps you identify the bird you just saw with what is often amazing accuracy. The new online tool "Merlin Photo ID" can help you identify a bird from a photograph you have taken.

I use a combination of these resources. I typically rely on the apps on my smartphone while I am casually out and about, but I take a complete printed field guide with me on a long day in the field. In between field trips, I study the printed guides at home.

Online field guides and references

All About Birds

www.allaboutbirds.org
I often consult this Cornell Lab website to identify birds using the photos, range maps, songs, and calls; it also provides detailed information about their habitat, food sources, family life and similar birds.

Audubon Guide to North American Birds

www.audubon.org/field-guide
This excellent and visually appealing site helps you quickly find the bird you are interested in and all similar species. In addition to range maps and song recordings, it offers photos of each bird along with paintings by David Allen Sibley and texts by Kenn Kaufman.

Birds of North America Online

www.bna.birds.cornell.edu
I used this reference work extensively in compiling the detailed species information for this book. Maintained by the Cornell Lab of Ornithology and the American Ornithologists' Union, "Birds of North America Online" is accessible by subscription. The print work, completed in 2002, runs to more than 18,000 pages in 18 volumes; the online version also features recordings of songs and calls selected from the vast collections of Cornell's Macaulay Library for Natural Sounds.

eBird

www.ebird.org
eBird, another project of the Cornell Laboratory of Ornithology and the National Audubon Society, is a database of millions of bird sightings contributed by thousands of birders all over the world. You can submit your own sightings or explore the reports to find out what birds are being seen in your area. You can contribute sightings online or with the mobile eBird app; the "BirdsEye North America" app lets you see the latest sightings reported from any geographic area.

Macaulay Library of Natural Sounds at the Cornell Laboratory of Ornithology

www.macaulaylibrary.org
Want to hear the song of just about any bird? This is the place to do it. The Macaulay Library collects audio and video recordings documenting each species' behavior and natural history, and encourages their use in education, conservation, and research. You may also submit your own recordings and photos through eBird.

Xeno-canto

www.xeno-canto.org
Xeno-canto is dedicated to collecting and preserving bird sounds from all over the world. Anyone can explore the collection and download the songs, calls, and other sounds made by more than 9,000 bird species.

Wild Birds Unlimited
Educational resources and videos

www.wbu.com
This is a great place to start your research about feeding birds, finding products, solving problems, and much more.

Photographing birds on feeders and in landscape

I have spent many joyful hours photographing birds on feeders. Most of the photographs in this book that were taken by me required just a few basic pieces of equipment. I won't give you a full lesson in digital wildlife photography but will share a few hints. For more details, I recommend you study the many excellent books and online resources available for beginners to experts.

You have two primary choices with your bird feeder photography. Do you want to just document your guests, or do you want photos worthy of being in a magazine or product ad? Using a basic point and shoot camera with a built-in zoom lens plus a little effort to set up the scene, you can get great documentation of the birds at your feeders. However, better camera bodies such as DSLR and better lenses do result in better images.

Digital SLR cameras

I use Nikon bodies and lenses. Canon, Sony, and many others make very fine cameras and lenses, too. Since I started shooting digital more than 15 years ago, I have upgraded cameras every few years. Recently, I have been using a Nikon D810 FX 36.3 megapixel to photograph birds and landscapes. The high-resolution images are extraordinary in their detail, and can easily be cropped and enlarged as needed.

Telephoto lenses

Birds will be more comfortable and visit the feeders more often the farther away you are. My workhorse portable zoom lens is the AF-S NIKKOR 80-400 f/4.5-5.6G ED VR. My other main lens, which I use on a tripod, is an AF-S NIKKOR 200-400mm f/4G ED VR. This is a nice piece of glass that produces very clear images even in low light.

For even more magnification, I use the AF-S Nikkor 600mm 1:4 ED lens, a 16-pound behemoth

from the pre-digital age that still works great with digital cameras.

Big glass

The bigger the glass on your zoom lens, the more light it admits, letting you combine fast shutter speeds for a crisp image of your subject with low f-stops to blur the background. This background blur isolates the subject.

Bird portraits are usually most appealing with a sharply-focused subject and blurry background.

The background

Once you have a subject, the background is the most important thing to consider. In most bird portraits, you want the background to be blurry and the subject to stand out. This means that you will be using lower f-stops: higher f-stops tend to keep the background clear enough to compete with the subject. This portrait of a female Pileated Woodpecker was shot at f/ 5.3, so that she would be the sole focus of the photo, yet the blurry falling snow adds context as to the season. The background branches would be very distracting if they were also in focus.

I will often set-up a shot with the subject and background carefully selected, and then use a remote trigger so I can comfortably sip my coffee while waiting for the birds (opposite page).

This Black-billed Magpie does not show up very well against these busy branches.

This female Pileated Woodpecker on a suet feeder is intended to be a marketing product shot. At f/5, the background does not distract from the feeder and bird, but it is just visible enough to add seasonal context to the photo.

To use lower f-stops, you need lots of natural or artificial light or a big lens. Fortunately, today's digital cameras take excellent images at higher ISOs, so you can increase the ISO setting to permit the use of low f-stops in low light even with a smaller lens. And of course, you can always compensate for low light by using a flash.

Even a blurry background can be varied by moving just a few inches one direction or another. If you put your subject in front of that sunlit bush or evergreen 50 feet away, it will stand out nicely. Blurry flowers behind colorful birds such as hummingbirds and orioles can add beauty to a photo, but be sure to avoid annoying branches and tree trunks.

The background is better in this shot, but now there are distracting grasses in front of the tail and an annoying branch coming out of the bird's back.

This portrait shows the magpie on an interesting rock for foreground context; the blurry background emphasizes the subject.

This Lesser Goldfinch is isolated against a background of pines and rocks, chosen specially to be interesting when blurred.

An outdoor studio

Setting up the shot sometimes results in creating a photography studio around the feeders. I use real branches attached to poles near the feeders, I might have extra flashes on tripods to light the scene or fill in dark spaces or fill-flash backlit subjects, and I have my camera on a large tripod. I carefully choose both the background and the direction of the sunlight.

Choose one bird

Let a single bird be the focal point, or tell a story with an image of two birds' behavior towards each other. Look for a way to take the photo so that it emphasizes the bird's beauty, intelligence, or survival skills. A photo cluttered up with lots of feeders and lots of birds just won't be interesting unless you are intentionally trying to tell a story about lots of birds on lots of feeders. And remember: The eye of the bird must be in focus. If it isn't, delete the photo.

Have one feeder with food

Nothing is more frustrating than watching the birds go to all the feeders except the one you are focused on. Remove all food except for the target feeder or the feeder near your portrait site. Place one feeder close to the perch, and the birds will use your target perch on their way to and from the feeder. By the way, this is how I came to understand the importance of perching branches, one of the 12 Elements of a Thoughtful Bird Feeding Station (see Chapter 2, page 28).

Use a remote trigger

When my camera is on a tripod and focused on a particular feeder, I almost always use a remote wireless trigger. This eliminates camera shake, and the birds visit more often while I am inside enjoying a nice warm cup of coffee and snapping photos. I also use high-tech remote triggers that send wireless signals to my iPad, such as the CamRanger Wireless Camera Control. CamRanger can even be combined with a motorized tripod head so that I can sit inside with my iPad and point the camera at different feeders and adjust the focus and settings as needed.

When I am taking action shots and portraits, though, I need to be behind the lens and in control of composition, settings, focus, and shutter release. Hummingbirds pay no attention to humans in any event, so I am always behind the camera when I am photographing them.

I took photos remotely using the iPad to view and control the camera. In between birds, I was writing this book.

Bringing kids and nature together

Feeding the birds is a great way to introduce children to the wonders of nature. Children love to be involved in building their own feeders, buying food, and observing the birds as they fly in and out. Feeders can be made out of many household items, such as coffee cans, paper milk cartons, and plastic pop bottles. You can even use an empty half of a grapefruit, orange, or coconut. You can also make bird cookies and tree ornaments. Craft ideas and homemade recipes can be found in abundance online.

Fun feeder and birdhouse kits are available at retailers or online. One kit, Build a Bird feeder Kit by Toysmith, works well to immerse the child in the activity as it needs to be hammered together and includes paints so the feeder can be personalized. Spend an hour building a feeder with your child; as soon as they fill it with good bird seed, they will feel an instant attachment to "their" feeder and "their" birds. They just might look out the window in between looks at their digital screens.

Window feeders are a great way to get kids interested in watching birds, because the birds are just so close! Involve your child in filling the feeders,

cleaning them, and making a list of the birds and the foods they ate.

Another way to get kids involved is to encourage them and their class or troop to get involved in the Great Backyard Bird Count, organized by the Cornell Lab of Ornithology, National Audubon Society, and Bird Studies Canada, and sponsored by Wild Birds Unlimited. Over one weekend in February, thousands of people all over the world watch and count the birds in their yards or neighborhoods and report their findings to gbbc.birdcount.org. This "citizen science" project provides valuable data for scientists seeking to understand where the birds are and why. Even as little as 15 minutes of watching can result in an important report to be shared with researchers. This activity teaches many skills, from watching and identifying birds to using binoculars and the internet. Combine that with the joy of joining other kids and adults all over the world who are helping to protect our planet by learning about birds. All participants are encouraged to submit photos of their birds, another activity the kids can take part in.

Feeding the birds is a great way to get kids involved in watching and learning about nature.

Watch the birds when you're not at home

When you are away from home, you miss a lot of the action at your feeders. Even when you are home, it is difficult to see everything, but there are ways to see the birds on your own feeders or on other people's feeders.

Wingscapes bird feeder camera

The Wingscapes BirdCam Pro is a weatherproof, motion-activated digital camera that takes high-definition photos and videos of wildlife. It has a flash for low-light and nighttime photography. A really neat feature is that you can use a special SD card that automatically sends images to your computer or a website over your home wireless network, so you can view your images anywhere at any time. The BirdCam Pro can be attached to the pole to get it close to the feeders.

Live feeder cams

I started the Wild Birds Unlimited Bird FeederCam in 1995, when only a few dozen cameras were posting images to the internet. The camera was in our dining room, pointed at the feeders on our deck, and it posted a new image every 30 seconds. I still have a camera in the dining room pointing at our feeders, but it is streaming live images now. My wife, Nancy, is a very understanding person!

The easiest way to watch birds live online is to watch someone's streaming video. You can always check www.wbu.com to see if my cam is streaming. The Cornell Lab of Ornithology also has feeder and nest cams streaming live images at allaboutbirds. org. You can find many more by searching the internet for "bird feeder cams."

Live nest cams

I mounted a Barred Owl nest box 30 feet up a hickory tree in my backyard in 1997. I have had several cameras inside it over the years since, but in 2014, I installed a high-definition cam with a microphone and joined the Cornell Lab Nest Cam Network. A Barred Owl family uses the box in about two out of three years, from February to May, so check www.wbu.com or the Cornell Lab website allaboutbirds.org to see if it is operating. This is one of the most exciting things I have done in nature, and everyone who has followed the family from eggs to nestlings to fledging has experienced something very rewarding.

There are many other streaming nest cams on the Cornell Lab site and all over the world. You can watch Red-tailed Hawks, Bald Eagles, Great Blue Herons, Laysan Albatrosses, Ospreys, and dozens of other species raise their families on live streaming video. To see many more, search the web for "live nest cams" and enjoy the many options.

Get involved with citizen science

Birdwatchers can become participants in scientific research by sharing their observations with each other and with scientists. This sharing is called citizen science.

. . . .

eBird

eBird is one of the greatest mergers of a nature-based activity with computer-based scientific study. It is hard to use too many superlatives in describing the cleverness of the scientists who created this database or its usefulness to scientists and birdwatchers. It is very easy to set up an account, and you can use an eBird app on your smartphone to submit observations and study the data. eBird, at ebird.org, was launched by the Cornell Lab and the National Audubon Society in 2002 to collect the millions of bird observations made every year. Every participant's observations enter a massive database that helps educators, conservation biologists, and land managers better understand bird distribution around the world. *www.ebird.org*

Project FeederWatch

A joint program of the Cornell Lab of Ornithology and Bird Studies Canada, this is one of the longest-running citizen science activities, with origins reaching back to 1976. The project now has over 20,000 participants each year, who pay a small registration fee to cover administration costs. Project FeederWatch, at feederwatch.org, is a winter survey of the birds at feeders across North America. The data gathered helps scientists track the movements of wintering bird populations and identify long-term trends in distribution and abundance. Anyone can participate: children, families, classrooms, bird clubs, retired persons, and anyone else interested in birds. To see results from the

FeederWatch 2015/2016 season, go to page 410. There you will find the top 25 birds observed in the US and Canada listed by state and province. *www.feederwatch.org*

Great Backyard Bird Count?

The Great Backyard Bird Count takes place over one February weekend. It has been sponsored by Wild Birds Unlimited since its start in 1998. The project uses eBird to collect data from all over the world. In 2016, participants in more than 130 countries submitted nearly 162,000 bird lists. With 5,689 species reported, more than one-half of the total number of species in the world was counted.

Whether you participate or not, it is really informative to study the data showing you which birds were in your area during previous years' counts. This information can help you design your bird feeding station to attract both common and uncommon birds in your region. *gbbc.birdcount.org*

Other citizen science projects

The Cornell Lab of Ornithology conducts many other projects. You can get involved as an individual, or turn participation into an activity for a classroom or troop.

Habitat Network
The Habitat Network is the first interactive citizen scientist social network, where participants can

share maps and strategies for creating better wild-life habitats. The Habitat Network is a joint project of the Cornell Lab of Ornithology and The Nature Conservancy and is partly funded by The National Science Foundation.
content.yardmap.org

NestWatch

NestWatch tracks bird reproduction, including the timing of nesting, the number of eggs, and the survival of hatchlings. The data are compiled to study changes in breeding habits and populations over time resulting from habitat loss and climate change.
www.nestwatch.org

Celebrate Urban Birds

Celebrate Urban Birds is a year-round project that reaches diverse urban audiences that might not otherwise participate in citizen science. The project partners with community organizations to distribute educational kits and award mini-grants. Participants range from preschoolers to seniors. For many, the project represents their first intro-duction to the observation of wild birds.
www.celebrateurbanbirds.org

Acknowledgments

I HAVE SO MANY people to thank for helping this book become a reality that I cannot possibly name them all. Over the last 35 years I have learned so much about birds and the bird feeding hobby from the customers of Wild Birds Unlimited. I will call out one customer to represent all WBU customers and that is Ree Moores, who was one of the very first customers at my first store. Without Ree and millions of other customers like her, there would be no Wild Birds Unlimited.

I thank all of our franchise store owners, who are the front line face of Wild Birds Unlimited and who are passionate about sharing the joys of the hobby. They have taught me so much about birds and bird food preferences over all of North America.

My team at Wild Birds Unlimited Franchise Support Center is an incredible resource to our store owners, but also to me in writing this book. In particular, I want to thank our Chief Naturalist, John Schaust and our Product and Hobby Education Manager, Brian Cunningham for the many conversations we had about the overall content of the book and their detailed help with the descriptions of the birds in the bird guide section. Our Marketing Department, led by Bo Lowery with our Multimedia Design Specialist Jim Switzer and Marketing Production Assistant Mitch Jacki, were a tremendous help with recommending photos from our WBU photo library or the creation of illustrative photos for the book. Christy Barrett, our Graphic Design Manager, contributed timely design advice. Jim Lesch, our Director of Products and Merchandising and his team, including Andrea McNeely, our Merchandise Manager for Bird Food, gave important advice regarding bird food and feeders. My Executive Assistant, Sue Hernandez, my Indianapolis WBU Store Manager, Gina Jannazzo, our Chief Development Officer, Paul Pickett, and our COO, Pat Perkinson always encouraged my book writing endeavor and kept the company operating when I was busy with the book.

I want to thank the folks at the Cornell Lab of Ornithology for all that they have done to promote the involvement of citizen scientists in collecting data about birds and for the long-term relationship that Wild Birds Unlimited has had with their staff and programs. All of their resources, research and publications serve as a foundation for anyone writing about birds. I appreciate all the encouragement that John Fitzpatrick, Scott Sutcliffe, Mary Guthrie, David Bonter, Tim Gallagher and others at the Lab gave as I shared my thoughts and concepts for this book.

Behind the scenes, but very important, are all of the manufacturers of high quality bird feeding supplies. There are many producers of bird seed, but only a few that produce and deliver the very best quality to our stores and I appreciate their commitment to excellence. I want to thank Joe, Marilyn, Casey and Steve of Holscher Products, Inc. for 30 years of working together on hardware items such as the Advanced Pole System. I also want to thank Aspects, Inc., Arundale, Inc., Backyard Nature Products, Brome Bird Care, C&S Products, Droll Yankees, Inc., Gold Crest Distributing, Mr. Bird, Woodlink, Ltd. and many others for manufacturing bird feeders and bird food products that meet our high standards.

I want to pay a special tribute to two earlier authors on this topic. John K. Terres published *Songbirds in Your Garden* in 1953 and John V. Dennis published *A Complete Guide to Bird Feeding* in 1975. Both books informed and inspired me and still have relevant advice to any hobbyist. I also appreciate the friendship and corporate relationship we have had with all of the Thompsons at *Bird Watcher's Digest*, who have so diligently promoted the hobby of bird feeding and have informed the birding community about birds since 1978.

I want to thank my agent, Russell Galen, who gave me excellent advice on the organization of the book and who connected me with a superb publisher. I am especially indebted to George Scott, of Scott & Nix, Inc. for his incredible creation of the book, effectively communicating the joy of the hobby to the reader. Rick Wright, Amy K. Hooper, Harry Kidd, Paul Pianin, and George Scott IV assisted with editing the book and Paul Lehman and Erin Greb did excellent work on map revisions.

Most of all, I want to thank my wife, Nancy, for all she has done for me, our daughters and Wild Birds Unlimited. She helped me grow the company in the important early years and has been an essential advisor ever since. Nancy helped raise our daughters, Rebecca and Casey, to be fine young adults while also contributing her energies to local and global habitat preservation and human quality of life issues. And regarding this book, she encouraged me without reserve as I spent countless hours over the years taking photographs, researching and writing.

Image credits

KEY JRC = James R. Carpenter; WBU = Wild Birds Unlimited, Inc.; [T] = Top, [B] = Bottom, [L] = Left, [R] = Right, [TL] = Top Left, [TR] = Top Right, [TM] = Top Middle, [M] = Middle, [ML] = Middle Left, [MR] = Middle Right, [BL] = Bottom Left, [BM] = Bottom Middle, [BR] = Bottom Right. Pages with multiple images from one source are indicated by a single credit.

References and resources

T he following is a partial list of references that I used as the source of certain quotes, facts and figures or as general reference for the chapter topics. I also have used my own personal experience and observations and that which I have learned from my Wild Birds Unlimited staff, franchise store owners and customers.

Foreword

Lee, K.E., Williams, K.J.H., Sargent, L.D., Williams, N.S.G., Johnson, K.A. 2015. 40-second green roof views sustain attention: The role of micro-breaks in attention restoration. *Journal of Environmental Psychology* 42:182-189 http://dx.doi.org/10.1016/j.jenvp.2015.04.003

Welcome to Subirdia, John M. Marzluff. 2014, Yale University Press. Quote reprinted by permission of Yale University Press.

Feeding Wild Birds in America: Culture, Commerce & Conservation, Paul J. Baicich, Margaret A. Barker, and Carrol L. Henderson. 2015, Texas A&M University Press

Brittingham, M.C., Temple, S.A.. 1992, Use of Winter Bird Feeders by Black-Capped Chickadees. *Journal of Wildlife Management* 56(1):103 – 110

Robb, G.N., McDonald, R.A, Chamberlain, D.E., Reynolds, S. J., Harrison, T. J. E. & Bearhop, S. 2008. Winter feeding of birds increases productivity in the subsequent breeding season. *The Royal Society Biology Letters* 4, 220-223. doi:10.1098/rsbl.2007.0622

Wilcoxen T.E., Horn D.J., Hogan B.M., Hubble C.N., Huber S.J., Flamm J., Knott M., Lundstrom L., Salik F., Wassenhove S.J., Wrobel E.R. 2015. Effects of bird-feeding activities on the health of wild birds. *Conservation Physiology* 3, 1-13 http://dx.doi.org/10.1093/conphys/cov058

Chapter 2

Scott, S.R., Will, T., Loss, S.S., Marra, P.P. 2014. Bird–building collisions in the United States: Estimates of annual mortality and species vulnerability. *The Condor* 116(1):8-23. http://dx.doi.org/10.1650/CONDOR-13-090.1

American Bird Conservancy Cats Indoors Campaign website: www.abcbirds.org/threat cats-and-other-invasives

Chapter 3

The Birds of North America Online (A.Poole, Ed.). Ithaca: Cornell Lab of Ornithology: www.birds.cornell.edu/bna

Cornell Lab of Ornithology, All About Birds website: www.allaboutbirds.org

National Audubon Society, Guide to North American Birds website: www.audubon.org/bird-guide

Lives of North American Birds, Kenn Kaufman. 1996, Houghton Mifflin

The Sibley Guide to Bird Life & Behavior, Illustrated by David Allen Sibley. Edited by Chris Elphick, John B. Dunning, Jr., David Allen Sibley. 2001, Alfred A. Knopf

The Sibley Guide to Birds, David Allen Sibley. 2000, Alfred A. Knopf

Smithsonian Field Guide to the Birds of North America, Ted Floyd. 2008, HarperCollins Publishers

The FeederWatcher's Guide to Bird Feeding, Margaret A. Barker and Jack Griggs. 2000, HarperCollins Publishers

Guide to the Backyard Birds of North America, Jonathan Alderfer and Paul Hess. 2011, National Geographic Society

Northeastern Birds Backyard Guide, Bill Thompson III, 2013, Cool Springs Press

The Birder's Handbook, Paul R. Ehrlich, David S. Dobkin, and Darryl Wheye. 1988, Simon & Schuster

American Wildlife & Plants, Alexander C. Martin, Herbert S. Zim and Arnold L. Nelson. 1951, McGraw-Hill Book Company

The Audubon Society Encyclopedia of North American Birds, John K. Terres. 1980 Alfred A. Knopf

Songbirds in Your Garden, John K. Terres. 1953, Thomas Y. Crowell Company

A Complete Guide to Bird Feeding, John V. Dennis. 1988, Alfred A. Knopf

Audubon North American Birdfeeder Guide, Robert Burton and Stephen W. Kress. 2005, DK Publishing

Chapter 4

Horn, D.J., Johansen, S.M., Wilcoxen, T.E. 2013. Seed and Feeder Use by Birds in the United States and Canada. *Wildlife Society Bulletin* 1-8 http://dx.doi.org/10.1002/wsb.365

PROJECT WILDBIRD—*Food and Feeder Preferences of Wild Birds in the United States and Canada*, Wild Bird Feeding Industry Research Foundation. 2005 to 2008. Dr. David J. Horn, Principal Investigator

Birds at Your Feeder: A Guide to Feeding Habits, Behavior, Distribution, and Abundance, Erica H. Dunn & Diane L. Tessaglia-Hymes. 1999. W.W. Norton & Company

A Complete Guide to Bird Feeding, John V. Dennis. 1988, Alfred A. Knopf

USDA National Nutrient Database for Standard Reference website: https://Ndb.nal.usda.gov/ndb

Nutrition Information regarding Nutrasaff: www.safflowertech.com

Information regarding winter hummingbirds: www.hummingbirdresearch.net/

Dhondt, A., Hochachka, W.M. 2001. Variations in calcium use by birds during the breeding season. *The Condor* 103(3):595-598 http://dx.doi.org/10.1650/0010-5422(2001)103[0592:-VICUBB]2.0.CO;2

Curtis, P. D., Rowland, E. D., Curtis, G. B., and Dunn, J. A. 2000. Capsaicin-treated seed as a squirrel deterrent at birdfeeders (2000). *Wildlife Damage Management Conferences* —Proceedings. Paper 18. http://digitalcommons.unl.edu/icwdm_wdmconfproc/18

Chapter 7
Maine Department of Inland Fisheries and Wildlife website regarding feeding deer in winter: www.maine.gov/ifw/wildlife/species/mammals/feeding_deer.html

New Jersey Audubon website regarding hawks at your bird feeders: www.njaudubon.org/SectionNatureNotes/SuburbanSurvivalGuides/HawksKillingBirdsatYourFeeders.aspx

American Bird Conservancy Cats Indoors Campaign website: www.abcbirds.org/threat/cats-and-other-invasives

Chapter 8
American Bird Conservancy window strike website: www.abcbirds.org/threat/bird-strikes

General information and links to rehabilitators
National Wildlife Rehabilitators Association www.nwrawildlife.org

Humane Society of the United States www.humanesociety.org/animals/resources/tips/find-a-wildlife-rehabilitator

Information about orphaned birds
Cornell Lab of Ornithology www.birds.cornell.edu/AllAboutBirds/faq/master_folder/attracting/challenges/orphaned

Chapter 10
Cornell Laboratory of Ornithology and Bird Studies Canada FeederWatch website about bird diseases: www.feederwatch.org/learn/sick-birds-and-bird-diseases

National Wildlife Heath Center website about wild bird diseases: www.nwhc.usgs.gov/disease_information

Live nest and feeder cams
Wild Birds Unlimited Bird FeederCam www.livestream.com/watch and search for Wild Birds Unlimited FeederCam

Wild Birds Unlimited Barred Owl Box Cam cams.allaboutbirds.org/channel/43/Barred_Owls/

Cornell Laboratory of Birds - All About Birds Nest and Feeder Cams cams.allaboutbirds.org/

Other general resources
Wild Birds Unlimited Educational Resources: www.wbu.com

Hummingbird migration maps Spring hummingbird migration map www.hummingbirds.net/map.html

Fall hummingbird migration map Journey North Hummingbirds www.learner.org/jnorth/humm

Wild Birds Unlimited store directory

UNITED STATES

ALABAMA

Wild Birds Unlimited
1580 Montgomery Hwy
Birmingham, AL 35216
(205) 823-6500

Wild Birds Unlimited
4800 Whitesburg Dr., Ste. 9B
Huntsville, AL 35802
(256) 536-9128

Wild Birds Unlimited
6345-C Airport Blvd.
Mobile, AL 36608
(251) 380-0280

Wild Birds Unlimited
1550 Opelika Rd., Suite #7
Auburn, AL 36830
(334) 826-9230

ARKANSAS

Wild Birds Unlimited
1818 N. Taylor St.
Little Rock, AR 72207
(501) 666-4210

Wild Birds Unlimited
2011 Promenade Blvd., Ste. 430
Rogers, AR 72758
(479) 246-0217

Wild Birds Unlimited
745 E. Joyce Blvd.
Fayetteville, AR 72703
(479) 435-6366

ARIZONA

Wild Birds Unlimited
6546 E. Tanque Verde Rd., Ste. #150
Tucson, AZ 85715
(520) 299-9585

Wild Birds Unlimited
7645 N. Oracle Rd., Ste. #110
Tucson, AZ 85704
(520) 878-9585

Wild Birds Unlimited
2136 East Baseline Rd., Ste. 2
Mesa, AZ 85204
(480) 507-2473

Wild Birds Unlimited
7001 N. Scottsdale Rd., Ste. 174
Scottsdale, AZ 85253
(480) 306-5153

CALIFORNIA

Wild Birds Unlimited
2624 El Camino Real, Ste. F
Carlsbad, CA 92008
(760) 720-1906

Wild Birds Unlimited
692 Contra Costa Blvd.
Pleasant Hill, CA 94523
(925) 798-0303

Wild Birds Unlimited
71 Brookwood Ave.
Santa Rosa, CA 95404
(707) 576-0861

Wild Birds Unlimited
25416 Crenshaw Blvd.
Torrance, CA 90505
(310) 326-2473

Wild Birds Unlimited
17611 Yorba Linda Blvd.
Yorba Linda, CA 92886
(714) 985-4928

Wild Birds Unlimited
3940 Broad St., Ste. F-6
San Luis Obispo, CA 93401
(805) 547-0242

Wild Birds Unlimited
2561 Fair Oaks Blvd.
Sacramento, CA 95825
(916) 971-0719

Wild Birds Unlimited
119 Neal St.
Grass Valley, CA 95945
530-272-7744

Wild Birds Unlimited
24451 Alicia Pkwy., Unit 9B
Mission Viejo, CA 92691
(949) 472-4928

Wild Birds Unlimited
10450 Magnolia Ave.
Riverside, CA 92505
(951) 352-2020

Wild Birds Unlimited
104 Vintage Way, Ste. A-7
Novato, CA 94945
(415) 893-0500

Wild Birds Unlimited
720 N. Moorpark Rd.
Thousand Oaks, CA 91360
(805) 379-3901

Wild Birds Unlimited
911 W. Foothill Blvd.
Claremont, CA 91711
(909) 626-2266

Wild Birds Unlimited
10549 Scripps Poway Pkwy., Ste. B-3
San Diego, CA 92131
(858) 271-8457

Coming Soon
Wild Birds Unlimited
Huntington Beach, CA

Wild Birds Unlimited
Roseville, CA

Wild Birds Unlimited
Ventura, CA

COLORADO

Wild Birds Unlimited
7370 West 88th Ave., Unit A
Arvada, CO 80021
(303) 467-2644

Wild Birds Unlimited
3350 N. Union Blvd.
Colorado Springs, CO 80907
(719) 596-1819

Wild Birds Unlimited
2720 S. Wadsworth
Denver, CO 80227
(303) 987-1065

Wild Birds Unlimited
3636 S. College Ave., Ste. C
Ft. Collins, CO 80525
(970) 225-2557

Wild Birds Unlimited
2454 Hwy 6 & 50, #116
Grand Junction, CO 81505
(970) 242-2843

Wild Birds Unlimited
18666 E. Hampden Ave.
Aurora, CO 80013
(720) 519-1374

Wild Birds Unlimited
320 W. Allen St.
Castle Rock, CO 80108
(303) 660-6334

CONNECTICUT

Wild Birds Unlimited
2848A Main St.
Griswold Shopping Plaza
Glastonbury, CT 06033
(860) 633-5211

Wild Birds Unlimited
356 Heights Rd.
Darien, CT 06820
(203) 202-2669

Wild Birds Unlimited
190 Flanders Rd., Unit 1
Niantic, CT 06357
(860) 739-7302

Wild Birds Unlimited
317 Federal Rd, Ste. D1
Brookfield, CT 06804
(203) 775-4888

Wild Birds Unlimited
320 West Main St., Ste. 5
Westridge Shops
Avon, CT 06001-3687
(860) 677-0181

Coming Soon
Wild Birds Unlimited
Fairfield, CT

DELAWARE

Wild Birds Unlimited
7411 Lancaster Pike
Hockessin, DE 19707
(302) 239-9071

FLORIDA

Wild Birds Unlimited
13140 N Dale Mabry
Tampa, FL 33618
(813) 280-9970

Wild Birds Unlimited
S. Beach Reg Shopping Ctr
4138 South Third St.
Jacksonville Beach, FL 32250
(904) 246-6832

Wild Birds Unlimited
4212 NW 16th Blvd.
Gainesville, FL 32605
(352) 381-1997

Wild Birds Unlimited
450 State Road 13 N., Ste. 108
St. Johns, FL 32259
(904) 230-3242

Wild Birds Unlimited
5687 Red Bug Lake Rd.
Winter Springs, FL 32708
(407) 695-0526

Wild Birds Unlimited
2098 Thomasville Rd.
Tallahassee, FL 32308
(850) 576-0002

Wild Birds Unlimited
2455 Martin Luther King Jr Blvd
Panama City, FL 32405
(850) 640-1354

Wild Birds Unlimited
2868 David Walker Dr.
Eustis, FL 32726
(352) 602-4208

GEORGIA

Wild Birds Unlimited
1050 E. Piedmont Rd.
Marietta GA 30062
(770) 565-9841

Wild Birds Unlimited
3000 Old Alabama Rd., #116
Alpharetta, GA 30022
(770) 410-0799

Wild Birds Unlimited
8108 Abercorn St., Ste. 210
Savannah, GA 31406
(912) 961-3455

Wild Birds Unlimited
Chastain Square Shopping Ctr
4279 Roswell Rd., Ste. 603
Atlanta, GA 30342
(404) 257-0084

Wild Birds Unlimited
3830 Washington Rd., Ste. 12
Augusta, GA 30907
(706) 855-1955

Wild Birds Unlimited
1630 Hwy 124, Ste. U
Snellville, GA 30078
(770) 982-2650

Wild Birds Unlimited
Dean Taylor Crossing
2133 Lawrenceville-Suwanee Rd.
#9
Suwanee, GA 30024
(678) 442-9691

Wild Birds Unlimited
1025 Rose Creek Dr., Ste. 760
Woodstock, GA 30189
(770) 928-3014

Wild Birds Unlimited
100 N. Peachtree Pkwy., Ste. 4
Peachtree City, GA 30269
(770) 486-1599

Wild Birds Unlimited
425 Quill Dr., Ste 100
Dawsonville, GA 30534
(706) 429-0077

Wild Birds Unlimited
80 Seven Hills Blvd., #303
Dallas, GA 30132
(770) 975-3423

Wild Birds Unlimited
2980 Cobb Pkwy., Ste. 103
Atlanta, GA 30339
(770) 433-2676

IOWA

Wild Birds Unlimited
801 73rd
Des Moines, IA 50324
(515) 222-1234

Wild Birds Unlimited
3616 Eastern Ave.
Davenport, IA 52807
(563) 445-3555

Wild Birds Unlimited
213 Duff Ave., Ste. 4
Ames IA 50010
(515) 956-3145

IDAHO

Wild Birds Unlimited
296 W. Sunset Ave., #22
Coeur d'Alene, ID 83815
(208) 765-8787

Wild Birds Unlimited
10480 Overland Rd.
Boise, ID 83709
(208) 376-6862

ILLINOIS

Wild Birds Unlimited
321 Rand Rd.
Arlington Heights, IL 60004
(847) 259-7286

Wild Birds Unlimited
1460 Waukegan Rd.
Glenview, IL 60025
(847) 729-4688

Wild Birds Unlimited
1891 2nd St.
Highland Park, IL 60035
(847) 432-3384

Wild Birds Unlimited
1149 Essington Rd.
Joliet, IL 60435
(815) 744-3800

Wild Birds Unlimited
1601 Ogden Ave.
Lisle, IL 60532
(630) 968-6332

Wild Birds Unlimited
13012 S. LaGrange
Palos Park, IL 60464
(708) 361-8726

Wild Birds Unlimited
2657 N. Illinois St.
Swansea, IL 62226
(618) 235-3370

Wild Birds Unlimited
631 South Perryville
Rockford, IL 61108
(815) 484-9281

Wild Birds Unlimited
1930 S. MacArthur Blvd.
Springfield, IL 62704
(217) 789-6468

Wild Birds Unlimited
1520 E. College Ave., Ste. I
Normal, IL 61761
(309) 454-3455

Wild Birds Unlimited
206 South Main St.
Galena, IL 61036
(815) 777-2883

Wild Birds Unlimited
7323 N. Radnor Rd.
Peoria, IL 61615
(309) 690-3232

Wild Birds Unlimited
2216 Troy Rd.
Edwardsville, IL 62025
(618) 307-9604

Wild Birds Unlimited
Hilander Village Shopping Center
4902 Hononegah Rd.
Roscoe, IL 61073
(815) 623-1407

INDIANA

Wild Birds Unlimited
3956 E 82nd St.
Indianapolis, IN 46240
(317) 578-0770

Wild Birds Unlimited
801 Northcrest Shopping Ctr
Ft. Wayne, IN 46805
(260) 484-3000

Wild Birds Unlimited
2902 Calumet Ave.
Valparaiso, IN 46383
(219) 465-0508

Wild Birds Unlimited
421 E. University Dr.
Granger, IN 46530
(574) 247-0201

Wild Birds Unlimited
8100 East US Hwy. 36, Ste. O
Avon, IN 46123
(317) 272-0780

Wild Birds Unlimited
9830 A North Michigan Rd.
Carmel, IN 46032-7925
(317) 334-1883

Wild Birds Unlimited
14753 Hazel Dell Crossing
Ste. 400
Noblesville, IN 46062
(317) 566-8222

Wild Birds Unlimited
5620 E. Virginia St.
Evansville, IN 47715-2639
(812) 476-2473

Wild Birds Unlimited
331 S. State Road 135
Ste. B
Greenwood, IN 46142
(317) 884-9632

Wild Birds Unlimited
138 US HWY 41
Schererville, IN 46375
(219) 319-0126

KANSAS

Wild Birds Unlimited
11711 Roe Ave.
Leawood, KS 66211
(913) 491-4887

Wild Birds Unlimited
13222 W. 62nd Terrace
Shawnee, KS 66216
(913) 962-0077

KENTUCKY

Wild Birds Unlimited
152 N. Locust Hill Dr.
Lexington, KY 40509
(859) 268-0114

Wild Birds Unlimited
4987 Houston Rd.
Florence, KY 41042
(859) 283-2473

Wild Birds Unlimited
1100 US 127 S, Unit B3
Frankfort, KY 40601
(502) 352-2891

LOUISIANA

Wild Birds Unlimited
137 Arnould Blvd.
Lafayette, LA 70506
(337) 993-2473

Wild Birds Unlimited
8342 Perkins Rd., Ste. L
Baton Rouge, LA 70810
(225) 408-0600

MASSACHUSETTS

Wild Birds Unlimited
301 Newbury St.
Danvers, MA 01923
(978) 774-9819

Wild Birds Unlimited
386 Columbia Rd. Rte.#53
Hanover, MA 02339
(781) 826-1640

Wild Birds Unlimited
1462 Fall River Ave.
Seekonk, MA 02771
(508) 336-4043

Wild Birds Unlimited
513A Boston Post Rd., Rte 20
Sudbury Plaza
Sudbury, MA 01776
(978) 443-1739

Wild Birds Unlimited
1198 Main St., Route 28
South Yarmouth, MA 02664
(508) 760-1996

Wild Birds Unlimited
Franklin Village Mall
215 Franklin Village Dr.
Franklin, MA 02038
(508) 541-6800

Wild Birds Unlimited
175 Littleton Rd., Unit L
Westford, MA 01886
(978) 692-7932

MARYLAND

Wild Birds Unlimited
7820 Wormans Mill Rd., Ste. J
Frederick MD 21701
(301) 360-9910

Wild Birds Unlimited
1304 Main Chapel Way
Gambrills, MD 21054
(410) 451-6876

Wild Birds Unlimited
2438 Broad Ave.
Timonium, MD 21093
(410) 561-1215

Wild Birds Unlimited
Boulevard at Box Hill-Ste. 104
3491 Merchant Boulevard
Abingdon, MD 21009
(410) 569-2299

Wild Birds Unlimited
46400 Lexington Village #106
Lexington Park, MD 20653
(301) 863-2473

MAINE

Wild Birds Unlimited
400 Expedition Dr., Ste. F
Scarborough, ME 04074
(207) 771-2473

MICHIGAN

Wild Birds Unlimited
2208 S. Main St.
Ann Arbor, MI 48103
(734) 665-7427

Wild Birds Unlimited
G4208 Corunna Rd.
Flint, MI 48532
(810) 732-0100

Wild Birds Unlimited
3085 Broadmoor S.E.
Kentwood, MI 49512
(616) 957-0366

Wild Birds Unlimited
20381 Mack Ave.
Grosse Pointe Woods, MI 48236
(313) 881-1410

Wild Birds Unlimited
3015 Oakland Dr.
Kalamazoo, MI 49008
(269) 353-7550

Wild Birds Unlimited
3032 Walton Blvd.
Rochester Hills, MI 48309
(248) 375-5202

Wild Birds Unlimited
28558 Woodward Ave.
Royal Oak, MI 48067
(248) 548-2424

Wild Birds Unlimited
1211 East Front St.
Traverse City, MI 49686
(231) 946-0431

Wild Birds Unlimited
975 S. Main
Frankenmuth, MI 48734
(989) 652-8830

Wild Birds Unlimited
2200 Coolidge Rd., Ste. 17
East Lansing, MI 48823
(517) 337-9920

Wild Birds Unlimited
47760 Grand River Ave.
Novi, MI 48374
(248) 374-4000

Wild Birds Unlimited
41816 Ford Rd.
Canton, MI 48187
(734) 983-9130

Wild Birds Unlimited
20241 Hall Rd.
Macomb, MI 48044
(586) 229-2798

MINNESOTA

Wild Birds Unlimited
5115 Burning Tree Rd., Unit 311
Duluth, MN 55811
(218) 722-5658

Wild Birds Unlimited
2020A Ford Parkway
St. Paul, MN 55116
(651) 690-9525

Wild Birds Unlimited
Tower Square
582 Prairie Center Dr.
Eden Prairie, MN 55344
(952) 944-3272

Wild Birds Unlimited
11210 Wayzata Blvd.
Minnetonka, MN 55305
(952) 525-9365
Wild Birds Unlimited
Miracle Mile Center
20–17th Ave. NW
Rochester, MN 55901
(507) 292-9266

Wild Birds Unlimited
5805 Egan Dr.
Savage, MN 55378
(952) 226-2010

Coming Soon
Wild Birds Unlimited
Brighton, MI

MISSOURI

Wild Birds Unlimited
1739 Clarkson Rd.
Chesterfield, MO 63017
(636) 537-5574

Wild Birds Unlimited
9987 Manchester Rd.
Warson Woods, MO 63122
(314) 821-2266

Wild Birds Unlimited
Parkcrest Shopping Ctr.
3849 S. Campbell
Springfield, MO 65807
(417) 882-8801

Wild Birds Unlimited
1983 Zumbehl Rd.
St. Charles, MO 63303
(636) 949-9191

Wild Birds Unlimited
Surrey Plaza 1
2644 N. Highway 67
Florissant, MO 63033
(314) 830-3533

Wild Birds Unlimited
8708 North Flintlock Rd.
Kansas City, MO 64157
(816) 415-4303

Wild Birds Unlimited
6074 Telegraph Rd.
St. Louis, MO 63129
(314) 293-1300

Wild Birds Unlimited
650 N. Branson Landing Blvd.
Branson, MO 65616
(417) 336-2473

MISSISSIPPI

Wild Birds Unlimited
4800 I-55 North, Ste. 19B
Jackson, MS 39211
(601) 366-9973

MONTANA

Wild Birds Unlimited
2727 South 3rd West
Missoula, MT 59804
(406) 543-3333

Wild Birds Unlimited
111 S. 24th St. W., Ste. 27
Billings, MT 59102
(406) 245-1640

Wild Birds Unlimited
2047 Oak St., #105
Bozeman, MT 59718
(406) 219-2066

NORTH CAROLINA

Wild Birds Unlimited
10 Crispin Court, Ste. D102
Asheville, NC 28803
(828) 687-9433

Wild Birds Unlimited
1848 Galleria Blvd., Ste. F
Charlotte, NC 28270
(704) 844-8426

Wild Birds Unlimited
2040 Kildaire Farm Rd.
Cary, NC 27518
(919) 233-9370

Wild Birds Unlimited
568 Hanes Mall Blvd.
Winston-Salem, NC 27103
(336) 774-1906

Wild Birds Unlimited
2920-A Martinsville Rd.
Greensboro, NC 27408
(336) 282-4458

Wild Birds Unlimited
2029 South Glenburnie Rd.
Crossroads Shopping Ctr.
New Bern, NC 28562
(252) 637-6604

Wild Birds Unlimited
638 Spartanburg Highway
Ste. 60
Hendersonville, NC 28792
(828) 694-0081

Wild Birds Unlimited
518 Greenville Blvd. SE, Unit A
Greenville, NC 27858
(252) 493-0340

Wild Birds Unlimited
4412-110 Falls of Neuse Rd.
Raleigh, NC 27609
(919) 876-4498

Wild Birds Unlimited
Woodcroft Shopping Ctr.
4711 Hope Valley Rd., Ste 6D
Durham, NC 27707
(919) 401-4928

Wild Birds Unlimited
3014 North Center St.
Hickory, NC 28601
(828) 441-2473

Wild Birds Unlimited
1806 Martin Luther King Blvd.
Chapel Hill, NC 27514
(919) 969-6778

Wild Birds Unlimited
476 Shotwell, Ste. 101
Clayton, NC 27520
(919) 553-7973

Wild Birds Unlimited
124 Brucewood Rd.
Southern Pines, NC 28387
(910) 246-0002

Wild Birds Unlimited
8609 Concord Mills Blvd.
Concord, NC 28027
(704) 979-3443

Wild Birds Unlimited
1589 Skeet Club Rd., Ste. 134
High Point, NC 27265
(336) 841-2572

Wild Birds Unlimited
3916 E. Franklin Blvd., Ste. 150
Gastonia, NC 28056
(704) 823-1988

Wild Birds Unlimited
9719-B Sam Furr Rd.
Huntersville, NC 28078
(704) 892-3209

Wild Birds Unlimited
946 Merrimon Ave., #120
North Asheville, NC 28804
(828) 575-2081

NEBRASKA

Wild Birds Unlimited
10923 Elm St.
Omaha, NE 68144
(402) 399-9976

NEW HAMPSHIRE

Wild Birds Unlimited
650 Amherst St.
Nashua, NH 03063
(603) 886-5091

Wild Birds Unlimited
37 Plaistow Rd., #10
Plaistow, NH 03865
(603) 382-3354

Wild Birds Unlimited
250 Indian Brook Dr.
Somersworth, NH 03878
(603) 743-4928

NEW JERSEY

Wild Birds Unlimited
2520 Highway 22 East
Scotch Plains, NJ 07076
(908) 233-5004

Wild Birds Unlimited
Classic Plaza
1619 N. Kings Highway
Cherry Hill, NJ 08034
(856) 428-1200

Wild Birds Unlimited
189 Route 17 South
Paramus, NJ 07652
(201) 599-0099

Wild Birds Unlimited
844 Route 35
Middletown, NJ 07748
(732) 671-3155

Wild Birds Unlimited
941 Route 37 West, #2
Toms River, NJ 08755
(732) 281-2473

NEW MEXICO

Wild Birds Unlimited
7200 Montgomery N.E.
Ste. G-3
Albuquerque, NM 87109
(505) 883-0324

Wild Birds Unlimited
Cordova Center
518-B Cordova Rd.
Santa Fe, NM 87505
(505) 989-8818

Wild Birds Unlimited
2001 E. Lohman Ave.
Ste. 130
Las Cruces, NM 88001
(575) 523-5489

Wild Birds Unlimited
10701 Corrales Rd. NW
Ste. 5
Albuquerque, NM 87114
(505) 717-1385

NEVADA

Wild Birds Unlimited
1100 West Moana Ln.
Reno, NV 89509
(775) 825-0600

Wild Birds Unlimited
11301 South Virginia St.
Reno, NV 89511
(775) 853-1319

Wild Birds Unlimited
7655 Pyramid Hwy.
Sparks, NV 89436
(775) 425-4300

NEW YORK

Wild Birds Unlimited
551 North Bedford Rd.
Bedford Hills, NY 10507
(914) 241-0721

Wild Birds Unlimited
314 Towne Dr.
Fayetteville, NY 13066
(315) 637-0710

Wild Birds Unlimited
800 Valley Plaza, Ste. 7
Johnson City, NY 13790
(607) 770-4920

Wild Birds Unlimited
3835 McKinley Pkwy, Ste. 1
Blasdell, NY 14219
(716) 823-7889

Wild Birds Unlimited
159 Sapsucker Woods Rd.
Ithaca, NY 14850
(607) 266-7425

Wild Birds Unlimited
950 County Rd. 64, Ste. 600
Elmira, NY 14903
(607) 739-8157

Wild Birds Unlimited
3084 Route 50, Ste. 1
Saratoga Springs, NY 12866
(518) 226-0071

Wild Birds Unlimited
911 Montauk Highway
Oakdale, NY 11769
(631) 218-2473

Coming Soon
Wild Birds Unlimited
Buffalo, NY

Wild Birds Unlimited
Syosset, NY

OHIO

Wild Birds Unlimited
9887 Montgomery Rd.
Cincinnati, OH 45242
(513) 891-2199

Wild Birds Unlimited
6654 Sawmill Rd.
Columbus, OH 43235
(614) 766-2103

Wild Birds Unlimited
4027 Far Hills Ave.
Kettering, OH 45429
(937) 299-1102

Wild Birds Unlimited
5736 Mayfield Rd.
Mayfield Heights, OH 44124
(440) 449-3324

Wild Birds Unlimited
26791 Brookpark Extension
North Olmsted, OH 44070
(440) 777-1233

Wild Birds Unlimited
5236 Monroe St., Ste. D
Toledo, OH 43623
(419) 841-7219

Wild Birds Unlimited
720 North State St.
Westerville, OH 43082
(614) 899-9453

Wild Birds Unlimited
90 Boardman-Canfield Rd.
Boardman, OH 44512
(330) 629-2473

Wild Birds Unlimited
1196 West Kemper Rd.
Forest Park, OH 45240
(513) 825-7777

Wild Birds Unlimited
14178 Pearl Rd.
Strongsville, OH 44136
(440) 846-6443

Wild Birds Unlimited
28728 Wolf Rd.
Bay Village, OH 44140
(440) 835-9422

Wild Birds Unlimited
6839 E. Broad St.
Columbus, OH 43213
(614) 860-1133

Wild Birds Unlimited
4428 Milan Rd.
Sandusky, OH 44870
(419) 626-5843

Wild Birds Unlimited
6496 Glenway Ave.
Cincinnati, OH 45211
(513) 598-4645

Wild Birds Unlimited
597 Howe Ave.
Cuyahoga Falls, OH 44221
(330) 922-4990

Wild Birds Unlimited
734 N. Main St.
Springboro, OH 45066
(937) 748-8979

Wild Birds Unlimited
34500 Euclid Ave., #5
Willoughby, OH 44094
(440) 918-1996

Wild Birds Unlimited
7712 Voice of America Ctr. Dr.
West Chester, OH 45069
(513) 847-6580

OKLAHOMA

Wild Birds Unlimited
7501 N. May
Oklahoma City, OK 73116
(405) 842-9910

Wild Birds Unlimited
Brookhaven Village
3770 W. Robinson, Ste. 104
Norman, OK 73072
(405) 321-8686

Wild Birds Unlimited
Kings Pointe Village Shopping Ctr
5960 S. Yale Ave.
Tulsa, OK 74135
(918) 477-7408

OREGON

Wild Birds Unlimited
961 Medford Center
Medford, OR 97504
(541) 772-2107

Wild Birds Unlimited
1935 NW 9th St.
Corvallis, OR 97330
(541) 757-0120

Wild Birds Unlimited
1210 Commercial St. SE
Salem, OR 97302
(503) 363-9744

Wild Birds Unlimited
2680 NE Hwy. 20, Ste. 310
Bend, OR 97701
(541) 617-8840

Wild Birds Unlimited
2510 Willamette St.
Eugene, OR 97405
(541) 844-1788

PENNSYLVANIA

Wild Birds Unlimited
4920 York Rd.
Buckingham, PA 18912
(215) 794-3888

Wild Birds Unlimited
Village West #17
3330 W. 26th St.
Erie, PA 16506
(814) 838-5145

Wild Birds Unlimited
1775 N. Highland Rd.
Pittsburgh, PA 15241
(412) 833-9299

Wild Birds Unlimited
12019 Perry Hwy., Rte. #19
Wexford, PA 15090
(724) 935-0051

Wild Birds Unlimited
60 Shillington Rd.
Sinking Spring, PA 19608
(610) 670-5508

Wild Birds Unlimited
Dreshertown Plaza
1650 Limekiln Pike
Dresher, PA 19025
(215) 654-1993

Wild Birds Unlimited
3848 William Penn Hwy.
Monroeville, PA 15146
(412) 374-0678

Wild Birds Unlimited
4251 Tilghman St.
Allentown, PA 18104
(610) 366-1725

Wild Birds Unlimited
Dallas Shopping Center
Memorial Hwy
Dallas, PA 18612
(570) 675-9900

Wild Birds Unlimited
1947 Fruitville Pike Foxshire Plaza
Lancaster, PA 17601
(717) 208-6881

Wild Birds Unlimited
6391 Carlisle Pike
Mechanicsburg, PA 17050
(717) 697-9000

Wild Birds Unlimited
100 Evergreen Dr, Ste. 109
Glen Mills, PA 19342
(484) 800-4941

Coming Soon
Wild Birds Unlimited
Wynnewood, PA

RHODE ISLAND

Wild Birds Unlimited
1000 Bald Hill Rd.
Warwick, RI 02886
(401) 826-0606

SOUTH CAROLINA

Wild Birds Unlimited
626 Congaree Rd.
Congaree Center #4
Greenville, SC 29607
(864) 234-2150

Wild Birds Unlimited
468 E. Main St.
Spartanburg, SC 29302
(864) 585-0409

Wild Birds Unlimited
1085 Lake Murray Blvd
Irmo, SC 29063
(803) 781-3480

Wild Birds Unlimited
4711 Forest Dr., Ste. 10
Columbia, SC 29206-3125
(803) 782-5700

Wild Birds Unlimited
435 Columbia Ave.
Lexington, SC 29072
(803) 951-2070

Wild Birds Unlimited
The Village at Sandhill
130-3 Forum Dr.
Columbia, SC 29229
(803) 736-4810

Wild Birds Unlimited
Moultrie Plaza 624 Coleman Blvd.
Mt. Pleasant, SC 29464
(843) 216-8800

Wild Birds Unlimited
St. Andrews Shopping Ctr.
975 Savannah Hwy
Charleston, SC 29407
(843) 571-3771

Wild Birds Unlimited
2734 Celanese Rd.
Rock Hill, SC 29732
(803) 981-9282

Wild Birds Unlimited
8703 US Hwy 17 Bypass, Ste. E
Surfside Beach, SC 29575
(843) 748-0989

Coming Soon
Wild Birds Unlimited
Hilton Head, SC

TENNESSEE

Wild Birds Unlimited
6025 E. Brainerd Rd., Ste. 102
Chattanooga, TN 37421
(423) 892-3816

Wild Birds Unlimited
704 S. Mendenhall
Memphis, TN 38117
(901) 681-9837

Wild Birds Unlimited
2813 Bransford Ave.
Nashville, TN 37204
(615) 385-2426

Wild Birds Unlimited
806 Meadow Lark Lane
Goodlettsville, TN 37072
(615) 859-7597

Wild Birds Unlimited
Battlewood Shopping Ctr
2176 Hillsboro Rd., Ste.110
Franklin, TN 37064
(615) 591-6962

Wild Birds Unlimited
5929 Hixson Pike Shop, #100
Hixson, TN 37343
(423) 847-1120

Wild Birds Unlimited
7240 Kingston Pike, Ste. 164
Knoxville, TN 37919
(865) 337-5990

TEXAS

Wild Birds Unlimited
5715 West Lovers Lane
Dallas, TX 75209
(214) 891-9793

Wild Birds Unlimited
Wood Ridge Plaza
27590 I-45 North
Conroe, TX 77385
(281) 298-7900

Wild Birds Unlimited
3535 Bee Caves Rd., Ste. A
Austin, TX 78746
(512) 328-9453

Wild Birds Unlimited
14032 Memorial Dr.
Houston, TX 77079
(281) 293-0959

Wild Birds Unlimited
14602 Huebner Rd., Ste. 114
San Antonio, TX 78230
(210) 479-2473

Wild Birds Unlimited
12320 Barker Cypress Rd., Ste. 500
Cypress, TX 77429
(281) 246-1200

Wild Birds Unlimited
14010 US 183 N., Ste. 515
Austin, TX 78717
(512) 335-1700

Wild Birds Unlimited
6333 E. Mockingbird Ln., Ste. 101
Dallas, TX 75214
(214) 821-7400

Wild Birds Unlimited
1507 Wooded Acres
Waco, TX 76710
(254) 741-9630

Wild Birds Unlimited
855 Junction Highway
Kerrville, TX 78028
(830) 895-7393

Wild Birds Unlimited
3820 FM3009, Ste. 152
Schertz, TX 78154
(210) 566-8808

Wild Birds Unlimited
3701 Fairway, Ste. 110
Wichita Falls, TX 76310
(940) 234-2473

Wild Birds Unlimited
2704 Cross Timbers Rd., Ste. #118
Flower Mound, TX 75028
(972) 874-1111

Wild Birds Unlimited
1660 W. Randoll Mill Rd.
Arlington, TX 76012
(817) 275-1000

Wild Birds Unlimited
9910 West Loop 1604 North
Ste. 120
San Antonio, TX 78254
(210) 375-3611

Wild Birds Unlimited
1013 W. University Ave., Ste. 330
Georgetown, TX 78628
(512) 763-1081

Wild Birds Unlimited
3819 Bellaire Blvd.
Houston, TX 77025
(713) 668-6440

Coming Soon
Wild Birds Unlimited
Katy, TX

Wild Birds Unlimited
Keller, TX

Wild Birds Unlimited
Kingwood, TX

Wild Birds Unlimited
McKinney, TX

Wild Birds Unlimited
New Braunfels, TX

Wild Birds Unlimited
Pearland, TX

UTAH

Wild Birds Unlimited
1967 E. Murray Holladay Rd.
Salt Lake City, UT 84117
(801) 878-4449

VIRGINIA

Wild Birds Unlimited
2437 N. Harrison St.
Arlington, VA 22207
(703) 241-3988

Wild Birds Unlimited
12631 Stone Village Way
Midlothian, VA 23113
(804) 323-0353

Wild Birds Unlimited
620 Hilltop W. Shopping Ctr.
Virginia Beach, VA 23451
(757) 422-3215

Wild Birds Unlimited
Settlers Market
4625 Casey Blvd., Ste. 300
Williamsburg, VA 23188
(757) 253-0873

Wild Birds Unlimited
Greenbrier Marketctr, Ste. 570
1244 Greenbrier Parkway
Chesapeake, VA 23220
(757) 436-4472

Wild Birds Unlimited
3120 Kiln Creek Pkwy., Unit A
Yorktown, VA 23693
(757) 875-1936

Wild Birds Unlimited
3404 Pump Rd.
Henrico, VA 23233
(804) 934-9200

Wild Birds Unlimited
1510 Seminole Trail 29th Place
Charlottesville, VA 22901
(434) 973-5850

Wild Birds Unlimited
3103 Valley Ave., Ste. 110
Winchester, VA 22601
(540) 722-9407

Wild Birds Unlimited
44110 Ashburn Plaza Shopping Ctr,
#174
Ashburn, VA 20147
(703) 687-4020

Wild Birds Unlimited
1937 Carl D. Silver Parkway
Fredericksburg, VA 22401
(540) 548-9393

WASHINGTON

Wild Birds Unlimited
5565 Van Barr Place, Ste. AB
Freeland, WA 98249
(360) 341-1404

Wild Birds Unlimited
275953 Highway 101
Gardiner, WA 98382
(360) 797-7100

Wild Birds Unlimited
3120 ½ Harborview Dr.
Gig Harbor, WA 98335
(253) 851-2575

Wild Birds Unlimited
17171 Bothell Way NE, #A007
Lake Forest Park, WA 98155
(206) 367-1950

Wild Birds Unlimited
15155 NE 24th St.
Redmond, WA 98052
(425) 747-8908

Wild Birds Unlimited
4821 Evergreen Way
Everett, WA 98203
(425) 252-2220

Wild Birds Unlimited
Cooper Point Mktpl, Ste. 304
1200 Cooper Point Rd. SW
Olympia, WA 98502
(360) 352-5458

Wild Birds Unlimited
19915 State Rt. 2
Monroe, WA 98272
(360) 863-9173

Wild Birds Unlimited
15858 First Ave. S., #106
Burien, WA 98148
(206) 241-3201

Wild Birds Unlimited
27177 185th
Ave. SE, Ste. D109
Covington, WA 98042
(253) 639-6378

Wild Birds Unlimited
4621 S. Meridian St.
Ste. 825
Puyallup, WA 98373
(253) 845-5434

WISCONSIN

Wild Birds Unlimited
3000 Milton Ave., #102
Janesville, WI 53545
(608) 758-2565

Wild Birds Unlimited
8402 Old Sauk Rd.
Middleton, WI 53562
(608) 664-1414

Wild Birds Unlimited
11004 N. Port Washington Rd.
Mequon, WI 53092
(262) 241-8483

Wild Birds Unlimited
4454 S. 108th St.
Milwaukee, WI 53228
(414) 529-4644

Wild Birds Unlimited
19555 W. Bluemound Rd., Ste. #4
Brookfield, WI 53045
(262) 789-8226

Wild Birds Unlimited
4326 Mormon Coulee Rd.
La Crosse, WI 54601
(608) 781-5088

Wild Birds Unlimited
3173 Golf Rd.
Delafield, WI 53018
(262) 646-4128

Wild Birds Unlimited
4121 Rib Mountain Dr.
Wausau, WI 54401
(715) 298-3140

Wild Birds Unlimited
2285 South Oneida St., Ste. D
Green Bay, WI 54304
(920) 489-2684

WEST VIRGINIA

Wild Birds Unlimited
1074 Suncrest Towne Center Dr.
Morgantown, WV 26505
(304) 241-4370

CANADA

ALBERTA

Wild Birds Unlimited
12204 107th Ave. N.W.
Edmonton AB T5M 4A8
(587) 521-2473

BRITISH COLUMBIA

Wild Birds Unlimited
2421 King George Blvd.
Surrey BC V4P 1H8
(604) 536-4011

Wild Birds Unlimited
1302 W. Broadway (at Birch)
Vancouver BC V6H 1H2
(604) 736-2676

Wild Birds Unlimited
1190 Marine Dr.
North Vancouver BC V7P1S8
(604) 988-2121

Wild Birds Unlimited
3631 Shelbourne St.
Victoria BC V8P 4H1
(250) 595-3595

Wild Birds Unlimited
#2–6131 200th St.
Langley BC V2Y 1A2
(604) 510-2035

Wild Birds Unlimited
#13-33324 S. Fraser Way
Abbotsford BC V2S 2B4
(604) 852-1960

Wild Birds Unlimited
8810-C Young Rd.
Chilliwack BC V2P 4P5
(604) 792-1239

ONTARIO

Wild Birds Unlimited
5468 Dundas Street West
Toronto ON M9B 6E3
(416) 233-3558

Wild Birds Unlimited
951 Gordon St.
Guelph ON N1G 4S1
(519) 821-2473

Wild Birds Unlimited
Blue Heron Mall
1500 Bank St.
Ottawa ON K1H 7Z1
(613) 521-7333

Wild Birds Unlimited
Unit-4 7690 Yonge St.
Thornhill ON L4J 1W1
(905) 709-3775

Wild Birds Unlimited
502 Springbank Dr.
London ON N6J 1G8
(519) 657-0745

Wild Birds Unlimited
3350 Fairview St.
Burlington ON L7N 3L5
(905) 634-7700

Wild Birds Unlimited
16655 Yonge St. Unit #2
Newmarket ON L3X 1V6
(905) 868-9696

Wild Birds Unlimited
515 Bryne Dr., Unit B
Barrie ON L4N 9P7
(705) 726-7600

MANITOBA

Wild Birds Unlimited
Unit 45 11 Reenders Dr.
Winnipeg MB R2C 5K5
(204) 667-2161

SASKATCHEWAN

Wild Birds Unlimited
330A 2600 8th St East
Saskatoon SK S7H 0V7
(306) 955-2473

Feeder Birds checklist

This checklist includes the 180 feeder birds included in the *Guide to Feeder Birds* section of *The Joy of Bird Feeding* followed by the page number where it appears.

GEESE AND DUCKS
☐ Canada Goose, 80
☐ Mallard, 81

CHACALACA
☐ Plain Chachalaca, 82

QUAIL AND OTHER GAMEBIRDS
☐ California Quail, 83
☐ Gambel's Quail, 84
☐ Northern Bobwhite, 84
☐ Mountain Quail, 85
☐ Scaled Quail, 85
☐ Ring-necked Pheasant, 86
☐ Montezuma Quail, 87
☐ Wild Turkey, 87

DOVES AND PIGEONS
☐ Rock Pigeon, 88
☐ Band-tailed Pigeon, 89
☐ Eurasian Collared-Dove, 89
☐ Inca Dove, 90
☐ Common Ground-Dove, 90
☐ White-winged Dove, 91
☐ Mourning Dove, 91
☐ White-tipped Dove, 92

HUMMINGBIRDS
☐ Magnificent Hummingbird, 94
☐ Ruby-throated Hummingbird, 95
☐ Black-chinned Hummingbird, 96
☐ Anna's Hummingbird, 97
☐ Costa's Hummingbird, 98
☐ Broad-tailed Hummingbird, 99
☐ Rufous Hummingbird, 100
☐ Allen's Hummingbird, 101
☐ Calliope Hummingbird, 102
☐ Broad-billed Hummingbird, 103

WOODPECKERS
☐ Lewis's Woodpecker, 105
☐ Red-headed Woodpecker, 105
☐ Acorn Woodpecker, 106
☐ Gila Woodpecker, 106
☐ Golden-fronted Woodpecker, 107
☐ Red-bellied Woodpecker, 107
☐ Yellow-bellied Sapsucker, 108
☐ Red-naped Sapsucker, 108
☐ Red-breasted Sapsucker, 109
☐ White-headed Woodpecker, 109
☐ Hairy Woodpecker, 110
☐ Downy Woodpecker, 111
☐ Nuttall's Woodpecker, 112
☐ Ladder-backed Woodpecker, 112
☐ Northern Flicker, 113
☐ Pileated Woodpecker, 114

ESCAPED EXOTICS
☐ Peach-faced Lovebird, 116
☐ Red-crowned Parrot, 117
☐ Monk Parakeet, 117

FLYCATCHERS
☐ Black Phoebe, 118
☐ Eastern Phoebe, 119
☐ Vermilion Flycatcher, 119

JAYS, MAGPIE, NUTCRACKER, CROWS, AND RAVEN
☐ Gray Jay, 120
☐ Green Jay, 121
☐ Pinyon Jay, 121
☐ Steller's Jay, 122
☐ Blue Jay, 122
☐ Florida Scrub-Jay, 123
☐ California and Woodhouse's Scrub-Jays, 123
☐ Mexican Jay, 124
☐ Black-billed Magpie, 124
☐ Clark's Nutcracker, 125
☐ American Crow, 126
☐ Fish Crow, 126
☐ Northwestern Crow, 126
☐ Common Raven, 127

CHICKADEES
☐ Carolina Chickadee, 129
☐ Black-capped Chickadee, 129
☐ Mountain Chickadee, 130
☐ Mexican Chickadee, 130
☐ Chestnut-backed Chickadee, 131
☐ Boreal Chickadee, 131

TITMICE
☐ Bridled Titmouse, 132
☐ Oak Titmouse, 133
☐ Juniper Titmouse, 133
☐ Tufted Titmouse, 134
☐ Black-crested Titmouse, 134
☐ Verdin, 135
☐ Bushtit, 135

NUTHATCHES AND CREEPER
☐ Red-breasted Nuthatch, 136
☐ White-breasted Nuthatch, 137
☐ Pygmy Nuthatch, 137
☐ Brown-headed Nuthatch, 138
☐ Brown Creeper, 138

WRENS
☐ House Wren, 139
☐ Carolina Wren, 140
☐ Bewick's Wren, 140
☐ Cactus Wren, 141

KINGLETS
- [ ] Golden-crowned Kinglet, 142
- [ ] Ruby-crowned Kinglet, 142

BLUEBIRDS
- [ ] Eastern Bluebird, 143
- [ ] Western Bluebird, 144
- [ ] Mountain Bluebird, 144

THRUSHES
- [ ] Veery, 145
- [ ] Gray-cheeked Thrush, 145
- [ ] Swainson's Thrush, 146
- [ ] Hermit Thrush, 146
- [ ] Wood Thrush, 146
- [ ] American Robin, 147
- [ ] Varied Thrush, 147

CATBIRD, THRASHERS, AND MOCKINGBIRD
- [ ] Gray Catbird, 148
- [ ] Curve-billed Thrasher, 149
- [ ] Brown Thrasher, 149
- [ ] California Thrasher, 150
- [ ] Crissal Thrasher, 150
- [ ] Northern Mockingbird, 151

WAXWINGS
- [ ] Bohemian Waxwing, 152
- [ ] Cedar Waxwing, 152

WARBLERS
- [ ] Orange-crowned Warbler, 153
- [ ] Palm Warbler, 153
- [ ] Yellow-rumped Warbler, 154
- [ ] Townsend's Warbler, 154
- [ ] Yellow-throated Warbler, 155
- [ ] Pine Warbler, 155
- [ ] Hermit Warbler, 155

TOWHEES
- [ ] Green-tailed Towhee, 156
- [ ] Spotted Towhee, 156
- [ ] Eastern Towhee, 157
- [ ] Canyon Towhee, 157
- [ ] California Towhee, 158
- [ ] Abert's Towhee, 158

SPARROWS
- [ ] Rufous-crowned Sparrow, 160
- [ ] American Tree Sparrow, 160
- [ ] Chipping Sparrow, 161
- [ ] Field Sparrow, 161
- [ ] Lark Sparrow, 162
- [ ] Black-throated Sparrow, 162
- [ ] Fox Sparrow, 163
- [ ] Song Sparrow, 163
- [ ] Lincoln's Sparrow, 164
- [ ] Vesper Sparrow, 164
- [ ] Golden-crowned Sparrow, 165
- [ ] Harris's Sparrow, 165
- [ ] White-crowned Sparrow, 166
- [ ] White-throated Sparrow, 166
- [ ] House Sparrow, 167
- [ ] Eurasian Tree Sparrow, 167

DARK-EYED JUNCOS
- [ ] "Slate-colored" Junco, 169
- [ ] "White-winged" Junco, 169
- [ ] "Oregon" Junco, 170
- [ ] "Pink-sided" Junco, 170
- [ ] "Gray-headed" Junco, 171
- [ ] "Red-backed" Junco, 171

CARDINALS
- [ ] Pyrrhuloxia, 172
- [ ] Northern Cardinal, 173

GROSBEAKS
- [ ] Rose-breasted Grosbeak, 174
- [ ] Black-headed Grosbeak, 175
- [ ] Blue Grosbeak, 176
- [ ] Pine Grosbeak, 176
- [ ] Evening Grosbeak, 177

BUNTINGS
- [ ] Snow Bunting, 178
- [ ] Lazuli Bunting, 179
- [ ] Indigo Bunting, 180
- [ ] Painted Bunting, 181

BLACKBIRDS AND STARLING
- [ ] European Starling, 182
- [ ] Red-winged Blackbird, 183
- [ ] Yellow-headed Blackbird, 184
- [ ] Rusty Blackbird, 184
- [ ] Brewer's Blackbird, 185
- [ ] Common Grackle, 185
- [ ] Boat-tailed Grackle, 186
- [ ] Great-tailed Grackle, 186
- [ ] Brown-headed Cowbird, 187

ORIOLES
- [ ] Hooded Oriole, 188
- [ ] Scott's Oriole, 189
- [ ] Orchard Oriole, 189
- [ ] Bullock's Oriole, 190
- [ ] Baltimore Oriole, 191

FINCHES
- [ ] Gray-crowned Rosy-Finch, 192
- [ ] Black Rosy-Finch, 193
- [ ] Brown-capped Rosy-Finch, 193
- [ ] House Finch, 194
- [ ] Purple Finch, 195
- [ ] Cassin's Finch, 196
- [ ] Red Crossbill, 197
- [ ] White-winged Crossbill, 197
- [ ] Common Redpoll, 198
- [ ] Hoary Redpoll, 198
- [ ] Pine Siskin, 199
- [ ] Lesser Goldfinch, 200
- [ ] Lawrence's Goldfinch, 201
- [ ] American Goldfinch, 202

Project FeederWatch

Operated by the Cornell Lab of Ornithology and Bird Studies Canada, Project FeederWatch is a winter-long survey of birds that visit feeders. Project participants periodically identify and count the birds at their feeders from November–April, learning about their feeder friends all the while. Using an easy online system, participants can enter their counts and create colorful and easy-to-understand graphs and summaries of the birds in their backyard. Since 1987, FeederWatch data have been giving scientists a better understanding of how bird populations are changing at home and across the continent. Thee is a small participation fee that helps support the program.

Anyone interested in birds can participate; you don't have to be an expert. All you need is a window and a yard with feeders, plantings, and/or water that attracts birds.

Increase your enjoyment and knowledge of birds and contribute to science at the same time. Learn more and sign up at www.feederwatch.org. Participants receive:

▸ FeederWatch Handbook & Instructions with bird-ID and bird-feeding tips

▸ Full-color poster of common feeder birds

▸ FeederWatch calendar

▸ Subscription to *Winter Bird Highlights*, our annual publication

▸ A newsletter subscription from the Cornell Lab or Bird Studies Canada

Please consider contributing your observations to this decades-long dataset while learning about the feathered friends in your own backyard.

Top 25 Birds Listing

The listings on the following pages show the top 25 types of birds most frequently reported at feeders across the United States and Canada.

It's easy to participate. Just sign up with a small participation fee, then:

▸ Put up a feeder

▸ Count the birds

▸ Enter your data

Anyone can study study reports about the birds for one or many years. You can learn which birds were sighted in your region, their flock size and the percent of feeders visited.

UNITED STATES

ALABAMA

1. Northern Cardinal
2. Tufted Titmouse
3. Carolina Chickadee
4. American Goldfinch
5. Mourning Dove
6. Dark-eyed Junco
7. Carolina Wren
8. House Finch
9. Red-bellied Woodpecker
10. Blue Jay
11. American Robin
12. White-throated Sparrow
13. Downy Woodpecker
14. Northern Mockingbird
15. Chipping Sparrow
16. Brown Thrasher
17. Spotted/Eastern Towhee
    (Rufous-sided Towhee)
18. Yellow-rumped Warbler
19. White-breasted Nuthatch
20. Red-winged Blackbird
21. Brown-headed Cowbird
22. American Crow
23. Pine Warbler
24. Brown-headed Nuthatch
25. Eastern Bluebird

ALASKA

1. Black-capped Chickadee
2. Common Redpoll
3. Red-breasted Nuthatch
4. Black-billed Magpie
5. Pine Grosbeak
6. Boreal Chickadee
7. Hairy Woodpecker
8. Downy Woodpecker
9. Gray Jay
10. Dark-eyed Junco
11. Steller's Jay
12. Common Raven
13. Hoary Redpoll
14. Pine Siskin
15. Chestnut-backed Chickadee
16. Northern Shrike
17. Sharp-shinned Hawk
18. American Robin
19. Bald Eagle
20. Bohemian Waxwing
21. Northwestern Crow

22. Song Sparrow
23. Ruffed Grouse
24. Brown Creeper
25. White-crowned Sparrow

ARIZONA

1. House Finch
2. Mourning Dove
3. White-crowned Sparrow
4. House Sparrow
5. Lesser Goldfinch
6. Gambel's Quail
7. Anna's Hummingbird
8. Curve-billed Thrasher
9. Eurasian Collared-Dove
10. Gila Woodpecker
11. Verdin
12. Cooper's Hawk
13. Pine Siskin
14. Dark-eyed Junco
15. Abert's Towhee
16. Yellow-rumped Warbler
17. Northern Cardinal
18. Cactus Wren
19. Common Raven
20. Northern Mockingbird
21. White-winged Dove
22. Ruby-crowned Kinglet
23. Costa's Hummingbird
24. American Robin
25. Ladder-backed Woodpecker

ARKANSAS

1. Carolina Chickadee
2. American Goldfinch
3. Northern Cardinal
4. Mourning Dove
5. Downy Woodpecker
6. Tufted Titmouse
7. White-throated Sparrow
8. Carolina Wren
9. Red-bellied Woodpecker
10. Dark-eyed Junco
11. American Robin
12. Blue Jay
13. House Finch
14. White-breasted Nuthatch
15. Northern Mockingbird
16. House Sparrow
17. Eastern Bluebird
18. American Crow
19. Pine Siskin

20. Purple Finch
21. Northern Flicker
22. Brown-headed Cowbird
23. Red-winged Blackbird
24. Chipping Sparrow
25. Common Grackle

CALIFORNIA

1. House Finch
2. Anna's Hummingbird
3. Mourning Dove
4. White-crowned Sparrow
5. *Aphelocoma* species (scrub jays)
6. Dark-eyed Junco
7. Lesser Goldfinch
8. California Towhee
9. Pine Siskin
10. Golden-crowned Sparrow
11. American Robin
12. Oak/Juniper Titmouse
    (Plain Titmouse)
13. Yellow-rumped Warbler
14. American Goldfinch
15. House Sparrow
16. Black Phoebe
17. Spotted/Eastern Towhee (Rufous-sided Towhee)
18. American Crow
19. Chestnut-backed Chickadee
20. Northern Mockingbird
21. Bewick's Wren
22. Bushtit
23. *Selasphorus* species (hummingbirds)
24. Northern Flicker
25. Ruby-crowned Kinglet

COLORADO

1. Dark-eyed Junco
2. House Finch
3. Northern Flicker
4. Black-capped Chickadee
5. Eurasian Collared-Dove
6. Downy Woodpecker
7. American Robin
8. House Sparrow
9. Black-billed Magpie
10. American Goldfinch
11. Mountain Chickadee
12. Red-breasted Nuthatch
13. European Starling
14. American Crow
15. Blue Jay

16. White-breasted Nuthatch
17. Red-winged Blackbird
18. Pine Siskin
19. Mourning Dove
20. *Aphelocoma* species (scrub jays)
21. Bushtit
22. Hairy Woodpecker
23. Cooper's Hawk
24. Steller's Jay
25. Sharp-shinned Hawk

CONNECTICUT

1. Black-capped Chickadee
2. Dark-eyed Junco
3. Tufted Titmouse
4. Downy Woodpecker
5. White-breasted Nuthatch
6. Mourning Dove
7. Northern Cardinal
8. Blue Jay
9. American Goldfinch
10. Red-bellied Woodpecker
11. House Finch
12. White-throated Sparrow
13. Hairy Woodpecker
14. House Sparrow
15. American Robin
16. Carolina Wren
17. Song Sparrow
18. American Crow
19. Common Grackle
20. Northern Flicker
21. European Starling
22. Brown-headed Cowbird
23. Red-winged Blackbird
24. Cooper's Hawk
25. Purple Finch

DELAWARE

1. Dark-eyed Junco
2. Mourning Dove
3. House Finch
4. Northern Cardinal
5. Common Grackle
6. Red-winged Blackbird
7. Tufted Titmouse
8. American Goldfinch
9. Brown-headed Cowbird
10. Carolina/Black-capped Chickadee
11. Downy Woodpecker
12. Carolina Wren
13. Red-bellied Woodpecker

14. European Starling
15. White-throated Sparrow
16. Blue Jay
17. Song Sparrow
18. American Robin
19. House Sparrow
20. White-breasted Nuthatch
21. Northern Mockingbird
22. Northern Flicker
23. Hairy Woodpecker
24. Cooper's Hawk
25. Chipping Sparrow

FLORIDA

1. Northern Cardinal
2. Mourning Dove
3. Blue Jay
4. Red-bellied Woodpecker
5. Tufted Titmouse
6. Northern Mockingbird
7. Carolina Wren
8. American Goldfinch
9. Yellow-rumped Warbler
10. Carolina Chickadee
11. Gray Catbird
12. Downy Woodpecker
13. Chipping Sparrow
14. House Finch
15. Ruby-throated Hummingbird
16. Common Grackle
17. American Robin
18. Pine Warbler
19. American Crow
20. Palm Warbler
21. Red-winged Blackbird
22. Eastern Phoebe
23. Painted Bunting
24. Brown Thrasher
25. Brown-headed Cowbird

GEORGIA

1. Northern Cardinal
2. Carolina Chickadee
3. Tufted Titmouse
4. Carolina Wren
5. Mourning Dove
6. House Finch
7. American Goldfinch
8. Downy Woodpecker
9. Red-bellied Woodpecker
10. Blue Jay
11. Eastern Bluebird

12. White-breasted Nuthatch
13. Dark-eyed Junco
14. Chipping Sparrow
15. Spotted/Eastern Towhee (Rufous-sided Towhee)
16. Brown Thrasher
17. Pine Warbler
18. Northern Mockingbird
19. Brown-headed Nuthatch
20. American Robin
21. White-throated Sparrow
22. Yellow-rumped Warbler
23. Pine Siskin
24. Song Sparrow
25. American Crow

HAWAII*

1. Spotted Dove
2. Red-vented Bulbul
3. Common Waxbill
4. Zebra Dove
5. Red-whiskered Bulbul
6. Red-crested Cardinal
7. Common Myna
8. Red-billed Leiothrix
9. House Finch
10. Northern Cardinal
11. Java Sparrow
12. Japanese White-eye
13. Pacific Golden-Plover
14. White-rumped Shama

A total of 1 FeederWatchers reported data from this region.

IDAHO

1. Dark-eyed Junco
2. House Finch
3. Black-capped Chickadee
4. Red-breasted Nuthatch
5. Northern Flicker
6. American Goldfinch
7. House Sparrow
8. Mourning Dove
9. Mountain Chickadee
10. Pine Siskin
11. Eurasian Collared-Dove
12. Downy Woodpecker
13. American Robin
14. Sharp-shinned Hawk
15. Song Sparrow
16. California Quail
17. Black-billed Magpie

18. European Starling
19. Red-winged Blackbird
20. Steller's Jay
21. White-crowned Sparrow
22. Cooper's Hawk
23. Cedar Waxwing
24. Lesser Goldfinch
25. Brown Creeper

ILLINOIS
1. Northern Cardinal
2. Dark-eyed Junco
3. Carolina/Black-capped Chickadee
4. House Sparrow
5. Downy Woodpecker
6. Mourning Dove
7. House Finch
8. American Goldfinch
9. White-breasted Nuthatch
10. Red-bellied Woodpecker
11. American Robin
12. European Starling
13. Blue Jay
14. Red-winged Blackbird
15. Common Grackle
16. Cooper's Hawk
17. Hairy Woodpecker
18. American Tree Sparrow
19. Brown-headed Cowbird
20. White-throated Sparrow
21. American Crow
22. Tufted Titmouse
23. Song Sparrow
24. Pine Siskin
25. Purple Finch

INDIANA
1. Dark-eyed Junco
2. Northern Cardinal
3. Downy Woodpecker
4. Carolina/Black-capped Chickadee
5. House Finch
6. American Goldfinch
7. Mourning Dove
8. White-breasted Nuthatch
9. Blue Jay
10. Red-bellied Woodpecker
11. Tufted Titmouse
12. House Sparrow
13. European Starling
14. American Robin
15. Hairy Woodpecker

16. Carolina Wren
17. Song Sparrow
18. Red-winged Blackbird
19. American Tree Sparrow
20. Brown-headed Cowbird
21. Northern Flicker
22. American Crow
23. Common Grackle
24. Cooper's Hawk
25. Pileated Woodpecker

IOWA
1. Dark-eyed Junco
2. Northern Cardinal
3. House Sparrow
4. Black-capped Chickadee
5. Downy Woodpecker
6. Red-bellied Woodpecker
7. American Goldfinch
8. Blue Jay
9. White-breasted Nuthatch
10. House Finch
11. American Robin
12. Mourning Dove
13. Hairy Woodpecker
14. European Starling
15. Common Grackle
16. Purple Finch
17. American Tree Sparrow
18. American Crow
19. Tufted Titmouse
20. Northern Flicker
21. Cooper's Hawk
22. Red-winged Blackbird
23. White-throated Sparrow
24. Pine Siskin
25. Brown-headed Cowbird

KANSAS
1. Dark-eyed Junco
2. Northern Cardinal
3. Blue Jay
4. American Goldfinch
5. Downy Woodpecker
6. Red-bellied Woodpecker
7. House Finch
8. House Sparrow
9. Carolina/Black-capped Chickadee
10. Mourning Dove
11. European Starling
12. American Robin
13. Northern Flicker

14. Tufted Titmouse
15. White-breasted Nuthatch
16. Carolina Wren
17. Common Grackle
18. Red-winged Blackbird
19. American Crow
20. Hairy Woodpecker
21. Harris's Sparrow
22. Cooper's Hawk
23. Eastern Bluebird
24. Eurasian Collared-Dove
25. Brown-headed Cowbird

KENTUCKY
1. Northern Cardinal
2. Mourning Dove
3. Dark-eyed Junco
4. Tufted Titmouse
5. Downy Woodpecker
6. American Goldfinch
7. House Finch
8. Blue Jay
9. Red-bellied Woodpecker
10. White-breasted Nuthatch
11. European Starling
12. Carolina Chickadee
13. White-throated Sparrow
14. American Robin
15. Carolina Wren
16. Song Sparrow
17. House Sparrow
18. Northern Mockingbird
19. Common Grackle
20. Brown-headed Cowbird
21. Purple Finch
22. Hairy Woodpecker
23. Red-winged Blackbird
24. Northern Flicker
25. American Crow

LOUISIANA
1. Carolina Chickadee
2. Northern Cardinal
3. Mourning Dove
4. American Goldfinch
5. Blue Jay
6. Tufted Titmouse
7. House Finch
8. Carolina Wren
9. House Sparrow
10. Northern Mockingbird
11. Downy Woodpecker

12. Cedar Waxwing
13. White-throated Sparrow
14. Chipping Sparrow
15. Yellow-rumped Warbler
16. Red-bellied Woodpecker
17. Red-winged Blackbird
18. Dark-eyed Junco
19. American Robin
20. Eurasian Collared-Dove
21. Brown-headed Cowbird
22. Pine Siskin
23. White-winged Dove
24. Eastern Bluebird
25. Pine Warbler

MAINE

1. Black-capped Chickadee
2. Downy Woodpecker
3. American Goldfinch
4. Mourning Dove
5. Dark-eyed Junco
6. White-breasted Nuthatch
7. Blue Jay
8. Hairy Woodpecker
9. Tufted Titmouse
10. Northern Cardinal
11. Purple Finch
12. American Crow
13. Red-breasted Nuthatch
14. Song Sparrow
15. American Robin
16. Common Grackle
17. House Finch
18. Red-winged Blackbird
19. American Tree Sparrow
20. European Starling
21. Wild Turkey
22. Pine Siskin
23. Red-bellied Woodpecker
24. Pileated Woodpecker
25. Fox Sparrow

MARYLAND

1. Northern Cardinal
2. Dark-eyed Junco
3. Carolina/Black-capped Chickadee
4. Mourning Dove
5. Tufted Titmouse
6. Downy Woodpecker
7. House Finch
8. American Goldfinch
9. Carolina Wren

10. Blue Jay
11. Red-bellied Woodpecker
12. White-breasted Nuthatch
13. American Robin
14. White-throated Sparrow
15. House Sparrow
16. European Starling
17. Common Grackle
18. Red-winged Blackbird
19. Song Sparrow
20. Brown-headed Cowbird
21. American Crow
22. Hairy Woodpecker
23. Northern Flicker
24. Chipping Sparrow
25. Northern Mockingbird

MASSACHUSETTS

1. Black-capped Chickadee
2. Dark-eyed Junco
3. Northern Cardinal
4. Downy Woodpecker
5. Tufted Titmouse
6. White-breasted Nuthatch
7. Blue Jay
8. Mourning Dove
9. American Goldfinch
10. House Finch
11. House Sparrow
12. Red-bellied Woodpecker
13. American Robin
14. Hairy Woodpecker
15. Song Sparrow
16. Common Grackle
17. White-throated Sparrow
18. European Starling
19. American Crow
20. Carolina Wren
21. Red-winged Blackbird
22. Northern Flicker
23. Brown-headed Cowbird
24. Purple Finch
25. American Tree Sparrow

MICHIGAN

1. Black-capped Chickadee
2. American Goldfinch
3. Blue Jay
4. Downy Woodpecker
5. Dark-eyed Junco
6. White-breasted Nuthatch
7. Mourning Dove

8. Northern Cardinal
9. Red-bellied Woodpecker
10. Tufted Titmouse
11. House Finch
12. Hairy Woodpecker
13. House Sparrow
14. American Robin
15. European Starling
16. American Tree Sparrow
17. Red-winged Blackbird
18. Pine Siskin
19. American Crow
20. Common Grackle
21. Cooper's Hawk
22. Purple Finch
23. Brown-headed Cowbird
24. Song Sparrow
25. Northern Flicker

MINNESOTA

1. Black-capped Chickadee
2. Downy Woodpecker
3. White-breasted Nuthatch
4. Dark-eyed Junco
5. Hairy Woodpecker
6. Blue Jay
7. American Goldfinch
8. Northern Cardinal
9. Red-bellied Woodpecker
10. American Crow
11. House Finch
12. Pileated Woodpecker
13. American Robin
14. Common Redpoll
15. House Sparrow
16. Mourning Dove
17. European Starling
18. Red-winged Blackbird
19. Purple Finch
20. Red-breasted Nuthatch
21. Pine Siskin
22. Common Grackle
23. American Tree Sparrow
24. Wild Turkey
25. Northern Flicker

MISSISSIPPI

1. Northern Cardinal
2. Tufted Titmouse
3. Mourning Dove
4. Carolina Chickadee
5. American Goldfinch

6. Carolina Wren
7. Dark-eyed Junco
8. Blue Jay
9. Northern Mockingbird
10. House Finch
11. Red-bellied Woodpecker
12. White-throated Sparrow
13. Chipping Sparrow
14. Red-winged Blackbird
15. House Sparrow
16. American Robin
17. Cedar Waxwing
18. Pine Siskin
19. Yellow-rumped Warbler
20. Brown Thrasher
21. Brown-headed Cowbird
22. Purple Finch
23. Downy Woodpecker
24. Eurasian Collared-Dove
25. Eastern Bluebird

MISSOURI
1. Northern Cardinal
2. Dark-eyed Junco
3. Downy Woodpecker
4. Mourning Dove
5. Carolina/Black-capped Chickadee
6. American Goldfinch
7. Blue Jay
8. House Finch
9. Red-bellied Woodpecker
10. Tufted Titmouse
11. White-breasted Nuthatch
12. American Robin
13. Carolina Wren
14. European Starling
15. White-throated Sparrow
16. House Sparrow
17. Northern Flicker
18. Hairy Woodpecker
19. Common Grackle
20. Purple Finch
21. Northern Mockingbird
22. Red-winged Blackbird
23. Eastern Bluebird
24. Brown-headed Cowbird
25. Song Sparrow

MONTANA
1. Black-capped Chickadee
2. Black-billed Magpie
3. House Finch

4. Northern Flicker
5. Downy Woodpecker
6. Mountain Chickadee
7. Dark-eyed Junco
8. American Robin
9. Hairy Woodpecker
10. Eurasian Collared-Dove
11. House Sparrow
12. Red-breasted Nuthatch
13. European Starling
14. Pine Siskin
15. Common Redpoll
16. Red-winged Blackbird
17. American Goldfinch
18. White-breasted Nuthatch
19. Song Sparrow
20. Clark's Nutcracker
21. Steller's Jay
22. Sharp-shinned Hawk
23. American Crow
24. Pileated Woodpecker
25. Evening Grosbeak

NEBRASKA
1. Northern Cardinal
2. Downy Woodpecker
3. American Goldfinch
4. Dark-eyed Junco
5. House Finch
6. Blue Jay
7. House Sparrow
8. Red-bellied Woodpecker
9. American Robin
10. Black-capped Chickadee
11. European Starling
12. White-breasted Nuthatch
13. Mourning Dove
14. Northern Flicker
15. Hairy Woodpecker
16. Common Grackle
17. Cooper's Hawk
18. Eurasian Collared-Dove
19. American Crow
20. Sharp-shinned Hawk
21. American Tree Sparrow
22. Purple Finch
23. Red-winged Blackbird
24. Carolina Wren
25. Cedar Waxwing

NEVADA
1. House Finch
2. White-crowned Sparrow
3. Mourning Dove
4. Dark-eyed Junco
5. Lesser Goldfinch
6. American Robin
7. Northern Flicker
8. European Starling
9. Cooper's Hawk
10. House Sparrow
11. American Goldfinch
12. Eurasian Collared-Dove
13. California Quail
14. *Aphelocoma* species (scrub jays)
15. Mountain Chickadee
16. Yellow-rumped Warbler
17. Spotted/Eastern Towhee (Rufous-sided Towhee)
18. Pine Siskin
19. Rock Pigeon
20. Cassin's Finch
21. Bewick's Wren
22. Downy Woodpecker
23. Sharp-shinned Hawk
24. Northern Mockingbird
25. Ruby-crowned Kinglet

NEW HAMPSHIRE
1. Black-capped Chickadee
2. Dark-eyed Junco
3. Tufted Titmouse
4. American Goldfinch
5. Blue Jay
6. Downy Woodpecker
7. White-breasted Nuthatch
8. Mourning Dove
9. Hairy Woodpecker
10. Northern Cardinal
11. Purple Finch
12. American Robin
13. American Crow
14. Red-bellied Woodpecker
15. House Finch
16. Song Sparrow
17. Red-winged Blackbird
18. American Tree Sparrow
19. Red-breasted Nuthatch
20. European Starling
21. House Sparrow
22. Pine Siskin
23. Eastern Bluebird

24. White-throated Sparrow
25. Common Grackle

NEW JERSEY
1. Dark-eyed Junco
2. Northern Cardinal
3. Mourning Dove
4. Carolina/Black-capped Chickadee
5. Downy Woodpecker
6. Blue Jay
7. Tufted Titmouse
8. House Finch
9. White-breasted Nuthatch
10. Red-bellied Woodpecker
11. American Goldfinch
12. White-throated Sparrow
13. House Sparrow
14. American Robin
15. Carolina Wren
16. Common Grackle
17. European Starling
18. Song Sparrow
19. Red-winged Blackbird
20. Brown-headed Cowbird
21. Hairy Woodpecker
22. American Crow
23. Cooper's Hawk
24. Northern Mockingbird
25. Chipping Sparrow

NEW MEXICO
1. Dark-eyed Junco
2. House Finch
3. Pine Siskin
4. American Robin
5. White-winged Dove
6. Northern Flicker
7. House Sparrow
8. White-crowned Sparrow
9. *Aphelocoma* species (scrub jays)
   Eurasian Collared-Dove
10. Bushtit
11. Lesser Goldfinch
12. Canyon Towhee
13. Curve-billed Thrasher
14. Mourning Dove
15. Ladder-backed Woodpecker
16. Spotted/Eastern Towhee (Rufous-sided Towhee)
17. White-breasted Nuthatch
18. Cooper's Hawk
19. Western Bluebird

20. American Goldfinch
21. Common Raven
22. Bewick's Wren
23. Mountain Chickadee
24. Yellow-rumped Warbler

NEW YORK
1. Black-capped Chickadee
2. Dark-eyed Junco
3. Blue Jay
4. Downy Woodpecker
5. Mourning Dove
6. Northern Cardinal
7. White-breasted Nuthatch
8. American Goldfinch
9. Tufted Titmouse
10. Red-bellied Woodpecker
11. House Finch
12. Hairy Woodpecker
13. House Sparrow
14. European Starling
15. American Robin
16. American Crow
17. Common Grackle
18. Red-winged Blackbird
19. Song Sparrow
20. American Tree Sparrow
21. White-throated Sparrow
22. Purple Finch
23. Brown-headed Cowbird
24. Carolina Wren
25. Northern Flicker

NORTH CAROLINA
1. Northern Cardinal
2. Tufted Titmouse
3. Mourning Dove
4. Carolina Wren
5. American Goldfinch
6. Dark-eyed Junco
7. Carolina Chickadee
8. Downy Woodpecker
9. House Finch
10. Red-bellied Woodpecker
11. White-throated Sparrow
12. White-breasted Nuthatch
13. Blue Jay
14. American Robin
15. Spotted/Eastern Towhee (Rufous-sided Towhee)
16. Eastern Bluebird
17. Yellow-rumped Warbler

18. Song Sparrow
19. Northern Mockingbird
20. American Crow
21. Chipping Sparrow
22. Brown-headed Nuthatch
23. Brown Thrasher
24. Pine Warbler
25. Pine Siskin

NORTH DAKOTA
1. House Sparrow
2. Black-capped Chickadee
3. Downy Woodpecker
4. Dark-eyed Junco
5. White-breasted Nuthatch
6. Hairy Woodpecker
7. Common Redpoll
8. Blue Jay
9. House Finch
10. Pine Siskin
11. Eurasian Collared-Dove
12. American Robin
13. American Goldfinch
14. Common Grackle
15. Mourning Dove
16. European Starling
17. Red-winged Blackbird
18. American Crow
19. Northern Cardinal
20. Cedar Waxwing
21. Wild Turkey
22. Gray Partridge
23. Pine Grosbeak
24. Purple Finch
25. Hoary Redpoll

OHIO
1. Northern Cardinal
2. Carolina/Black-capped Chickadee
3. Dark-eyed Junco
4. Downy Woodpecker
5. Mourning Dove
6. Red-bellied Woodpecker
7. House Finch
8. Blue Jay
9. American Goldfinch
10. White-breasted Nuthatch
11. Tufted Titmouse
12. House Sparrow
13. European Starling
14. American Robin
15. Song Sparrow

16. Hairy Woodpecker
17. Common Grackle
18. Carolina Wren
19. Red-winged Blackbird
20. Brown-headed Cowbird
21. American Tree Sparrow
22. American Crow
23. Cooper's Hawk
24. White-throated Sparrow
25. Northern Flicker

OKLAHOMA

1. American Goldfinch
2. Dark-eyed Junco
3. Northern Cardinal
4. Blue Jay
5. Mourning Dove
6. House Finch
7. Carolina Chickadee
8. Downy Woodpecker
9. House Sparrow
10. Tufted Titmouse
11. American Robin
12. Red-bellied Woodpecker
13. Carolina Wren
14. Red-winged Blackbird
15. European Starling
16. Northern Flicker
17. Northern Mockingbird
18. Harris's Sparrow
19. Cedar Waxwing
20. American Crow
21. Eurasian Collared-Dove
22. Purple Finch
23. Brown-headed Cowbird
24. White-throated Sparrow
25. White-breasted Nuthatch

OREGON

1. Dark-eyed Junco
2. Black-capped Chickadee
3. Pine Siskin
4. Northern Flicker
5. House Finch
6. Spotted/Eastern Towhee (Rufous-sided Towhee)
7. Anna's Hummingbird
8. American Robin
9. *Aphelocoma* species (scrub jays)
   Steller's Jay
10. Song Sparrow
11. Varied Thrush

12. Chestnut-backed Chickadee
13. Red-breasted Nuthatch
14. Downy Woodpecker
15. Mourning Dove
16. Bushtit
17. European Starling
18. Lesser Goldfinch
19. Golden-crowned Sparrow
20. American Goldfinch
21. American Crow
22. House Sparrow
23. White-crowned Sparrow
24. Fox Sparrow

PENNSYLVANIA

1. Carolina/Black-capped Chickadee
2. Dark-eyed Junco
3. Northern Cardinal
4. Mourning Dove
5. Tufted Titmouse
6. Downy Woodpecker
7. Blue Jay
8. House Finch
9. White-breasted Nuthatch
10. American Goldfinch
11. Red-bellied Woodpecker
12. American Robin
13. Song Sparrow
14. House Sparrow
15. European Starling
16. Carolina Wren
17. Hairy Woodpecker
18. White-throated Sparrow
19. American Crow
20. Brown-headed Cowbird
21. Common Grackle
22. Red-winged Blackbird
23. Northern Flicker
24. Purple Finch
25. Eastern Bluebird

RHODE ISLAND

1. Black-capped Chickadee
2. Northern Cardinal
3. Downy Woodpecker
4. Dark-eyed Junco
5. American Goldfinch
6. Tufted Titmouse
7. Mourning Dove
8. House Finch
9. White-breasted Nuthatch
10. House Sparrow

11. Blue Jay
12. White-throated Sparrow
13. Red-bellied Woodpecker
14. Common Grackle
15. American Robin
16. Song Sparrow
17. Hairy Woodpecker
18. Northern Flicker
19. Red-winged Blackbird
20. Brown-headed Cowbird
21. European Starling
22. Carolina Wren
23. American Crow
24. Cooper's Hawk
25. Purple Finch

SOUTH CAROLINA

1. Northern Cardinal
2. Carolina Chickadee
3. Tufted Titmouse
4. Carolina Wren
5. Mourning Dove
6. House Finch
7. American Goldfinch
8. Chipping Sparrow
9. Red-bellied Woodpecker
10. Northern Mockingbird
11. Eastern Bluebird
12. Blue Jay
13. Downy Woodpecker
14. White-throated Sparrow
15. Dark-eyed Junco
16. Yellow-rumped Warbler
17. American Robin
18. Pine Warbler
19. Brown Thrasher
20. Brown-headed Nuthatch
21. White-breasted Nuthatch
22. Pine Siskin
23. American Crow
24. Song Sparrow
25. Spotted/Eastern Towhee (Ru-
    fous-sided Towhee)

SOUTH DAKOTA

1. American Goldfinch
2. Downy Woodpecker
3. Dark-eyed Junco
4. House Sparrow
5. House Finch
6. European Starling
7. Black-capped Chickadee

8. Hairy Woodpecker
9. Blue Jay
10. White-breasted Nuthatch
11. American Robin
12. Eurasian Collared-Dove
13. Common Grackle
14. Northern Cardinal
15. Pine Siskin
16. Sharp-shinned Hawk
17. American Crow
18. Northern Flicker
19. Mourning Dove
20. Common Redpoll
21. Cooper's Hawk
22. Red-winged Blackbird
23. Cedar Waxwing
24. Purple Finch
25. Red-bellied Woodpecker

TENNESSEE
1. Northern Cardinal
2. Carolina/Black-capped Chickadee
3. Mourning Dove
4. Tufted Titmouse
5. House Finch
6. Downy Woodpecker
7. American Goldfinch
8. Dark-eyed Junco
9. Blue Jay
10. Red-bellied Woodpecker
11. Carolina Wren
12. American Robin
13. White-throated Sparrow
14. White-breasted Nuthatch
15. Spotted/Eastern Towhee (Rufous-sided Towhee)
16. Northern Mockingbird
17. European Starling
18. Brown-headed Cowbird
19. American Crow
20. Song Sparrow
21. Eastern Bluebird
22. Common Grackle
23. Red-winged Blackbird
24. Purple Finch
25. House Sparrow

TEXAS
1. Northern Cardinal
2. Carolina Chickadee
3. American Goldfinch
4. House Finch

5. Carolina Wren
6. Northern Mockingbird
7. White-winged Dove
8. Blue Jay
9. House Sparrow
10. Mourning Dove
11. Tufted Titmouse
12. Chipping Sparrow
13. American Robin
14. Dark-eyed Junco
15. Red-bellied Woodpecker
16. Downy Woodpecker
17. Cedar Waxwing
18. Yellow-rumped Warbler
19. Pine Siskin
20. Red-winged Blackbird
21. Ruby-crowned Kinglet
22. Brown-headed Cowbird
23. American Crow
24. Orange-crowned Warbler
25. Eastern Bluebird

UTAH
1. Dark-eyed Junco
2. House Finch
3. House Sparrow
4. Eurasian Collared-Dove
5. Black-capped Chickadee
6. American Goldfinch
7. Northern Flicker
8. American Robin
9. Lesser Goldfinch
10. European Starling
11. Downy Woodpecker
12. Mourning Dove
13. Black-billed Magpie
14. *Aphelocoma* species (scrub jays)
    Sharp-shinned Hawk
15. California Quail
16. Pine Siskin
17. Mountain Chickadee
18. Spotted/Eastern Towhee (Rufous-sided Towhee)
19. Red-breasted Nuthatch
20. Cassin's Finch
21. Ruby-crowned Kinglet
22. Red-winged Blackbird
23. Cooper's Hawk
24. Yellow-rumped Warbler

VERMONT
1. American Goldfinch
2. Black-capped Chickadee
3. Dark-eyed Junco
4. Blue Jay
5. Downy Woodpecker
6. White-breasted Nuthatch
7. Mourning Dove
8. Hairy Woodpecker
9. Purple Finch
10. Tufted Titmouse
11. Northern Cardinal
12. American Robin
13. American Crow
14. Red-breasted Nuthatch
15. American Tree Sparrow
16. House Finch
17. Red-winged Blackbird
18. Song Sparrow
19. Red-bellied Woodpecker
20. European Starling
21. Pine Siskin
22. Common Grackle
23. House Sparrow
24. Pileated Woodpecker
25. Wild Turkey

VIRGINIA
1. Carolina/Black-capped Chickadee
2. Northern Cardinal
3. Dark-eyed Junco
4. Tufted Titmouse
5. Mourning Dove
6. American Goldfinch
7. Carolina Wren
8. Downy Woodpecker
9. House Finch
10. Red-bellied Woodpecker
11. Blue Jay
12. White-throated Sparrow
13. White-breasted Nuthatch
14. American Robin
15. Song Sparrow
16. American Crow
17. European Starling
18. House Sparrow
19. Eastern Bluebird
20. Brown-headed Cowbird
21. Common Grackle
22. Red-winged Blackbird
23. Northern Mockingbird
24. Northern Flicker

25. Hairy Woodpecker

WASHINGTON
1. Dark-eyed Junco
2. Black-capped Chickadee
3. Spotted/Eastern Towhee (Rufous-sided Towhee)
4. Northern Flicker
5. Song Sparrow
6. Chestnut-backed Chickadee
7. Anna's Hummingbird
8. Steller's Jay
9. Pine Siskin
10. House Finch
11. Red-breasted Nuthatch
12. American Robin
13. Varied Thrush
14. Downy Woodpecker
15. Bushtit
16. American Crow
17. Golden-crowned Sparrow
18. House Sparrow
19. Bewick's Wren
20. Fox Sparrow
21. European Starling
22. American Goldfinch
23. White-crowned Sparrow
24. Cooper's Hawk
25. Mourning Dove

WEST VIRGINIA
1. Carolina/Black-capped Chickadee
2. Tufted Titmouse
3. Northern Cardinal
4. White-breasted Nuthatch
5. American Goldfinch
6. Dark-eyed Junco
7. Downy Woodpecker
8. Red-bellied Woodpecker
9. Blue Jay
10. Mourning Dove
11. Carolina Wren
12. House Finch
13. American Robin
14. Song Sparrow
15. European Starling
16. American Crow
17. White-throated Sparrow
18. Purple Finch
19. House Sparrow
20. Hairy Woodpecker
21. Red-winged Blackbird

22. Brown-headed Cowbird
23. Common Grackle
24. Pileated Woodpecker
25. Chipping Sparrow

WISCONSIN
1. Black-capped Chickadee
2. Dark-eyed Junco
3. Downy Woodpecker
4. White-breasted Nuthatch
5. American Goldfinch
6. Northern Cardinal
7. Blue Jay
8. Mourning Dove
9. Red-bellied Woodpecker
10. Hairy Woodpecker
11. House Finch
12. House Sparrow
13. American Robin
14. American Crow
15. Pine Siskin
16. Common Redpoll
17. European Starling
18. American Tree Sparrow
19. Red-winged Blackbird
20. Red-breasted Nuthatch
21. Purple Finch
22. Cooper's Hawk
23. Common Grackle
24. Tufted Titmouse
25. Song Sparrow

WYOMING
1. House Finch
2. Eurasian Collared-Dove
3. House Sparrow
4. European Starling
5. Dark-eyed Junco
6. American Robin
7. American Goldfinch
8. Northern Flicker
9. Black-capped Chickadee
10. Downy Woodpecker
11. Pine Siskin
12. Black-billed Magpie
13. Sharp-shinned Hawk
14. American Crow
15. Mountain Chickadee
16. Hairy Woodpecker
17. Red-winged Blackbird
18. Rosy-finch species
19. Rock Pigeon

20. Blue Jay
21. Red-breasted Nuthatch
22. White-breasted Nuthatch
23. Wild Turkey
24. Song Sparrow
25. Mourning Dove

CANADA

ALBERTA
1. Black-capped Chickadee
2. Black-billed Magpie
3. Downy Woodpecker
4. Blue Jay
5. Common Redpoll
6. House Sparrow
7. Red-breasted Nuthatch
8. White-breasted Nuthatch
9. Hairy Woodpecker
10. Northern Flicker
11. House Finch
12. Dark-eyed Junco
13. Pine Grosbeak
14. Pine Siskin
15. American Robin
16. American Crow
17. Red Crossbill
18. White-winged Crossbill
19. Bohemian Waxwing
20. Common Raven
21. Hoary Redpoll
22. European Starling
23. Boreal Chickadee
24. Pileated Woodpecker
25. Rock Pigeon

BRITISH COLUMBIA
1. Dark-eyed Junco
2. Northern Flicker
3. Song Sparrow
4. Downy Woodpecker
5. Black-capped Chickadee
6. Steller's Jay
7. Pine Siskin
8. Spotted/Eastern Towhee (Rufous-sided Towhee)
9. Red-breasted Nuthatch
10. House Finch
11. American Robin
12. Chestnut-backed Chickadee
13. Anna's Hummingbird

14. Varied Thrush
15. Fox Sparrow
16. European Starling
17. Hairy Woodpecker
18. House Sparrow
19. Bushtit
20. Common Redpoll
21. American Goldfinch
22. Pileated Woodpecker
23. Eurasian Collared-Dove
24. American Crow
25. Red-winged Blackbird

MANITOBA

1. Black-capped Chickadee
2. Common Redpoll
3. Downy Woodpecker
4. White-breasted Nuthatch
5. Blue Jay
6. Hairy Woodpecker
7. Dark-eyed Junco
8. House Sparrow
9. Pine Grosbeak
10. American Crow
11. Pine Siskin
12. Hoary Redpoll
13. American Robin
14. Black-billed Magpie
15. Purple Finch
16. Pileated Woodpecker
17. Evening Grosbeak
18. House Finch
19. European Starling
20. American Tree Sparrow
21. Common Raven
22. Northern Shrike
23. Merlin
24. White-throated Sparrow
25. Sharp-shinned Hawk

NEW BRUNSWICK

1. American Goldfinch
2. Black-capped Chickadee
3. Blue Jay
4. Mourning Dove
5. Downy Woodpecker
6. Dark-eyed Junco
7. Hairy Woodpecker
8. American Crow
9. Purple Finch
10. European Starling
11. Common Grackle

12. Song Sparrow
13. American Robin
14. Red-breasted Nuthatch
15. American Tree Sparrow
16. Red-winged Blackbird
17. Pine Siskin
18. Rock Pigeon
19. Northern Cardinal
20. Common Redpoll
21. Pileated Woodpecker
22. Evening Grosbeak
23. Ring-necked Pheasant
24. Common Raven
25. Northern Flicker

NEWFOUNDLAND & LABRADOR

1. Black-capped Chickadee
2. Dark-eyed Junco
3. American Goldfinch
4. Blue Jay
5. American Crow
6. Common Redpoll
7. Purple Finch
8. Pine Siskin
9. European Starling
10. Pine Grosbeak
11. Hairy Woodpecker
12. House Sparrow
13. Northern Flicker
14. Boreal Chickadee
15. Common Grackle
16. Downy Woodpecker
17. Red-breasted Nuthatch
18. Sharp-shinned Hawk
19. Rock Pigeon
20. American Robin
21. Gray Jay
22. Fox Sparrow
23. Ruffed Grouse
24. Song Sparrow
25. White-winged Crossbill

NORTHWEST TERRITORIES

1. Black-capped Chickadee
2. Common Raven
3. Boreal Chickadee
4. Pine Grosbeak
5. Black-billed Magpie
6. Willow Ptarmigan
7. Dark-eyed Junco
8. Hairy Woodpecker
9. Common Redpoll

10. Hoary Redpoll
11. Common/Hoary Redpoll
12. Bohemian Waxwing
13. Evening Grosbeak
14. Gray Jay
15. American Crow
16. Downy Woodpecker
17. American Three-toed Woodpecker
18. Red-breasted Nuthatch

NOVA SCOTIA

1. Black-capped Chickadee
2. Blue Jay
3. American Goldfinch
4. Mourning Dove
5. Dark-eyed Junco
6. American Crow
7. Downy Woodpecker
8. European Starling
9. Purple Finch
10. Song Sparrow
11. Hairy Woodpecker
12. American Robin
13. Pine Siskin
14. Common Grackle
15. White-throated Sparrow
16. Northern Flicker
17. American Tree Sparrow
18. Red-winged Blackbird
19. Ring-necked Pheasant
20. Northern Cardinal
21. White-breasted Nuthatch
22. Red-breasted Nuthatch
23. Sharp-shinned Hawk
24. Rock Pigeon
25. Fox Sparrow

NUNAVUT

No data available

ONTARIO

1. Black-capped Chickadee
2. Dark-eyed Junco
3. Downy Woodpecker
4. Blue Jay
5. American Goldfinch
6. Mourning Dove
7. White-breasted Nuthatch
8. Northern Cardinal
9. Hairy Woodpecker
10. European Starling
11. American Robin

12. Common Grackle
13. American Tree Sparrow
14. House Finch
15. House Sparrow
16. Red-winged Blackbird
17. American Crow
18. Red-breasted Nuthatch
19. Purple Finch
20. Pine Siskin
21. Song Sparrow
22. Brown-headed Cowbird
23. Red-bellied Woodpecker
24. Common Redpoll
25. Cooper's Hawk

PRINCE EDWARD ISLAND
1. Blue Jay
2. Black-capped Chickadee
3. American Crow
4. European Starling
5. Mourning Dove
6. American Goldfinch
7. Dark-eyed Junco
8. Downy Woodpecker
9. Hairy Woodpecker
10. Song Sparrow
11. Common Grackle
12. Red-breasted Nuthatch
13. American Robin
14. Northern Flicker
15. Common Redpoll
16. Cedar Waxwing
17. Pine Siskin
18. Red-winged Blackbird
19. Ruffed Grouse
20. Bohemian Waxwing
21. House Sparrow
22. Gray Partridge
23. Rock Pigeon
24. Evening Grosbeak
25. Common Raven

QUEBEC
1. Black-capped Chickadee
2. Downy Woodpecker
3. American Goldfinch
4. Blue Jay
5. Dark-eyed Junco
6. Hairy Woodpecker
7. Mourning Dove
8. Purple Finch
9. Northern Cardinal

10. White-breasted Nuthatch
11. European Starling
12. American Crow
13. Pine Siskin
14. American Robin
15. Common Grackle
16. Song Sparrow
17. Red-winged Blackbird
18. American Tree Sparrow
19. House Finch
20. Common Redpoll
21. House Sparrow
22. Red-breasted Nuthatch
23. Pileated Woodpecker
24. Cooper's Hawk
25. Brown-headed Cowbird

SASKATCHEWAN
1. Black-capped Chickadee
2. Downy Woodpecker
3. Common Redpoll
4. Black-billed Magpie
5. House Sparrow
6. Dark-eyed Junco
7. Hairy Woodpecker
8. Blue Jay
9. Pine Grosbeak
10. White-breasted Nuthatch
11. Evening Grosbeak
12. Red-breasted Nuthatch
13. American Robin
14. Common Raven
15. House Finch
16. Hoary Redpoll
17. American Crow
18. Northern Flicker
19. Merlin
20. Gray Jay
21. Boreal Chickadee
22. Ruffed Grouse
23. Bohemian Waxwing
24. American Tree Sparrow
25. Pileated Woodpecker

YUKON TERRITORY
1. Common Redpoll
2. Black-capped Chickadee
3. Boreal Chickadee
4. Gray Jay
5. Black-billed Magpie
6. Pine Grosbeak
7. Hoary Redpoll

8. Common Raven
9. Hairy Woodpecker
10. Red Crossbill
11. Red-breasted Nuthatch
12. Mountain Chickadee
13. Downy Woodpecker
14. Ruffed Grouse
15. Pileated Woodpecker
16. Sharp-shinned Hawk
17. Northern Shrike
18. Northern Goshawk
19. Spruce Grouse
20. Red-breasted Sapsucker

Index

Notes